Penguin Education

Mathematics for Technology: 1
John Dobinson

Mathematics
for Technology: 1

John Dobinson

Penguin Books

Penguin Books Ltd, Harmondsworth,
Middlesex, England
Penguin Books, 625 Madison Avenue,
New York, New York 10022, U.S.A.
Penguin Books Australia Ltd, Ringwood,
Victoria, Australia
Penguin Books Canada Ltd, 41 Steelcase Road West,
Markham, Ontario, Canada
Penguin Books (N.Z.) Ltd, 182–190 Wairau Road,
Auckland 10, New Zealand

First published as *O.N. Mathematics: 1* 1968
Reprinted with amendments 1972
Reprinted 1973, 1975, 1976
Copyright © John Dobinson, 1968, 1972

Filmset in Monophoto Times by Oliver Burridge
Filmsetting Ltd, Crawley, England, and made and
printed by Hazell Watson & Viney Ltd, Aylesbury, Bucks

Contents

Preface

The two volumes of *Mathematics for Technology* are intended to meet the requirements of students taking the two-year O.N.C. courses in mathematics, volume 1 covering a suitable first-year syllabus and volume 2 the syllabus of the final year.

In each book the chapters are in the order in which it is suggested the various sections be worked. It is an order which is designed to add interest and variety to the course but there is nothing rigid about it. Indeed, with the variations in syllabuses of different colleges students are not expected to study every topic in the two volumes. Some teachers, and students, may prefer to complete the different sections on algebra, trigonometry, calculus, and so on in turn but, as the report of the Mathematical Association on the teaching of mathematics in technical colleges points out, the success of the teacher of part-time students depends to a great extent on his ability to provide links between the different branches of mathematics in each class period. A teacher would be advised to share his allotted weekly time between two or more sections of the course and so keep his students doing weekly exercises in more than one branch of mathematics.

Each topic, as far as possible, is broken up into small parts followed by a set of fairly straightforward exercises. In this way a small amount of theory can be complemented by examples which the student works for himself. The miscellaneous exercises at the end of each chapter are mostly from actual examination papers, and are designed to test the work of the whole chapter.

In this volume the approach to the calculus is by gradients, followed by rates of change. In volume 2 the calculus is started from its beginnings again with a more systematic treatment. Also in the second volume, to cover the variations in syllabuses, are topics not necessarily in all National Certificate courses: as an example the expansions of e^x and $\log(1+x)$ are derived from the binomial theorem for those who need this, whilst students who omit this section are introduced independently to the logarithmic and exponential functions by way of the calculus in the next chapter and this explains the alternative treatment. Numerical methods introduced with the desk calculating machine in volume 1 are extended in volume 2 to various iterative methods with an introduction to the preparation of flow diagrams. Sections on statistics, probability and complex numbers are added for students who require them in their course or for further general reading.

Thanks are due to the following examining bodies who have kindly allowed me to use questions from their examination papers; the East Midland Educational Union (denoted by E.M.E.U.), the Northern Counties Technical Examinations Council (N.C.T.E.C.), the Union of Educational Institutions (U.E.I.), the Union of Lancashire and Cheshire Institutes (U.L.C.I.) and the Director, Naval Education Service for H.M. Dockyard Technical Colleges (D.T.C.). Thanks are also due to my colleague Mr B. P. Lisgarten, Senior Lecturer, for preparing diagrams and checking some answers, and to my wife for typing the manuscript.

John Dobinson
1968

1 Logarithms and the slide rule

It is hoped that much of this chapter will be in the nature of revision for the student. We start by developing those rules which are known as the laws of indices. These laws should already be known for indices which are positive whole numbers. The rules have now to be extended to include fractional, negative, and zero indices.

1a The laws of indices

Instead of writing $a \times a \times a \times a \times a$ we write a^5. In a^5 there are five factors multiplied together. In the same way if n represents a positive integer (a whole number) then

$a^n = a \times a \times a \ldots$ to n factors

From this simple definition we build up the following rules.

Rule 1 $\quad a^m \times a^n = a^{m+n}$ where m and n are positive integers.

By definition $a^m = a \times a \times a \ldots$ to m factors
Also $\qquad a^n = a \times a \times a \ldots$ to n factors
Thus $\quad a^m \times a^n = (a \times a \times a \ldots m \text{ factors}) \times (a \times a \times a \ldots n \text{ factors})$
$\qquad\qquad\quad = a \times a \times a \ldots$ to $m+n$ factors
$\qquad\qquad\quad = a^{m+n}$ by our original definition
For example $2^4 \times 2^3 = 2^{4+3} = 2^7$
Similarly $a^m \times a^n \times a^p = a^{m+n+p}$

Rule 2 $\quad \dfrac{a^m}{a^n} = a^{m-n}$ where m and n are positive integers and m is greater than n
(i.e. $m > n$).

By definition $\dfrac{a^m}{a^n} = \dfrac{a \times a \times a \ldots m \text{ factors}}{a \times a \times a \ldots n \text{ factors}}$

As there are more factors in the numerator than in the denominator cancelling will leave $m-n$ factors in the numerator.

Thus $\qquad \dfrac{a^m}{a^n} = a \times a \times a \ldots$ to $(m-n)$ factors

$\qquad\qquad\quad = a^{m-n}$ by definition

Similarly $\quad \dfrac{a^n}{a^m} = \dfrac{1}{a^{m-n}} \qquad m > n$

Thus $\qquad \dfrac{3^5}{3^3} = 3^2 = 9$

Rule 3 $\quad a^0 = 1$

If in rule 2 we let $m = n$ we get

$$\dfrac{a^m}{a^m} = a^{m-m} = a^0$$

i.e. $1 = a^0$

Rule 4 $\quad a^{-n} = \dfrac{1}{a^n}$

If we wish a^{-n} to obey the three previous rules then

$$a^{-n} \times a^n = a^{-n+n} = a^0 = 1$$

Thus $a^{-n} = \dfrac{1}{a^n}$

For example $2^{-3} = \dfrac{1}{2^3} = \dfrac{1}{8}$

Rule 5 $\quad (a^m)^n = a^{mn}$

$(a^m)^n = a^m \times a^m \times a^m \ldots$ to n terms
$\qquad\ = (a \times a \times a \ldots m \text{ factors}) \times (a \times a \times a \ldots m \text{ factors}) \ldots n \text{ brackets}$
$\qquad\ = a \times a \times a \ldots$ to mn factors
$\qquad\ = a^{mn}$ by definition

For example $(2^3)^2 = 2^6$. Notice that this is not the same as $2^3 \times 2^2$ which is 2^5 by Rule 1.

Rule 6 $\quad a^{p/q} = \sqrt[q]{a^p}$

We can extend these laws of indices to give a meaning to fractional indices. Assuming that Rule 1 is obeyed by fractional indices then

$a^{p/q} \times a^{p/q} = a^{2p/q}$ where p and q are positive integers

Similarly $\quad a^{p/q} \times a^{p/q} \times a^{p/q} \ldots$ to q factors $= a^{p/q \times q}$

$$= a^p$$

Taking the qth root of each side we have

$$a^{p/q} = \sqrt[q]{a^p}$$

If $\quad p = 1$ and putting $q = n$

$$a^{1/n} = \sqrt[n]{a}$$

For example $\quad 8^{\frac{1}{3}} = \sqrt[3]{8} = 2$

and $\qquad\qquad 8^{\frac{2}{3}} = (\sqrt[3]{8})^2 = 2^2 = 4$

or $\qquad\qquad\quad = (8^2)^{\frac{1}{3}} = \sqrt[3]{64} = 4$

Example Simplify (a) $\dfrac{10^4 \times 10^3 \times 10^{-2}}{10^5 \times 10^{-1}}$ (b) $(8^{\frac{1}{2}} \times 3^{\frac{3}{2}})^{\frac{2}{3}}$

(c) $\dfrac{2^n . 4^{n+2}}{8^{n-1}}$

(a) $\dfrac{10^4 \times 10^3 \times 10^{-2}}{10^5 \times 10^{-1}} = \dfrac{10^{4+3-2}}{10^{5-1}} = \dfrac{10^5}{10^4} = 10^1 = 10$

(b) $(8^{\frac{1}{2}} \times 3^{\frac{3}{2}})^{\frac{2}{3}} = (2^{\frac{3}{2}} \times 3^{\frac{3}{2}})^{\frac{2}{3}} = 2^1 \times 3^1 = 6$

(c) $\dfrac{2^n \times 4^{n+2}}{8^{n-1}} = \dfrac{2^n . (2^2)^{n+2}}{(2^3)^{n-1}} = \dfrac{2^{n+2n+4}}{2^{3n-3}}$

$$= 2^{3n+4-(3n-3)} = 2^7 = 128$$

Exercise 1a

Write down in their simplest form

1   $16^{\frac{1}{4}}$

2   $16^{\frac{3}{4}}$

3   $2^{\frac{1}{2}} \times 2^{\frac{1}{2}}$

4   $8^{\frac{2}{3}}$

5   $27^{\frac{2}{3}}$

6   3^{-2}

7   $4^{\frac{1}{2}} \times 4^{-\frac{1}{2}}$

8   $x^3 \times x^2$

9   $(x^2)^3$

10   $\left(\dfrac{1}{3^2}\right)^{-1}$

11   $4^{\frac{3}{2}}$

12   $25^{-\frac{1}{2}}$

13   $125^{-\frac{2}{3}}$

14   $3^{\frac{1}{2}} \times 9^{\frac{1}{4}}$

15   $16^{0.5}$

16   $\left(\dfrac{1}{4}\right)^{-2.5}$

17   $16^{-0.25}$

18   $8^{\frac{4}{3}}$

Simplify

19   $(27x^3 y^{-6})^{\frac{1}{3}}$

20   $\dfrac{3^{-n} 9^{2n-1}}{3^{3n-1} 9^{-2}}$

13   The laws of indices

21 $\dfrac{4^3 \times 3^{\frac{1}{2}}}{4^2 \times 3^{-\frac{1}{2}}}$ 　　　　**22** $(a^{-\frac{1}{3}}b^3 c^{-\frac{2}{3}})^{\frac{1}{2}} \div (a^{\frac{1}{2}} b^{\frac{3}{2}} c^{-1})^{\frac{1}{3}}$

A number is said to be in *standard form* when it is expressed as a number between 1 and 10 multiplied by a power of 10. For example 27 100 is written $2\cdot71 \times 10^4$ and 0·0256 is written $2\cdot56 \times 10^{-2}$ when in standard form.

23 Express in standard form

(a) 36 000 　　(b) 0·000 067 23 　　(c) $\dfrac{2\cdot5 \times 10^2}{0\cdot25 \times 0\cdot002}$

24 Express the following in standard form and hence evaluate without the use of tables

(a) $\dfrac{33\,000\,000 \times 0\cdot4}{1\cdot1 \times 30}$ 　　(b) $\dfrac{70 \times 1\cdot6 \times 200}{2240 \times 0\cdot01}$

1b　Laws of logarithms

Logarithms will already have been used by the students and will have been found of great practical value in calculations. The theory of logarithms is developed from the laws of indices, given in the previous section.

Definition of a logarithm

If a number N can be written in the form a^x then the index x is called the logarithm of N to base a.

If　$N = a^x$ then $\log_a N = x$

That these two statements are equivalent is the first principle to be learnt.

Since 　　　$81 = 3^4$ then $\log_3 81 = 4$
Since 　　$0\cdot001 = 10^{-3}$ then $\log_{10} 0\cdot001 = -3$
Thus 　$\log_2 32 = 5$ and $\log_2 (\frac{1}{8}) = -3$
Notice that since $a^0 = 1$ then $\log_a 1 = 0$
Thus whatever the base the logarithm of 1 is zero.

Rule 1 　$\log_a MN = \log_a M + \log_a N$

Let $\log_a M = x$ and $\log_a N = y$
Then by definition 　$M = a^x$ and $N = a^y$
$\therefore$ 　　　　　　$MN = a^x a^y = a^{x+y}$
Hence 　　　$\log_a MN = x + y = \log_a M + \log_a N$

Example 　$\log_a 15 = \log_a 5 + \log_a 3$

14　**Logarithms and the slide rule**

It follows that $\log_a MNP = \log_a MN + \log_a P$
$$= \log_a M + \log_a N + \log_a P$$

This may be continued to any number of factors

Thus $\log_a 42 = \log_a 2 \times 3 \times 7 = \log_a 2 + \log_a 3 + \log_a 7$

Rule 2 $\log_a \dfrac{M}{N} = \log_a M - \log_a N$

As before let $\log_a M = x$ and $\log_a N = y$
Then $M = a^x$ and $N = a^y$
$\therefore \qquad \dfrac{M}{N} = \dfrac{a^x}{a^y} = a^{x-y}$

$\therefore \quad \log_a \dfrac{M}{N} = x - y = \log_a M - \log_a N$

Thus $\log 2\frac{3}{7} = \log \frac{17}{7} = \log 17 - \log 7$ to any base
and $\log 2\frac{1}{7} = \log \frac{15}{7} = \log 5 + \log 3 - \log 7$

Rule 3 $\log_a N^r = r \log_a N$

Let $\log_a N = x$. As before $N = a^x$

Raising each side to the power r we get
$$N^r = (a^x)^r = a^{rx}$$
$\therefore \qquad \log_a N^r = rx = r \log_a N$
Thus $\log_{10} 3^4 = 4 \log_{10} 3$

Notice that $\log_a \sqrt[r]{N} = \log_a N^{1/r} = \dfrac{1}{r} \log_a N$

This follows from rule 3.

For example $\log_{10} \sqrt[3]{2} = \frac{1}{3} \log_{10} 2$

Example 1 $\log \left(\dfrac{3^5 \times \sqrt[3]{2}}{\sqrt{5}} \right) = \log 3^5 + \log 2^{\frac{1}{3}} - \log 5^{\frac{1}{2}}$
$$= 5 \log 3 + \tfrac{1}{3} \log 2 - \tfrac{1}{2} \log 5$$

We need not state any base for the logarithms as the result is true no matter what base is chosen.

Example 2 $\log \dfrac{324}{\sqrt[5]{64}} = \log 324 - \tfrac{1}{5} \log 64$

$$= \log (2^2 \times 3^4) - \tfrac{1}{5} \log 2^6$$
$$= 2 \log 2 + 4 \log 3 - \tfrac{6}{5} \log 2$$
$$= \tfrac{4}{5} \log 2 + 4 \log 3$$

Exercise 1b

Write down the answers to questions 1–12

1   $\log_3 27$ 2 $\log_2 16$ 3 $\log_{10} 1000$

4   $\log_5 125$ 5 $\log_{10} 0{\cdot}1$ 6 $\log_{10} 0{\cdot}01$

7   $\log_2 \frac{1}{8}$ 8 $\log_3 \frac{1}{27}$ 9 $\log_4 8$

10   $\log_8 2$ 11 $\log_{25} 5$ 12 $\log_{\frac{1}{2}} 8$

Write questions 13–18 down in terms of log 2, log 3 and log 5 to any base

13   $\log 8$ 14 $\log 15$ 15 $\log 270$

16   $\log \dfrac{27 \times \sqrt[3]{5}}{16}$ 17 $\log \dfrac{216}{\sqrt[3]{32}}$ 18 $\log 648 \sqrt{125}$

19   Find x if (a) $\log_{10} x = 2$ (b) $\log_4 x = 2\frac{1}{2}$
               (c) $\log_3 x = -2$ (d) $2^x = 64$
               (e) $2^x \times 3^x = 216$ (f) $2^x = \frac{1}{8}$

20   Given $\log_{10} 2 = 0{\cdot}3010$ give the values of
     (a) $\log_{10} 20$ (b) $\log_{10} 200$ (c) $\log_{10} 8$
     (d) $\log_{10} 0{\cdot}02$ (e) $\log_{10} 2 \times 10^6$

21   Solve the equation $\log x^3 - \log x^2 = \log 5x - \log 4x$

22   Given that $\log_{10} 2 = 0{\cdot}3010$ and $\log_{10} 3 = 0{\cdot}4771$, calculate $\log_{10} 8$ and $\log_{10} 18$ without using tables.

1c   Common logarithms

These are logarithms to base 10 and are the logarithms which we use in practice. From now on in this section if we do not state a base for a logarithm then it must be taken that the base is 10.

Suppose we know that $\log_{10} 3{\cdot}452 = 0{\cdot}5381$
i.e. that $3{\cdot}452 = 10^{0{\cdot}5381}$

Such logarithms can be calculated by methods used in advanced mathematics.

If $\log 3{\cdot}452 = 0{\cdot}5381$
then $\log 345{\cdot}2 = \log 3{\cdot}452 \times 100 = \log 100 + \log 3{\cdot}452$
                   $= 2 + 0{\cdot}5381$ since $100 = 10^2$
Thus $\log 345{\cdot}2 = 2{\cdot}5381$
Similarly $\log 3452 = 3{\cdot}5381$

In the same way $\log 0.034\,52 = \log \dfrac{3.452}{100}$

$$= \log 3.452 - \log 100$$
$$= 0.5381 - 2$$

This we write as $\overline{2}.5381$

The minus sign is put over the 2 to show that it alone is negative and we read this as 'bar 2'.

In a logarithm the whole number before the decimal point is called the *characteristic* and the decimal part the *mantissa*.

In logarithms to base 10 all numbers which have the same sequence of digits will have the same mantissa. Only the characteristic will differ depending on the position of the decimal point. In compiling a table of logarithms the mantissa only is given and the characteristic is picked out by inspection according to the following rules.

Rule 1   The characteristic for a number greater than one is positive and is one less than the number of digits before the decimal point.

Rule 2   The characteristic for a number less than one is negative and is numerically one more than the number of cyphers or zeros immediately after the decimal point.

Thus if $\log 2 = 0.3010$
   $\log 2000 = 3.3010$
and $\log 0.02 = \overline{2}.3010$

Example 1   Find the value of $\dfrac{15.58 \times 0.4572}{32.38 \times 0.0068}$

Let $x = \dfrac{15.58 \times 0.4572}{32.38 \times 0.0068}$

Taking logarithms
$\log x = \log 15.58 + \log 0.4572 - \log 32.38 - \log 0.0068$
$\quad = 1.1925 + \overline{1}.6601 - 1.5103 - \overline{3}.8325$
$\quad = 0.8526 - \overline{1}.3428$
$\quad = 1.5098$
$\quad x = 32.34$

Example 2   Find the value of $\dfrac{(352 \times \frac{1}{28})^5}{\sqrt[3]{(58 \times 2.752)}}$

Let the value be x and taking logs

$\log x = 5 \log 352 - 5 \log 28 - \frac{1}{3} \log 58 - \frac{1}{3} \log 2.752$

Number	Log
352	2·5465
28	1·4472
	1·0993
	5
	5·4965
	0·7343
	4·7622 = log x
x =	57 840

Number	Log
58	1·7634
2·752	0·4396
	3)2·2030
	0·7343

Exercise 1c

Evaluate questions 1–8 using logarithms

1 $\dfrac{0.373 \times 24.62}{0.013\,79}$

2 $\dfrac{179}{\sqrt[3]{(0.8112)}}$

3 $\dfrac{22.37 \times \sqrt{(0.2371)}}{(0.4316)^3}$

4 $\dfrac{49.35 \times \sqrt{(0.2543)}}{(41.35)^2}$

5 $\dfrac{5769 \times \sqrt[3]{(3462)}}{\sqrt{231}}$

6 $\dfrac{\sqrt[3]{(0.0664)} \times 123.1}{(4.636)^3}$

7 $\sqrt{\dfrac{(0.348)^2}{169}}$

8 $\dfrac{22.22 \times \sqrt[3]{(0.0876)}}{(0.0962)^2}$

9 In the formula $P = \sqrt{\left(\dfrac{2gQ \sin \theta}{R}\right)}$ find P when

$g = 32.2, Q = 2.25, \sin \theta = 0.3063$ and $R = 0.0612$

10 An alternating current, I, is found from the formula

$I = \dfrac{E}{\sqrt{(W^2 L^2 + R^2)}}$ where $W = 2\pi f$

Find the value of R which will make I equal to 7 when $E = 210, f = 90,$
$L = 0.04, \pi = 3.142$.

1d Napierian logarithms and change of base

To convert from one system of logarithms to another

Suppose we are given $\log_a N$ and we wish to find $\log_b N$.

Let $\log_b N = x$. Then by definition $N = b^x$

Taking logarithms to base a

$$\log_a N = \log_a (b^x)$$
$$= x \log_a b \text{ by rule 3 (laws of logarithms), page 15}$$

Hence $\quad x = \dfrac{\log_a N}{\log_a b}$

i.e. $\quad \log_b N = \dfrac{1}{\log_a b} \times \log_a N$

Thus to convert logarithms to base a into logarithms to base b we multiply by the factor $\dfrac{1}{\log_a b}$ which is a constant for this transformation.

Notice in the above result that if we put $N = a$

then $\log_b a = \dfrac{1}{\log_a b}$ since $\log_a a = 1$

There are two main types of logarithms:
(a) Common logarithms which are logarithms to base 10, and
(b) Hyperbolic or Napierian logarithms which are logarithms to base e where $e = 2.71828\ldots$

Students should get a little practice in looking up logarithms to base e in the tables.

To convert from common to Napierian logarithms

$$\log_e N = \frac{1}{\log_{10} e} \times \log_{10} N = \frac{1}{\log 2.718} \times \log_{10} N$$

$$= \frac{1}{0.4343} \log_{10} N = 2.303 \log_{10} N$$

To convert from Napierian to common logarithms

$$\log_{10} N = \frac{1}{\log_e 10} \times \log_e N = \log_{10} e \times \log_e N$$

$$= 0.4343 \log_e N$$

To avoid confusion between $\log_{10} N$ and $\log_e N$ the latter may be written $\ln N$; thus $\ln 10 = 2.303$.

1e Indicial equations

Example 1 Solve the equation $2^{x+1} = 3^{x-1}$

19   Indicial equations

Taking logarithms

$$(x+1) \log 2 = (x-1) \log 3$$
$$(x+1)\, 0{\cdot}3010 = (x-1)\, 0{\cdot}4771$$
$$x(0{\cdot}4771 - 0{\cdot}3010) = 0{\cdot}3010 + 0{\cdot}4771$$
$$x = \frac{0{\cdot}7781}{0{\cdot}1761}$$
$$= 4{\cdot}420$$

Number	Log
0·7781	$\bar{1}$·8911
0·1761	$\bar{1}$·2457
4·420 ←	0·6454

Example 2 Calculate $\log_3 5$

$$\log_3 5 = \frac{1}{\log_{10} 3} \times \log_{10} 5$$
$$= \frac{0{\cdot}6990}{0{\cdot}4771} = \frac{6{\cdot}99}{4{\cdot}771}$$
$$= 1{\cdot}465$$

Number	Log
6·990	0·8445
4·771	0·6786
1·465 ←	0·1659

Example 3 Evaluate $(0{\cdot}4256)^{2{\cdot}31}$

$$\log \text{(answer)} = 2{\cdot}31 \times \log 0{\cdot}4256$$
$$= 2{\cdot}31 \times \bar{1}{\cdot}6290$$
$$= 2{\cdot}31 \times (-1) + 2{\cdot}31 \times 0{\cdot}6290$$
$$= -2{\cdot}31 + 1{\cdot}453$$
$$= -0{\cdot}8570$$
$$= \bar{1}{\cdot}1430$$
$$\text{Answer} = 0{\cdot}1390$$

Number	Log
2·31	0·3636
0·6290	$\bar{1}$·7937
1·453 ←	0·1623

Exercise 1e

1 Test the rule $\log_a b \times \log_b a = 1$ when

$a = 10$ and $b = 2{\cdot}718 = e$

2 Using logarithms to base 10 find $\log_e 3{\cdot}435$ taking $e = 2{\cdot}718$

3 Calculate (a) $\log_{5{\cdot}2} 27{\cdot}31$
             (b) $\log_{9{\cdot}51} 52{\cdot}63$
             (c) $\log_e 20{\cdot}68$

4 Evaluate (a) $(289{\cdot}5)^{1{\cdot}23}$
             (b) $(20{\cdot}78)^{2{\cdot}34}$
             (c) $(0{\cdot}5316)^{1{\cdot}32}$

5 Evaluate (a) $(30{\cdot}83)^{2{\cdot}25}$
             (b) $(0{\cdot}514)^{-1{\cdot}2}$
             (c) $(0{\cdot}0427)^{-2{\cdot}33}$

6   Solve the equation $(4 \cdot 37)^x = 8 \cdot 934$

7   Solve the equation $5^{x+2} = 8^{2x-1}$

8   Solve the equation $2^x \times 5^{x-1} = 8^{2x+1}$

9   Solve the equation $4 \times 2^{2-x} = 5^{6x-4}$

10 Solve $2^x.3^y = 100; \quad 3^x.2^y = 50$

1f   The slide rule

Slide rules vary depending on their purpose and designer, and a book of instruction for use is invariably provided with each rule. As the slide rule is equivalent to a table of logarithms, a section following the principles of logarithms seems a suitable place to deal with it.

The slide rule consists of three main parts: the body, the slide, and the cursor or sliding marker. The rule has four basic scales, A, B, C, and D, each usually 25 cm long.

The C and D scales are identical and are divided into lengths proportional to the logarithms of numbers from 1 to 10.

Figure 1

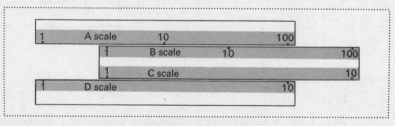

Number = x	1	2	3	4	5	6	7	8	9	10
$\log_{10} x$	0	0·301	0·477	0·602	0·699	0·778	0·845	0·903	0·954	1·0
Proportional to $\log_{10} x$	0	301	477	602	699	778	845	903	954	1,000

In the table we have the logarithms of the numbers 1 to 10 and below that numbers proportional to these values. The C and D scales of 25 cm each may be regarded as being divided into 1000 equal parts with the number 1 placed over the left-hand end of each scale. A figure 2 is placed over the 301st division, a 3 over the 477th division and so on. Thus the distance of any graduation from the end represents the logarithm of that number to a common scale.

The actual distance of any number, say 6, from the end is $25 \log_{10} 6 = 25 \times 0.778 = 19.45$ cm from the left-hand end.

The A and B scales are the logarithms of numbers 1 to 100 plotted to the scale of 25 cm $= \log_{10} 100 = 2$ which is exactly half the scale used for the lower scales C and D.

Example   Find the distance between the 3·1 graduation and the 3·7 graduation on the C scale.

$$3\cdot7 \text{ is at a distance } 25 \log_{10} 3\cdot7 \text{ along the scale } = 25 \times 0\cdot5682$$
$$= 14\cdot205$$
$$3\cdot1 \text{ is at a distance } 25 \log_{10} 3\cdot1 \text{ along the scale } = 25 \times 0\cdot4914$$
$$= 12\cdot285$$

Distance between graduations $= 14\cdot205 - 12\cdot285 = 1\cdot92$ cm

Note that on the A and B scales the corresponding distances would be halved and the final answer would be 0·96 cm.

Figure 2

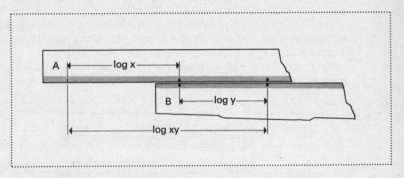

Multiplication

Since $\log xy = \log x + \log y$ multiplication is converted to addition by taking logarithms. The addition is performed by moving two similar scales relatively to each other until a length corresponding to the logarithm of one of the numbers is placed to end where the length corresponding to the logarithm of the other begins. The combined length will correspond to the logarithm of their product.

Suppose $x = 3$ and $y = 5$ and we use the two upper scales A and B. We move the slide until 1 on B is under 3 on A and then 5 on B will be under the product which is 15 on A.

Division

To divide any number x by another number y we reverse the above process since $\log (x \div y) = \log x - \log y$

Thus to divide 8 by 4 we set the divisor 4 on *B* under the 8 on *A* and the result 2 is read on *A* opposite the 1 of the slide.

Beginners should first try many simple calculations whose answers can be checked mentally. The slide rule is usually used to produce the significant figures of an answer only. If there is any doubt about the position of the decimal point, a rough calculation should be made to estimate its position.

Students will soon learn to carry out multiplications and divisions alternately to avoid unnecessary movements of the slide and cursor.

Square roots and squares

Readings on scale *A* are the squares of exactly opposite readings on scale *D*. Thus 9 on *A* is exactly opposite 3 on *D*. This is because twice the logarithm of a number equals the logarithm of the square of that number. Thus to get the square of any number, set the cursor line over the given number on *D* and take the reading under the cursor line on *A*.

To find the square root of any number we set the cursor line over the given number on scale *A* and read the answer on scale *D*. Care is necessary in determining square roots to choose the correct range, 1 to 10 or 10 to 100, on scale *A* for the given number.

Once the use of the basic scales is understood and mastered, other calculations can be made using the more advanced scales such as the log–log scales, following the examples in the instruction booklet.

With all calculating machines it is useful training to set out a work programme.

Example   Evaluate $\dfrac{4 \cdot 63 \times 2 \cdot 86}{8 \cdot 73 \times 5 \cdot 45}$

Programme
1 Move cursor to 4·63 on *A* scale.
2 Move 8·73 of *B* scale to cursor.
3 Move cursor to 2·86 on *B* scale.
4 Move 5·45 of *B* scale to cursor.
5 Slide cursor to 10 on *B* scale or to end of *B* scale.
6 Read off answer 278 on *A* scale.
7 Rough check: $4 \times 3 \div 9 \times 5 \simeq \frac{1}{4} = 0 \cdot 25$
8 Write answer 0·278.

1g   The desk calculating machine

Desk calculating machines are increasingly available in schools and colleges and these greatly improve the speed and accuracy of numerical work. They vary from hand-operated lever or keyboard setting machines where the results are read from registers to electrically-operated keyboard machines which print results on a paper roll.

Figure
3

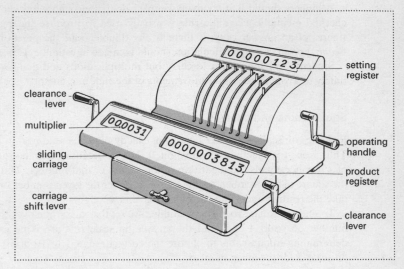

The simple hand machine is one that the student will most probably use. This has three registers: (i) the keyboard or setting register, (ii) the counter or multiplier register, (iii) the product register or accumulator. A number put on the setting register can be transferred to the accumulator by one turn of the operating handle while three turns will put thrice the number into the accumulator and also show a three in the counter register. Thus three rotations is equivalent to three additions of the number into the accumulator. A backward rotation of the operating handle is equivalent to subtraction and is used when dividing. A shift lever moves the carriage carrying product and multiplier registers to the left or right, enabling multiplication by tens, hundreds, and so on to be performed.

Study of the operations manual and some practice soon gives skill in the basic operations of addition, subtraction, multiplication and division.

For a series of calculations or a solution of a particular problem it is useful to set out a programme or flow diagram for the operation.

Example A group of 75 boys were each weighed and the results are shown tabulated in intervals of 1 kg from 39·5 kg to 47·5 kg. Find the average weight for the group assuming the weight of each boy to be equal to that at the centre of the interval in which he is grouped.

Centre of interval in kg	40	41	42	43	44	45	46	47
Number of boys	1	7	10	17	19	11	8	2

Here we have to work out the total weight of the 75 boys given by $40 \times 1 + 41 \times 7 + 42 \times 10 + \ldots + 47 \times 2$.

These products are added stage by stage into the accumulator. By dividing the total by 75 we get the average to be 43·61 kg.

The method of procedure is set out in the following simple flow diagram where straightforward sequences are enclosed in rectangular frames and the steps in the sequence indicated by arrows.

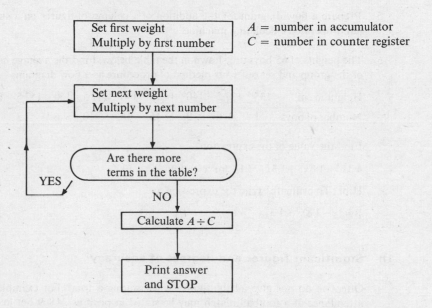

$A =$ number in accumulator
$C =$ number in counter register

Where the next step in the sequence is not automatic, the conditions, usually in the form of a question, are enclosed in a different frame, in this example an oval. The flow diagram has a loop circuit to one answer to the question and this repeats the sequence of operations until the answer changes. Then the sequence continues along the main line.

Exercise 1g

1 Explain in simple language how you would perform the following calculations
(a) using a slide rule   (b) using a desk calculating machine.

    i $\dfrac{25\cdot6 \times 14\cdot7}{6\cdot75}$

    ii $\dfrac{27\cdot5^2 + 48\cdot3^2}{455}$

2   Explain how a slide rule is graduated and state what reading on the *A* scale will be directly opposite 6·1 on the *D* scale.

3   Calculate the distance of the number 4 from the 1 on the *D* scale of a 25 cm slide rule.

4   What is the distance between the 6 and the 9 on a 25 cm slide rule?

5   Prepare a flow diagram for the addition of a column of figures on a simple hand-operated calculating machine.

6   The heights of 65 boys are shown in the table below. Find the average height of the group and set out your method of procedure as a flow diagram.

Height in cm	135	137·5	140	142·5	145	147·5	150	152·5	Total
Number of boys	1	6	9	15	16	10	6	2	65

7   Find the value of the expression

$$4\cdot3x^3 - 1\cdot8x^2 + 1\cdot3x - 3\cdot1 \quad \text{for } x = 1\cdot9$$

Hint: To evaluate, write the expression as

$$\{(4\cdot3x - 1\cdot8)x + 1\cdot3\}x - 3\cdot1$$

1h   Significant figures and degrees of accuracy

Often we do not give all the figures when stating a total. For example the attendance at a football match may be stated in print as 24 869 but in conversation we are more likely to give it as 25 thousand. The numbers retained (i.e. 25) are known as *significant figures* and the attendance of 25 000 is said to be correct to two significant figures. To three significant figures the attendance would be 24 900.

For numbers less than one, any zeros at the beginning do not count. Thus 0·045 87 is 0·0459 to three significant figures and 0·046 to two significant figures.

Example   Express correct to 3 significant figures
    30 756; 3·0756; 0·030 756; 500·2; 0·020 65

Answers   30 800; 3·08;   0·0308;   500;   0·0207

Degree of accuracy

If we are given that the length of a brass rod is 8·43 cm correct to 3 significant figures then we must realize that the 8·43 could be the approximation for lengths lying between 8·425 to 8·435 cm. The true measurement could lie between 8·43±0·005 cm. The error permitted in accurate practical work is called the tolerance.

Thus if a shaft is to be turned to a diameter of 2 cm with a 'tolerance' of 5 thousandths, the finished work must lie between 1·995 and 2·005 cm in diameter.

In calculations which involve approximated numbers we must be careful to assess the degree of accuracy of the result.

For example, in calculating the area of a plate of length 11·16 cm and breadth 5·87 cm where one is correct to 4 and the other correct to 3 significant figures, if we multiply 11·16 by 5·87 we get 65·5092.

Since the length could lie between 11·155 and 11·165 and the breadth between 5·865 and 5·875 then the area can lie anywhere between 65·424 075 and 65·594 375, i.e. between 65·4 and 65·6 to 3 significant figures.

This shows that we can only obtain the answer accurately to two significant figures.

The number of significant figures which can be depended upon in the final result is generally less than the least number of significant figures among the numbers employed. Thus multiplying

a(to 3 significant figures) × b(to 4 significant figures) × c(to 3 significant figures) = abc (to 2 significant figures)

Example 1   Find the error, the relative error and the percentage error in taking a diameter of 3·572 cm as 3·6 cm giving the answers correct to three significant figures.

True error or absolute error = stated value − true value
$$= 3·6 - 3·572$$
$$= 0·0280 \text{ cm}$$

Relative error $= \dfrac{\text{error}}{\text{correct value}} = \dfrac{0·028}{3·572}$

$$= 0·007\,84$$

Percentage error = relative error × 100%

$$= 0·784\%$$

Number	Log
0·028	$\bar{2}$·4472
3·572	·5529
·007 839 ←	$\bar{3}$·8943

Example 2   In the formula $\dfrac{pv}{273+t} = k$ which relates to the pressure, volume and temperature of a gas, make t the subject of the formula.

Determine the value of t to 3 significant figures given $p = 233$, $v = 42·6$, and $k = 21·5$.

Multiplying both sides of the formula by $273+t$ we get

$$pv = k(273+t) \quad \text{from which}$$

$$\frac{pv}{k} = 273+t$$

and $t = \dfrac{pv}{k}-273$

Substituting the given values

$$t = \frac{233 \times 42 \cdot 6}{21 \cdot 5}-273$$

$$= 461 \cdot 7-273$$
$$= 188 \cdot 7$$

Answer $t = 189$

Number	Log
233	2·3674
42·6	1·6294
	3·9968
21·5	1·3324
461·7 ←	2·6644

Exercise 1h

1   The mass of the earth in g is given by the formula $\dfrac{G.M}{R^2} = 980$ where G, the gravitational constant, is $6 \cdot 66 \times 10^{-8}$, R, the radius of the earth, is $6 \cdot 36 \times 10^8$. Calculate M to 3 significant figures stating the result in standard form.

2   The dimensions of a rectangular block of metal are 5·23 cm by 4·61 cm by 2·24 cm. These dimensions are correct to within $\pm 0 \cdot 01$ cm.
    Find the greatest and the least possible values of the volume and state the volume of the block to an accurate number of significant figures.

3   Make t the subject of the formula

$$s = \sqrt{\left(\frac{t-q}{t+2q}\right)}$$ and find the value of t to 3 significant figures if $s = \dfrac{2}{7}$ and $q = 20\,000$.
Give your answer in standard form.

4   Make h the subject of the following formulae

(a) $T = \dfrac{R}{\pi}\left(\dfrac{1}{h}-\dfrac{1}{s}\right)$

(b) $x = l+\sqrt{(l^2+2hl)}$

(c) $P = f\left(\dfrac{\pi h^2}{4}-T\right)$

5   Calculate the value of P to 2 significant figures from the formula

$$P = \frac{fA}{1 + a\left(\dfrac{l}{k}\right)^2}$$

given that $f = 21$, $a = \dfrac{1}{7500}$, $l = 40$, $k = 4.44$ and $A = 38.38$.

6   The sag y at the centre of a wire length S supported at 2 points distance L apart is given by

$$y = \sqrt{\left\{\frac{3L(S-L)}{8}\right\}}$$

Find the value of $S - L$ to three significant figures if $L = 150\,\text{m}$ and $y = 0.5\,\text{m}$.

7   Make r the subject of the formula

$$p = \frac{v}{\sqrt{\left(\dfrac{r}{tE} + \dfrac{1}{2k}\right)}}$$

Calculate the value of r to 3 significant figures if $t = 0.01$, $E = 30 \times 10^6$, $v = 4$, $k = 3 \times 10^5$ and $p = 1000$.

Miscellaneous exercises 1

1   (a) Evaluate correct to 3 significant figures

   i $(0.265)^{-\frac{1}{4}}$
   ii $\log_e 263.4$

   (b) If $y = \dfrac{wl^4}{16Eab^3}$ calculate y to 3 significant figures when $w = 0.22$, $l = 140$, $E = 30 \times 10^6$, $a = 2.0$, $b = 2.8$. Express your answer as a product of a number between 1 and 10 and a power of 10.

2   (a) Given that $\log_{10} 3 = 0.4771$ and that $\ln 10 = 2.303$, both values being correct to four significant figures, obtain the value of $\ln 3$.
   (b) Solve the equation $4^x = 6$ correct to three significant figures.

   U.L.C.I.

3   (a) Write down i the square root of $169a^4b^6$
                   ii the cube root of $125a^9b^6$
   (b) Simplify

   $$\frac{nm^{\frac{1}{3}}\, m^2 \sqrt{n}}{\sqrt{\dfrac{n}{81}}\ \sqrt[3]{m^{-1}}}\, (m^{\frac{1}{3}})^{-2}$$

(c) Use logarithms to evaluate the following

$$\frac{0 \cdot 0265^{\frac{1}{4}} \times 5 \cdot 6^{-3} \times 20 \cdot 6^2}{0 \cdot 006^2}$$

U.L.C.I.

4   (a) Solve the equations
      i $\log x + \log (x+2) = \log 3$
      ii $2^{x+1} = 3^x$
   (b) Evaluate i $3 \cdot 27^{2 \cdot 2}$
      ii $\left(\dfrac{1}{2}\right)^{-1 \cdot 2}$

5   (a) If $\log (x+y) = \log x + \log y$ find the value of y if $x = 1 \cdot 1568$.
   (b) Use Napierian logarithms to find
      i $\log_e 0 \cdot 476$
      ii the number whose Napierian logarithm is $\overline{5} \cdot 686$.
   (c) Rewrite the following expression to give W

$$\log_e 32 \cdot 8 = \log_e 16 \cdot 87 + \frac{W}{16 \cdot 87 \times 180}$$

   and hence find the value of W.

U.E.I.

6   (a) Evaluate $5 \cdot 73^{-3 \cdot 42}$
   (b) If $pv^n = C$, find the value of v when $C = 350, p = 95$ and $n = 1 \cdot 4$
   (c) Without using Napierian logarithm tables, find the value of Q when
      $T = 550$ from the following formula

$$Q = \log_e \frac{T}{460} + \frac{1420}{T} - 0 \cdot 68$$

U.E.I.

7   (a) Use Napierian logarithms to find
      i $\log_e 0 \cdot 658$
      ii the number whose Napierian logarithm is $\overline{4} \cdot 762$.
   (b) Evaluate H in the following formula

$$H = \frac{bd}{4} (\log_e m^2 + \log_e n^2)$$

   when $b = 23 \cdot 4, d = 0 \cdot 285, m = 5 \cdot 3$ and $n = 4 \cdot 2$

U.E.I.

8   (a) Evaluate p from the expression $\dfrac{p}{q} = e^{b\theta}$

   when $e = 2 \cdot 718, b = 0 \cdot 25, \theta = 1 \cdot 88$ and $(p-q) = 555$

(b) Express the formula

$$L = 2c\left(\log_e \frac{b}{a} + 1\right)$$

in terms of logarithms to the base 10 and then transpose the formula to give b in terms of the other quantities.

E.M.E.U.

9 The following expression gives the self-inductance, L, of parallel conductors, radius r, distance d apart:

$$L = 0.000\,644\left(\log_e \frac{d}{r} + \frac{1}{4}\right)$$

Re-arrange this expression to give r in terms of the other quantities, and evaluate r when $L = 0.003\,22$ and $d = 80$, using logarithms to base 10.

10 (a) If $vk = \sqrt{\left\{\dfrac{1 + \left(\dfrac{1}{x} + 1\right)^2}{lg}\right\}}$

use logarithms to evaluate v when $x = 0.85$, $k = 1.26$, $l = 48.5$, and $g = 32.2$.

(b) Obtain an expression for x in terms of the other symbols.

U.L.C.I.

11 Use logarithms to evaluate f, given that

$$f = \frac{1}{2\pi}\sqrt{\left(\frac{1}{LC} - \frac{R^2}{L^2}\right)}$$

and $L = 4.25 \times 10^{-3}$, $C = 2.48 \times 10^{-5}$ and $R = 3.58$.

Find, to the nearest whole number, the percentage error involved in calculating f from the simplified expression

$$f = \frac{1}{2\pi}\sqrt{\frac{1}{LC}}$$

U.L.C.I.

12 (a) Transpose

$$q = \sqrt{\left\{\frac{2ghDA^2}{d\,(S^2 - A^2)}\right\}}$$

to give A in terms of the other symbols.

(b) If $\log_e\left(\dfrac{b}{a}\right) = 0.985$ and $a = 1.75$, find b.

U.L.C.I.

31   Miscellaneous exercises 1

13 (a) From the formula $S = \dfrac{1}{k}\log_e\left(\dfrac{L}{L-V^2}\right)$

prove $\qquad\qquad V^2 = L(1-e^{-ks})$

(b) The quantities p and v are connected by the equation $pv^n = c$.

If $p = 14$ when $v = 26$, and $p = 33$ when $v = 12$, find the values of n and c.

D.T.C.

14 (a) Show that $\log_a M^n = n \log_a M$.

(b) Without using tables, find the value of

   i $\log_{32} 64$ and   ii $\dfrac{\log_3 64}{\log_3 32}$

(c) Solve the equation $5^{-2x} = 625^{\frac{3}{4}}$

(d) Find the value of $(1 \cdot 163)^{-1 \cdot 2}$

D.T.C.

15 (a) Evaluate $\dfrac{243^{\frac{2}{5}} - 32^{\frac{2}{5}}}{3125^{\frac{2}{5}}}$ without using tables.

(b) Solve the equation $\log_{10} x = \frac{1}{3}(1 \cdot 5 - 4 \cdot 4040)$ for x.

(c) Show that $\log_a N = \log_a b \log_b N$, and hence find the value of $\log_e 3$ given that $\log_{10} 3 = 0 \cdot 4771$ and that $e = 2 \cdot 718$.

(d) Evaluate $(0 \cdot 026)^{-0 \cdot 3}$

D.T.C.

16 The minimum diameter d of a shaft subjected to a bending moment M and a torque T is given by the formula

$$d^2 = \frac{16}{\pi f}\{M + \sqrt{(M^2 + T^2)}\}.$$

(a) Find the value of d when $f = 8400$, $M = 12\,560$ and $T = 25\,000$.

(b) Also transpose the formula to make T the subject.

17 Explain how a slide rule is graduated and how the upper and lower scales can be used for finding squares and square roots.

Calculate the distance between the marks $3 \cdot 6$ and $7 \cdot 8$ on the C and D scales of a 25 cm slide rule.

18 Explain how a slide rule is used for multiplication and division.

Find the reading on the scale which lies halfway between the graduations 3 and 4.

19 Six weights are attached to a light rod at points indicated in the table.

Weight w (kg)	2·4	4·6	3·2	6·9	5·3	3·5
Distance from end x (cm)	62	113	175	223	285	323

The distance $\bar{x}$ of the centre of gravity of the system from the end of the rod is calculated from the formula

$$\bar{x} = \frac{w_1 x_1 + w_2 x_2 + \ldots + w_6 x_6}{w_1 + w_2 + \ldots + w_6}$$

Set out your method of procedure as a flow diagram and calculate $\bar{x}$.

2 Quadratic and other equations

2a Surds

All quantities can be divided into two classes, *commensurable* and *incommensurable*.

An incommensurable quantity is one which cannot be expressed either as a multiple or as a fraction of any unit; e.g. $\pi = 3 \cdot 14159\ldots$ cannot be expressed as a fraction and the decimal may be continued indefinitely.
All other quantities are said to be commensurable.

Surds belong to the family of incommensurables and consist of roots of numbers which cannot be exactly determined.

Thus $\sqrt{2} = 1 \cdot 41421\ldots$ where its value may be obtained to as many decimal places as one pleases.

An expression containing one or more surds is said to be *irrational*. A *rational* expression is one in which no root sign is necessarily involved.

The root sign $\sqrt{}$ is called the radical sign and the number written over the radical sign, for example $\sqrt[2]{}, \sqrt[3]{}, \sqrt[4]{}$, etc. denotes respectively square root, cube root, fourth root, and so on. In the case of the square root the 2 is omitted.

Since $\sqrt{(a \times b \times c)} = \sqrt{a} \times \sqrt{b} \times \sqrt{c}$ a surd may be simplified if it can be split up into factors.

Thus
$$\sqrt{363} = \sqrt{(121 \times 3)} = \sqrt{121} \times \sqrt{3} = 11\sqrt{3}$$
and
$$\sqrt{48} = \sqrt{(16 \times 3)} = \sqrt{16} \times \sqrt{3} = 4\sqrt{3}$$
Also
$$\sqrt{12} \times \sqrt{6} = \sqrt{72} = \sqrt{(36 \times 2)} = 6\sqrt{2}$$
Note that $\sqrt{(a+b+c)}$ is not equal to $\sqrt{a} + \sqrt{b} + \sqrt{c}$

Example 1   Simplify $3\sqrt{12} + 10\sqrt{3} - 6\sqrt{\frac{1}{3}}$

$$
\begin{aligned}
3\sqrt{12} + 10\sqrt{3} - 6\sqrt{\tfrac{1}{3}} &= 3\sqrt{(4 \times 3)} + 10\sqrt{3} - \sqrt{\tfrac{36}{3}} \\
&= 6\sqrt{3} + 10\sqrt{3} - 2\sqrt{3} \\
&= 14\sqrt{3}
\end{aligned}
$$

Example 2   Compare for magnitude the surds $\sqrt[3]{5}, \sqrt[4]{9}, \sqrt[6]{26}$.
The l.c.m. (least common multiple) of 3, 4, and 6 is 12.

Hence express the surds all to the 12th order and write the roots in the form of indices:

$$\sqrt[3]{5} = 5^{\frac{1}{3}} = 5^{\frac{4}{12}} = (5^4)^{\frac{1}{12}} = \sqrt[12]{625}$$

$$\sqrt[4]{9} = 9^{\frac{1}{4}} = 9^{\frac{3}{12}} = (9^3)^{\frac{1}{12}} = \sqrt[12]{729}$$

$$\sqrt[6]{26} = 26^{\frac{1}{6}} = 26^{\frac{2}{12}} = (26^2)^{\frac{1}{12}} = \sqrt[12]{676}$$

Thus $\sqrt[4]{9}$ is the greatest and $\sqrt[3]{5}$ is the least.

Rationalization

In evaluating fractions containing surds it helps if the surd in the denominator can be removed without altering the value of the expression. This is known as rationalizing the denominator.

For example to evaluate $\dfrac{3}{\sqrt{2}}$ we could say $\dfrac{3}{\sqrt{2}} = \dfrac{3}{1\cdot41421}$ approximately and then find the value of the expression by division, but a much shorter method is to rationalize the denominator as follows:

$$\frac{3}{\sqrt{2}} = \frac{3}{\sqrt{2}} \times \frac{\sqrt{2}}{\sqrt{2}} = \frac{3\sqrt{2}}{2} = \frac{3 \times 1\cdot41421}{2} = 2\cdot1213 \text{ correct to 4 decimal places.}$$

Exercise 2a

Simplify (questions 1–15)

1   $\sqrt{32}$ 2 $\sqrt{75}$ 3 $\sqrt{243}$ 4 $\sqrt[3]{81}$

5   $\sqrt[3]{16}$ 6 $\sqrt[3]{(-16)}$ 7 $\sqrt{507}$ 8 $\sqrt{500}$

9   $\sqrt{18} + 3\sqrt{2}$ 10 $2\sqrt{75} - 3\sqrt{3}$

11   $\sqrt{5} + 15\sqrt{\frac{1}{5}}$ 12 $2\sqrt{12} - \sqrt{75} + \sqrt{27}$

13   $2\sqrt{12} + \sqrt{48} - 4\sqrt{3} + 5\sqrt{147}$ 14 $3\sqrt{80} + \sqrt{245} - \sqrt{3125}$

15   $\sqrt[3]{108} + 4\sqrt[3]{32} - \sqrt[3]{500}$ 16   If $\sqrt{50} + \sqrt{162} - \sqrt{98} = x\sqrt{2}$ find x

17   Express $3\sqrt{24} - 5\sqrt{54} + \sqrt{150}$ in the form $k\sqrt{6}$

Calculate to three decimal places the value of the following (questions 18–22) given that $\sqrt{2} = 1\cdot41421$, $\sqrt{3} = 1\cdot73205$, $\sqrt{6} = 2\cdot44949$

18   $\dfrac{6}{\sqrt{2}}$ 19 $\dfrac{2}{\sqrt{3}}$ 20 $\dfrac{6\sqrt{2}}{\sqrt{3}}$ 21 $\dfrac{12}{\sqrt{6}} + \dfrac{1}{\sqrt{3}}$ 22 $\dfrac{\sqrt{2}+1}{\sqrt{3}}$

If an expression containing surds has two or more terms it is called a compound surd.

e.g. $3\sqrt{5}-\sqrt{2}$ and $2\sqrt{3}-\sqrt{7}+4$

The first is called a binomial surd and the second a trinomial surd.

In multiplying two compound surds multiply each term of one by each term of the other as in ordinary algebraic multiplication.

e.g. $(2\sqrt{5}+3\sqrt{2})\times(2\sqrt{5}-\sqrt{2})$
$= (2\sqrt{5}+3\sqrt{2})\times 2\sqrt{5}-(2\sqrt{5}+3\sqrt{2})\times\sqrt{2}$
$= 20+6\sqrt{10}-2\sqrt{10}-6$
$= 14+4\sqrt{10}$

Conjugate binomial surds are two surds of the form

$a\sqrt{b}+c\sqrt{d}$ and $a\sqrt{b}-c\sqrt{d}$

Their product contains no surd – that is, it is rational.

For example $(\sqrt{3}+\sqrt{2})(\sqrt{3}-\sqrt{2}) = (\sqrt{3})^2-(\sqrt{2})^2 = 3-2 = 1$
just as $(x+y)(x-y) = x^2-y^2$
Thus $(\sqrt{x}+\sqrt{y})(\sqrt{x}-\sqrt{y}) = x-y$
$(a\sqrt{b}+c\sqrt{d})(a\sqrt{b}-c\sqrt{d}) = a^2b-c^2d$
$(2\sqrt{5}+3\sqrt{2})(2\sqrt{5}-3\sqrt{2}) = 4\times5-9\times2 = 2$

This property of conjugate surds is used in evaluating fractions. We rationalize the denominator by multiplying numerator and denominator by the conjugate surd of the denominator.

Example 1 Find the value of $\dfrac{1}{2-\sqrt{3}}$ correct to 3 decimal places given $\sqrt{3} = 1{\cdot}7321$

Since $(2-\sqrt{3})(2+\sqrt{3}) = 2^2-3 = 1$ we multiply numerator and denominator by $2+\sqrt{3}$

$$\frac{1}{2-\sqrt{3}} = \frac{1}{(2-\sqrt{3})}\times\frac{(2+\sqrt{3})}{(2+\sqrt{3})} = \frac{2+\sqrt{3}}{2^2-3} = 2+\sqrt{3}$$
$$= 3{\cdot}7321 = 3{\cdot}732 \text{ to 3 decimal places}$$

Example 2 Calculate to 3 decimal places the value of $\dfrac{\sqrt{3}+2\sqrt{2}}{4+\sqrt{6}}$ given $\sqrt{2} = 1{\cdot}4142$

$$\frac{\sqrt{3}+2\sqrt{2}}{4+\sqrt{6}} = \frac{\sqrt{3}+2\sqrt{2}}{4+\sqrt{6}}\times\frac{4-\sqrt{6}}{4-\sqrt{6}} = \frac{4\sqrt{3}+8\sqrt{2}-3\sqrt{2}-4\sqrt{3}}{16-6}$$
$$= \frac{5\sqrt{2}}{10} = \frac{\sqrt{2}}{2} = 0{\cdot}707 \text{ to 3 decimal places}$$

2b   Irrational equations

If an algebraic equation contains the variable under the root sign then the equation must be rationalized.

Example   Solve $\sqrt{(2x-1)} - x + 2 = 0$

We put the term containing the radical on one side of the equation and square it as follows:

$$\sqrt{(2x-1)} = x-2$$

Squaring both sides
$$2x-1 = (x-2)^2$$
$$2x-1 = x^2 - 4x + 4$$
i.e.
$$x^2 - 6x + 5 = 0$$
This equation factorizes to give

$$(x-5)(x-1) = 0$$

Either $x-5 = 0$ giving $x = 5$
or $x-1 = 0$ giving $x = 1$

Squaring an equation often introduces an extra solution so that we must test both $x = 5$ and $x = 1$ to see if they satisfy the original equation.

Putting $x = 5$ in the original equation gives for the left-hand side $\sqrt{(2 \times 5 - 1)} - 5 + 2 = 3 - 5 + 2$ which is zero.

Thus $x = 5$ is a solution.

Putting $x = 1$ in the original equation gives

$$\sqrt{(2 \times 1 - 1)} - 1 + 2 = 1 - 1 + 2 = 2$$

and $x = 1$ is not a solution. It is actually a solution of $-\sqrt{(2x-1)} - x + 2 = 0$

Exercise 2b

Simplify (questions 1–10)

1   $(\sqrt{3}-1)(\sqrt{3}+1)$

2   $(\sqrt{5}+\sqrt{3})(\sqrt{5}-\sqrt{3})$

3   $(\sqrt{7}+2)(\sqrt{7}-2)$

4   $(2\sqrt{3}-\sqrt{2})(2\sqrt{3}+\sqrt{2})$

5   $(4\sqrt{6}+2)(\sqrt{3}+\sqrt{2})$

6   $(8\sqrt{2}+5\sqrt{3})(8\sqrt{2}-5\sqrt{3})$

7   $(1+\sqrt{2}+\sqrt{3})(2+\sqrt{3})$

8   $(4\sqrt{7}+\sqrt{15})(\sqrt{7}-\sqrt{3})$

9   $\{x+\sqrt{(x^2-y^2)}\}\{x-\sqrt{(x^2-y^2)}\}$

10   $\{t+\sqrt{(t^2-1)}\}\{t-\sqrt{(t^2-1)}\}$

Rationalize the denominators in questions 11–19 and express them in their simplest forms

11   $\dfrac{1}{2+\sqrt{3}}$

12   $\dfrac{\sqrt{2}-1}{\sqrt{2}+1}$

13   $\dfrac{1}{3+2\sqrt{2}}$

14   $\dfrac{4}{\sqrt{5}-1}$

15    $\dfrac{3}{2\sqrt{7}+\sqrt{13}}$ 16 $\dfrac{4(\sqrt{3}-1)}{3\sqrt{2}-4}$ 17 $\dfrac{2-4\sqrt{7}}{2\sqrt{7}-1}$ 18 $\dfrac{1}{2+\sqrt{3}}+\dfrac{1}{\sqrt{3}-1}$

19    $\dfrac{3\sqrt{2}}{\sqrt{3}+\sqrt{6}}-\dfrac{4\sqrt{3}}{\sqrt{6}+\sqrt{2}}+\dfrac{\sqrt{6}}{\sqrt{2}+\sqrt{3}}$

Taking $\sqrt{2}=1{\cdot}41421$, $\sqrt{3}=1{\cdot}73205$, $\sqrt{5}=2{\cdot}23607$ calculate to three decimal places the values of questions 20–24

20    $\dfrac{1}{\sqrt{5}+\sqrt{3}}$ 21 $\dfrac{2}{3+2\sqrt{2}}$ 22 $\dfrac{2\sqrt{2}+1}{2\sqrt{2}-1}$ 23 $\dfrac{5}{2\sqrt{3}-2}$

24    $\dfrac{1}{2-\sqrt{3}}+\dfrac{1}{\sqrt{3}+1}$

Solve the equations in questions 25–27

25    $\sqrt{x}+x-2=0$ 26 $2\sqrt{(x+1)}-x+2=0$ 27 $\sqrt{(2x-3)}=x-9$

2c   Ratio and proportion

We speak of the relative sizes of two quantities of the same kind as a *ratio*.

Thus the ratio of *a* to *b* is the quotient obtained by dividing *a* by *b*. It is written $\dfrac{a}{b}$ or sometimes $a:b$.

For example the ratio of two centimetres to one metre is the ratio of 2 centimetres to 100 centimetres.

i.e. $\dfrac{2\text{ cm}}{100\text{ cm}}=\dfrac{1}{50}$ or $1:50$

The idea of ratio is not restricted to two quantities only. If we say that three quantities are in the ratio $2:3:5$ we mean that the first quantity is $\dfrac{2}{2+3+5}=\dfrac{2}{10}$ of the whole, the second quantity is $\frac{3}{10}$ of the whole and the third is $\frac{5}{10}$ of the whole.

Example 1   A certain alloy contains 70% copper, 18% zinc and 12% tin by weight. Calculate the weight of tin in 20 kg of alloy.

The weights of copper, zinc, and tin are in the ratio $70:18:12$ respectively.

Thus the weight of tin is $\dfrac{12}{70+18+12}=\dfrac{12}{100}$ of the whole.

38   **Quadratic and other equations**

$$\therefore \qquad \text{weight of tin in 20 kg of alloy} = \frac{12}{100} \times 20$$
$$= 2{\cdot}4 \text{ kg.}$$

Example 2   If $\dfrac{4x-3y}{3x+y} = \dfrac{6}{11}$ find the ratio $x:y$

By cross multiplication

$$11(4x-3y) = 6(3x+y)$$
$$44x-33y = 18x+6y$$
$$26x = 39y$$
$$\therefore \qquad \frac{x}{y} = \frac{39}{26} = \frac{3}{2}$$

When the ratio of two quantities equals the ratio of a second pair a *proportion* is formed.

Thus four numbers a, b, c, d are in proportion when the ratio of the first pair equals the ratio of the second.

This is denoted by $\dfrac{a}{b} = \dfrac{c}{d}$

It is sometimes written $a:b::c:d$ but this notation is becoming obsolete.

If $\dfrac{a}{b} = \dfrac{c}{d}$ various other proportions follow

1. $\dfrac{a}{c} = \dfrac{b}{d}$

2. $\dfrac{b}{a} = \dfrac{d}{c}$ since $\dfrac{1}{\dfrac{a}{b}} = \dfrac{1}{\dfrac{c}{d}}$

3. $\dfrac{a+b}{b} = \dfrac{c+d}{d}$ since $\dfrac{a}{b}+1 = \dfrac{c}{d}+1$

4. $\dfrac{a-b}{b} = \dfrac{c-d}{d}$ since $\dfrac{a}{b}-1 = \dfrac{c}{d}-1$

5. $\dfrac{a+b}{a-b} = \dfrac{c+d}{c-d}$ from 3. and 4.

Many quite impressive properties of ratios are easily proved by taking some single letter k to represent each of several equal ratios as in the following:

If $\dfrac{a}{b} = \dfrac{c}{d} = \dfrac{e}{f}$ then each of these ratios is equal to $\left(\dfrac{pa^n+qc^n+re^n}{pb^n+qd^n+rf^n}\right)^{\frac{1}{n}}$

where p, q and r are any constants.

Let $\dfrac{a}{b} = \dfrac{c}{d} = \dfrac{e}{f} = k$

Then $a = bk, c = dk, e = fk$

Substituting these values in $\left(\dfrac{pa^n + qc^n + re^n}{pb^n + qd^n + rf^n}\right)^{\frac{1}{n}}$ we get

$$\left(\frac{pb^n k^n + qd^n k^n + rf^n k^n}{pb^n + qd^n + rf^n}\right)^{\frac{1}{n}} = (k^n)^{\frac{1}{n}} = k$$

$$= \frac{a}{b} = \frac{c}{d} = \frac{e}{f}$$

Exercise 2c

1 A brass contains 7 parts by weight of copper to 3 of zinc. Find the weight of copper in 500 kg of the brass.

2 Find the quantities in cubic metres of cement, sand, and aggregate respectively to cover a rectangular area of 5 m by 4 m to a depth of 25 cm if the concrete mixture is in the ratio $1:3:6$.

3 For what value of x will the ratio $\dfrac{7+x}{12+x}$ equal the ratio $\dfrac{5}{6}$?

4 If $\dfrac{5x-4y}{3x-2y} = 4$, find the ratio of x to y

5 If $\dfrac{x}{4} = \dfrac{y}{7}$, find the ratio of $x+4$ to $y+7$

6 If $\dfrac{x}{y} = \dfrac{3}{5}$, find the value of $\dfrac{x+y}{y-x}$

7 If $6x^2 + 6y^2 = 13xy$, what is the ratio of x to y?

8 If $\dfrac{a}{b} = \dfrac{c}{d} = \dfrac{e}{f}$, prove

(a) $\dfrac{2a^3 + 3a^2c + c^2e}{2b^3 + 3b^2d + d^2f} = \dfrac{a^3}{b^3}$

(b) $\dfrac{ae + 2c^2}{bf + 2d^2} = \dfrac{a^2 + c^2}{b^2 + d^2}$

(c) $\dfrac{2a + 3c - 4e}{2b + 3d - 4f} = \dfrac{2a - 3c + 4e}{2b - 3d + 4f} = \dfrac{a}{b}$

9 Two numbers are in the ratio $\dfrac{3}{4}$. When each is increased by 5 they have the ratio $\dfrac{4}{5}$. Find the numbers.

10   Find two numbers whose sum is 91 and whose ratio is $\dfrac{6}{7}$

11   Divide 72 in the ratio $\dfrac{7}{11}$

12   Two tanks contain mixtures of oil and petrol in ratios 1 to 10 and 2 to 9. In what ratio must liquid be drawn from each tank to give a mixture of oil and petrol in the ratio 1 to 8?

13   The marks gained by 3 candidates in an examination paper for which the maximum marks were 65, were 53, 42 and 37. What would these marks be if the maximum is changed to 100?

14   An alloy contains a mixture of 55% copper, 27% zinc and 18% nickel. How many kilogrammes of each are needed to make 2 Mg of the alloy?

2d   Variation

Direct variation

When the ratio of two quantities remains constant however much their values may alter one is said to *vary directly* as the other.

Thus when $\dfrac{y}{x} =$ a constant ratio $= k$

or $y = kx$,   then y is said to vary directly as x.
This is sometimes written $y \propto x$.

While ratio is only applicable to quantities of the same kind we can state that one quantity varies or is proportional to another even when they are of different kinds.

Thus the tension in newtons in an elastic string is proportional to the extension in metres up to a certain limit known as the elastic limit.

We can say $T = kx$ where T stands for the tension and x for the extension. The constant k will now involve the units N and m.

Inverse variation

If one quantity y is said to vary inversely as the other quantity x, then y varies directly as the reciprocal of x.

Thus if y varies inversely as x

$$y = \dfrac{k}{x}$$

or $xy = k$

Joint variation

When one quantity varies directly as the product of a number of other quantities it is said to vary jointly as the others.

Thus if y varies jointly as x and z

then $\qquad y = kxz$

If $\qquad y = k\dfrac{xz}{w}$, y is said to vary jointly as x and z and inversely as w.

Example 1 A spring is stretched 10 cm by a weight of 4 N. What extension will be caused by a weight of 5 N?

Let T stand for the tension and x for the extension.

We may write $\quad T = kx$

Putting $\qquad T = 4\,\text{N and } x = 10\,\text{cm}$

we get $\qquad 4\,\text{N} = k\,10\,\text{cm}$

Thus $\qquad k = \dfrac{4\,\text{N}}{10\,\text{cm}}$

and $\qquad T = \dfrac{4\,\text{N}}{10\,\text{cm}}\,x$

When $\qquad T = 5\,\text{N}\quad$ we get $\quad 5\,\text{N} = \dfrac{4\,\text{N}}{10\,\text{cm}}\,x$

Whence $\qquad x = \dfrac{5 \times 10}{4} = 12\cdot5\,\text{cm}.$

Answer: extension $= 12\cdot5$ cm.

In problems of this type it is as well to put in the units to prevent any confusion.

Example 2 If y is equal to the sum of two quantities one of which varies directly as x and the other inversely as x, and if $y = 4$ when $x = 1$ and $y = 8$ when $x = 5$, find the relation between x and y. Also find the value of y when $x = 3$.

$y = p+q$ where $\quad p \propto x$; i.e. $\quad p = kx$

$$\text{and} \quad q \propto \frac{1}{x}\,; \text{i.e.} \quad q = \frac{c}{x}$$

Hence $\quad y = kx + \dfrac{c}{x}\quad$ where k and c are constants.

When $\quad x = 1\ \ y = 4\quad$ Hence $\quad 4 = k+c\ \ \ldots(2.1)$

When $\quad x = 5\ \ y = 8\quad$ Hence $\quad 8 = 5k + \dfrac{c}{5}\ldots(2.2)$

We have two simultaneous equations in k and c.

42 Quadratic and other equations

Multiply equation (2.2) by 5 and subtract equation (2.1) from it.

$$40 - 4 = 25k - k \quad \therefore \ k = \frac{36}{24} = 1\tfrac{1}{2}$$

Substitute $k = 1\tfrac{1}{2}$ in equation (2.1) to give

$$c = 4 - 1\tfrac{1}{2} = 2\tfrac{1}{2}$$

Thus $\qquad y = \dfrac{3}{2}x + \dfrac{5}{2x}$

When $\quad x = 3 \cdot \ y = \dfrac{3 \times 3}{2} + \dfrac{5}{2 \times 3} = 4\tfrac{1}{2} + \tfrac{5}{6}$

$$= 5\tfrac{1}{3}$$

Example 3 The resistance R of a wire to electric current is directly proportional to the length L and inversely proportional to its area of cross-section A. Express this as a formula.

If the resistance of 2000 m of wire of cross-section 0·002 sq. cm is 36 ohms, calculate the resistance of a wire of similar material of length 80 m and cross-section 0·015 sq. cm.

The formula connecting R, L, and A is

$$R = \frac{kL}{A}$$

Substituting $\quad R = 36, L = 2000$ and $A = 0·002$

we get $\quad 36 = \dfrac{k \times 2000}{0·002} \quad \therefore \ k = \dfrac{36 \times 0·002}{2000}$

$$\therefore \qquad k = \frac{36}{1\,000\,000}$$

Thus $\quad R = \dfrac{36}{10^6} \cdot \dfrac{L}{A},$ where R is in ohms, L is in metres, and A is in square centimetres, so for L equalling 80 m and A equalling 0·015 sq. cm

$$R = \frac{36}{10^6} \times \frac{80}{0·015} \text{ ohms}$$

$$= \frac{\overset{12}{\cancel{36}}\ \overset{16\,000}{\cancel{80\,000}}}{10^6 \quad \underset{3}{\cancel{15}}} = \frac{12 \times 16}{10^3} = \frac{192}{1000}$$

$$= 0·192 \text{ ohms}$$

Exercise 2d

1   If $y \propto x$ and $y = 2$ when $x = 3$, find the equation between x and y and give the value of y when $x = 9$.

2   If $y \propto \dfrac{1}{x}$ and $y = 3$ when $x = 4$, find y when $x = 2$.

3   z varies directly as x and inversely as y. If $z = 8$ when $x = 12$ and $y = 15$, find the value of z when $x = 2$ and $y = 5$.

4   y varies as the sum of two quantities, one of which varies directly as x and the other varies inversely as x. If $y = 4\frac{1}{2}$ when $x = 1$ and $y = 12\frac{3}{8}$ when $x = 4$, find the relation between x and y.

5   If x varies as r^2 and y varies as r^5, show that x^5 varies as y^2.

6   The volume V of a given mass of gas varies directly as the absolute temperature T and inversely as the pressure P. If V is 7 when $T = 350$ and $P = 15$ find V when $T = 550$ and $P = 50$ units.

7   The mass of a hemisphere varies as the cube of its radius. If the mass of a hemisphere of radius 30 cm is 12 kg, find the weight of a hemisphere of the same material of radius 45 cm.

8   If the tension of a stretched spring is proportional to its extension and a spring 20 cm long is stretched to 25 cm by a weight of 8 N, find its length under a weight of 12 N.

9   The weight of a cylinder of given material varies as the square of its diameter if its height is constant, and varies as its height, when the diameter is constant. The diameter of one cylinder is $\frac{2}{3}$ that of a second cylinder and its height is $\frac{3}{4}$ that of the second. If the first cylinder weighs 6 N, find the weight of the second.

10   The distance of the visible horizon at sea varies as the square root of the height of the eye above sea level. If the distance is 5 km when the height is 2 m., find the distance of the visible horizon from the top of a lighthouse which is 72 m above the sea.

11   The weight of a cone of given material varies directly as the square of the diameter of the base and also as the height. A cone of base diameter 60 cm and height 80 cm weighs 54 N. Find the diameter of the base of a second cone of similar material of height 50 cm and weight 15 N.

44   Quadratic and other equations

12 The expenses of a hostel are partly constant and partly proportional to the number of students in residence. When the hostel contains 80 students the expenses are £6450 and when there are 95 students the expenses for the same period of time are £7575. Find the relationship between expenses and numbers.

2e Quadratic equations

A quadratic *expression* in x is an expression of the form $ax^2 + bx + c$.

A quadratic *equation* in x is an expression of the form $ax^2 + bx + c = 0$.

A quadratic equation has 2 solutions, that is, it is true for two values of x.

Thus the equation $3x^2 + 5x - 2 = 0$ is true for $x = \dfrac{1}{3}$ and for $x = -2$.

No other value of x substituted in the left hand side of this equation will make it zero.

These two values are called the *roots* of the equation and finding the roots is known as solving the equation.

Solution by factors

If we can factorize the equation when all its terms are on one side then we can find the roots by putting each factor in turn equal to zero.

Thus $2x^2 - x - 3 = 0$ factorizes into

$(2x - 3)(x + 1) = 0$

For this to be zero then one of the factors must be zero.

Either $2x - 3 = 0$ giving $x = \dfrac{3}{2}$

or $x + 1 = 0$ giving $x = -1$

The roots are $\dfrac{3}{2}$ and -1.

Solution by the method of completing the square

Since $\left(x + \dfrac{a}{2}\right)^2 = x^2 + ax + \dfrac{a^2}{4}$

we can make $x^2 + ax$ into a perfect square by adding $\left(\dfrac{a}{2}\right)^2$, that is, by adding the square of half the coefficient of x.

Thus $x^2 + 3x$ becomes a perfect square by adding $\left(\dfrac{3}{2}\right)^2$

for $\quad x^2+3x+\left(\dfrac{3}{2}\right)^2 = \left(x+\dfrac{3}{2}\right)^2$

This can be useful in solving quadratic equations.

Example Solve $2x^2+6x-9 = 0$

Dividing by 2 we have

$$x^2+3x-4\tfrac{1}{2} = 0$$
i.e. $\quad x^2+3x \qquad = 4\tfrac{1}{2}$

Add $\left(\dfrac{3}{2}\right)^2$ to both sides to make the terms containing x a perfect square

$$x^2+3x+\left(\dfrac{3}{2}\right)^2 = 4\tfrac{1}{2}+\left(\dfrac{3}{2}\right)^2$$

$$\left(x+\dfrac{3}{2}\right)^2 = \dfrac{27}{4}$$

Taking the square root of each side and remembering that the square root can be either positive or negative:

$$x+\dfrac{3}{2} = \pm\sqrt{\left(\dfrac{27}{4}\right)} = \pm\dfrac{3\sqrt{3}}{2}$$

Thus $\quad x = -\dfrac{3}{2}\pm\dfrac{3\sqrt{3}}{2}$

$$= -1\cdot5\pm2\cdot598$$
$$= 1\cdot098 \text{ or } -4\cdot098$$

Solution by formula

The standard form of a quadratic equation is

$$ax^2+bx+c = 0$$

Dividing by a we get $\quad x^2+\dfrac{b}{a}x+\dfrac{c}{a} = 0$

i.e. $\qquad\qquad\qquad\qquad x^2+\dfrac{b}{a}x = -\dfrac{c}{a}$

Adding $\left(\dfrac{b}{2a}\right)^2$ to each side to make the left-hand side a perfect square we get

$$x^2+\dfrac{b}{a}x+\left(\dfrac{b}{2a}\right)^2 = \left(\dfrac{b}{2a}\right)^2-\dfrac{c}{a}$$

i.e. $\left(x+\dfrac{b}{2a}\right)^2 = \dfrac{b^2-4ac}{4a^2}$

$$\therefore\; x+\dfrac{b}{2a} = \dfrac{\pm\sqrt{(b^2-4ac)}}{2a}$$

$$\therefore\; x = -\dfrac{b}{2a}\pm\dfrac{\sqrt{(b^2-4ac)}}{2a}$$

$$= \dfrac{-b\pm\sqrt{(b^2-4ac)}}{2a}$$

This may be memorized as a formula to give the roots of a quadratic equation.

Some students prefer to write the standard form of the quadratic equation as $x^2+2px+q = 0$ which leads to the formula $x = -p\pm\sqrt{(p^2-q)}$ to give the roots. Whichever formula is used the student should be able to derive it for himself.

The two solutions or roots of $ax^2+bx+c = 0$ which we denote by α and β are

$$\alpha = \dfrac{-b+\sqrt{(b^2-4ac)}}{2a} \quad \text{and} \quad \beta = \dfrac{-b-\sqrt{(b^2-4ac)}}{2a}$$

The nature of the roots depends very much on the term $\sqrt{(b^2-4ac)}$. If this term is zero, the roots are equal and each will be $-\dfrac{b}{2a}$.

If b^2-4ac is negative, then as we cannot find a number which is the square root of a negative quantity we say that the roots are not real. $\sqrt{(b^2-4ac)}$ is said to be *imaginary* and the root is called a *complex number*.

Example 1 Solve the equation $x^2+x-3\tfrac{3}{4} = 0$ by the method of completing the square.

$$x^2+x-3\tfrac{3}{4} = 0$$
$$x^2+x = 3\tfrac{3}{4}$$

Adding the square of half the coefficient of x to each side

$$x^2+x+\left(\frac{1}{2}\right)^2 = 3\tfrac{3}{4}+\left(\frac{1}{2}\right)^2$$

$$\left(x+\frac{1}{2}\right)^2 = 4$$

$$x+\frac{1}{2} = \pm 2$$

$$x = -\frac{1}{2}+2 \quad \text{or} \quad -\frac{1}{2}-2$$

Thus $\qquad x = 1\frac{1}{2}$ or $-2\frac{1}{2}$

Example 2 Given that $y = \sqrt{\left(\dfrac{5x^2}{P+3x}\right)}$ find the values of x when $y = 2$ and $P = 10$

Substituting for y and P we get

$$2 = \sqrt{\left(\frac{5x^2}{10+3x}\right)}$$

Squaring both sides $\quad 4 = \dfrac{5x^2}{10+3x}$

$$4(10+3x) = 5x^2$$

i.e. $\qquad 5x^2 - 12x - 40 = 0$

Using the formula $\quad x = \dfrac{12 \pm \sqrt{\{(-12)^2 - 4.5.(-40)\}}}{2 \times 5}$

$$= \frac{12 \pm \sqrt{(144+800)}}{10}$$

$$= \frac{12 \pm 30{\cdot}72}{10}$$

$$= 4{\cdot}272 \quad \text{or} \quad -1{\cdot}872$$

Exercise 2e(i)

Complete the equations in questions 1–5:

1   $x^2 + 6x + \quad = (x + \quad)^2$ 2 $x^2 + 4x + \quad = (x + \quad)^2$

3   $x^2 - 6x + \quad = (x - \quad)^2$ 4 $2x^2 - x + \quad = 2(x - \quad)^2$

5   $3x^2 + x + \quad = 3(x + \quad)^2$

Solve the equations in questions 6–21:

6   $x^2 - 5x + 6 = 0$ 7 $x^2 + 10x + 21 = 0$

8   $x(x-4) = 5$ 9 $x(x+4) = 6(x+4)$

10   $x - \dfrac{9}{2} + \dfrac{2}{x} = 0$ 11 $x^2 - 0{\cdot}5x + 0{\cdot}06 = 0$

12   $m(m-7) + 12 = 0$ 13 $z^2 + 1{\cdot}1z - 1{\cdot}8 = 0$

14   $t(t-6) = 15$ 15 $\dfrac{6}{t} + \dfrac{10}{t+1} = 5$

16    $x^2 - 4x + 1 = 0$ 17 $5x^2 - 9x + 4 = 0$

18    $x^2 - \sqrt{3}x - 6 = 0$ 19 $15(x-3)^2 + 79(x-2) + 11 = 0$

20    $(x + \frac{1}{2})^2 - 4(x+2) + 1 = 0$ 21 $\dfrac{x+3}{x} - \dfrac{3-x}{2(x+1)} = \dfrac{7}{3}$

22   If α and β are the roots of the equation $2x^2 + 8x + 7 = 0$ write down the values of i $\alpha + \beta$ ii $\alpha\beta$

        Without solving the equation for α and β find the value of $\alpha^2 + \beta^2$

23   Find the possible values of a, if one root of the equation $ax^2 - 9x + 3a + 3 = 0$ is twice the other.

24   Find the value of k for which the equation $4x^2 - 12x + 13 = k$ has equal roots.

25   If the roots of the equation $4x^2 - (k-2)x + 1 = 0$ are real, find the numbers between which k must lie.

26   In the equation $3^{2x} - 4.3^x + 3 = 0$, put $y = 3^x$ to obtain a quadratic equation in y.

        Solve this equation for y and so find values of x which are solutions of the equation.

.27   Solve the equation $2^{2x} - 7.2^x + 10 = 0$ by using the substitution $y = 2^x$

28   Solve the equation $x^4 - 3x^2 + 2 = 0$

29   The formula $M = \dfrac{wx(l-x)}{2}$ gives the bending moment M at a point in a beam.

        If $M = 70, l = 20$, and $w = 1\frac{1}{2}$ find the values of x.

30   A solid cylinder is 70 cm high and has a total surface area of $7.2\ \text{m}^2$. Calculate its diameter.

31   The formula $l = \dfrac{8y^2}{3x} + x$ gives the sag y in a cable of length l stretching between two supports, distance x apart.

        Find x when $l = 80$ and $y = 3$

49   **Quadratic equations**

32 The stress p set up in a bar of length l, cross-section A, by a weight W falling a distance h is given by the formula

$$p^2 - \frac{2W}{A}p - \frac{2WEh}{Al} = 0$$

If $E = 13\,000$, find the large value of p when $l = 120$, $h = \frac{1}{2}$, $W = 2\cdot23$ and $A = 3\cdot142$.

Solution by graph

Most students will have plotted graphs of quadratic expressions, graphs of $y = x^2$, $y = 2x^2 - x + 3$, and so on, and will be familiar with the shape of these curves, which are all parabolas. A quadratic equation may be solved graphically, but this method is not as accurate as the algebraic methods.

As an example we will solve by a graphical method the equation

$$x^2 + x - 3\tfrac{3}{4} = 0$$

We plot a graph of $y = x^2 + x - 3\frac{3}{4}$ for a range of values of x, say -3 to $+3$

x	-3	-2	-1	0	1	2	3
x^2	9	4	1	0	1	4	9
x	-3	-2	-1	0	1	2	3
$-3\frac{3}{4}$	$-3\frac{3}{4}$	$-3\frac{3}{4}$	$-3\frac{3}{4}$	$-3\frac{3}{4}$	$-3\frac{3}{4}$	$-3\frac{3}{4}$	$-3\frac{3}{4}$
y	$2\frac{1}{4}$	$-1\frac{3}{4}$	$-3\frac{3}{4}$	$-3\frac{3}{4}$	$-1\frac{3}{4}$	$2\frac{1}{4}$	$8\frac{1}{4}$

Figure 4

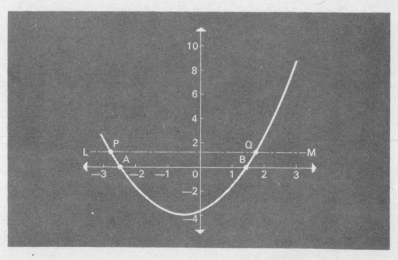

Where the curve cuts the x axis we have $y = 0$. At these points marked A and B, $x^2 + x - 3\frac{3}{4} = 0$. The values of x at these points, namely $x = -2\frac{1}{2}$ and $1\frac{1}{2}$, clearly make $x^2 + x - 3\frac{3}{4}$ equal to zero.

Therefore $x = -2\frac{1}{2}$ and $x = 1\frac{1}{2}$ are roots of the equation.

Incidentally, we can use this graph to solve a similar equation, such as $x^2 + x - 3\frac{3}{4} = k$.

Consider the equation $x^2 + x - 5 = 0$. If we rearrange this we may write it

as $x^2 + x - 3\frac{3}{4} - 1\frac{1}{4} = 0$
or $x^2 + x - 3\frac{3}{4} = 1\frac{1}{4}$

If we draw the line $y = 1\frac{1}{4}$ as represented by LM in the graph, where this cuts the graph $y = x^2 + x - 3\frac{3}{4}$ we have

$$x^2 + x - 3\frac{3}{4} = 1\frac{1}{4}$$
i.e. $x^2 + x - 5 = 0$

Thus the values of x at P and Q are values which make

$$x^2 + x - 3\frac{3}{4} = 1\frac{1}{4}$$
i.e. $x^2 + x - 5 = 0$

From the graph these are -2.8 and 1.8

Notice that the formula gives a more accurate result:

$$x = \frac{-1 \pm \sqrt{(1 + 4 \times 5)}}{2} = -\frac{1}{2} \pm \frac{\sqrt{21}}{2} = -\frac{1}{2} \pm \frac{4.583}{2}$$

$$= -2.792 \quad \text{or} \quad 1.792$$

Consider what happens if we try to solve the equation

$$x^2 + x - 3\frac{3}{4} = -5 \quad \text{i.e.} \quad x^2 + x + 1\frac{1}{4} = 0$$

We draw a horizontal line through the value $y = -5$ and where this line cuts the parabola $y = x^2 + x - 3\frac{3}{4}$ would give the values of x which satisfy the equation $x^2 + x + 1\frac{1}{4} = 0$

As the line $y = -5$ does not meet the graph of $y = x^2 + x - 3\frac{3}{4}$ then there is no real value of x satisfying the equation

$$x^2 + x - 3\frac{3}{4} = -5 \quad \text{or} \quad x^2 + x + 1\frac{1}{4} = 0$$

This quadratic equation has no real roots. This is the case of imaginary or complex roots.

Comparing with $ax^2 + bx + c = 0$ we see that

$$b^2 - 4ac = 1^2 - 4 \times 1\frac{1}{4} = -4 \quad \text{i.e.} \quad b^2 - 4ac \text{ is negative.}$$

If we draw the graph of $y = x^2 + x + 1\frac{1}{4}$ we see that it does not cut the x axis (see fig. 5).

The equation $x^2 + x + 1\frac{1}{4} = 0$ has no real roots.

Figure
5

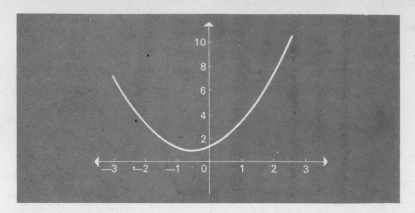

Exercise 2e(ii)

Graphical problems

1 Plot the graph of $y = x^2 - 5x + 2 \cdot 25$ from $x = -2$ to $x = 6$
   From this graph obtain the roots of the equation

   $$x^2 - 5x + 2 \cdot 25 = 0$$

2 Plot the graph of $y = x^2 - x - 3\frac{3}{4}$ from $x = -3$ to $x = 4$
   From the graph find the least value of $x^2 - x - 3\frac{3}{4}$
   Use the graph to solve the equation $x^2 - x - 3\frac{3}{4} = 0$

3 Plot the graph of $y = 2x^2 - x + 1$ from values of x from -3 to $+3$. From the
   graph find the following
   (a) the minimum value of $2x^2 - x + 1$
   (b) the roots of $2x^2 - x + 1 = 0$
   (c) the roots of $2x^2 - x - 3 = 0$

4 Using the same axes, plot the graphs of $y = x^2$ and $y = 2x + 3 \cdot 5$. From the
   graphs find the solutions of $x^2 - 2x - 3 \cdot 5 = 0$

5 Draw the graph of $y = x^2 - 3x + 4 = 0$ and find the minimum value of
   $x^2 - 3x + 4$. Use your graph to show that $x^2 - 3x + 4 = 0$ has no real roots.

6 On the same axes and to the same scales, plot graphs of the functions
   $17 - 4x - 2x^2$ and $2x + 16$ between the values of $x = -4$ and $x = 2$
   Use the graphs to solve the equation $2x^2 + 6x - 1 = 0$

52   Quadratic and other equations

2f   First and second degree simultaneous equations

Solving two simultaneous linear or first degree equations in two unknowns should be a fairly easy problem to the student. For example, the solution of the simultaneous equations $x+y = 3$; $3x-2y = 4$ is easily found to be $x = 2, y = 1$.

With three unknowns we require three independent equations. The solution takes a little longer than with two unknowns, but the method is basically the same.

Example 1   Solve the equations
$$2x-y+z = 7 \ldots (2.3)$$
$$3x-2y-2z = 5 \ldots (2.4)$$
$$4x+2y+3z = 4 \ldots (2.5)$$

First we eliminate z from equations (2.3) and (2.4)
Multiplying (2.3) by 2 $4x-2y+2z = 14$
Adding (2.4) $3x-2y-2z = \ \ 5$

$$7x-4y = 19 \ldots (2.6)$$

Next we eliminate z from equations (2.3) and (2.5)
Multiplying (2.3) by 3 $6x-3y+3z = 21$
Subtracting (2.5) $4x+2y+3z = \ \ 4$

$$2x-5y \ \ \ \ = 17 \ldots (2.7)$$

We have now reduced the problem to the easier one of solving two simultaneous equations in two unknowns; that is, of solving equations (2.6) and (2.7).

Multiplying equation (2.6) by 5 $35x-20y = 95$
Multiplying equation (2.7) by 4 and subtracting $8x-20y = 68$

$$27x \ \ \ \ \ \ \ = 27 \ldots (2.8)$$

Hence $x = 1$; and substituting this value of x in equation (2.6) we get $7-4y = 19$ i.e. $y = -3$

Substituting $x = 1$ and $y = -3$ in equation (2.3) we get $2+3+z = 7$ from which $z = 2$

Thus the required solution is $x = 1, y = -3, z = 2$

It is wise to check that these values satisfy equations (2.4) and (2.5).

If we have to solve simultaneous equations of degree higher than the first degree then we generally find more than one solution; in general the number of different solutions is equal to the product of the degrees of the equations.

Example 2   Solve the equations
$$2x+y = 8 \ldots (2.9)$$
$$xy = 6 \ldots (2.10)$$

From equation (2.9) $y = 8 - 2x$ and substituting this value for y in equation
(2.10) $(8 - 2x)x = 6$

$$8x - 2x^2 = 6$$
$$2x^2 - 8x + 6 = 0$$

Thus $\qquad 2(x-1)(x-3) = 0$

giving $\qquad x = 1 \quad$ or $\quad x = 3$

When $\qquad x = 1, y = 8 - 2 \times 1 = 6$

and when $\quad x = 3, y = 8 - 2 \times 3 = 2$

The required solutions are $x = 1, y = 6$ and $x = 3, y = 2$

Example 3 Solve the equations $\quad 9x^2 + y^2 = 52 \dots (2.11)$
$$xy = \quad 8 \dots (2.12)$$

From equation (2.12) we get $y = \dfrac{8}{x}$ and substituting this in equation (2.11)

$$9x^2 + \frac{64}{x^2} = 52$$

Multiplying both sides by x^2 and putting all the terms on one side

$$9x^4 - 52x^2 + 64 = 0$$

We factorize this as a quadratic equation in x^2 as the variable

$$(9x^2 - 16)(x^2 - 4) = 0$$

Thus $\quad x^2 = \dfrac{16}{9} \quad$ or $\quad 4 \quad$ and taking square roots

$$x = \frac{4}{3} \quad \text{or} \quad \frac{-4}{3} \quad \text{or} \quad 2 \quad \text{or} \quad -2$$

Since $\quad y = \dfrac{8}{x} \quad$ corresponding values of y are $6, -6, 4, -4$

Thus $\quad \left. \begin{matrix} x = \frac{4}{3} \\ y = 6 \end{matrix} \right\} \quad \left. \begin{matrix} x = \frac{-4}{3} \\ y = -6 \end{matrix} \right\} \quad \left. \begin{matrix} x = 2 \\ y = 4 \end{matrix} \right\} \quad \text{and} \quad \left. \begin{matrix} x = -2 \\ y = -4 \end{matrix} \right\} \quad$ are the solutions.

2g Linear equations: solution by desk calculating machine

The method is illustrated by setting out as follows the solution to example 1,
worked at the beginning of the discussion on first and second degree simultaneous equations (see page 53).

54 Quadratic and other equations

The equations for solution were

$$2x - y + z = 7 \ldots (2.3)$$
$$3x - 2y - 2z = 5 \ldots (2.4)$$
$$4x + 2y + 3z = 4 \ldots (2.5)$$

When using a machine the layout consists of the numbers only, the procedure being the same as that used in the previous solution. (See worked example 1, page 53.)

Equation number	Operation	Coefficient of			r.h.s.	Sum
		x	y	z		
(2.3)		2	-1	1	7	9
(2.4)		3	-2	-2	5	4
(2.5)		4	2	3	4	13
(2.6)	$(2.3) \times 2 + (2.4)$	7	-4		19	22
(2.7)	$(2.3) \times 3 - (2.5)$	2	-5		17	14
(2.8)	$(2.6) \times 5 - (2.7) \times 4$	27			27	54

$$\therefore x = \frac{27}{27} = 1$$

From (2.7) $\quad -5y = 17 - 2 \quad \therefore y = -3$
From (2.3) $\quad\quad z = 7 - 2 - 3 = 2$

Check: from equation (2.4)

$$3x - 2y - 2z = 3 - 2(-3) - 2.2 = 5$$

Note the use of the last column which contains the sum of the rest of the terms in that row. Each operation is carried out on this column as on other columns and at each stage we check that the sum column agrees with the sum of the remaining columns. This provides a constant check on the arithmetic until the first unknown is found.

In practical problems the coefficients in equations are not usually whole or exact numbers and the solution of such equations can be long and tedious unless a calculating machine is used.

Example 2 Solve the equations

$$2 \cdot 73x + 0 \cdot 92y + 1 \cdot 33z = 5 \cdot 40 \ldots (2.13)$$
$$0 \cdot 45x - 1 \cdot 13y + 2 \cdot 12z = 18 \cdot 7 \ldots (2.14)$$
$$1 \cdot 65x + 0 \cdot 82y + 0 \cdot 47z = 10 \cdot 3 \ldots (2.15)$$

We eliminate z from the equations by selecting equation (2.14) as the 'pivotal' equation as it has the largest coefficient of z ($= 2 \cdot 12$). This equation is multiplied throughout by $0.4717 \left(= \dfrac{1}{2.12} \right)$ and is then used to eliminate z from equation (2.13) and (2.15). The table illustrates the method.

Equation number	Operation	Coefficient of			r.h.s.	Sum
		x	y	z		
(2.13)		2·73	0·92	1·33	5·40	10·38
(2.14)		0·45	−1·13	2·12	18·70	20·14
(2.15)		1·65	0·82	0·47	10·30	13·24
(2.16)	(2.14) × 0·4717	0·212	−0·533	1	8·821	9·500
(2.17)	(2.13) − 1·33 × (2.16)	2·448	1·629		−6·332	−2·255
(2.18)	(2.15) − 0·47 × (2.16)	1·550	1·071		6·154	8·775
(2.19)	(2.17) × 0·614	1·503	1		−3·888	−1·385
(2.20)	(2.18) − 1·07 × (2.19)	−0·060			10·318	10·258

From equation (2.20) we have

$$x = -\frac{10.318}{0.060} = -172.0$$

Equation (2.19) gives $y = -3.888 - 1.503x = 254.6$
Equation (2.16) gives $z = 8.821 - 0.212x + 0.533y = 181.0$
    As a final check we substitute these values into equation (2.13)

l.h.s. $= -2.73 \times 172.0 + 0.92 \times 254.6 + 1.33 \times 181.0 = 5.40 =$ r.h.s.

Solution: $x = -172, y = 255, z = 181$

Exercise 2g

1   Solve the simultaneous equations $\dfrac{x}{3} + \dfrac{y}{2} = 4$

$$\frac{2x}{3} - \frac{y}{4} = 3$$

2   Find the values of M_1 and M_2 which satisfy the equations

$$M_1 + \frac{M_2}{3} = 4.4$$

$$3M_1 - 4M_2 = 10.2$$

3   Solve the equations $\dfrac{2}{x}+\dfrac{3}{y} = 1\frac{1}{15}$

$$\dfrac{5}{x}-\dfrac{4}{y} = \dfrac{1}{9}$$

4   For a simple lifting machine the effort P to lift a load W is given by the formula $P = aW+b$, when W is 100 N, P is 24 N, and when W is 250 N, P is 42 N. By substituting these values in turn in the equation $P = aW+b$, obtain two simultaneous equations in a and b, and solve these to find the values of the constants a and b.

The equation $P = aW+b$ is known as the law of the load–effort graph.

5   Solve the simultaneous equations

$x+2y+3z = 5$
$3x+y+2z = 6$
$2x+3y+z = 1$

6   Solve the simultaneous equations

$3l+2m-n = 1$
$2l-m+3n = 20$
$-l+m+2n = 3$

7   Solve the following simultaneous equations for

$\dfrac{1}{a}, \dfrac{1}{b}, \dfrac{1}{c}$ and hence find a, b, c:

$\dfrac{1}{a}+\dfrac{1}{b}+\dfrac{2}{c} = 6$

$\dfrac{2}{a}-\dfrac{3}{b}-\dfrac{1}{c} = 7$

$\dfrac{3}{a}+\dfrac{1}{b}+\dfrac{1}{c} = 10$

8   The following relationships between currents exist in a network. Find the values of i_1, i_2, i_3.

$10i_1-4i_2 = 4$
$20i_1+10i_2+5i_3 = 11{\cdot}5$
$4i_2-15i_3 = 4$

9   The equation of a curve is given by $y = ax^2+bx+c$ where a, b and c are constants. The curve passes through the points $(-2, 15)$, $(-1, 6)$, $(1, 0)$. Find the equation of the curve.

57   Linear equations: solution by desk calculating machine

10   If $x = 3, x = 1$ and $x = -2$ are roots of the equation $ax^3 + bx^2 + cx + 18 = 0$ find the values of a, b, and c.

11   Solve the simultaneous equations

$$2x + y = 7 \qquad xy = x + y - 1$$

12   Solve the equations $4x^2 + y^2 = 17$
$$2x + y = 5$$

13   Solve the equations $x^2 + 9y = 18$
$$xy = 3$$

14   Solve the equations $4x^2 + y^2 = 17$
$$xy = 2$$

15   Use a desk calculating machine to solve the following simultaneous equations, setting out the solution in tabular form.

$$1 \cdot 5x + 2 \cdot 3y - 0 \cdot 3z = 0 \cdot 4$$
$$2 \cdot 3x - 1 \cdot 9y + 2 \cdot 6z = 8 \cdot 3$$
$$1 \cdot 8x + 4 \cdot 1y - 2 \cdot 7z = -4 \cdot 1$$

2h   Functional notation and difference tables

If we write $y = x^2 - 2x - 3$ then y has different values as different values are given to x. Since the value of y depends on x we say y is a *function* of x. Thus the area of a circle is a function of the radius; the logarithm of a number is a function of the number.

To denote a function of a variable x we use a symbol such as $f(x)$, or $F(x)$ or sometimes $\phi(x)$.

Instead of $y = x^2 - 2x - 3$ we could write $f(x) = x^2 - 2x - 3$

If we want to indicate the value of y when a specific value is given to x such as $x = 2$ we write $f(2)$.

Thus if $f(x) = x^2 - 2x - 3$
$$f(2) = 2^2 - 2.2 - 3 = -3$$
Similarly $f(3) = 3^2 - 2.3 - 3 = 0$
$$f(0) = 0^2 - 2.0 - 3 = -3$$
$$f(h) = h^2 - 2h - 3$$
$$f(x + h) = (x + h)^2 - 2(x + h) - 3$$
etc.

Example 1   If $f(x) = x^3 - 2x^2 - 5x + 6$ find $f(2), f(0), f(-2)$ and $f(3)$.

$$f(2) = 2^3 - 2.2^2 - 5.2 + 6 = -4$$
$$f(0) = 0^3 - 2.0^2 - 5.0 + 6 = 6$$
$$f(-2) = (-2)^3 - 2(-2)^2 - 5(-2) + 6 = 0$$
$$f(3) = 3^3 - 2.3^2 - 5.3 + 6 = 0$$

Example 2   If $f(x) = x^2 - 2x$ find the value of

(a) $f(x+h)$ (b) $\dfrac{f(x+h) - f(x)}{h}$

(a) $f(x+h) = (x+h)^2 - 2(x+h) = x^2 + 2xh + h^2 - 2x - 2h$

(b) $\dfrac{f(x+h) - f(x)}{h} = \dfrac{x^2 + 2xh + h^2 - 2x - 2h - (x^2 - 2x)}{h}$

$$= \frac{2xh + h^2 - 2h}{h} = 2x + h - 2$$

Difference tables

For numerical work with calculating machines and computers, tabulated values of functions are required for a range of values of the variable x. Normal mathematical tables are examples of tabulated values of functions for equal intervals of the variable. In calculating values of $f(x)$ to prepare a table we can make use of the method of differences.

Consider the function tabulated below. This gives values of the function $f(x) = x^2 - 2x - 3$ for values of x from -3 to $+2$ in steps of 1. This is written $x = -3\,(1)\,2$

The third column is the differences between successive values of $f(x)$, the next column is the differences between these first differences, and so on.

x	$f(x)$	First differences	Second differences	Third differences
-3	12			
-2	5	-7		
-1	0	-5	$+2$	0
0	-3	-3	$+2$	0
1	-4	-1	$+2$	0
2	-3	$+1$	$+2$	

This table is known as a difference table. The first differences are written on a level intermediate to that of the function values, the second differences are intermediate to the first differences, and so on.

Notice that the second differences are all constant and that the third and any subsequent differences are all zero. Functions of the type $2x^3 - 6x^2 + 3x - 4$, $\frac{1}{4}x^4 + 3x^3 - 2x + 3$, etc., are known as *polynomials* and it is a property of all polynomials that one of the columns of differences is constant and all succeeding columns are zero. A polynomial of degree 3, where the highest power of x is x^3, will have the third differences constant.

We can make use of this property to tabulate polynomials. For example we can continue the table above for any values of x we require.

To continue the table we start with the second differences as $+2$ and work across the table from right to left noting that each term in the table is the sum of the number immediately above it and the number above and to the right.

x	$f(x)$	First differences	Second differences	Third differences
				0
1	−4		+2	
2	−3	+1		
			+2	
3	0	+3	+2	
4	5	+5	+2	
5	12	+7	+2	
6	21	+9	+2	
7	32	+11	+2	
8	45	+13	+2	
9	60	+15	+2	
10	77	+17		

We now have the complete table of values of $f(x) = x^2 - 2x - 3$ for $x = -3\,(1)\,10$

Example Complete the following table of values of a polynomial for $x = 0\,(0\cdot1)\,1$

x	0	0·1	0·2	0·3	0·4
$f(x)$	0	0·031	0·128	0·297	0·544

The table is set out below. Note that the decimal point has not been recorded in the difference columns where the units are to 3 decimal places.

x	$f(x)$	First differences	Second differences	Third differences
0	0			
0·1	0·031	31	66	
0·2	0·128	97	72	6
0·3	0·297	169	78	6
0·4	0·544	247	84	6
0·5	0·875	331	90	6
0·6	1·296	421	96	6
0·7	1·813	517	102	6
0·8	2·432	619	108	6
0·9	3·159	727	114	6
1·0	4·000	841		

The third differences are found to be constant and since the function is a polynomial we continue the table from the broken line onwards by writing down the third difference as 6 each time and working across from right to left as before.

Since the third differences are constant $f(x)$ must be of the form

$$ax^3 + bx^2 + cx + d$$

Exercise 2h

1 If $f(x) = x^2 + 4x - 3$, find $f(2), f(0), f(1)$ and $f(-1)$

2 If $f(x) = x^3 - 2x^2 - 13x - 10$, find $f(1), f(-1), f(2), f(-2)$ and $f(0)$

3 If $f(x) = \dfrac{x^2 + 3}{\sqrt{x}}$, find $f(1), f(4)$ and $f(9)$

4 If $f(x) = x^4 + 2x^2$, find $f(2)$ and $f(-2)$. Show that $f(h) = f(-h)$

5 If $f(x) = 2x^2 - x$, find (a) $f(x+h)$ (b) $\dfrac{f(x+h) - f(x)}{h}$

6 If $f(x) = \dfrac{1}{2x}$, find $\dfrac{f(x+h) - f(x)}{h}$

7 Evaluate $f(x) = x^3 - 2x^2 + x$ from $x = -1\,(1)\,4$ and, by the method of differences, tabulate $f(x)$ for $x = 5\,(1)\,12$

8 Evaluate $f(x) = 2x^3 - 6x$ for $x = 0\,(0{\cdot}1)\,0{\cdot}4$. Hence tabulate $f(x)$ for $x = 0{\cdot}4\,(0{\cdot}1)\,1$ and check the final value by calculating $2x^3 - 6x$ when $x = 1$

9 Tabulate $f(x) = 3x^2 - 5x + 2$ for $x = 0\,(0{\cdot}1)\,2$

10 Show that the second differences are constant for the following table and hence $f(x)$ must be of the form $ax^2 + bx + c$. Find a, b and c by substituting in $ax^2 + bx + c$ the given values at $x = 0, 1, 2$

x	0	1	2	3	4	5
$f(x)$	-1	-2	1	8	19	34

11 Find the relation between s and t from the following table.

t seconds	0	0·2	0·4	0·6	0·8	1·0	1·2	1·4	1·6
s metres	0	0·36	0·64	0·84	0·96	1·0	0·96	0·84	0·64

61 Functional notation and difference tables

2i   The remainder theorem

If we solve the quadratic equation $x^2-2x-3=0$ we get $x=3$ as one root, for the expression has a factor $x-3$ and may be written $(x+1)(x-3)=0$. Clearly, putting $x=3$ makes the left hand side of the equation zero.

If we write $x^2-2x-3=f(x)$ then $f(3)=0$.

We may conclude that if the substitution of 3 for x makes $F(x)$ zero, then it will have a factor $x-3$

This is an example of the *factor theorem*: if in such algebraic expressions we substitute a for x and the expression is zero then we may say $x-a$ is a factor.

If $F(a)=0$ then $F(x)$ has a factor $(x-a)$

Thus x^3-4x^2+6x-4 is equal to zero when $x=2$

for $F(2)=2^3-4.2^2+6.2-4=0$

and so x^3-4x^2+6x-4 has a factor $x-2$

This factor theorem follows from the *remainder theorem* which may be illustrated by an example:

Suppose we divide ax^3+bx^2+cx+d by $x-p$ until the remainder is independent of x. We set it out as follows:

$$x-p\,)\,ax^3+bx^2+cx+d \qquad (ax^2+(ap+b)\,x+ap^2+bp+c$$
$$\underline{ax^3-apx^2}$$
$$(ap+b)\,x^2+cx$$
$$\underline{(ap+b)\,x^2-(ap^2+bp)\,x}$$
$$(ap^2+bp+c)\,x+d$$
$$\underline{(ap^2+bp+c)\,x-(ap^3+bp^2+cp)}$$
$$ap^3+bp^2+cp+d=\text{remainder}$$

We find that the remainder may be obtained by substituting p for x in the original expression.

If for the original expression we write $F(x)$ then the remainder is $F(p)$.

This rule still holds when $F(x)$ is of higher degree than the above. Thus the remainder when x^4-3x^2+2x-7 is divided by $x-2$ is $(2)^4-3\,(2)^2+2\,(2)-7=1$

If the remainder $F(p)$ is zero then $(x-p)$ divides into $F(x)$ without any remainder, that is $(x-p)$ is a factor.

Example 1   Find the remainders when

$x^3-7x^2+11x-5$ is divided by

(a) $x-3$ (b) $x-2$ (c) $x+3$ (d) $x+2$

(a) Remainder $=(3)^3-7\,(3)^2+11\,(3)-5=-8$
(b) Remainder $=(2)^3-7\,(2)^2+11\,(2)-5=-3$
(c) Remainder $=(-3)^3-7\,(-3)^2+11\,(-3)-5=-128$
(d) Remainder $=(-2)^3-7\,(-2)^2+11\,(-2)-5=-63$

Example 2 Factorize $2x^3 + 3x^2 - 1$

Let $F(x) \equiv 2x^3 + 3x^2 - 1$

We try factors $(x-1)$, $(x+1)$, $(x-2)$, $(x+2)$, etc. until we find the remainder is zero.

$F(1) = 2(1)^3 + 3(1)^2 - 1 = 4$ $\therefore$ $x-1$ is not a factor.
$F(-1) = 2(-1)^3 + 3(-1)^2 - 1 = 0$ $\therefore$ $x+1$ is a factor.

Dividing $2x^3 + 3x^2 - 1$ by $x+1$

$$
\begin{array}{r}
2x^2 + x - 1 \\
x+1 \overline{)\, 2x^3 + 3x^2 - 1} \\
\underline{2x^3 + 2x^2} \\
x^2 - 1 \\
\underline{x^2 + x} \\
-x - 1 \\
\underline{-x - 1}
\end{array}
$$

But $2x^2 + x - 1$ has factors $(2x-1)(x+1)$
Hence $2x^3 + 3x^2 - 1 = (x+1)^2 (2x-1)$

Example 3   For what value of p is $x^2 - (p+2)x + 6$ divisible by $x-p$ without remainder?

The remainder when $x^2 - (p+2)x + 6$ is divided by $x-p$ is given by substituting p for x and is

$p^2 - (p+2)p + 6$

This remainder has to be zero

$\therefore p^2 - (p+2)p + 6 = 0$
$p^2 - p^2 - 2p + 6 = 0$
$\therefore -2p + 6 = 0$
and $p = 3$

Exercise 2i

1   Find the remainder when $2x^3 + 7x^2 - 9x + 2$ is divided by

(a) $x-3$ (b) $x+2$ (c) $x+1$

2   For what value of p is $3x^3 - 7x^2 - 9x - p$ divisible by $x-3$ without remainder?

Use the remainder theorem to find one factor of each of the following and by division find the other factors:

3   $x^3 + 6x^2 + 11x + 6$

63   The remainder theorem

4    $x^3 - 3x^2 - 4x + 12$ 5 $x^3 - 3x^2 - 10x + 24$

6    $x^3 - 9x^2 + 23x - 15$ 7 $x^3 - 5x^2 + 2x + 8$

8    $2x^3 - 7x^2 + 7x - 2$ 9 $x^3 - 7x^2 + 36$

10   Find the values of a and b if $f(x) = 3x^4 + ax^3 + 12x^2 + bx + 4$ is divisible by $(x - 1)$ and has a remainder of 18 when divided by $(x + 2)$.

Miscellaneous exercises 2

1   (a) Simplify the expression

$$\frac{x^{2n+1}\sqrt{(x^{n-\frac{1}{2}})}}{x^{n-\frac{1}{2}}\sqrt{(x^{3n})}}$$

Give your answer as a single power of x without root signs.

(b) Solve the simultaneous equations

$2x - y = 11$
$4x - 5z = 5$
$3y + 2z = 3$ *D.T.C.*

2   (a) Resolve the following into factors

     i $y^3x + 6y^2x - 91yx$ ii $9b^2 - 6ab - 16 + a^2$
     iii $(3a + 2b)^2 - (2a - 3b)^2$ iv $27a^3 - 216b^3$

(b) Solve the equation $\sqrt{(x - 4)} + 3 = \sqrt{(x + 11)}$

(c) The volume V of a solid varies jointly as the height h and the area A of the base. If $V = 10$ when $h = 6$ and $A = 5$, find V in terms of A and h. Determine the value of V when $h = 8$ cm and $A = 9$ cm^2.

3   (a) Factorize the following

     i $a^2 - (3a - 2b)^2$ ii $105x^2 + 9x - 60$ iii $27a^3 - 125b^3$

(b) Solve the equation

$$\sqrt{(x + 2)} + \sqrt{(2x - 3)} = 3$$
                                                 U.E.I.

4   Solve   (a) $x + y = -40$
                 $xy = 256$
         (b) $x + y + z = 18$
               $x + 2y + 2z = 24$
               $2x + 2y - z = 45$
         (c) correct to two places of decimals,
              $2x^2 - 7x = 5$

5   (a) By the use of the remainder theorem, solve the equation

$$3x^3 - 5x^2 - 12x + 20 = 0$$

(b) The following relationships exist in an electrical network. Find the values of the currents i_1, i_2 and i_3.

$$15i_1 - 5i_2 = -3 \cdot 5$$
$$25i_1 + 10i_2 + 10i_3 = -1 \cdot 5$$
$$5i_2 - 20i_3 = 8$$

D.T.C.

6   (a) By the use of the remainder theorem, solve the equation

$$2x^3 - x^2 - 7x + 6 = 0$$

(b) Given that $4x^2 - 4x - 9 = c$, find the value of c if the roots of the equation differ by 2. Find the roots of the equation.

D.T.C.

7   (a) Solve the simultaneous equations

$$x + y - z = 3$$
$$2x - 3y + 9z = 60$$
$$7x + 3y + 3z = 69$$

(b) Solve the quadratic equation

$$12 \cdot 57x^2 - 27 \cdot 14x + 7 \cdot 776 = 0$$

giving your answer correct to two decimal places.

E.M.E.U.

8   (a) Given that $E = \dfrac{x^2 - 1}{x^2 + 1}$ and $x = \dfrac{a+b}{a-b}$

find a simplified expression for E in terms of a and b.

(b) By means of the remainder theorem, or otherwise, show that $(b-2)$ is a factor of the expression $2b^3 + b^2 - 13b + 6$. Find the remaining factors.

N.C.T.E.C.

9   (a) Find the value of a if $(x+2)$ is a factor of

$$x^3 - ax^2 + 7x + 10$$

(b) Factorize completely i $\ x^3 - 2x^2 - 5x + 6$

$$\text{ii } \pi d^3 - \frac{\pi}{27}$$

N.C.T.E.C.

10   Solve the simultaneous equations

(a) $a + 2b + 3c = 4$
$\ \ \ \ a + 3b - 4c = -2$
$\ \ \ \ a - 4b + 2c = -3$

65   Miscellaneous exercises 2

(b) $x^2 - 9y^2 = 24$

$x - 3y = 8$

N.C.T.E.C.

11 (a) Solve (correct to two decimal places) the following equation

$3x^2 - 5x - 7 = 0$

(b) A motorist makes a journey of 175 km. He returns by an alternative route which is 20 km longer, but he is able to increase his average speed by 5 km per hour and takes 7·5 minutes less than the outward journey. Find the average speed for each journey.

12 (a) Factorize the following

i $20x^2y + 26xy - 84y$ ii $(2a - 5b)^2 - 9b^2$ iii $64a^3 + 125b^3$

(b) A rectangular sheet of tinplate is 6 cm longer than it is wide. A square of edge 2 cm is cut from each corner. The area of the remaining tinplate is 150 cm². Find correct to two decimal places the length and width of the original sheet.

13 (a) Solve by factorization

$2x^2 + 4x - 6 = 0$

(b) Verify the result of (a) by using the method of completing the square.

(c) By a method other than completing the square or factorization, solve

$4x^2 + 3x - 5 = 0$

U.L.C.I.

14 Solve the following equations correct to two decimal places:

(a) $0·7 (2 + x) = 1·2 + x^2$

(b) $x^2 - 25y^2 = 36$

$x + 5y = 12$

(c) $2^{7x} = 8^{(5-x)}$

U.L.C.I.

15 Solve

(a) $x^2 - 7x + 3 = 0$

(b) $\dfrac{x}{12(x-4)} = \dfrac{3}{2x}$

(c) $x^2 - 25y^2 = 36$; $x = 5y + 12$

U.L.C.I.

3 The trigonometric ratios

3a Degrees and radians

In geometry the unit of angle is the right angle and a line rotating through four right angles makes a complete revolution.

In trigonometry the right angle is subdivided into 90 equal parts called degrees, each degree is divided into 60 equal parts called minutes, and each minute is divided into 60 equal parts called seconds.

Thus 1 complete revolution = 4 right angles = 360 degrees (written 360°)

$1° = 60$ minutes (written 60′)
$1′ = 60$ seconds (written 60″)

This system is known as the sexagesimal system and is the system usually adopted for practical work.

In the theoretical work in mathematics a second system is used. This is known as *circular measure*, where the unit is the *radian*.

Figure 6

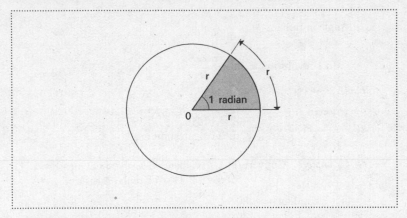

The radian is defined as the angle subtended at the centre of a circle by an arc whose length is equal to the radius.

Thus the radian measure or circular measure of an angle is the ratio of the arc it subtends to the radius of the circle in which it is the central angle.

If an arc of length s subtends an angle θ radians (written θ^c) at the centre of the circle

then $\quad \dfrac{s}{r} = \dfrac{\theta \text{ radians}}{1 \text{ radian}}$

Figure 7

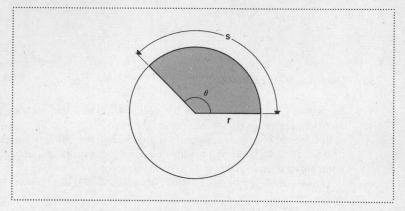

or arc $s = r\theta$. This is an important formula giving the relation between the sizes of arc, radius, and angle.

Note that the radian does not depend on the size of the circle chosen. Since the circumference of a circle is $2\pi \times$ radius then the radius can be spaced around the circumference 2π times, and hence there are 2π radians in one complete revolution. We set it out thus:

$$\text{Angle in radians} = \frac{\text{arc}}{\text{radius}}$$

In 1 revolution there are $\dfrac{2\pi r}{r} = 2\pi$ radians $= 360°$

2π radians $= 360°$

$1 \text{ radian} \quad = \dfrac{360°}{2\pi} = \dfrac{360}{2 \times 3 \cdot 1416} \fallingdotseq 57 \cdot 3°$

$\fallingdotseq 57° \; 18'$ to the nearest minute.

Example 1   Convert (a) 1·76 radians to sexagesimal measure
(b) 64° 11′ 33″ to circular measure.

(a) π radians $= 180°$

$1 \text{ radian} = \dfrac{180°}{\pi}$

$1 \cdot 76 \text{ radians} = \dfrac{180°}{\pi^c} \times 1 \cdot 76^c = 100 \cdot 8°$

(b) $180° = \pi$ radians

$$1° = \frac{\pi}{180} \text{ radians}$$

$$64{\cdot}1925° = \frac{\pi^c}{180°} \times 64{\cdot}1925°$$

$$= 1{\cdot}1204^c$$

$$\begin{array}{r|l} 60 & 33'' \\ \hline 60 & 11{\cdot}55' \\ \hline & {\cdot}1925° \end{array}$$

Example 2   Find the radius of a circle in which an arc of 12 cm subtends an angle of $20°$ at the centre.

Using the formula $s = r\theta$ we have

$$s = 12 \text{ cm}, \ \theta = 20° = \frac{20 \times \pi}{180} \text{ radians}$$

$$\therefore r = \frac{s}{\theta} = \frac{12 \times 180}{20 \times \pi} = \frac{108}{\pi} = 34{\cdot}4 \text{ cm}$$

Area of a sector of a circle

We can obtain a very simple formula for the area of a sector of a circle when the sector angle is in radians.

Since the areas of sectors in a circle are proportional to the arcs on which they stand

$$\frac{\text{area of sector } AOC}{\text{area of whole circle}} = \frac{\text{arc } AC}{\text{circumference of circle}}$$

$$\frac{\text{area of sector}}{\pi r^2} = \frac{s}{2\pi r}$$

$$\therefore \qquad \text{area} = s \times \frac{\pi r^2}{2\pi r} = \frac{1}{2} rs$$

Figure 8

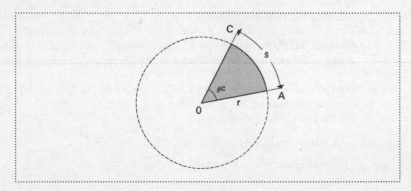

Since   arc $s = r\theta$ where θ is in radians then
area of sector $= \frac{1}{2}rs = \frac{1}{2}r^2\theta$

Example The radius of a sector is 10 m and the arc 14 m; find the angle of the sector and its area.

Angle of radians $= \dfrac{\text{arc}}{\text{radius}} = \dfrac{14 \text{ m}}{10 \text{ m}} = 1{\cdot}4$

Area $= \frac{1}{2}rs = \frac{1}{2}\ 10 \text{ m} \times 14 \text{ m} = 70 \text{ m}^2$

Exercise 3a

1. Express in radians the following angles:
   (a) 60°   (b) 175° 45′   (c) 58° 12′ 18″   (d) 540°

2. Express in degrees, minutes and seconds the angles
   (a) $\dfrac{\pi^c}{3}$ (b) $2{\cdot}58^c$ (c) $0{\cdot}64^c$ (d) $\dfrac{5\pi^c}{6}$

3. Find the magnitude in radians and degrees of the interior angle between adjacent sides of:
   (a) a regular pentagon (5 sides)   (b) a regular hexagon (6 sides)
   (c) a regular heptagon (7 sides)   (d) a regular octagon (8 sides)

4. Define a radian. Find in radians the angle between the hour hand and the minute hand of a clock at
   (a) half past one   (b) half past two.

5. Find the circular measure of an angle subtended at the centre of a circle of radius 4 cm by an arc 13 cm long.

6. Assuming the earth to be a sphere and the distance between two parallels of latitude subtending any angle of 1° at the centre of the earth to be 110 km, calculate the radius of the earth.

7. Find the difference in latitudes in degrees, minutes and seconds of two places if one is 200 km north of the other. Take the radius of the earth to be 6·3 Mm.

8. (a) The diameter of a circle is 20 cm and the angle of a sector is 30°. Find the area of the sector.
   (b) Find the area of a sector
      i whose angle is $\dfrac{2\pi^c}{3}$ and radius 12 cm
      ii whose arc is 30 m and radius 16 m

9   Find the radius of a sector
     (a) whose arc is 8 m and area 30 m^2
     (b) whose area is 40 m^2 and angle 56°.

10   A sector of radius 20 m has an area of 60 m^2. Find the angle of the sector
     in radians and degrees.

11   A band passes round three equal circles of radius 10cm that touch one another.
     Find the whole area enclosed by the band.

12   A piece of string is wound once round an equilateral triangle of side 6 units,
     starting and ending at one of the angular points.
         Find the length of, and area inside, the spiral traced out by the end of the
     string when it is unwound through one revolution.

3b   The basic trigonometric ratios

Consider two similar triangles as shown. It is a property of similar triangles
that their corresponding sides are proportional. Thus the ratio of $\dfrac{AB}{OA}$ is the

Figure
9

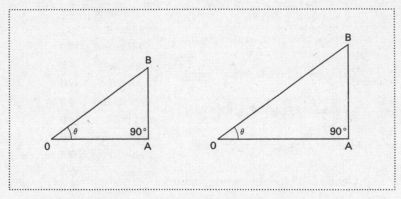

same for each triangle and for any other triangle similar to these. The ratio
does not depend on the size of the triangle but depends only on the value of
angle θ. As θ varies so does the ratio $\dfrac{AB}{OA}$.

     The ratio between any two sides of a right-angled triangle occurs so fre-
quently in problems that the various ratios between the sides are given names
and their values for different angles are tabulated in books of tables. Altogether
there are six different ratios between the sides; the student will have already
used some, if not all, of them.

71   The basic trigonometric ratios

Definitions of the ratios

In the right-angled triangle shown, the side opposite the right angle is called the hypotenuse, the side opposite angle θ is called the opposite and the remaining side is the adjacent.

Figure
10

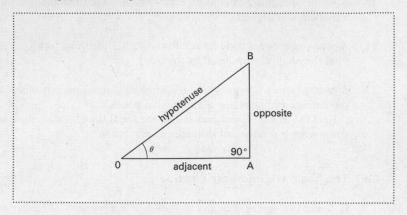

The ratios are defined as follows:

sine of angle θ, written sin θ $= \dfrac{\text{opposite}}{\text{hypotenuse}} = \dfrac{AB}{OB}$

cosine of angle θ, written cos θ $= \dfrac{\text{adjacent}}{\text{hypotenuse}} = \dfrac{OA}{OB}$

tangent of angle θ, written tan θ $= \dfrac{\text{opposite}}{\text{adjacent}} = \dfrac{AB}{OA}$

cosecant of angle θ, written cosec θ $= \dfrac{\text{hypotenuse}}{\text{opposite}} = \dfrac{OB}{AB}$

secant of angle θ, written sec θ $= \dfrac{\text{hypotenuse}}{\text{adjacent}} = \dfrac{OB}{OA}$

cotangent of angle θ, written cot θ $= \dfrac{\text{adjacent}}{\text{opposite}} = \dfrac{OA}{AB}$

From these definitions we see that

$$\text{cosec } \theta = \frac{1}{\sin \theta} \qquad \sec \theta = \frac{1}{\cos \theta} \qquad \cot \theta = \frac{1}{\tan \theta}$$

Trigonometric tables give the values of these ratios for all angles from 0° to 90° in 1′ intervals. Notice that the values of all the 'co'-ratios, that is, cosine, cosecant, cotangent, decrease as the angle increases to 90° and that the mean differences on the right-hand side of the tables have to be subtracted. In the following section we will use these tables in practical problems involving heights and distances, but before this we consider some relationships between the six ratios.

3c   Fundamental relationships between the ratios

The six ratios are not independent of one another. Consider the right-angled triangle in fig. 11.

Figure 11

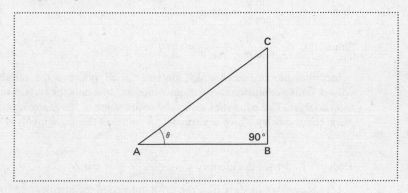

By the theorem of Pythagoras, $BC^2 + AB^2 = AC^2 \dots (3.1)$

If we divide both sides of this equation by AC^2 we get

$$\left(\frac{BC}{AC}\right)^2 + \left(\frac{AB}{AC}\right)^2 = 1$$

i.e. $(\sin \theta)^2 + (\cos \theta)^2 = 1$

It is customary to write $(\sin \theta)^2$ in the form $\sin^2 \theta$ and similarly for the other ratios.

Thus $\sin^2 \theta + \cos^2 \theta = 1$

If we divide equation (3.1) by AB^2 we get

$$\left(\frac{BC}{AB}\right)^2 + 1 = \left(\frac{AC}{AB}\right)^2$$

i.e. $(\tan \theta)^2 + 1 = (\sec \theta)^2$

so that $\tan^2 \theta + 1 = \sec^2 \theta$

Again dividing equation (3.1) by BC^2 we get

$$1 + \left(\frac{AB}{BC}\right)^2 = \left(\frac{AC}{BC}\right)^2$$

$1 + (\cot \theta)^2 = (\operatorname{cosec} \theta)^2$

giving $1 + \cot^2 \theta = \operatorname{cosec}^2 \theta$

These three relationships are basically Pythagoras' theorem in trigonometrical language and are sometimes called the *Pythagorean identities*.

Further since $\dfrac{\sin\theta}{\cos\theta} = \dfrac{\dfrac{BC}{AC}}{\dfrac{AB}{AC}} = \dfrac{BC}{AC}\times\dfrac{AC}{AB} = \dfrac{BC}{AB}$

$$= \tan\theta$$

then $\dfrac{\sin\theta}{\cos\theta} = \tan\theta$

Similarly $\dfrac{\cos\theta}{\sin\theta} = \dfrac{1}{\tan\theta} = \cot\theta$

Identities are equalities which are true for all values of the variables involved, unlike conditional equations which are true only for certain values of the variables. The equalities given above are some of the many identities of plane trigonometry which are true for all values of the angle involved.

Example 1 Prove the identity $\dfrac{\operatorname{cosec} A}{\cot A + \tan A} = \cos A$

It is customary to start with the left-hand side of the identity and by use of the standard identities proved above, change it into the right-hand side, setting out the working as follows:

l.h.s. $= \dfrac{\operatorname{cosec} A}{\cot A + \tan A}$

$= \dfrac{\dfrac{1}{\sin A}}{\dfrac{\cos A}{\sin A} + \dfrac{\sin A}{\cos A}}$ and multiplying numerator and denominator by $\sin A \cos A$

$= \dfrac{\sin A \cos A \left(\dfrac{1}{\sin A}\right)}{\sin A \cos A \left(\dfrac{\cos A}{\sin A} + \dfrac{\sin A}{\cos A}\right)}$

$= \dfrac{\cos A}{\cos^2 A + \sin^2 A}$ and since $\cos^2 A + \sin^2 A = 1$

$= \cos A = $ r.h.s.

Example 2 (a) If $\sin\theta = \dfrac{5}{13}$ find $\cos\theta$, $\tan\theta$, and $\sec\theta$

(b) If $\cos\theta = \dfrac{a}{b}$ find $\tan\theta$, $\operatorname{cosec}\theta$, and $\sin\theta$

Figure
12

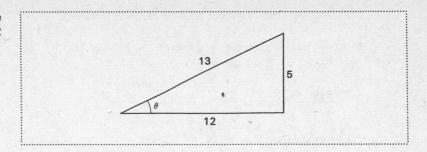

(a) Since $\sin \theta = \dfrac{\text{opposite}}{\text{hypotenuse}}$ draw a small right angled triangle with side opposite = 5 and hypotenuse = 13. By Pythagoras' theorem the adjacent side = $\sqrt{(13^2 - 5^2)} = 12$

Then $\cos \theta = \dfrac{12}{13}$ $\tan \theta = \dfrac{5}{12}$ $\sec \theta = \dfrac{13}{12}$

(b) In this case draw the triangle as shown with adjacent = a, hypotenuse = b. The side opposite the angle = $\sqrt{(b^2 - a^2)}$

Figure
13

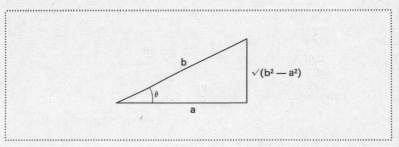

Then $\tan \theta = \dfrac{\sqrt{(b^2 - a^2)}}{a}$ $\operatorname{cosec} \theta = \dfrac{b}{\sqrt{(b^2 - a^2)}}$ $\sin \theta = \dfrac{\sqrt{(b^2 - a^2)}}{b}$

Exercise 3c

1 If $\sin \theta = \dfrac{3}{5}$ write down the values of the other trigonometric ratios.

2 If $\sec \theta = \dfrac{17}{8}$ find the values of the other ratios.

3 If $\tan \theta = \dfrac{p}{q}$ find the values of the other ratios.

75   Fundamental relationships between the ratios

4   If $\cos \theta = x$ find the values of the other ratios in terms of x.

Prove the following identities (questions 5 to 16):

5   $\cos^2 \theta - \sin^2 \theta = 1 - 2 \sin^2 \theta$

6   $\dfrac{\cos \theta \cot \theta \sec^2 \theta}{\operatorname{cosec} \theta} = 1$

7   $\sin \theta (\operatorname{cosec} \theta + \cot \theta) = 1 + \cos \theta$

8   $\dfrac{1 + \tan A}{1 + \cot A} = \tan A$

9   $\sec^4 \theta - \tan^4 \theta = \sec^2 \theta + \tan^2 \theta$

10 $\dfrac{\sec \theta + \tan \theta}{1 + \sin \theta} = \sec \theta$

11 $\dfrac{\sec \theta}{\tan \theta + \cot \theta} = \sin A$

12 $\dfrac{\tan \theta}{(1 + \tan^2 \theta)^2} + \dfrac{\cot \theta}{(1 + \cot^2 \theta)^2} = \sin \theta \cos \theta$

13 $(\tan A + \sec A)^2 = \dfrac{1 + \sin A}{1 - \sin A}$

14 $\sqrt{\left(\dfrac{1 - \sin \theta}{1 + \sin \theta}\right)} = \sec \theta - \tan \theta$

15 $(\sin \theta + \cos \theta)(\tan \theta + \cot \theta) = \sec \theta + \operatorname{cosec} \theta$

16 $(\tan \theta + \sin \theta)^2 - (\tan \theta - \sin \theta)^2 = 4\sqrt{(\tan^2 \theta - \sin^2 \theta)}$

17 If $\tan \theta = \dfrac{2t}{1 - t^2}$ find the values of all the other ratios.

18 If $\tan \theta = \dfrac{1}{\sqrt{5}}$ find the value of $\dfrac{\operatorname{cosec}^2 \theta - \sec^2 \theta}{\operatorname{cosec}^2 \theta + \sec^2 \theta}$

19 If $\tan \theta = \dfrac{4}{3}$ find the value of $\dfrac{5 \sin \theta + 6 \cos \theta}{7 \cos \theta - 3 \sin \theta}$

76   The trigonometric ratios

3d   Ratios of 0°, 30°, 45°, 60°, 90°

The exact values of the trigonometric ratios of these angles are useful in many branches of science and engineering, and we can find them by making use of Pythagoras' theorem.

Ratios of 45°

These can be found by drawing a right-angled triangle having angles as shown in fig. 14, where $OA = AB = 1$ unit (say).

Figure 14

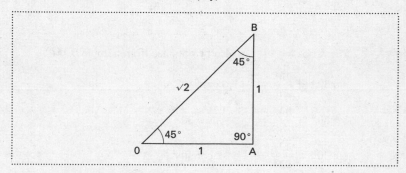

Then $OB = \sqrt{(1^2 + 1^2)} = \sqrt{2}$

Thus $\sin 45° = \dfrac{AB}{OB} = \dfrac{1}{\sqrt{2}}$ $\operatorname{cosec} 45° = \sqrt{2}$

$\cos 45° = \dfrac{OA}{OB} = \dfrac{1}{\sqrt{2}}$ $\sec 45° = \sqrt{2}$

$\tan 45° = \dfrac{AB}{OA} = 1$ $\cot 45° = 1$

Ratios of 30° and 60°

Consider the equilateral triangle ABC of side 2 units. Each angle will be 60°. Let BM be drawn perpendicular to AC. Then by geometry $AM = MC = 1$ unit and $BM = \sqrt{(2^2 - 1^2)} = \sqrt{3}$

$\sin 60° = \dfrac{BM}{AB} = \dfrac{\sqrt{3}}{2}$ and the other ratios are easily seen to be

$\cos 60° = \dfrac{1}{2}$ $\sec 60° = 2$ $\operatorname{cosec} 60° = \dfrac{2}{\sqrt{3}}$

$\tan 60° = \sqrt{3}$ $\cot 60° = \dfrac{1}{\sqrt{3}}$

Figure
15

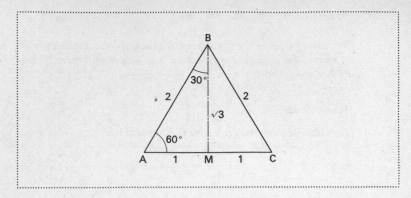

The ratios for 30° can also be obtained from triangle BAM

$$\sin 30° = \frac{AM}{AB} = \frac{1}{2} \qquad \operatorname{cosec} 30° = 2$$

$$\cos 30° = \frac{BM}{AB} = \frac{\sqrt{3}}{2} \qquad \sec 30° = \frac{2}{\sqrt{3}}$$

$$\tan 30° = \frac{AM}{BM} = \frac{1}{\sqrt{3}} \qquad \cot 30° = \sqrt{3}$$

Ratios of 0°

For ratios of 0° consider right-angled triangle OAB with angle $AOB = \theta$ where θ is very nearly equal to 0°, and let $OB = 1$ unit. OA and OB are very nearly equal and AB is very small

Figure
16

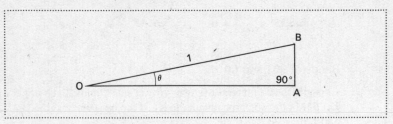

$$\sin \theta = \frac{AB}{OB} = AB \qquad \cos \theta = \frac{OA}{OB} = OA \qquad \tan \theta = \frac{AB}{OA}$$

As the angle θ approaches 0° (we write this $\theta \to 0°$) B will ultimately coincide with A. We write this as follows:

As $\theta \to 0°$, $AB \to 0$, and $OA \to OB = $ unity

Then $\sin 0° = 0, \cos 0° = 1, \tan 0° = 0$

And cosec $0° = \dfrac{1}{\sin 0°} = \dfrac{1}{0}$ which is infinite and is denoted by the symbol ∞

$$\sec 0° = \dfrac{1}{\cos 0°} = \dfrac{1}{1} = 1$$

$$\cot 0° = \dfrac{1}{\tan 0°} = \dfrac{1}{0} = \infty$$

Ratios of 90°

In fig. 17 let angle $AOB = \theta$ be an angle very nearly equal to 90°. Let OB = 1 unit.

Figure 17

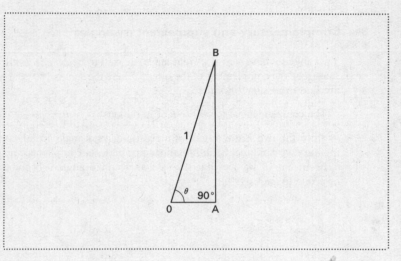

Then $\quad \sin \theta = \dfrac{AB}{OB} = AB$

$$\cos \theta = \dfrac{OA}{OB} = OA$$

$$\tan \theta = \dfrac{AB}{OA}$$

As angle $\theta \to 90°$ (approaches 90°) then $A \to 0$, $AB \to OB$ = unity and $OA \to 0$

Thus $\sin 90° = 1 \qquad \cos 90° = 0 \qquad \tan 90° = \dfrac{1}{0} = \infty$

and cosec $90° = 1 \qquad \sec 90° = \dfrac{1}{0} = \infty \qquad \cot 90° = \dfrac{0}{1} = 0$

The values of the ratios obtained in the above section should be committed to memory.

	0°	30°	45°	60°	90°
sin	0	$\dfrac{1}{2}$	$\dfrac{1}{\sqrt{2}}$	$\dfrac{\sqrt{3}}{2}$	1
cos	1	$\dfrac{\sqrt{3}}{2}$	$\dfrac{1}{\sqrt{2}}$	$\dfrac{1}{2}$	0
tan	0	$\dfrac{1}{\sqrt{3}}$	1	$\sqrt{3}$	∞

3e Complementary and supplementary angles

Two angles whose sum is a right angle are said to be *complementary*. Each is said to be the complement of the other. Where the sum is 180° the two angles are said to be *supplementary*.

The complement of θ is $90° - \theta$ or in radians $\dfrac{\pi^c}{2} - \theta$

Since the two acute angles of a right-angled triangle are always complementary we can quickly find relationships between complementary angles.

From fig. 18 we see that the side adjacent to angle θ becomes the side opposite to angle $90° - \theta$

Figure 18

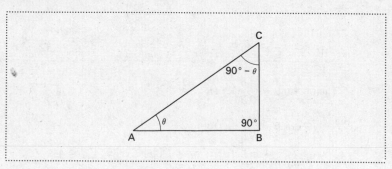

Hence
$$\sin(90°-\theta) = \frac{AB}{AC} = \cos\theta; \quad \cos(90°-\theta) = \frac{BC}{AC} = \sin\theta$$

$$\tan(90°-\theta) = \frac{AB}{BC} = \cot\theta; \quad \cot(90°-\theta) = \frac{BC}{AB} = \tan\theta$$

$$\sec(90°-\theta) = \frac{AC}{BC} = \operatorname{cosec}\theta; \quad \operatorname{cosec}(90°-\theta) = \frac{AC}{AB} = \sec\theta$$

Thus the sine of any angle is the cosine of its complement and the tangent of any angle is the cotangent of its complement and the secant of any angle is the cosecant of its complement.

We may also interchange sine and cosine, tangent and cotangent, secant and cosecant in the last sentence.

We can use tables of sines to find cosines, or tables of cosines to find sines. If we require $\cos 54°$ we may look up $\sin (90° - 54°) = \sin 36°$
In the same way $\cot 47° \ 30' = \tan (90° - 47° \ 30') = \tan 42° \ 30'$

Exercise 3e

1   (a) Using sine tables find the values of $\cos 32° \ 26'$, $\cos 46° \ 20'$, $\cos 64° \ 17'$, $\cos 55° \ 53'$. Check your answers direct from the cosine tables.
    (b) Using tangent tables find $\cot 54° \ 16'$, $\cot 18° \ 26'$, $\cot 81° \ 9'$, $\cot 36° \ 48'$ and check your answers from the cotangent tables.

2   Write down the complements and supplements of the angles:

$$45°, 60°, 49° \ 15', \frac{\pi}{5} \text{ radians}, 155°, -30°$$

3   Without using tables find the numerical value of
  (a) $3 \tan^2 45° - \sin^2 60° - \frac{1}{2} \cot^2 30° + \frac{1}{8} \sec^2 45°$

  (b) $\dfrac{\cot^2 30° - \tan^2 45°}{\tan^2 60° - \sec^2 45°}$

4   Show that $\dfrac{\tan 60° - \tan 30°}{1 + \tan 60° \tan 30°} = \tan 30°$

5   Verify that (a) $\sin 60° \cos 30° - \cos 60° \sin 30° = \sin 30°$
               (b) $\cos 60° \cos 30° + \sin 60° \sin 30° = \cos 30°$

6   Show that (a) $\sin^2 30° + \sin^2 45° + \sin^2 60° = \frac{3}{2}$
           (b) $\tan^2 30° + \tan^2 45° + \tan^2 60° = 4\frac{1}{3}$
           (c) $\cos^2 30° + \cos^2 45° + \cos^2 60° = \frac{3}{2}$

7   Verify that (a) $\sin 2A = 2 \sin A \cos A$

           (b) $\tan 2A = \dfrac{2 \tan A}{1 - \tan^2 A}$
  when $A = 30°$ and when $A = 45°$

8   Find θ when $\sin \theta = \sin^2 32° \ 42' \times \tan 54° \ 10'$

9   Calculate $\dfrac{\sin 62° \ 12' \times \tan 8° \ 46'}{\cos 79° \ 4'}$

81   Complementary and supplementary angles

10   If the vertical pressure V on a pier is given by

$$V = \frac{W}{2}\left(1 + \frac{\tan\theta}{\tan\alpha}\right) \text{ find } V \text{ when } W = 165, \theta = 66° \text{ and } \alpha = 52°$$

3f   Problems in heights and distances

Many practical problems involving calculation of distances and angles can be solved by breaking down the problem into one depending on the solution of right-angled triangles. A simple example of the type of example 1 leads on to examples 2 and 3.

Example 1   The angle of elevation of the top of a flagpole from a point on a level with its base and 60 m from it, is 37°. Find the height of the flagpole.

Figure 19

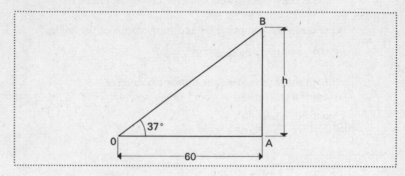

Let $AB = h$ m represent the flagpole

Then $\dfrac{h}{60} = \tan 37°$

$\therefore$ $h = 60 \tan 37° = 45\cdot2$
Height of flagpole $= 45\cdot2$ m

Example 2   A tower stands on a horizontal plane. The angle of elevation of the top of the tower from a point A on the plane is 22°. From a point B 80m nearer, the angle of elevation is found to be 34°. Find the height of the tower.

In fig. 20 let $CD = h$ m represent the tower.

Then $AC = h \cot 22°$
$\quad\quad\quad\; BC = h \cot 34°$
$\quad\quad\quad\; AB = AC—BC = h \cot 22° - h \cot 34°$
i.e. $80 = h(\cot 22° - \cot 34°)$

giving $h = \dfrac{80}{\cot 22° - \cot 34°} = 80\cdot6$

82   The trigonometric ratios

Figure
20

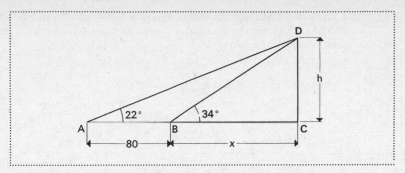

Example 3   A tower stands on a horizontal plane. The angle of elevation of the top from a point *A* due south of the tower is 30° and at a point *B* 100 m due west of *A*, it is 20°. Find the height of the tower.

Figure
21

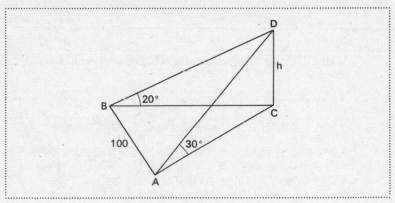

In fig. 21 *CD* represents the tower of height *h* m
Note that angle $CAB = 90°$
$$AC = h \cot 30°$$
$$BC = h \cot 20°$$
and since $BC^2 = AB^2 + AC^2$
$$(h \cot 20°)^2 = 100^2 + (h \cot 30°)^2$$
$$h^2 (\cot^2 20° - \cot^2 30°) = 100^2$$

$$h^2 = \frac{10\,000}{\cot^2 20° - \cot^2 30°} = \frac{10\,000}{2 \cdot 7475^2 - 3}$$

$$= \frac{10\,000}{4 \cdot 549}$$

Giving $h = \sqrt{\left(\frac{10\,000}{4 \cdot 549}\right)} = 46 \cdot 9$

Height of tower = 46·9 m

83   Problems in heights and distances

Example 4 Calculate the length of a thin belt which fits tightly round two pulleys in the same plane whose radii are 2 and 3 units respectively, and whose centres are 5 units apart.

Figure 22

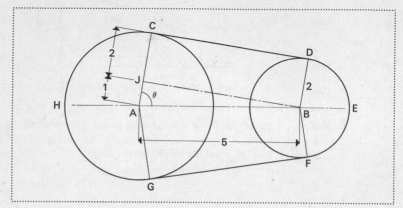

CDEFGH in fig. 22 represents the belt. Draw *BJ* parallel to *CD*, the common tangent.

Let angle $BAC = \theta$

Then $\quad \cos \theta = \dfrac{AJ}{AB} = \dfrac{1}{5}, \theta = 78° \, 28' = 1 \cdot 3695$ radians

Arc $DEF =$ radius $\times$ radians $= 2 \times 2\theta = 4 \times 1 \cdot 3695 = 5 \cdot 478$

Arc $CHG = 3 \times (2\pi - 2\theta) = 6 \, (3 \cdot 1416 - 1 \cdot 3695) = 10 \cdot 633$

$CD = GF = JB = \sqrt{(5^2 - 1^2)} = \sqrt{24} = 4 \cdot 899$

$\therefore \qquad$ Total length of belt $= 5 \cdot 478 + 10 \cdot 633 + 2 \times 4 \cdot 899$

$= 25 \cdot 9$ units

Exercise 3f

1 Find the height of a pole if the angle of inclination of its highest point from a point on the ground 30 m from the base of the pole is 20° 32′.

2 Vertical borings are made at points *A* and *B* which are a quarter of a km apart. If coal is found at depths 56 m and 78 m respectively, find the average dip of the coal seam from *A* to *B*.

3 From the top of a cliff 100 metres high, the angles of depression of the top and bottom of a lighthouse are observed to be 30° and 60°; find the height of the lighthouse.

4 The elevation of the top of a church spire is 45°. On walking 10 m towards the tower the elevation is 60°. Find the height of the tower assuming the ground is level.

84 The trigonometric ratios

5   From a point *A* on the deck of a ship the elevation of the top of a cliff is 50°. From the top of a mast 20 m vertically above *A*, the elevation is 35°. Calculate the height of the cliff above the deck to the nearest metre.

6   From a straight level road running east and west, a church tower *A* can be seen to the north. From a point *B* on the road, the bearing of the tower *A* is 32° west of north; and from a point *C*, 1500 metres further along the road, the bearing of *A* is 64° east of north. Find the shortest distance of the tower from the road.
Note. The bearing of an object from a point of observation is the angle that the line through the two points makes with the north and south line (or sometimes the east and west line) through the point of observation.

7   *B* is a point 423 m due east of *A*, and *C* is 320 m from *A* in a direction 47° 50′ east of north. Calculate the distance and bearing of *C* from *B*.

8   The angle of elevation of a mountain peak is 40°, and after walking 2 kilometres towards the peak up a slope inclined at 30° to the horizontal, the angle of elevation of the peak is found to be 70°. Find to the nearest metre the vertical height of the peak above the first point of observation.

9   A regular octagon is inscribed in a square of 60 cm side.
Calculate (a) the length of one side of the octagon,
           (b) the length of a diagonal of the octagon.

10 A thin belt passes over two pulleys whose diameters are 20 cm and 32 cm and whose centres are 60 cm apart.
Find the length, if it is (a) an open belt, (b) a crossed belt.

3g   Ratio of angles of any magnitude

Supposing angle θ is formed by the terminal line *OP* rotating about 0 from the initial line *OX*. If the rotation is counter-clockwise it is said to be positive and the angle θ is said to be positive.

Figure
23

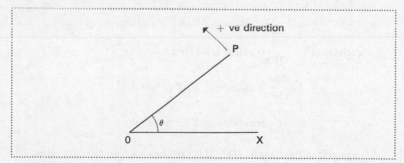

If the rotation of *OP* from the initial position is clockwise the angle formed is said to be negative.

Figure
24

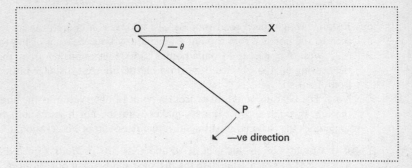

If the line *OP* revolves around 0 from position *OX* into any of the positions OP_1, OP_2, OP_3, OP_4 in any of the four quadrants and a perpendicular *PM* be drawn to *OX* or OX_1, then, no matter in which quadrant *OP* is drawn,

Figure
25

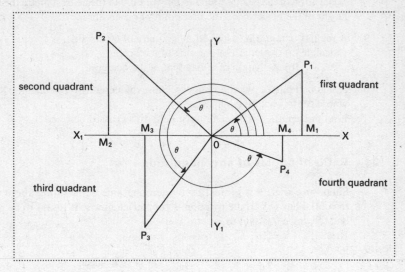

the ratio $\dfrac{MP}{OP}$ is called sin $X\hat{O}P$ or sin θ

$\dfrac{OM}{OP}$ is called cos $X\hat{O}P$ or cos θ

$\dfrac{MP}{OM}$ is called tan $X\hat{O}P$ or tan θ

provided the lengths *OM*, *MP*, *OP* are given appropriate signs.

86   The trigonometric ratios

In accordance with the usual convention OM is regarded as positive if M is to the right of the vertical YOY_1, that is, horizontal distances measured to the right of YOY_1 are positive. Also MP is regarded as being positive if P is above XOX_1 and negative if below XOX_1.

The rotating line OP is taken as positive in all positions.

We next consider the signs of the trigonometric ratios for the line OP in each of the four quadrants in turn.

Figure 26

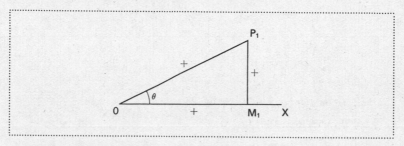

In the first quadrant: see fig. 26.

Here θ varies from $0°$ to $90°$.

In this quadrant all the distances are positive and hence all the ratios are positive.

Figure 27

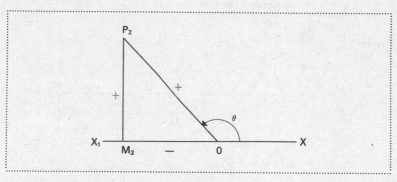

In the second quadrant: see fig. 27.

θ varies from $90°$ to $180°$.

$$\sin \theta = \frac{M_2 P_2}{OP_2} = \frac{+\text{quantity}}{+\text{quantity}} \text{ i.e. the sine is positive}$$

$$\cos \theta = \frac{OM_2}{OP_2} = \frac{-\text{quantity}}{+\text{quantity}} \text{ which is negative}$$

$$\tan \theta = \frac{M_2 P_2}{OM_2} = \frac{+\text{quantity}}{-\text{quantity}} \text{ which is negative}$$

Figure
28

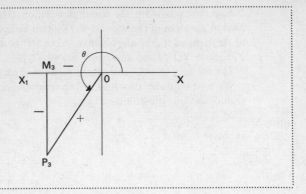

In the third quadrant: see fig. 28.

θ varies from 180° to 270°.

$$\sin \theta = \frac{-\text{quantity}}{+\text{quantity}} \quad \text{negative}$$

$$\cos \theta = \frac{-\text{quantity}}{+\text{quantity}} \quad \text{negative}$$

$$\tan \theta = \frac{-\text{quantity}}{-\text{quantity}} \quad \text{positive}$$

Figure
29

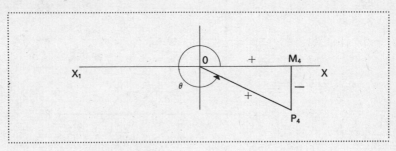

In the fourth quadrant: see fig. 29.

θ varies from 270° to 360°.

$$\sin \theta = \frac{-\text{quantity}}{+\text{quantity}} \quad \text{negative}$$

$$\cos \theta = \frac{+\text{quantity}}{+\text{quantity}} \quad \text{positive}$$

$$\tan \theta = \frac{-\text{quantity}}{+\text{quantity}} \quad \text{negative}$$

Thus the positive ratios in each respective quadrant are as shown in fig. 30. In all quadrants the ratios secant, cosecant, and cotangent will have the same signs as their reciprocals, the cosine, sine, and tangent respectively.

Figure 30

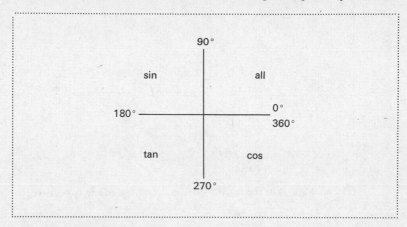

The numerical value of any ratio will be equal to the numerical value of that of the acute angle made by the line OP and the horizontal line XOX_1.

Thus cos 150° is negative since a positive rotation of line OP from OX will put it in the second quadrant.

It is numerically equal to cos (180° − 150°) = cos 30°

∴ cos 150° = − cos 30° = − 0·8660

Example 1   Find (a) tan 147°   (b) cosec 460°   (c) cos (− 54°)

(a) The bounding arm OP of 147° lies in the second quadrant where the tangent is negative.

Figure 31

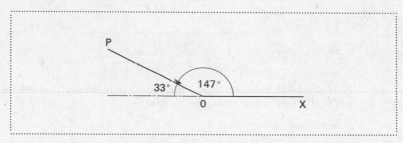

Thus tan 147° = − tan 33°
= − 0·6494

(b) The bounding arm is in the second quadrant where the sin and hence the cosec is positive.

Figure
32

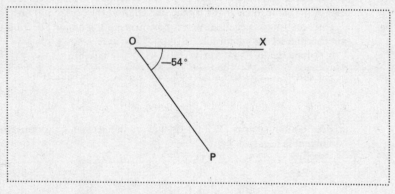

$$\text{cosec } 460° = \text{cosec } 80°$$
$$= 1·0154$$

(c) The angle is in the fourth quadrant and the cosine is positive.

$$\cos(-54°) = \cos 54°$$
$$= 0·5878$$

Figure
33

Example 2 Find (a) $\sin(-\theta)$, $\cos(-\theta)$, $\tan(-\theta)$
(b) $\sin(180°+\theta)$, $\cos(270°+\theta)$, $\tan(90°+\theta)$

(a) Treating θ as an acute angle, then $-\theta$ will lie in the fourth quadrant where only the cosine and secant are positive.

Hence $\sin(-\theta) = -\sin\theta$
$\cos(-\theta) = \cos\theta$
$\tan(-\theta) = -\tan\theta$

(b) $180°+\theta$ will lie in the third quadrant.
$\sin(180°+\theta) = -\sin\theta$

$270°+\theta$ is in the fourth quadrant and makes an angle of $90°-\theta$ with XOX_1

Thus $\cos (270° + \theta) = \cos (90° - \theta) = \sin \theta$

$90° + \theta$ is in the second quadrant and makes an angle of $90° - \theta$ with XOX_1

Hence $\tan (90° + \theta) = -\tan (90° - \theta) = -\cot \theta$

Exercise 3g

1 Using the tables find the values of
(a) $\sin 230°$ (b) $\tan 230°$ (c) $\sec (-130°)$ (d) $\tan (-60°)$ (e) $\cot (-250°)$
(f) $\sin 290°$ (g) $\cos 130°$ (h) $\sin 820°$ (i) $\tan 280°$ (j) $\csc (-190°)$

2 Find in terms of angle θ the values of
(a) $\sin (90° + \theta)$ (b) $\cos (90° + \theta)$ (c) $\tan (180° + \theta)$ (d) $\sin (270° + \theta)$
(e) $\tan (180° - \theta)$ (f) $\tan (\theta - 180°)$ (g) $\sin (270° - \theta)$ (h) $\sin (\theta - 270°)$

3 Show that $\dfrac{\tan 2\theta - \sec 4\theta}{\tan 4\theta + \sec 2\theta} = -1$ when $\theta = 60°$

$$\text{and} = \frac{1 + 2\sqrt{3}}{5} \text{ when } \theta = 75°$$

4 Find angles less than $360°$ whose (a) cosine is $-\dfrac{1}{2}$

(b) sine is $-\dfrac{\sqrt{3}}{2}$

(c) tangent is 1

5 Prove that
$\cos A + \sin (270° + A) - \sin (270° - A) + \cos (180° + A) = 0$

6 Prove that
$\sec (270° - A) \sec (90° - A) - \tan (270° - A) \tan (90° + A) + 1 = 0$

3h Graphs of trigonometric functions

Graph of sin x

We can find how the sine of an angle varies as the angle changes by plotting the graph of $y = \sin x$.

We prepare a table of values of $\sin x$ for any suitable intervals of x, say every $20°$ from $0°$ to $360°$.

$x°$	0	20	40	60	80	90	100	120	140	160	180
$y = \sin x$	0	0·342	0·643	0·866	0·985	1·0	0·985	0·866	0·643	0·342	0

$x°$	200	220	240	260	270	280	300	320	340	360
$y = \sin x$	−0·342	−0·643	−0·866	−0·985	−1	−0·985	−0·866	−0·643	−0·342	0

Figure 34

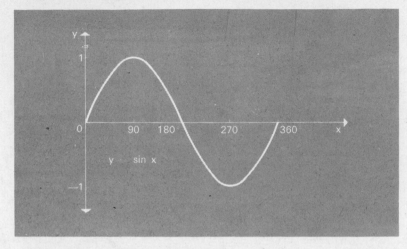

On plotting the values of y vertically against the values of x horizontally, we obtain the graph shown in fig. 34.

Notice that sin x increases from 0 to 1 as x goes from 0° to 90°; then it decreases from 1 to 0 at 180° and to −1 at 270°; then turns and increases, becoming zero at 360°.

If x is increased beyond 360° the curve repeats itself, going through the same series of changes every 360° or 2π radians. See fig. 35.

Figure 35

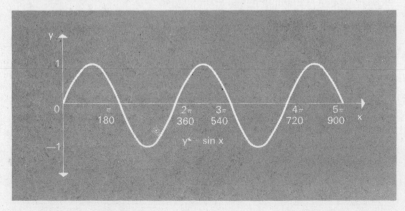

Because of this we say that the sine function is a periodic function and that its period is 360° or 2π radians.

Graph of cos x

To plot the graph of $y = \cos x$ we proceed as before by preparing a table of values.

$x°$	0	20	40	60	80	90	100	120	140	160	180
$y = \cos x$	1	0·940	0·766	0·50	0·174	0	−0·174	−0·50	−0·766	−0·940	−1

$x°$	200	220	240	260	270	280	300	320	340	360
$y = \cos x$	−0·940	−0·766	−0·50	−0·174	0	0·174	0·50	0·766	0·940	1

Figure 36

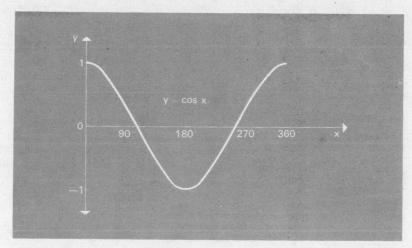

The graph is seen to be similar in shape to the sine graph but it starts at 1 when $x = 0$. The period of the cosine graph is also 2π radians; that is, it repeats itself every time the angle increases by 2π radians (fig. 36).

Graph of tan x

In the case of the tangent graph the tangent of 90°, 270°, 450°, etc. is infinity and we cannot complete the curve at these and similar points.

A table of values is prepared and the points plotted in the usual way.

$x°$	0	20	40	60	90	120	140	160	180
$y = \tan x$	0	0·364	0·839	1·732	∞	−1·732	−0·839	−0·364	0

$x°$	200	220	240	270	300	320	340	360
$y = \tan x$	0·364	0·839	1·732	∞	−1·732	−0·839	−0·364	0

Figure
37

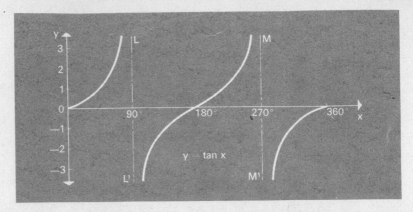

As x approaches 90°, tan x approaches the value infinity. Thus the graph gets closer and closer to the vertical line LL' drawn through the 90° mark and shown dotted in fig. 37. When x is slightly greater than 90° the tangent is large but negative and the curve reappears to the right of LL' on the negative side. At 270° the graph disappears to $+\infty$ on the left of MM' and reappears from $-\infty$ for x slightly greater than 270°.

Lines such as LL' and MM' to which the curve gets closer and closer as it moves off to an infinite distance are known as *asymptotes*.

The tangent graph goes through all its changes as the angle goes from 0° to 180° or to π radians. We say that the tangent is a periodic function of period π radians.

Graphs of sec x, cosec x, and cot x

The student should plot graphs of the remaining trigonometric functions sec x, cosec x, and cot x for himself. They are shown in small scale below. Notice the asymptotes in each case.

Figure
38

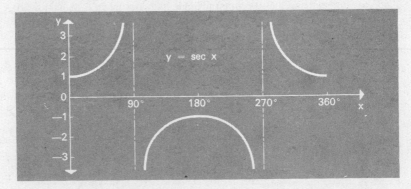

Figure
39

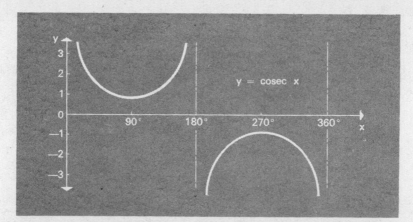

Figure
40

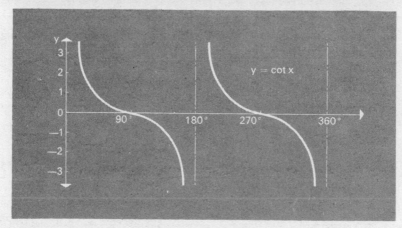

3i Periodic functions of the type $y = a \sin px$

The graph of $y = a \sin px$ is similar to that of the sine graph shown in figs. 34 and 35. Instead of varying or oscillating between $+1$ and -1, $a \sin px$ will vary between $+a$ and $-a$. a is called the *amplitude* and affects only the scale for y. The graph will repeat itself when the angle px increases by $360°$ or 2π radians,

i.e. when x increases by $\dfrac{360°}{p}$ or $\dfrac{2\pi}{p}$ radians.

Thus the period is $\dfrac{2\pi}{p}$ radians.

95   Periodic functions of the type $y = a \sin px$

The graph is shown below in fig. 41.

Thus $5 \sin 2x$ has a period of $\dfrac{2\pi}{2} = \pi$ radians and amplitude 5.

Figure
41

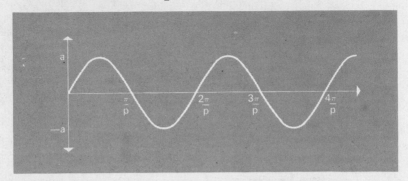

There are two complete waves between $0°$ and $360°$ for $y = 5 \sin 2x$.

In the same way $y = 4 \sin 3x$ is a sine curve varying between $+4$ and -4,

with a period for x of $\dfrac{360°}{3} = 120°$ or $\dfrac{2\pi}{3}$ radians.

The cosine function is very similar to the sine function; thus $y = a \cos px$

will repeat itself every $\dfrac{2\pi}{p}$ radians.

For certain purposes it is useful to be able to sketch the shape of trigonometric graphs without preparing a table and calculating the values.

Example 1   Sketch the graph of $y = 3 \sin 2x$ from $x = 0°$ to $360°$. On the same axes sketch $y = \sin x$. By adding ordinates sketch $y = 3 \sin 2x + \sin x$.

Figure
42

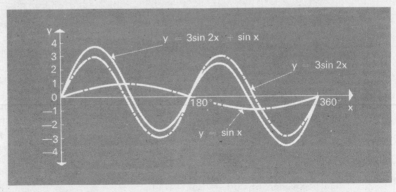

Example 2   For a complete wave or period sketch the graph of

$$y = 3 \sin \frac{x}{2} - \cos x$$

96   The trigonometric ratios

The period of $3 \sin \dfrac{x}{2}$ is 4π radians or $720°$.

The period of $\cos x$ is 2π radians or $360°$.

Thus to get a complete wave of $3 \sin \dfrac{x}{2} - \cos x$ we must include at least 4π radians or $720°$ on the x axis.

We first sketch the sine curve $y = 3 \sin \dfrac{x}{2}$, then the cosine curve $y = \cos x$.

We subtract the ordinates of $y = \cos x$ from $y = 3 \sin \dfrac{x}{2}$ to obtain points on the required curve. The sketch is shown in fig. 43 below.

Figure 43

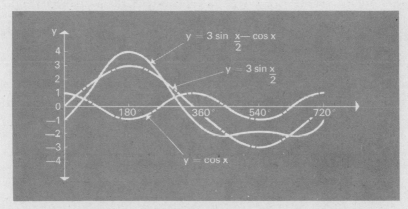

Example 3   Sketch the curve $y = 3 \sin (x + 60°)$

Figure 44

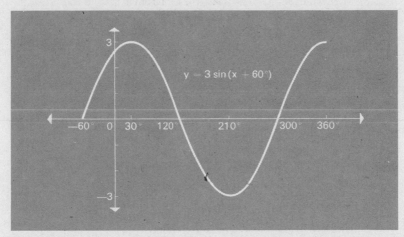

97   Periodic functions of the type $y = a \sin px$

We first sketch the curve $y = 3 \sin x$. The graph should be moved 60° to the left; or the y axis can be moved 60° to the right, which is equivalent, so that when $x = 0°$ y has the value of $3 \sin 60°$.

The function $y = 3 \sin (x + 60°)$ is said to have a *lead* of 60° since its values are those of $y = 3 \sin x$ with x increased by 60°.

$y = \sin (x - 60°)$ is said to *lag* 60° behind sin x.

Exercise 3i

1 State the amplitudes and the periods of the following functions of x, giving the periods in degrees and radians.

(a) $4 \sin 3x$ (b) $2 \cos 5x$ (c) $3 \sin \dfrac{x}{2}$

(d) $100 \cos \left(\dfrac{3x}{2} - \dfrac{\pi}{6} \right)$ (e) $5 \cos \left(2x + \dfrac{\pi}{3} \right)$ (f) $a \sin (wx + \alpha)$

2 Write down the periods of (a) $4 \tan 4x$ (b) $\cot 3x$ (c) $\tan px$

3 State the amplitude and period in radians of the following functions of t:

(a) $y = 15 \sin 20t$ (b) $v = 240 \sin 100\pi . t$

(c) $s = 3 \cdot 4 \cos (10t - 1 \cdot 5)$ (d) $y = y_0 \sin \left(\dfrac{at}{b} + c \right)$

4 Sketch on the same axes between 0° and 360° the graphs of $2 \sin x$, $\sin 3x$, $\sin \dfrac{x}{2}$

5 Draw the graph of $y = 4 \sin (\theta + 60°)$ from $\theta = 0°$ to 360°
Draw the lines $y = 2$ and $y = -2$ on the same axes.

    From the graphs find the values of θ between 0° and 360° which satisfy the equations (a) $4 \sin (\theta + 60°) = 2$
                           (b) $4 \sin (\theta + 60°) = -2$

6 Draw a rough sketch of the curve $y = 3 \tan 2x$ over two periods.

7 Sketch on the same axes between 0° and 360° the graphs of $y = \cos 2x$, $y = 2 \sin x$, $y = \cos 2x + 2 \sin x$

8 Sketch the graph of $\cos 2x - 2 \sin x$

9 Prepare a table of values and construct a graph of $y = \sin 2x - \sin x$ from $x = 0°$ to $x = 180°$. State the values of x which make the expression

(a) zero   (b) a maximum   (c) a minimum

10 Draw a graph of $y = 2 \sin x - \cos x$ for values of x from $0°$ to $180°$. By drawing the line $y = 0.4$ find a solution of the equation $2 \sin x - \cos x = 0.4$

Miscellaneous exercises 3

1 (a) Obtain i $\sin \dfrac{2}{3}\pi$

      ii $\cos 2.6$
      where the angles are measured in radians.

   (b) Given that $\sin A = \dfrac{3}{5}$ and $\cos B = \dfrac{12}{13}$ where A and B are acute angles, find without using tables the values of

      i $\sin A \cos B + \cos A \sin B$
      ii $\tan^2 A + \tan^2 B$

   (c) Prove that

      $\tan \theta + \tan (90 + \theta) + \tan (270 - \theta) + \cot (270 + \theta) = 0$

2 (a) If x is an acute angle such that $\cos x = 0.75$ evaluate, without the use of trigonometric tables, the value of $\tan^2 x$.

   (b) Simplify i $\dfrac{\tan A \sec A}{1 + \tan^2 A}$ ii $\dfrac{\sec^2 A - \operatorname{cosec}^2 A}{\tan^2 A - \cot^2 A}$

3 (a) Set out in tabular form the complements and supplements of the angles

      $62° \, 12', \dfrac{\pi}{6}$ radians, $136°$, $-50°$

   (b) Prove the identities

      i $(\sin \theta + \cos \theta)(\tan \theta + \cot \theta) = \sec \theta + \operatorname{cosec} \theta$
      ii $\sec^2 x + \operatorname{cosec}^2 x = \sec^2 x \operatorname{cosec}^2 x$

4 Define the radian and give an expression for converting degrees to radians.

    Find in radians the angle between the hour hand and the minute hand of a clock at half past three.

    If $\sin \theta = \dfrac{a}{b}$ find $\tan \theta$, $\sec \theta$, and $\cot \theta$

    Prove that $\dfrac{\operatorname{cosec} A}{\cot A + \tan A} = \cos A$

5 (a) Taking the radius of the earth as 6.3 Mm, find the difference in latitude of two places, one of which is 240 km north of the other.

   (b) Prove that $\dfrac{\tan \theta}{(1 + \tan^2 \theta)} + \dfrac{\cot \theta}{(1 + \cot^2 \theta)} = 2 \sin \theta \cos \theta$

6　Prove the following identities:
(a) $\sin \theta (1+\tan \theta)+\cos \theta (1+\cot \theta) = \sec \theta + \operatorname{cosec} \theta$
(b) $(\operatorname{cosec} A - \sin A)(\sec A - \cos A)(\tan A + \cot A) = 1$
(c) $\dfrac{1+\sin \theta}{1-\sin \theta} = (\sec \theta + \tan \theta)^2$

7　Two level tunnels AB and BC meet at point B, making an included angle of 120°. The angular junction is replaced by a curve, AB and BC being tangents to this curve. If the effect of this is to reduce the total length from A via B to C by 10 m, calculate the radius and the length of the curve.

8　From a certain point the elevation of the top of a spire is 42°. After walking 30 m towards the spire the elevation is found to be 60°. Find the height of the spire.

9　A tower, 20 m high, stands on the top of a mound. From a point on the ground the angles of elevation of the top and the bottom of the tower are found to be 75° and 45° respectively. Find the height of the mound.

10　A man walking along a straight road observes that the bearing of a distant beacon is 30° with the direction of the road. Two kilometres further on its bearing is 45°. How far from the road is the beacon?

11　A surveyor stands on a horizontal plane on which a flagpole is erected. To find the height of the flagpole he takes the angle of inclination from a point C to the top of the flagpole and finds the angle to be 32° 18′. He then walks a distance of 20 m to a point D which is directly in line between point C and the base of the flagpole. The angle of inclination from point D to the top of the flagpole is found to be 54° 24′. Calculate the height of the flagpole.

12　Two men standing in a straight line with a factory chimney, but on opposite sides of it, observe that the angles of elevation of the top of the chimney are 45° and 60° respectively. If the men are 100 m apart, find the height of the chimney.
　　If both men walk 15 m towards the base of the chimney, find the new angles of elevation.

13　From the top of a cliff 100 m high, the angles of depression of the top and bottom of a lighthouse are observed to be 40° and 60°. Find the height of the lighthouse.

14　Two ladders are used to reach a point on a vertical wall which is $13\frac{1}{3}$ m above ground level. The first ladder is 10 m long and makes an angle of 60° with the ground. The base of the second ladder which is also 10 m long, is secured to a point on the first ladder such that its uppermost end reaches the required position $13\frac{1}{3}$ m above the ground.

Calculate:

(a) the angle which the second ladder makes with the horizontal,

(b) the vertical height to the point where the two ladders are secured.

15 An aircraft flying horizontally at 400 km/h passes over an observer on the ground and has its angular elevations recorded as 72° and 38° at two instants 10 s apart. Find, in kilometres, the height at which the aircraft is flying.

16 From a point A a rock on a hillside is observed to have an angle of elevation of 45° 35′. After moving in the direction of the rock up a slope inclined at an angle of 31° 25′ to the horizontal for a distance of 875 m the observer finds the elevation of the rock to be 65° 45′. Find the vertical height of the rock above A.

17 On the same axes and with the same scales, plot the graphs of $y = 5 \sin \theta$ and $y = 2 \sin 3\theta$ between $\theta = 0°$ and $\theta = 360°$

State the amplitude and the period of each expression. By adding ordinates obtain the graph of $y = 5 \sin \theta + 2 \sin 3\theta$.

What is the period of this combined expression?

18 (a) Plot a graph of $y = 2 \sin x + \cos x$ between the values of 0° and 180°. (Take values of x at 15° intervals.)

(b) From the graph, determine the values of x between 0° and 180°, which satisfy the equation

$2 \sin x + \cos x = 1\cdot5$ $U.E.I.$

19 On the same figure draw the graphs of $y = \cos 3x$ and $y = 4 \sin x - 3 \cos x$ for the values of x from 0 to 60°. From your graphs obtain a solution of the equation

$4 \sin x - 3 \cos x = \cos 3x$

20 Plot a graph of $y = 2 \sin 2x - \cos x$ from $x = 0°$ to $x = 90°$ taking values of x at intervals of 10°. Find the value of x for which the function has its greatest value.

From your graph find two solutions of the equation

$2 \sin 2x - \cos x = 1$

4 Solution of triangles

4a Sine and cosine rules and the area of a triangle

Progressing from the properties of a right-angled triangle to those of any triangle we find various relations between the sides and the angles.

In accordance with the usual notation we denote the angles of any triangle ABC by A, B and C and the sides opposite these angles by a, b and c respectively.

The sine rule

$$\frac{a}{\sin A} = \frac{b}{\sin B} = \frac{c}{\sin C}$$

Suppose ABC is any triangle. There are two possible cases as shown in fig. 45 (a) and (b) where the angle C is taken as acute and obtuse respectively.

Figure 45

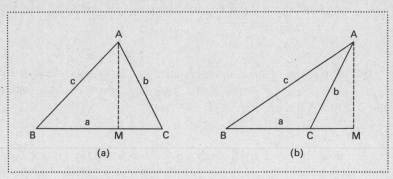

(a)   (b)

AM is drawn perpendicular to BC or BC produced.

(a) *Angle C acute: fig. 45(a)*

In triangle ACM $AM = AC \sin C = b \sin C$
In triangle ABM $AM = AB \sin B = c \sin B$

Equating these two values of AM we get

$$b \sin C = c \sin B$$

i.e. $\dfrac{b}{\sin B} = \dfrac{c}{\sin C}$

In a similar manner by drawing a perpendicular from C to AB

we get $\dfrac{a}{\sin A} = \dfrac{b}{\sin B}$

Hence $\dfrac{a}{\sin A} = \dfrac{b}{\sin B} = \dfrac{c}{\sin C}$

(b) *Angle C obtuse: fig. 45(b)*

In triangle ACM $\quad AM = AC \sin ACM$
$$= b \sin (180° - C)$$
$$= b \sin C$$

In triangle ABM $\quad AM = AB \sin B$
$$= c \sin B$$

Thus $\qquad\qquad b \sin C = c \sin B$

and $\qquad\qquad \dfrac{b}{\sin B} = \dfrac{c}{\sin C}$

Similarly by drawing a perpendicular from C to AB

$$\dfrac{a}{\sin A} = \dfrac{b}{\sin B}$$

and $\dfrac{a}{\sin A} = \dfrac{b}{\sin B} = \dfrac{c}{\sin C}$

and this rule holds in all cases.

Example In triangle ABC find the side AB if $AC = 5.4$ cm, $B = 70°$, $C = 80°$
In this example we are given $b(=AC)$, B and C and we require $c(=AB)$

Since $\dfrac{c}{\sin C} = \dfrac{b}{\sin B}$ we have sufficient information to find c

$$c = \frac{b \sin C}{\sin B} = \frac{5.4 \sin 80°}{\sin 70°} \text{ cm}$$

$$= 5.66 \text{ cm}$$

Number	Log
5·4	0·7324
sin 80°	$\bar{1}$·9934
	0·7258
sin 70°	$\bar{1}$·9730
5·659 ←	0·7528

The cosine rule

$$c^2 = a^2 + b^2 - 2ab \cos C$$

We consider the two cases as in the sine rule.

103   Sine and cosine rules and the area of a triangle

(a) *Triangle ABC acute-angled*

Figure
46

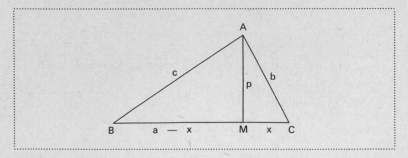

AM is drawn perpendicular to *BC*

Let $AM = p$ and $MC = x$

In triangle *ACM* $AC^2 = AM^2 + MC^2$
i.e. $b^2 = p^2 + x^2 \ldots (4.1)$
In triangle *ABM* $AB^2 = AM^2 + BM^2$
$$c^2 = p^2 + (a-x)^2$$
$$= p^2 + a^2 - 2ax + x^2$$
$$= a^2 + (p^2 + x^2) - 2ax \ldots (4.2)$$

From equation (4.1) we may substitute b^2 for $p^2 + x^2$ and

$x = MC = AC \cos ACM = b \cos C$

Equation (4.2) becomes

$c^2 = a^2 + b^2 - 2ab \cos C$

(b) *Triangle ABC obtuse-angled*

Figure
47

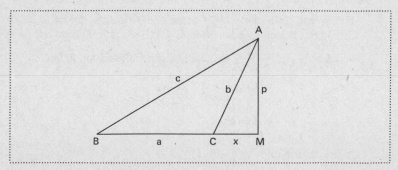

AM is drawn perpendicular to *BC* produced.
As before let $AM = p$ and $CM = x$

In triangle ACM $AC^2 = AM^2 + CM^2$

i.e. $b^2 = p^2 + x^2 \ldots (4.1)$

In triangle ABM $AB^2 = AM^2 + BM^2$

i.e. $c^2 = p^2 + (a + x)^2$

$$= p^2 + a^2 + 2ax + x^2 \ldots (4.3)$$

As before we may substitute b^2 for $p^2 + x^2$ and

$$x = CM = AC \cos ACM = b \cos (180° - C)$$
$$= -b \cos C \qquad \text{(see page 89)}$$

Equation (4.3) becomes $c^2 = a^2 + b^2 + 2a(-b \cos C)$

i.e. $c^2 = a^2 + b^2 - 2ab \cos C$

If $C = 90°$ then $\cos C = 0$ in which case $c^2 = a^2 + b^2$

Thus the cosine formula holds for all triangles, acute-angled, obtuse-angled and right-angled.

By the same method we could show that

$$a^2 = b^2 + c^2 - 2bc \cos A$$
and $b^2 = c^2 + a^2 - 2ca \cos B$

From the above we get also $\cos A - \dfrac{b^2 + c^2 - a^2}{2bc}$ $\cos B - \dfrac{c^2 + a^2 - b^2}{2ca}$

and $\cos C = \dfrac{a^2 + b^2 - c^2}{2ab}$

Notice that it is only necessary to memorize one formula. The other forms are quickly obtained by what is called *cyclic interchange*; that is 'a' changes into 'b', 'b' changes into 'c' and 'c' changes into 'a', and similarly for A, B and C.

Figure 48

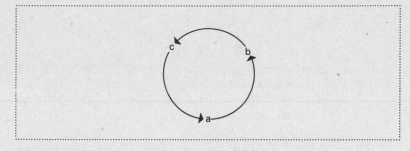

For example $a = b \cos C + c \cos B$ is true for any triangle. Then we obtain the following formulae by cyclic interchange of the letters:

$b = c \cos A + a \cos C$

$c = a \cos B + b \cos A$

Example The sides of a triangle are 7 cm, 8 cm, and 9 cm. Find the angle opposite the 9 cm side.

Figure
49

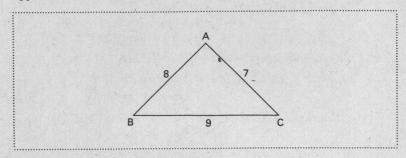

Letting the required angle be A we get

$$\cos A = \frac{b^2 + c^2 - a^2}{2bc} = \frac{7^2 + 8^2 - 9^2}{2 \times 7 \times 8}$$

$$= \frac{49 + 64 - 81}{2 \times 7 \times 8} = \frac{32}{2 \times 7 \times 8} = \frac{2}{7} = 0{\cdot}2857$$

Hence required angle $= 73° \ 24'$

Area of triangle

(a) Area $= \frac{1}{2}ab \sin C$

Figure
50

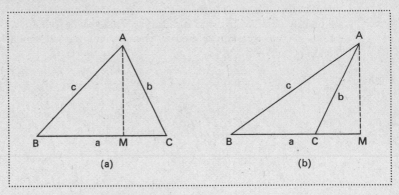

(a)   (b)

Area of triangle $= \frac{1}{2}$ base $\times$ height
$$= \frac{1}{2}BC \times AM$$

In right-angled triangle ACM

$AM = AC \sin C = b \sin C$
or $AM = AC \sin (180° - C) = b \sin C$

106   **Solution of triangles**

In each case area $= \frac{1}{2}ab \sin C$
Similarly   area $= \frac{1}{2}bc \sin A$
and   area $= \frac{1}{2}ca \sin B$

(b) Area $= \sqrt{\{s(s-a)(s-b)(s-c)\}}$ where $s = \dfrac{a+b+c}{2}$

If the three sides of the triangle are known we can obtain a second formula by substituting for $\sin C$ in $\frac{1}{2}ab \sin C$.

Since $\sin^2 C + \cos^2 C = 1$

$$\sin^2 C = 1 - \cos^2 C$$
$$= (1 + \cos C)(1 - \cos C)$$
$$= \left(1 + \frac{a^2 + b^2 - c^2}{2ab}\right)\left(1 - \frac{a^2 + b^2 - c^2}{2ab}\right)$$
$$= \left(\frac{2ab + a^2 + b^2 - c^2}{2ab}\right)\left(\frac{2ab - a^2 - b^2 + c^2}{2ab}\right)$$
$$= \frac{\{(a+b)^2 - c^2\}\{c^2 - (a-b)^2\}}{4a^2b^2}$$
$$= \frac{(a+b+c)(a+b-c)(c+a-b)(c-a+b)}{4a^2b^2}$$

Thus area $= \frac{1}{2}ab \sin C$

$$= \frac{1}{2}ab \frac{\sqrt{\{(a+b+c)(a+b-c)(a-b+c)(b+c-a)\}}}{2ab}$$
$$= \frac{1}{4}\sqrt{\{(a+b+c)(b+c-a)(a-b+c)(a+b-c)\}}$$

If we let $a+b+c = 2s$
then $a+b+c-2a = b+c-a = 2s-2a$
$\therefore$ $b+c-a = 2(s-a)$
Similarly $a-b+c = 2(s-b)$
and $a+b-c = 2(s-c)$
$\therefore$ area of triangle $= \frac{1}{4}\sqrt{\{2s.2(s-a)2(s-b)2(s-c)\}}$
i.e.   area $= \sqrt{\{s(s-a)(s-b)(s-c)\}}$

Example 1   Find the area of triangle ABC given that $a = 6$ cm $b = 5$ cm $c = 9$ cm

In this case $s = \frac{1}{2}(6+5+9) = 10$
$$s-a = 4$$
$$s-b = 5$$
$$s-c = 1$$
area $= \sqrt{(10 \times 4 \times 5 \times 1)} = \sqrt{200} = 14 \cdot 14$ cm^2

Example 2   Show that the area of a quadrilateral is given by $\frac{1}{2}l_1 l_2 \sin\theta$ where l_1 and l_2 are the lengths of the diagonals and θ is the angle between them.

In quadrilateral $ABCD$ let BL and DM be drawn perpendicular to AC (fig. 51).

Figure 51

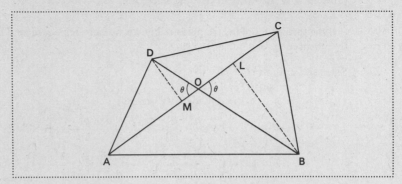

Area of quadrilateral $ABCD$ = area $\triangle ABC$ + area $\triangle ADC$
$$= \tfrac{1}{2}AC.BL + \tfrac{1}{2}AC.DM$$
$$= \tfrac{1}{2}AC(BL + DM)$$
$$= \tfrac{1}{2}AC(BO \sin\theta + DO \sin\theta)$$
$$= \tfrac{1}{2}AC.BD \sin\theta$$
$$= \tfrac{1}{2}l_1 l_2 \sin\theta \qquad \text{where } AC = l_1$$
$$BD = l_2$$

Exercise 4a

1   In triangle ABC (a) find a and b if $A = 60°$, $B = 80°$ and $C = 7.2$
    (b) find b if $a = 6.2$, $c = 4.8$, $B = 72°$

2   Find the area of triangle ABC if
    (a) $a = 6$ cm, $b = 9$ cm, $c = 67°$
    (b) $a = 10$ cm, $b = 9$ cm, $c = 6$ cm
    (c) $A = 52°30'$, $B = 63°$, $a = 14$ cm
    (d) $A = 52°30'$, $B = 63°$, $c = 14$ cm

3   If the area of triangle $ABC = 34$ cm^2 and $A = 70°$ and $b = 6$ cm, find c.

4   In triangle ABC if $a = 12$ cm, $b = 10$ cm and $c = 7$ cm find the area of the triangle and from it find the sine of the largest angle.

5   Verify the formula $\sqrt{\{s(s-a)(s-b)(s-c)\}}$ for the area of a triangle in the following cases by finding the area by a second method.
    (a) When the sides are 6, 8 and 10
    (b) When the sides are 12, 13 and 5
    (c) When the sides are each 2 cm

6   By drawing *AM* perpendicular to *BC* show that in triangle *ABC*
    $a = b \cos C + c \cos B$. By cyclic interchange of the letters write down the
    corresponding formula for *b* and for *c*.

7   Using the same construction as in exercise 6 above show that
    $$\tan B = \frac{b \sin C}{a - b \cos C}$$
    Write down the corresponding formula for tan *A* and for tan *C*.

8   The sides of a rhombus are 10 cm long and the smaller angle between adjacent
    sides is 72°. Find the area of the rhombus and the lengths of the diagonals.

9   Find the area of a parallelogram in which the lengths of adjacent sides are 12
    and 16 cm and the length of the shortest diagonal is 10 cm.

10 A metal plate is in the shape of a quadrilateral whose diagonals are 6 cm and
    8 cm. If the angle between the diagonals is 70° find the area.

4b   Solution of triangles

If we are given sufficient facts to fix the shape of a triangle then the unknown
sides or angles may be calculated using the sine and cosine rules. In general we
require three parts, such as the three sides or two sides and one angle, and then
the remaining three parts of the triangle can be found. In certain cases there
may be two possible triangles. The solution of these problems is known as
'solving the triangle' and there are four main cases as set out below.

Three angles are not sufficient to determine a triangle; we require at least
one side.

Case 1.   Given one side and two angles

Solve triangle *ABC* in which $A = 37°12'$, $B = 74°26'$, $a = 65 \cdot 2$

$c = 180° - 37°12' - 74°26'$
$ = 68°22'$

Figure
52

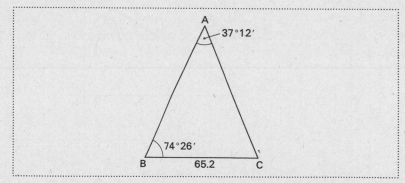

109   Solution of triangles

From the sine rule $\dfrac{a}{\sin A} = \dfrac{b}{\sin B} = \dfrac{c}{\sin C}$

we get $\dfrac{65\cdot2}{\sin 37°12'} = \dfrac{b}{\sin 74°26'} = \dfrac{c}{\sin 68°22'}$

$$b = \frac{65\cdot2 \sin 74°26'}{\sin 37°12'}$$

$$= 104$$

$$c = \frac{65\cdot2 \sin 68°22'}{\sin 37°12'}$$

$$= 100$$

Number	Log
65·2	1·8142
sin 74°26'	$\bar{1}$·9838
	1·7980
sin 37°12'	$\bar{1}$·7815
103·9 ←	2·0165
65·2	1·8142
sin 68°22'	$\bar{1}$·9683
	1·7825
sin 37°12'	$\bar{1}$·7815
100·2 ←	2·0010

Answers: $b = 104$, $c = 100$, $C = 68°22'$

Case 2. Given two sides and one angle (not the contained angle)

Solve triangle ABC in which $b = 63\cdot7$, $c = 29\cdot6$, $C = 27°22'$

From the sine rule $\sin B = \dfrac{b \sin C}{c}$

$$= \frac{63\cdot7 \sin 27°22'}{29\cdot6}$$

$B = 81°36'$ or $180° - 81°36'$

i.e. $B_1 = 81°36'$ or $B_2 = 98°24'$

Number	Log
63·7	1·8041
sin 27°22'	$\bar{1}$·6625
	1·4666
29·6	1·4713
sin 81°36' ←	$\bar{1}$·9953

Both solutions are possible as side b is greater than side c and thus angle B is greater than angle C.

Figure 53

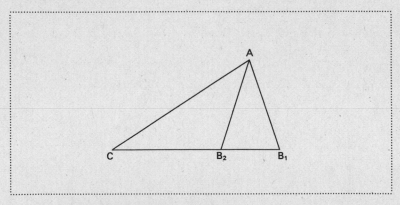

$A_1 = 180° - 27°22' - 81°36' = 71°2'$

and $A_2 = 180° - 27°22' - 98°24' = 54°14'$

For triangle ACB_1

$$a_1 = \frac{b \sin A_1}{\sin B_1} = \frac{63 \cdot 7 \sin 71°2'}{\sin 81°36'}$$
$$= 60 \cdot 9$$

For triangle ACB_2

$$a_2 = \frac{b \sin A_2}{\sin B_2} = \frac{63 \cdot 7 \sin 54°14'}{\sin 98°24'}$$
$$= 52 \cdot 3$$

Answers: $B_1 = 81°36'$, $A_1 = 71°2'$, $a_1 = 60 \cdot 9$
and $\qquad B_2 = 98°24'$, $A_2 = 54°14'$, $a_2 = 52 \cdot 3$

	Number	Log
	63·7	1·8041
sin 71°2'		$\overline{1}$·9758
		1·7799
sin 81°36'		$\overline{1}$·9953
	60·89 ←	1·7846
	63·7	1·8041
sin 54°14'		$\overline{1}$·9093
		1·7134
sin 98°24'		$\overline{1}$·9953
	52·25 ←	1·7181

Case 3. Given two sides and the contained angle

Solve triangle ABC in which $b = 43 \cdot 6$, $c = 29 \cdot 8$,
$A = 53°29'$

By the cosine rule we have $a^2 = b^2 + c^2 - 2bc \cos A$

$$a^2 = 43 \cdot 6^2 + 29 \cdot 8^2 - 2 \times 43 \cdot 6 \times 29 \cdot 8 \cos 53°29'$$
$$= 1901 + 888 - 1546$$
$$= 1243$$
$$a = \sqrt{1243} = 35 \cdot 25 = 35 \cdot 3$$

	Number	Log
	2·0	0·3010
	43·6	1·6395
	29·8	1·4742
cos 53°29'		$\overline{1}$·7745
	1546 ←	3·1892

Using the sine rule we find angle C which we know must be acute since side c is smaller than side b.

$$\sin C = \frac{c \sin A}{a} = \frac{29 \cdot 8 \sin 53°29'}{35 \cdot 3}$$
$$C = 42°43'$$
$$B = 180° - 42°43' - 53°29'$$
$$= 83°48'$$

Answers: $B = 83°48'$, $C = 42°43'$, $a = 35 \cdot 3$

	Number	Log
	29·8	1·4742
sin 53°29'		$\overline{1}$·9051
		1·3793
	35·3	1·5478
sin 42°43' ←		$\overline{1}$·8315

Case 4. Given the three sides

Solve triangle ABC in which $a = 26 \cdot 4$, $b = 19 \cdot 7$, $c = 36 \cdot 1$

There is no ambiguity in using the cosine rule to find an angle. If the angle is obtuse the cosine will be negative.

Using the cosine rule to find the largest angle

$$\cos C = \frac{a^2 + b^2 - c^2}{2ab} = \frac{26 \cdot 4^2 + 19 \cdot 7^2 - 36 \cdot 1^2}{2 \times 26 \cdot 4 \times 19 \cdot 7}$$

$$= \frac{697 \cdot 0 + 388 \cdot 1 - 1303 \cdot 0}{2 \times 26 \cdot 4 \times 19 \cdot 7}$$

$$= -\frac{217 \cdot 9}{2 \times 26 \cdot 4 \times 19 \cdot 7}$$

$$= -0 \cdot 2095$$

$$\therefore \ C = 180° - 77°54'$$

$$= 102°6'$$

Number	Log
2	0·3010
26·4	1·4216
19·7	1·2945
	3·0171
217·9	2·3383
	3·0171
0·2095	← $\overline{1}$·3212
26·4	1·4216
sin 77°54'	$\overline{1}$·9902
	1·4118
36·1	1·5575
sin 45°38'	← $\overline{1}$·8543

Since the sine rule is simpler to use we will use it for the next angle.

$$\sin A = \frac{a \sin C}{c} = \frac{26 \cdot 4 \sin 102°6'}{36 \cdot 1}$$

$$A = 45°38'$$

$$\therefore \ B = 180° - 45°38' - 102°6' = 32°16'$$

Answers: $A = 45°38'$, $B = 32°16'$, $C = 102°6'$

Exercise 4b

Solve the triangles in questions 1–4 and check your results by drawing the triangles to scale.

1    $A = 77°$ $B = 40°$ $b = 9 \cdot 9$

2    $a = 20$ $c = 24$ $B = 40°$

3    $a = 181$ $b = 131$ $c = 87$

4    $b = 4$ $c = 7$ $B = 15°$

Find the remaining sides and angles in the triangles 5–8. In number 8 find both solutions.

Figure 54

5

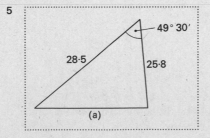

(a)

6

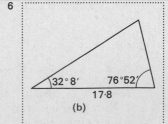

(b)

7

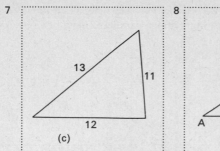

(c)

8

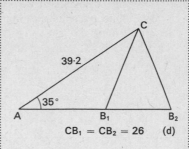

$CB_1 = CB_2 = 26$ (d)

9   A vertical mast AB, 5 m high, stands on ground which slopes at $10°$ to the horizontal. A tight stay connects the top of the mast B to a point C on the ground 4 m downhill from A, the foot of the mast. Calculate (a) the length of the stay (b) the angle which the stay makes with the ground.

4c   Projection of lines and areas

So far in this chapter we have used trigonometry to solve problems which could be called *two-dimensional*. A diagram giving the relations between the angles and distances could be drawn to scale on a sheet of paper. We proceed to problems in space involving three dimensions but before doing this we must define various angles.

When two lines intersect, the angle between their directions is found directly by using a protractor. But lines in space do not generally intersect; this can easily be verified by holding a long knitting needle in each hand, and moving them to various positions at random.

When two lines in space do not intersect they are called *skew* lines. We still talk about the angle between two skew lines. It is the angle between their directions, i.e. the angle between any two intersecting lines parallel to the given lines.

Figure 55

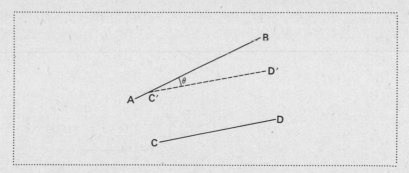

We may define the angle between two skew lines as the angle between one of the lines and a line meeting it drawn parallel to the other. This is shown as angle θ in fig. 55.

Figure 56

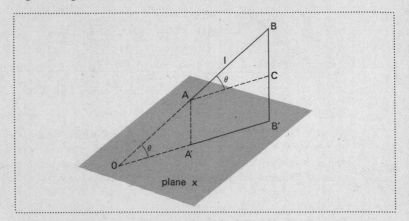

The angle between a line and a plane is defined as the angle between the line and its projection on the plane.

In fig. 56 if A is any point on the line then A', the foot of the perpendicular from A to the plane, is the projection of A on the plane. Thus line $A'B'$ is the projection of line AB on plane X.

θ, the angle at O where AB and $A'B'$ meet, is the angle between the line and its projection and is thus by definition the angle between the line and the plane.

Notice that if the length of the line AB is l then the length of its projection on the plane is $l \cos \theta$; for we have

$$\text{Length of projection} = A'B' = AC = l \cos \theta$$

as AC is drawn parallel to $A'B'$ so that angle $BAC = \theta$; and BB' is perpendicular to $A'B'$ so that ACB is a right-angled triangle.

When two planes in space are not parallel then they will intersect in a line which is called the line of intersection of the planes.

The angle between two planes is the angle between two straight lines, one

Figure 57

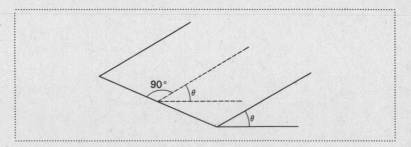

in each plane, and each drawn through a point on the line of intersection and perpendicular to that line of intersection (see fig. 57).

The angle between the two planes is also known as the *dihedral* angle.

If the planes are parallel the dihedral angle is zero.

A line of greatest slope in a given plane is any line in the plane perpendicular to any horizontal line in that plane. In effect it is the 'steepest' line in the plane.

Projection of an area

When an area on one plane is projected on to a second plane we often require the value of the projected area. Let S' be the projection on plane Y of any area S on plane X (see fig. 58). S' is formed by joining up the projections on plane Y of points all round the perimeter of S.

Figure 58

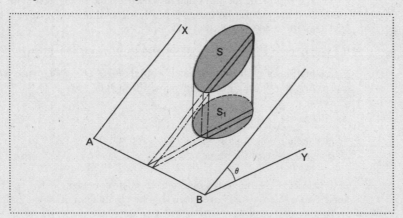

Consider the area S to be divided up into a series of narrow strips by lines drawn perpendicular to AB, the line of intersection of the two planes. The area S is the sum of the areas of these strips. The projections on Y of these strips are a series of similar strips whose lengths in a direction at right angles to AB are reduced by the multiplier $\cos \theta$. The widths of these strips in a direction parallel to AB are unchanged.

Thus the areas of the strips are reduced in the ratio $\cos \theta : 1$ and the sum of their areas are reduced in the same ratio.

Hence we get

Projected area $S' = S \cos \theta$

where θ is the angle between the planes.

Example 1 A hillside, which may be regarded as a plane, is inclined at $30°$ to the horizontal. A path on the hillside is inclined at $10°$ to a line of greatest slope and runs up the hill for a vertical height of 400 m. Find the length of the path and its inclination to the horizontal.

Figure
59

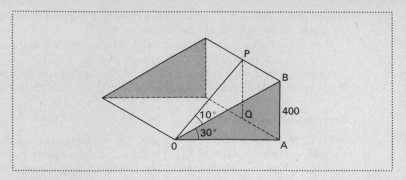

Let OP represent the path and let OB be a line of greatest slope through point O at the foot of the path. PB is a horizontal line.

Then $OB = 400$ cosec $30° = 800$ m

Length of path $OP = OB$ sec $10° = 800$ sec $10° = 812$ m approx.

Inclination of path to horizontal $=$ angle $POQ = \angle POQ$ where OQ is the projection of OP on a horizontal plane through O.

$$\sin POQ = \frac{PQ}{OP} = \frac{400 \text{ m}}{812 \text{ m}} = \frac{1}{2\cdot03}$$

Hence inclination of path $= \angle POQ = 29°30'$
The sign $\angle$ is used for angle.

Example 2 V is the vertex of a right circular cone, height $12\frac{1}{2}$ cm, radius of base 5 cm. Points ABC are taken on the circumference of the base so that $\angle BAC = 30°$, $\angle ABC = 70°$, $\angle BCA = 80°$

Figure
60

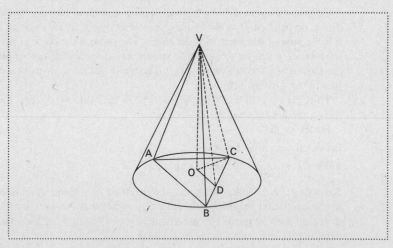

Find (a) the inclination of CV to the base of the cone.

      (b) the length of side BC

      (c) the angle CVB

      (d) the inclination of plane VBC to the base of the cone.

Let O be the foot of the perpendicular from vertex V to the base. Since the cone is symmetrical O will be the centre of the circle forming the base and $OC = OB = 5$ cm.

(a) Inclination of CV to base $= \angle VCO$

    where $\tan VCO = \dfrac{VO}{OC} = \dfrac{12\frac{1}{2}}{5} = 2 \cdot 5$

    $\therefore \quad \angle VCO = 68°12'$

(b) Triangle BOC is equilateral since $\angle BOC = 2 \times \angle BAC = 60°$, and $OB = OC = 5$ cm.

Thus length of side $BC = 5$ cm.

(c) Let D be the mid point of BC

Then $\quad DC = 2\frac{1}{2}$ cm

$$VC^2 = VO^2 + OC^2 = 12\tfrac{1}{2}^2 + 5^2 = 156\tfrac{1}{4} + 25 = 181\tfrac{1}{4} \text{ cm}^2$$

$\therefore \qquad VC = \sqrt{181\tfrac{1}{4}} = 13 \cdot 46$ cm

$\quad \sin CVD = \dfrac{2 \cdot 5}{13 \cdot 46} = 0 \cdot 1858$

$\therefore \quad \angle CVD = 10°42'$

Thus $\angle CVB = 21°24'$

(d) The inclination of plane VBC to the base of the cone is given by angle VDO

    $\tan VDO = \dfrac{VO}{OD}$

      $OD^2 = OC^2 - CD^2 = 5^2 - 2\tfrac{1}{2}^2 = 25 - 6\tfrac{1}{4} = 18\tfrac{3}{4}$

      $OD = \sqrt{(18 \cdot 75)} = 4 \cdot 33$ cm

    $\tan VDO = \dfrac{12\frac{1}{2}}{4 \cdot 33} = 2 \cdot 887$

$\therefore \angle VDO = 70°54'$

Inclination of plane VBC to base $= 70°54'$

Exercise 4c

1   Find the angle between a diagonal of a cube and any face which it meets.

2   Find the area of the shadow cast on the ground by a square plate of side 2 m held at right-angles to the sun's rays when the sun's altitude (i.e. angle above the horizontal) is $52°$.

3   A circular cylinder of diameter 10 cm is cut by a plane inclined at an angle of 40° to the axis of the cylinder. Find the area of the section.

4   Find the area of the shadow cast by a horizontal circular disc, diameter 10 m, on a vertical wall facing the sun, when the sun's altitude is 50°.

5   A hut H on a flat hillside sloping north at 30° to the horizontal plane is 120 m from a straight path running east and west. From a point A on this path a man walks north-east to reach the hut. Find (a) the distance AH and (b) the angle AH makes with the horizontal plane.

6   A seam of coal is $1\frac{1}{2}$ m thick and is inclined at an angle of 18° to the horizontal. Find the volume of coal in cubic metres under a 15 hectare field.

7   A 60° set square is held in a vertical plane with its shortest side in a horizontal plane. The plane of the set square makes an angle of 45° with a second vertical plane S. Find the angle between the longest side of the set square and the plane S.

8   An equilateral triangle ABC lying in a horizontal plane is rotated through an angle of 30° about the side AB. Find (a) the angle between AC and its original position (b) the inclination of AC to the horizontal plane.

9   A right pyramid $VABCD$ stands on a square base $ABCD$ of side 2 m and is of height 4 m. Find
     (a) the inclination of VA to the base, and
     (b) the angle between VAB and the base plane.

10   Explain how the angle between (a) a plane and a straight line (b) two planes, is measured. A right pyramid $VABC$ stands on base ABC which is an equilateral triangle of side a. The vertex V is equidistant from A, B and C and its height above the base is $3a$. Find (a) the inclination of edge VA to the base (b) the angle between faces VAB and ABC.

4d   Useful trigonometric limits

If θ radians represents an angle less than one right angle then we will show that

$$\sin \theta < \theta < \tan \theta$$

where the sign $<$ means 'less than'.

Consider a sector AOP of a circle of radius r and let the angle of the sector be θ radians where θ is acute.

Join chord AP and let PT be drawn at right angles to radius OP to cut OA produced at T.

Considering the areas of triangle AOP, sector AOP and triangle TOP we have

Figure
61

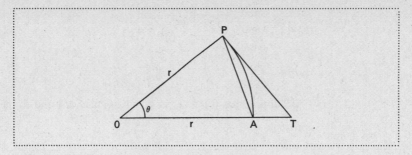

Triangle AOP < sector AOP < triangle TOP
Area of triangle $AOP = \frac{1}{2}r^2 \sin \theta$ (Refer $\frac{1}{2}ab \sin C$.)
Area of sector AOP $= \frac{1}{2}r^2\theta$ (See page 70.)
Area of triangle $TOP = \frac{1}{2}OP \times PT = \frac{1}{2}r \times r \tan \theta$
                       $= \frac{1}{2}r^2 \tan \theta$

Hence $\frac{1}{2}r^2 \sin \theta < \frac{1}{2}r^2\theta < \frac{1}{2}r^2 \tan \theta$
i.e. $\sin \theta < \theta < \tan \theta$

We next consider the value of the ratio $\dfrac{\theta}{\sin \theta}$ as θ gets smaller and smaller.
From $\sin \theta < \theta < \tan \theta$ if we divide throughout by $\sin \theta$ we have
$$1 < \frac{\theta}{\sin \theta} < \frac{\tan \theta}{\sin \theta}$$
Since $\tan \theta = \dfrac{\sin \theta}{\cos \theta}$ then $\dfrac{\tan \theta}{\sin \theta} = \dfrac{1}{\cos \theta} = \sec \theta$

i.e. $1 < \dfrac{\theta}{\sin \theta} < \sec \theta$

Since the secant of a small angle is very close to unity and since $\sec 0 = 1$ then as θ approaches 0 the closer will $\sec \theta$ approach 1 and also the closer will $\dfrac{\theta}{\sin \theta}$ approach 1.

We say the limit or the limiting value of $\dfrac{\theta}{\sin \theta}$ as θ approaches 0 is 1. This is written

$$\lim_{\theta \to 0} \frac{\theta}{\sin \theta} = 1$$

In the same way we can show $\lim\limits_{\theta \to 0} \dfrac{\theta}{\tan \theta} = 1$ for if we divide each term of $\sin \theta < \theta < \tan \theta$ by $\tan \theta$ we get $\dfrac{\sin \theta}{\tan \theta} < \dfrac{\theta}{\tan \theta} < 1$

119   **Useful trigonometric limits**

and as $\dfrac{\sin\theta}{\tan\theta} = \dfrac{\sin\theta}{\dfrac{\sin\theta}{\cos\theta}} = \cos\theta$ then

$$\cos\theta < \frac{\theta}{\tan\theta} < 1$$

The nearer θ approaches 0 the nearer $\cos\theta$ approaches 1 and so the nearer $\dfrac{\theta}{\tan\theta}$ approaches 1.

Thus we can write $\lim\limits_{\theta\to 0}\dfrac{\theta}{\tan\theta} = 1$

These two limits will be found very useful in later work in mathematics and science problems.

They are also useful in finding sines and tangents of very small angles since $\sin\theta$ and $\tan\theta$ are both very nearly equal to θ when θ is small and measured in radians.

Example Find the value of $\sin 40'$

$$40' = \frac{40°}{60} = \frac{2°}{3}\times\frac{\pi}{180°}\text{ radians}$$

$$= \frac{3\cdot141\,592\,6}{3\times 90}\ldots = 0\cdot011\,635\,5\ldots$$

$$\simeq \sin 40'$$

Exercise 4d

Given $\pi = 3\cdot141\,592\,65$;
Find to 5 places of decimals without using tables the value of

1 $\sin 9'$ 2 $\sin 26''$

3 $\tan 12'$ 4 $\tan 41'$

5 $\cos 89°45'$ 6 $\cot 89°50'$

7 Find approximately the distance of a lighthouse of height 22 m which subtends an angle of $3\frac{1}{2}'$ at the eye.

8 Find the height of a tower which at a distance of 4 km subtends an angle of $10'$ at the eye.

Miscellaneous exercises 4

1 Find the angles and area of a triangle ABC whose sides are $a = 346$, $b = 288$, $c = 568$.

2 In triangle ABC $b = 227$, $c = 175$, $A = 14°26'$. Find the remaining side and angles and calculate the area.

3 ABC is a triangular field where $A = 42°18'$, $a = 34.8$ m, $b = 49.2$ m. The third side is the shortest of the three. Calculate the length of this side, the other angles, and the area in square metres.

4 In triangle ABC $a = 6.3$, $b = 8.9$, $A = 43°$. Show by a sketch that there are two possible triangles and then solve them completely.

D.T.C.

5 The area of an acute-angled triangle is 160 cm^2. The sides a and b are 15 cm and 24 cm respectively. Calculate the three angles and the length of the remaining side.

6 An unworked part of a 2 m level seam of coal is triangular in shape, having sides of 325 m, 245 m and 204 m respectively. Assuming 100 per cent extraction and that the coal weighs 1.3 tonne/m^3, calculate the tonnes available.

7 (a) Show that $\tan (45° + A) = \dfrac{\cos A + \sin A}{\cos A - \sin A}$

(b) ABC is a triangle in which $AB = 4$ cm, $BC = 6$ cm, $CA = 5$ cm. Calculate the angles A, B and C to the nearest minute, and the length of the perpendicular from A on to BC to the nearest 0.01 cm.

8 (a) If $\sin x = -0.8817$, find the values of x between $0°$ and $360°$. Give answers in both degree and radian measure.
(b) Two roads leave point A. One is level and goes due east. On it is a point B which is exactly 0.75 km from A. The other road slopes uniformly downwards at an angle of $8°$ to the horizontal, and goes due south. On it is a point C which is exactly 0.5 km from A. A straight road with uniform slope joins B and C. Determine the length of the road BC and find its slope.

9 (a) Two straight roads cross at right-angles and a chimney stack stands along one of them. From the cross-roads, the elevation of the top of the stack is

$\theta°$, and from a point on the other road, distance x from the cross-roads, the elevation is $\alpha°$. Show that the height of the stack is

$$\frac{x}{\sqrt{(\cot^2 \alpha - \cot^2 \theta)}}$$

(b) Two ships A and B leave the same port at the same time. A steams along a course 078° at 9 km/hr and B along a course 150° at 12 km/hr. Find the distance between the ships after they have steamed for 3 hours.

10 A hip roof of uniform pitch is rectangular in plan, 7 m long and 4 m wide. The ridge is 1·6 m above the plane of the eaves. Calculate (a) the pitch of the roof, (b) the length and inclination of a hip rafter, (c) the length of the ridge, (d) the angle between the hip and the eaves line, (e) the total surface area of the roof surfaces.

11 During a survey observations are made of two positions A and B from a third position C. The horizontal projection of angle ACB is 42°24′, the distance CA is 363 m and CB is 428 m. The angle of elevation of A from C is 44°18′ and the angle of elevation of B from C is 33°24′. Determine the horizontal distance between A and B and the difference in level between them.

12 D is the summit of a mountain peak due east of an observation post B. From B the angle of elevation of D is β. A is due south of B and is at the same horizontal level as B. $AB = a$. The elevation of D from A is α.

If h is the height of D above the level of A and B,

show that $h^2(\cot^2 \alpha - \cot^2 \beta) = a^2$.

Calculate h in metres if $a = 0·5$ km, $\alpha = 40°34′$ and $\beta = 52°28′$.

13 A tower AB stands on the top of a hill which slopes upwards uniformly at an angle of 15° to the horizontal. From two points P and Q on the hill and in the same vertical plane as the tower, the elevations, measured rom the horizontal, of the top of the tower are 63° and 77° respectively. The distance PQ is 110 m. Calculate the height of the tower.

14 The sides of a railway cutting slope at an angle of 35° to the horizontal, and the top of the cutting is 15 m above the level of the track. Drains are to be laid in the surface of the bank, each making a straight line at an angle of 50° to the line of greatest slope and stretching from the bottom to the top of the bank.

Find the length of any one drain and its angle of inclination to the horizontal.

15 (a) *ABCD* is the base of a cube of side *a*; *AE*, *BF*, *CG* and *DH* are the vertical edges. *X*, *Y* and *Z* are the midpoints of the sides *AE*, *BF* and *GH* respectively. *O* is the centroid of the base. Find the ratio of the areas of the triangles *XYZ* and *XYO*.

(b) Sketch the curves of $3 \sin \theta$ and $2 \cos \theta$ on the same scales and axes. (Use a scale of $2 \text{ cm} = \dfrac{\pi^c}{2}$ on the θ scale, and $2 \text{ cm} = 1$ unit on the $f(\theta)$ scale.)

Hence, again using the same scale and axes, sketch the curve of $3 \sin \theta - 2 \cos \theta$ for values of θ from 0 to $2\pi^c$.

Hence or otherwise state: (i) the amplitude; (ii) the period; (iii) the phase angle of the function $3 \sin \theta - 2 \cos \theta$.

Indicate each of these quantities on your sketch.

D.T.C.

16 Two rectangular boards *ABCD* and *ABEF*, in which *BC* = *BE*, rest with *CD* and *EF* on horizontal ground. *AB* = 4 m, *BC* = 3 m, and *CE* = 2 m. Calculate

(a) the inclination of each board to the horizontal
(b) the inclination of *AC* to the horizontal
(c) the angle *CAE*.

17 In a crank mechanism, lying in a plane, the arm *OA* of length 1 m rotates in a circle about the fixed point *O*. Connecting rod *AB* is of length $3\frac{1}{2}$ m and end *B* moves in a straight line *OX*. If *OA* rotates through 90° from the position in which angle *AOX* is 40° to that in which it is 130°, find the distance moved by *B*.

18 The horizontal base *OBC* of a tetrahedron *OABC* is a right-angled triangle in which the angle *BOC* is a right angle; *OB* = 4 cm and *OC* = 3 cm. *OA* is perpendicular to the base *OBC* and *OA* = 5 cm. Calculate

(a) the length of the perpendicular from *O* to *BC*
(b) the inclination of the face *ABC* to the horizontal
(c) the length of the perpendicular from *A* to *BC*.

5 Co-ordinate systems and equations of curves

5a Co-ordinates

The use of graphs to show the relationships between two sets of quantities should, by now, be familiar to the student. The system of co-ordinates generally used is known as the *Cartesian system* and is illustrated in the figure.

Figure 62

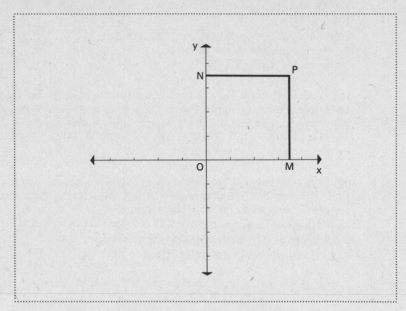

The position of a point P in a plane is stated in terms of its perpendicular distances NP and MP from two straight lines Ox and Oy which are at right angles. These distances are known as co-ordinates.

The lines Ox and Oy are called the axes of reference, Ox being the x axis and Oy the y axis. O is called the origin.

NP, the distance of P from Oy, is called the abscissa of P, and
MP, the distance of P from Ox, is called the ordinate of P.

If $NP = 3$ and $MP = 2$ we speak of P as being the point whose abscissa is 3 and whose ordinate is 2 and we usually abbreviate this and write P is the point (3, 2), always putting the abscissa first.

Co-ordinates may be positive or negative and obey the following rules. (See fig. 63.)

Distances measured upwards from xOx_1 are positive and distances below xOx_1 are negative.

Distances measured to the right of yOy_1 are positive and distances to the left of yOy_1 are negative.

Thus in fig. 63

Figure 63

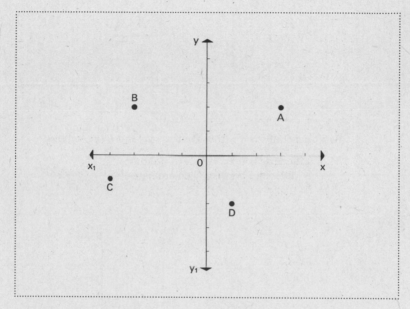

A is the point (3, 2)
B is the point $(-3, 2)$
C is the point $(-4, -1)$
D is the point $(1, -2)$

Example   Plot the points A (1, 3) and B (3, -2) and calculate the distance AB.

From the figure $CB = 3-1 = 2$
$$AC = 3+2 = 5$$

By applying Pythagoras' theorem

$AB^2 = AC^2 + CB^2 = 5^2 + 2^2 = 29$
$\therefore AB = \sqrt{29} = 5 \cdot 385$

Figure
64

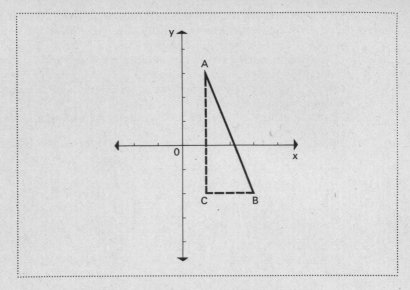

More generally, if A is the point (x_1, y_1) and B (x_2, y_2) then

$AB^2 = $ (difference between the x co-ordinates)^2
$\qquad$ $+$ (difference between y co-ordinates)^2
$\quad = (x_2 - x_1)^2 + (y_2 - y_1)^2$

Figure
65

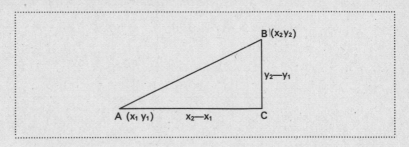

This formula may easily be obtained when required, from the 'conventional diagram' shown in fig. 65. A and B may be in any of the four quadrants and the formula is still true.

The polar system

This is a second system of plotting points.

A point O, called the pole, and a line Ox, called the initial line, are chosen. The position of a point P in the plane is stated in terms of its distance from the pole O and in terms of the angle which this distance makes with Ox.

Figure
66

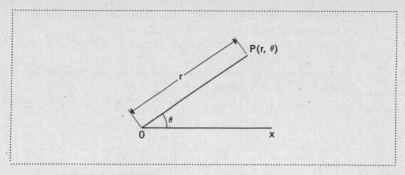

Thus if $OP = r$, and angle $xOP = \theta$, then the polar co-ordinates of P are r and θ.

P is called the point (r, θ).

r is called the radius vector of P and θ the vectorial angle. As in Cartesian co-ordinates we adopt a rule for the signs of r and θ.

The vectorial angle θ is positive when it has been traced out by an anti-clockwise rotation from the initial line.

It is negative when it has been obtained by a clockwise rotation from Ox.

The radius vector r is positive when with the initial line it forms the bounding arms of the vectorial angle.

The radius vector is negative when it has to be produced backwards in order to form one of the bounding arms of the vectorial angle. It is customary to make the radius vector positive and adjust the angle if necessary.

Thus $(-3, 40°)$ is better written $(3, 220°)$

Example   (a) Plot the following points : $A\,(2, 30°)$ $B\,(4, -20°)$ $C\,(5, 135°)$
$D\,(3, 250°)$
(b) The point P is given as $(-3, 60°)$.

Figure
67

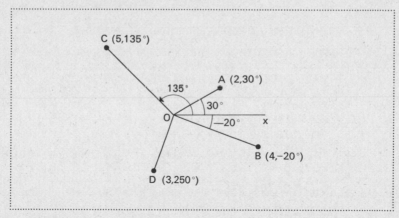

Give its co-ordinates in a form with the radius vector positive.

(a) Points A, B, C and D are shown in fig. 67.

(b) To find P we first obtain OP' at 60° and produce it backwards a distance 3 to point P (fig. 68).

P may be expressed as $(-3, 60°)$ or, as can be seen from the figure, $(3, 240°)$ which is the form required.

Figure 68

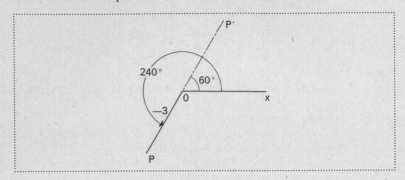

Exercise 5a

1 Draw two axes Ox and Oy and mark positions of the following points:
A (3, 4), B $(-3, 2)$, C $(-4, -3)$, D (4, -2), E (0, -4), F $(-3, -3)$, G (5, 0), H $(-4, -2)$

2 Draw an initial line Ox and mark positions of the following points:
J (4, 45°), K (3, $-60°$), L (2, 240°), M (5, 300°), N (4, $-300°$), P $(-3, 60°)$, Q $(-2, -30°)$, R (4, 0°)

3 (a) P has polar co-ordinates (5, 30°). Calculate its Cartesian co-ordinates.
(b) Q has Cartesian co-ordinates (3, 4). Calculate its polar co-ordinates.

4 Find the polar co-ordinates of points A $(-3, 4)$, B $(-3, -4)$, and C (3, -4)

5 Find the Cartesian co-ordinates of the following points:
(4, $-60°$), (2, 240°), (5, 300°)

6 On a diagram plot the following pairs of points and calculate the distance between each pair.
(a) (1, 3) and (4, 7)   (b) (6, 5) and $(-6, 0)$
(c) $(-4, -3)$ and (0, 0)   (d) (5, -3) and $(-3, 3)$

7 Find the lengths of the sides of triangle ABC if A is the point (2, 1), B is (4, 5) and C is $(-2, 5)$

8 Show that the triangle formed by joining the points (3, 1), $(-1, 4)$ and $(-1, -1)$ is isosceles and state the lengths of the sides.

9   Prove that the triangle joining the points A (7, 2), B (−1, 4) and C (6, −2) is right-angled and calculate its area.

10   Using the cosine rule calculate the distances between the following pairs of points.
     (a) (5, 30°) and (7, 80°) (b) (2, −30°) and (3, 210°) (c) (3, 45°) and (4, 330°)

11   (a) Find the polar co-ordinates of the points whose rectangular co-ordinates are (6, 8) and (−3, 4).
     (b) Find the rectangular co-ordinates of the points (4, 135°) and (6, −30°).

5b   Graphs of functions

In discussing the solution of quadratic equations by graph (page 50) we plotted the graph of

$$y = x^2 + x - 3\tfrac{3}{4}$$

and used it to solve the equation $x^2 + x - 3\tfrac{3}{4} = 0$

The equation $y = x^2 + x - 3\tfrac{3}{4}$ expressed a relationship between the two variables x and y. When $x = -3$ we calculated the value of y to be $2\tfrac{1}{4}$. Thus the point $(-3, 2\tfrac{1}{4})$ was plotted as a point on the curve. Other points found: $(-2, -1\tfrac{3}{4})$, $(-1, -3\tfrac{3}{4})$, $(0, -3\tfrac{3}{4})$ and so on, were also plotted. When the points were joined together by a smooth curve we obtained the

graph of the equation $y = x^2 + x - 3\tfrac{3}{4}$

For every pair of values of x and y which fit the equation there is a point on the graph, and conversely for every point on the graph there is a pair of values of x and y which fits the equation.

As y is given in terms of x, x is called the *independent variable* and y is called the *dependent variable*. As we have already explained in the discussion of quadratic functions (see page 58) y is said to be a *function* of x and the graph is the *graph of the function*.

By calculating a few values of a function of x it is often possible to sketch the general shape of the graph of the function.

Example 1   Sketch the graphs of (a) $y = x^3$, (b) $y = \tfrac{1}{3}x^3$ and (c) $y = x^3 - 10$

Preparing a table of corresponding values of x and y

(a)

x	−3	−2	−1	0	1	2	3
y	−27	−8	−1	0	1	8	27

The graph is shown by the continuous line in fig. 69.

(b) For $y = \tfrac{1}{3}x^3$ the values of y are $\tfrac{1}{3}$ of the values for $y = x^3$. The graph is shown by the broken line.

129   **Graphs of functions**

Figure 69

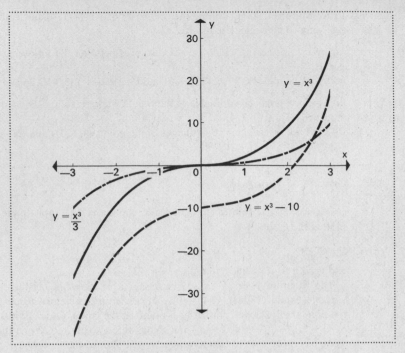

(c) For $y = x^3 - 10$ the values of y are 10 less than the values of y for $y = x^3$. This graph is shown by the dotted line.

Example 2 Draw graphs of the functions in each of the following sections, between the values $x = -3$ and $x = +3$, putting the graphs for each section on one diagram.

(a) $y = x$ $y = x+1$ $y = x-1$ $y = x+2$

(b) $y = 2x$ $y = 2x-3$ $y = 2x+4$

(a)

x	-3	-2	-1	0	1	2	3
$x+1$	-2	-1	0	1	2	3	4
$x+2$	-1	0	1	2	3	4	5
$x-1$	-4	-3	-2	-1	0	1	2

The table shows corresponding values of x and y.

The points are plotted on graph paper and joined for each of the functions. The graphs are as shown in fig. 70.

Notice that the straight lines are all parallel.

(b) The graphs are as shown in fig. 71.

130   Co-ordinate systems and equations of curves

Figure
70

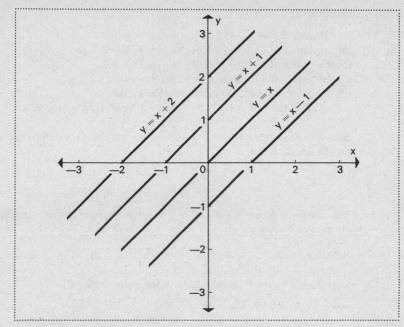

Figure
71

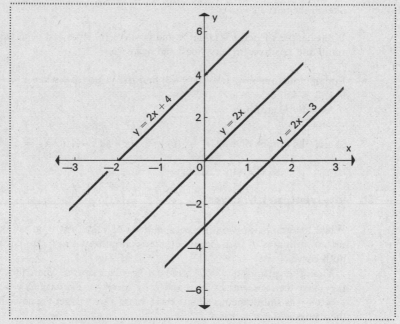

131 **Graphs of functions**

Exercise 5b

1 For the curve $y = 4 - x^2$ find
   (a) the values of y corresponding to $x = 1, 2, -2, -4$
   (b) the values of x corresponding to $y = 0, -5, 3$
   (c) the points at which the graph cuts the x axis
   (d) the point at which the graph cuts the y axis
   (e) which of the points $(1, 3), (-1, 4), (-2, 0), (2, 1)$ lie on the graph.

2 Between the values $x = -3$ to $x = +3$ draw graphs of the following equations on the one diagram

$$y = \frac{x}{2}, \quad y = \frac{x}{2} + 2, \quad y = \frac{x}{2} - 3$$

3 Between the values $x = -4$ to $x = +4$ sketch graphs of the following functions on the one diagram

$$y = x, y = 2x, y = \frac{x}{2}, y = -x, y = x+1$$

4 Sketch on the one diagram graphs of the following functions

$$y = x^2, y = x^2 + 2, y = -x^2, y = 2x^2$$

5 Sketch the curve $y = \dfrac{4}{x}$

   What happens when x is (a) large and positive, (b) large and negative, (c) very small and positive, (d) very small and negative.

6 For the function $y = x(x-1)(x-3)$ find the values of y when $x = -2, -1,$ 0, 1, 2, 3, 4 and 5.
   Sketch the graph.

7 Sketch the graphs of (a) $y = \dfrac{8}{x^2}$, (b) $y = x(x+1)(x-1)$, (c) $xy = 6$

5c Intersection of curves

When the graphs of two different functions of x are drawn on the same axes the co-ordinates of their points of intersection must satisfy the equations of both curves.

Thus if the graphs of $y = 2x^2$ and $y = x+3$ are drawn, where they intersect they have the same values for x and y. By solving the equations $y = 2x^2$ and $y = x+3$ as simultaneous equations in x and y we will get the co-ordinates of their points of intersection.

$$y = 2x^2 \ldots (5.1)$$
$$\text{and} \quad y = x+3 \ldots (5.2)$$

Substituting the value of y from equation (5.2) in equation (5.1) we get

$$x+3 = 2x^2$$
i.e. $\quad 2x^2 - x - 3 = 0$
$\therefore (2x-3)(x+1) = 0$
$$x = 1\tfrac{1}{2} \text{ or } -1$$

and from equation (5.2) the corresponding values of y are

$4\tfrac{1}{2}$ and 2

Thus the points of intersection are $(1\tfrac{1}{2}, 4\tfrac{1}{2})$ and $(-1, 2)$

Example Find the points of intersection of the graphs of $y = x^2 - x$ and $y = 3x + 12$

Since the points of intersection lie on both graphs then at these points

$y = x^2 - x \ldots (5.3)$
$y = 3x + 12 \ldots (5.4)$

must be true simultaneously.

Solving, we get

$$x^2 - x = 3x + 12$$
$$x^2 - 4x - 12 = 0$$
$$(x-6)(x+2) = 0$$

$x = 6$ or -2 and $y = 30$ or 6.
The points of intersection are $(6, 30)$ and $(-2, 6)$

Exercise 5c

1 Find the points of intersection of the graphs of $y = 2x$ and $y = x^2 - 3$

2 Calculate the points of intersection of the curves $y = x^2 + 1$ and $y = 2(x+1)$

3 Find the points of intersection of the curves $y = 3x(5x-1)$ and $y = 4(x+9)$

4 Prove that the straight lines $x + y = 1$, $3y - x + 1 = 0$ and $x + 5y - 1 = 0$ all pass through one point, and find their point of intersection.

5 Find the points of intersection of the curves $y = 3x(1-x)$ and $y = x^2(1-x)$

6 Prove that the line $y = 4x - 2$ does not meet the curve $y = x^2 - x + 5$

133 **Intersection of curves**

5d Gradients

The student will have probably realized by now that the graph of an equation of the form $y = ax+b$ where a and b are constants is always a straight line. (Refer to Example 2 of graphs of functions (see page 130). An equation of the form $y = ax+b$ is called an *equation of the first degree* as it contains no terms of degree higher than 1 (i.e. no terms like x^2, xy, y^2 etc.) As the graph is always a straight line it is also called a *linear equation* and the graph can be drawn with a ruler using only 2 points on the graph.

Consider the graph of $2y = x+2$ which may be written

$$y = \frac{x}{2}+1$$

Let x increase by 1

The new value of y is $\dfrac{x+1}{2}+1 = \dfrac{x}{2}+1+\frac{1}{2}$

and so y increases by $\frac{1}{2}$

Whatever value of y we start with, each time x increases by 1 then y increases by $\frac{1}{2}$. Thus the graph rises in equal steps and is a straight line. See fig. 72.

Figure 72

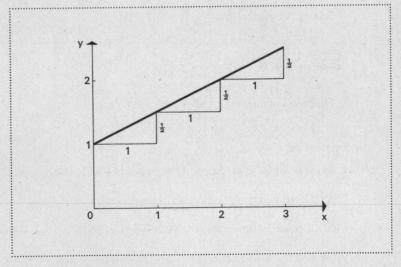

If we consider the graph of $y = ax+b$, then each time x increases by 1 the new value of y is

$$y = a(x+1)+b = ax+b+a$$

and we see that y increases by a (fig. 73).

Figure
73

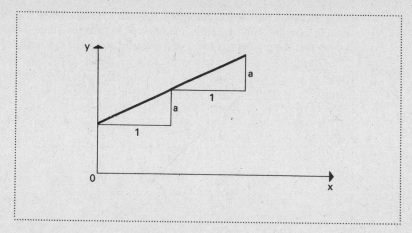

This increase in y for an increase of 1 in x is called the *gradient* of the line and it indicates the steepness of the line. Thus in $y = \frac{1}{2}x + 1$ the gradient is $\frac{1}{2}$ while the gradient of $y = ax + b$ is a.

$$\text{The gradient of a line} = \frac{\text{vertical rise } LQ}{\text{horizontal distance } PL}$$

$$= \frac{\text{increase in } y}{\text{increase in } x}$$

Figure
74

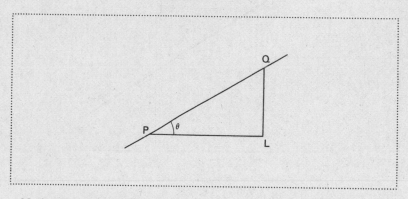

Notice that the gradient $= \tan \theta$ where θ is the angle the line makes with the horizontal direction (fig. 74).

Gradients of roads on hills and of railways are more usually given as the $\dfrac{\text{vertical rise } LQ}{\text{distance on the hill } PQ}$ and the student will realize that this equals $\sin \theta$ where θ is the angle the road or railway makes with the horizontal. This definition of gradient (i.e. $\sin \theta$) is not used in graphical work.

135   Gradients

Fig. 75 shows part of the graph of $y = -2x + 3$. Notice here that, by considering triangles *ABC* or *DEF*, an increase of 1 in x gives a *decrease* of 2 in y. We say that the gradient of this line is negative and write gradient $= -2$.

Figure 75

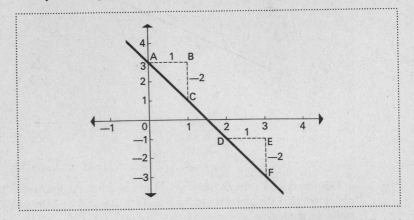

Example Find the gradient of the line joining the points $A(-2, 3)$ and $B(1, 1)$ and obtain the angle between the line and the positive direction of the x axis.

Figure 76

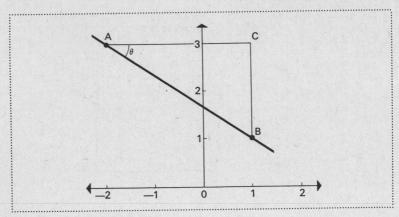

Gradient of $AB = \dfrac{CB}{AC} = \dfrac{-2}{3} = -\dfrac{2}{3}$

$\tan \theta = \dfrac{2}{3}$ $\therefore \theta = 33°41'$ (from tables)

The angle the line makes with the positive direction of the x axis is also given as negative:

$\theta = -33°41'$

136 Co-ordinate systems and equations of curves

Exercise 5d

1 Write down the gradients of the following lines
    (a) $y = 4x - 3$ (b) $y - 2x = 1$ (c) $2x - 3y + 2 = 0$
    (d) $x + 3y + 2 = 0$ (e) $ax + by + c = 0$ (f) $px + qy = 1$

2 Find the angles the following lines make with the positive direction of the
  x axis.
    (a) $y = x + 2$ (b) $2y = x - 3$ (c) $x + y = 1$
    (d) $3x + 2y = 5$ (e) $2x + y + 3 = 0$

3 Find the gradients of the lines joining the points
    (a) $(1, 2)$ and $(5, 8)$ (b) $(5, 1)$ and $(1, 4)$ (c) $(-2, -1)$ and $(2, 3)$
    (d) $(-2, 3)$ and $(1, -1)$

4 Show that the lines $y = \dfrac{2}{3}x + 1$, $3y - 2x + 5 = 0$, and $4x - 6y + 1 = 0$ are all
  parallel.

5 Prove that the points $(0, -1)$, $(2, 0)$, $(4, 1)$ and $(8, 3)$ lie in a straight line.

6 Prove that the gradient of the line joining the points whose co-ordinates are
  (x_1, y_1) and (x_2, y_2) is given by $\dfrac{y_2 - y_1}{x_2 - x_1}$

5e   The straight line $y = ax + b$

We have seen in the previous section that the graph of $y = ax + b$ is a straight
line and that the value of 'a' gives the gradient. Students may now ask, 'What
does "b" represent?' If we work out values of y corresponding to values of x
we find that when $x = 0$, $y = b$

Figure
77

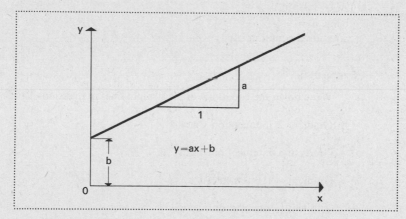

137   The straight line $y = ax + b$

This point $(0, b)$ lies on the y axis. It is thus the point where the line cuts the y axis.

The graph of the line $y = ax + b$ is shown in fig. 77.

We say that the line has an *intercept* b on the y axis.

The line $y = 2x + 3$ has a gradient 2 and makes an intercept of 3 on the y axis.

The line $y = x - 2$ has a gradient 1 and cuts the y axis at a distance 2 below the origin. Its intercept is -2 on the y axis.

It is useful to be able to find the equation of a line given certain geometrical facts. We can use the form $y = ax + b$ and then we have to find the values of a and b from the given information.

Example 1　Find the equation of the straight line making an angle of 45° with the x axis and cutting the y axis at a point 2 above the origin.

Here the gradient is obviously equal to tan 45° = 1
The intercept on the y axis is $+2$

Hence we put $a = 1$ and $b = 2$ in $y = ax + b$ giving the required equation as $y = x + 2$

Example 2　Find the equation of the straight line of gradient 3 and passing through the point (2, 1)

Starting with the equation of the line as $y = ax + b$ we know

$a = 3$
giving the equation $y = 3x + b$
We have now to find the value of b

As the point (2, 1) lies on this line then putting 2 for x and 1 for y in $y = 3x + b$ the equation must be true.

Thus　$1 = 3(2) + b$
giving $b = -5$
$\therefore$ required equation is $y = 3x - 5$

Exercise 5e

Write down the equations of the straight lines in questions 1 to 5.

1　Gradient 2, intercept on y axis 3

2　Gradient 3, intercept on y axis -2

3　Gradient -1, intercept on y axis $2\frac{1}{2}$

4　Gradient $\frac{1}{3}$, intercept on x axis 1

5   Gradient 2, intercept on x axis 2

6   Find the equation of the straight line passing through the point (0, 4) and having a gradient of 2.

7   State the gradient of the line $2y = 3x - 8$ and give the point where it cuts the y axis. Sketch the graph.

8   Find the equation of the straight line having a gradient of -1 and passing through the point (1, 2)

9   If the line $y = mx + c$ passes through the point $(x_1 y_1)$ show that $c = y_1 - mx_1$.
    By substituting this value of c in the equation $y = mx + c$ prove that the equation of the line passing through point $(x_1 y_1)$ with gradient m is $y - y_1 = m(x - x_1)$.

10 Use the formula $y - y_1 = m(x - x_1)$ of the previous example to obtain the equation of the lines
    (a) passing through the point (2, 1) and having a gradient 2
    (b) passing through the point $(-1, 2)$ and having a gradient $-\frac{2}{3}$

5f   Parallel lines and perpendicular lines

Two lines are parallel if they have the same gradients.
    Thus $y = 2x - 1$, $y = 2x + 3$ and $y = 2x + 7$ are all parallel since each has a gradient of 2.
    The relationship between the gradients of perpendicular lines can be obtained from fig. 78.

Figure 78

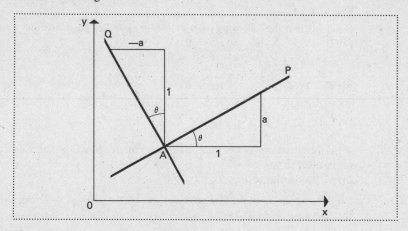

AP and *AQ* are perpendicular lines.

Gradient of $\quad AP = \tan \theta = a$ (say)

Then gradient of $AQ = \tan (90 + \theta)$

$$= -\cot \theta$$

$$= -\frac{1}{a}$$

Thus if a given line has a gradient of '*a*' any perpendicular line has a gradient of $-\dfrac{1}{a}$

Thus the lines $y = 2x + 1$ and $y = -\frac{1}{2}x + 3$ are perpendicular.

Example Give the equation of the line having an intercept -3 on the *y* axis and perpendicular to the straight line $x + 2y = 3$

Let the required line be of the form

$$y = ax + b$$

b is the intercept on the *y* axis

$$\therefore b = -3$$

The gradient of $x + 2y = 3$ is $-\frac{1}{2}$ since the line can be rearranged and written $y = -\frac{1}{2}x + \frac{3}{2}$

Any line perpendicular to this line must have a gradient *a*

where $a = \dfrac{-1}{-\frac{1}{2}} = 2$

$\therefore$ required line has equation $y = 2x - 3$

Exercise 5f

1 State whether the following pairs of lines are parallel, perpendicular or neither.
   (a) $2y = 3x - 2 \quad 6x - 4y + 5 = 0$
   (b) $2x + 3y + 2 = 0 \quad 3x - 2y + 2 = 0$
   (c) $x = y - 1 \quad x + y = 2$
   (d) $4y - 7x = 2 \quad 7x - 4y + 3 = 0$
   (e) $ax + by = 1 \quad ay - bx = 1$
   (f) $\dfrac{x}{4} + \dfrac{y}{3} = 1 \quad 4y = 1 - 3x$

2 Find the equations of the lines making an intercept of 2 on the *y* axis and
   (a) parallel to $y = 3x + 7$
   (b) perpendicular to $y = 3x + 7$

3 Find the equation of the line passing through the point $(0, -2)$ and parallel to the line $x + y - 3 = 0$.

4 Find the equation of the line perpendicular to the line $y = \frac{3}{4}x - 2$ and passing through the point (1, 2).

5 Show that the line joining points $(-1, 1)$ and $(3, 2)$ is perpendicular to the line joining points $(-1, 5)$ and $(1, -3)$.

Miscellaneous exercises 5

1 Define polar co-ordinates and explain how a point may have more than one pair of polar co-ordinates.

Plot the points $(2, 30°)$, $(3·86, 45°)$ and find the area of the triangle formed by the pole and these two points.

2 (a) Plot the points whose rectangular co-ordinates are (3, 3), $(-2, 2)$ and $(1, -1)$. Find the area of the triangle formed by these three points.

(b) Plot the points whose polar co-ordinates are $(3, 30°)$ and $(2, 135°)$. Join these points by a straight line and write down the co-ordinates of the midpoint of this line.

3 (a) A line of gradient 1 cuts off an intercept of 2 units on the y axis and a second line of gradient 2 cuts off an intercept of 1 unit on the x axis. Draw the lines and find (i) their point of intersection and (ii) the area of the triangle the lines form with the y axis.

(b) Plot the points on the graph $r = 2 \cos \theta$ using polar co-ordinates in the range $\theta = 0$ to $\theta = 90°$ and show that they lie on a circle.

D.T.C.

4 Plot a graph of $y = 6\,\dfrac{x+2}{x^2+5}$ from $x = -2$ to $x = 8$.

Find the maximum value of the expression for the portion plotted.

5 Draw on the same set of axes the graphs of $y = x^2$ and $y = 2x + 15$ between the limits $x = -5$ and $x = +5$.

Find the points of intersection and show that they are solutions of the equation $x^2 - 2x - 15 = 0$.

6 (a) What is the gradient of the line joining the points (4, 2) and (12, 4)?

(b) For a small lifting machine the effort P and the load W are connected by a law of the form $P = aW + b$. Find the values of a and b if an effort of 2 N will just lift a load of 4 N and an effort of 4 N will just lift a load of 12 N.

7 Find the gradient of the straight line $x - 2y + 3 = 0$. Where does this line cut the y axis?

What is the equation of the straight line which is parallel to the line $x - 2y + 3 = 0$ and passes through the point (0, 2)?

8   Plot a graph of the function $y = 2x^2 - 12x + 13$ for values of x from -1 to 6.
From the graph find (a) the values of x when $y = 5$
(b) the minimum value of y
Draw the tangent to the graph at the point $(4, -3)$ and measure its gradient.

9   In an experiment on a machine the following corresponding values of the effort P and the load W were found.

W	5	10	15	20	25	30
P	4·5	6·0	7·0	8·5	9·5	11·0

Taking values of W along the horizontal axis and values of P along the vertical axis plot a graph to show the relationship between P and W.

Show that the values lie approximately on a line whose equation is $P = 0.26W + 3.2$.

10   Plot the graphs of

$$y = x^2 - 1.9x$$

$$y = 3.3 - \frac{6}{x}$$

on the same axes, taking values of x from 3 to -3. What values of x are common to both equations?

E.M.E.U.

11   Plot the graphs of $y = 3x^2$ and $y = 5 - 8x$ for values of x from -5 to $+5$. Hence solve the equation $3x^2 + 8x - 5 = 0$. Also calculate the roots of the equation accurately to two decimal places.

U.L.C.I.

12   The equation of a curve is given by $y = ax^2 + bx + c$ where a, b and c are constants. The curve passes through the points $(-2, 12)$, $(-1, 3)$ and $(\frac{1}{2}, -3)$. Find the equation of the curve.

D.T.C.

13   Plot the graph of $y = 2\sqrt{x}$ from $x = 0$ to $x = 2$ using quarter units for x. On the same axes plot the graph of $y = 5x - 3$ and write down the abscissae of the points of intersection.

Show that these values are solutions of the equation $2\sqrt{x} = 5x - 3$ and check the values found by solving this equation.

D.T.C.

6 Progressions and series

6a Series

Consider the following sequences of numbers.

(1) 1, 2, 3, 4, 5   (3) 1, 2, 4, 8, 16
(2) 1, 4, 7, 10, 13   (4) 1, 4, 9, 16, 25

It is easy to see that there is a definite order in forming each member of the set. The next numbers in the sequence are:

(1) 6
(2) 16, since each number is formed by adding 3 to the previous number
(3) 32, since each number is twice the previous one
(4) 36, since the numbers are the squares of 1, 2, 3, etc.

By continuing the process we should get an unending set of numbers all of which are determined by the application of a rule or law and not written down at random.

The indicated sum of such an ordered set of numbers is called a *series* and any particular number is called a *term*.

Thus $1+4+7+10+13+ \ldots$ is a series in which the law determining it is that each number exceeds the previous one by 3.

When a series finishes after a certain number of terms, it is said to be a *finite* series. When there is an unending number of terms, the series is said to be *infinite*.

Example   Find the law governing the series $2+4\frac{1}{2}+7+9\frac{1}{2}+ \ldots$ Write down the next two terms and find a formula for the general or n^{th} term.

The series may be written

$$2+(2+2\tfrac{1}{2})+(2+2\times2\tfrac{1}{2})+(2+3\times2\tfrac{1}{2})+ \ldots$$

The law is that each number is formed by adding $2\frac{1}{2}$ to the preceding term.

The fifth term is thus $2+4\times2\tfrac{1}{2} = 12$
The sixth term is thus $2+5\times2\tfrac{1}{2} = 14\tfrac{1}{2}$
and the nth term is $2+(n-1)2\tfrac{1}{2} = 2\tfrac{1}{2}n-\tfrac{1}{2}$

Exercise 6a

Find the law and the next two terms in questions 1–7

1 $2, 5, 8, 11, \ldots$ 3 $3, 6, 12, 24, \ldots$ 5 $2, 1, \frac{1}{2}, \frac{1}{4}, \ldots$

2 $27, 23, 19, 15, \ldots$ 4 $24, -12, 6, -3, \ldots$ 6 $1, -3, 9, -27, \ldots$

7 $1, 2, 3, 5, 8, 13, \ldots$

8 What are the nth terms in the series

   (a) $2+4+6+8+ \ldots$ (b) $1+3+5+7+ \ldots$ (c) $1+4+9+16+ \ldots$

9 If the nth term of a series is $2n+3$, what are the first four terms?

10 If the nth term of a series is $3 \times 2^{n-1}$, write down the first four terms.

6b Arithmetical progression

A series of quantities is said to be in arithmetical progression when each term is formed from the preceding term by adding a constant quantity which may be positive or negative.

This constant quantity is called the *common difference*.

Thus the common difference = second term−first term
= third term−second term
= fourth term−third term   and so on

$1, 4, 7, 10$ are the terms of an a.p. whose common difference is 3.
$27, 23, 19, 15$ are the terms of an a.p. whose common difference is -4.
$a, 3a, 5a, 7a$ are the terms of an a.p. whose common difference is $2a$.

The standard form of an a.p.

Let the first term be a and the common difference be d. Then the terms of the a.p. are

$a, a+d, a+2d, a+3d$, etc.

To find the nth term of an a.p.

The first term is a
second term is $a+d$
third term is $a+2d$
fourth term is $a+3d$

and continuing in this way the nth term is $a+(n-1)d$.

Letting T_n stand for the nth term we have

$$T_n = a+(n-1)d$$

To find a formula for the sum of n terms of an a.p.

Let $a =$ the first term.
 $d =$ the common difference.
 $l =$ the last term.
 $S_n =$ the sum of the first n terms.

Then $S_n = a+(a+d)+(a+2d)+ \ldots +(l-d)+l$

Writing the terms in the reverse order

$$S_n = l+(l-d)+(l-2d)+ \ldots +(a+d)+a$$

By addition

$$2S_n = (a+l)+(a+l)+(a+l)+ \ldots +(a+l)+(a+l)$$
$$= n(a+l)$$
$$\therefore S_n = \frac{n}{2}(a+l)$$

This gives the rule that the sum to n terms is the number of terms × average of the end terms.

Since the last term $l = a+(n-1)d$

$$S_n = \frac{n}{2}\{2a+(n-1)d\}$$

Example 1   Find the tenth term and the sum of the first twelve terms of the series $2+5+8+11+ \ldots$

Here $a = 2$ and $d = 3$
tenth term $= a+9d = 2+9 \times 3 = 29$

Since $S_n = \frac{n}{2}\{2a+(n-1)d\}$

the sum to twelve terms $= \dfrac{12}{2}(2 \times 2+11 \times 3)$

$$= 6(4+33)$$
$$= 222$$

Example 2 The third term of an a.p. is -6 and the eleventh term is -18. Find the twentieth term and the sum of thirty terms.

$$\text{third term} = a+2d = -6$$
$$\text{eleventh term} = a+10d = -18$$
$$\text{Subtracting} \quad 8d = -12$$
$$d = \frac{-12}{8} = -1\tfrac{1}{2}$$
$$\text{and} \quad a = -6-2d = -6+3 = -3$$
$$\text{twentieth term} = a+19d = -3+19\,(-1\tfrac{1}{2}) = -31\tfrac{1}{2}$$
$$\text{Sum of thirty terms} = \frac{n}{2}\{2a+(n-1)d\}$$

$$= \frac{30}{2}\{2\times-3+29\,(-1\tfrac{1}{2})\}$$

$$= -742\tfrac{1}{2}$$

Arithmetic means

When three quantities are in arithmetic progression the middle term is called the *arithmetic mean* of the other two.

If we place a number of terms between two quantities a and b such that they form an arithmetical progression with a and b then all these terms are called *arithmetic means* of a and b.

Example 1   Find the arithmetic mean between a and b.

Let A be the required mean.
Then $\quad A-a = b-A$
$$\therefore 2A = a+b$$
and $\qquad A = \dfrac{a+b}{2}$

Example 2   Insert five arithmetic means between 5 and 20.

We regard   5 as the first term of an a.p.
and   20 becomes the seventh term.

$$\text{seventh term} = a+6d = 20$$
$$\text{first term} = a \quad\;\; = 5$$
$$\text{Subtracting} \quad 6d = 15$$
$$d = \frac{15}{6} = 2\tfrac{1}{2}$$

Thus the means are $7\tfrac{1}{2}$, 10, $12\tfrac{1}{2}$, 15, $17\tfrac{1}{2}$.

Exercise 6b

1   Find the twelfth term and the sum of the series of

$3+7+11+ \ldots$ to 20 terms.

2 Find the eighth term and the sum of the first 12 terms of
$3+4\frac{1}{2}+6+\ldots$

3 Find the twentieth term of $1\cdot2, 1\cdot35, 1\cdot5, \ldots$

Find the last term and the sum of the series in questions 4–8.

4 $2+3\frac{1}{4}+4\frac{1}{2}+\ldots$ to twelve terms.

5 $\frac{1}{2}+\frac{1}{3}+\frac{1}{6}+\ldots$ to eight terms.

6 $\frac{1}{2}+\frac{3}{5}+\frac{7}{10}+\ldots$ to sixteen terms.

7 $0\cdot5+0\cdot62+0\cdot74+\ldots$ to twenty-five terms.

8 $\frac{1}{2}+\frac{1}{5}-\frac{1}{10}-\ldots$ to twenty-one terms.

9 The fourth term of an a.p. is 12 and the ninth is 27; find the series.

10 The tenth term of an a.p. is 33 and the sixteenth is 9; find the series.

11 Find the sum of the odd numbers from 1 to 99 inclusive.

12 Find the sum of all the whole numbers from 1 to 50.

13 How many terms are there in the a.p. $5+9+13+\ldots+85$?

14 Insert six arithmetic means between 11 and 53.

15 Insert four arithmetic means between 12 and 27.

16 Find the arithmetic mean between $\frac{1}{2}$ and $\frac{1}{3}$.

17 An employee begins with a salary of £240 per annum and receives an annual increment of £18. What is his salary in the eighth year and how much will he have received in the first ten years?

18 Estimate the cost of sinking a shaft 12 m deep if the charge is £5 for sinking the first m with an increase in price of 20p per metre for each succeeding metre.

19 Find the sum of the first n natural numbers (i.e. $1+2+3+\ldots+n$). Deduce the sum of the numbers 63 to 85 inclusive.

20 A body falling freely falls 4·9 m in the first second, 14·7 m in the second second, 24·5 m in the third second, 34·3 m in the fourth second and so on.
(a) How far does it fall in the tenth second?
(b) What is the total distance fallen in the 10 seconds?

147　Arithmetical progression

6c   Geometrical progression

A series of quantities is said to be in geometrical progression when each term is formed from the preceding term by multiplying by a constant factor.

This constant factor is called the *common ratio*.

Thus 2, 4, 8, 16, 32, ... are terms of a g.p. whose common ratio is 2.

$4, -2, 1, -\frac{1}{2}, \frac{1}{4}, \ldots$ are terms of a g.p. whose common ratio is $-\frac{1}{2}$.

The standard form of a g.p.

We take the first term to be a and the common ratio to be r.

Then the terms are

$a, ar, ar^2, ar^3, \ldots$ etc.

To find the nth term of a g.p.

$$\begin{aligned} \text{The first term is} \quad & a \\ \text{second term is} \quad & ar \\ \text{third term is} \quad & ar^2 \\ \text{fourth term is} \quad & ar^3 \\ \text{and so the } n^{th} \text{ term is} \quad & ar^{n-1} \end{aligned}$$

Letting T_n stand for the nth term we have

$T_n = ar^{n-1}$

Example 1   Write down (a) the sixth term of $1, \frac{4}{3}, \frac{16}{9}, \ldots$

(b) the eighth term of $27, -9, 3, \ldots$

(a) $a = 1, r = \dfrac{4}{3}$

sixth term $T_6 = ar^5 = 1 \times \left(\dfrac{4}{3}\right)^5 = \dfrac{1024}{243}$

(b) $a = 27, r = -\dfrac{1}{3}$

eighth term $T_8 = ar^7 = 27\left(-\dfrac{1}{3}\right)^7 = -\dfrac{1}{81}$

Example 2   If the second term of a g.p. is 2·4 and the sixth term is 0·003 84 find the first term and the common ratio.

second term $= ar = 2\cdot4$

sixth term $= ar^5 = 0\cdot003\,84$

Dividing, $r^4 = \dfrac{0\cdot003\,84}{2\cdot4} = 0\cdot0016$

Thus $r = \sqrt[4]{(0\cdot0016)} = 0\cdot2$

and $a = \dfrac{2\cdot4}{0\cdot2} = 12$

To find a formula for the sum of n terms of a g.p.

Let a be the first term and r the common ratio.
Let S_n = sum of first n terms.

$$S_n = a + ar + ar^2 + ar^3 + \ldots + ar^{n-2} + ar^{n-1}$$

Multiply both sides by r

$$rS_n = ar + ar^2 + ar^3 + \ldots + ar^{n-2} + ar^{n-1} + ar^n$$

Subtracting

$$S_n - rS_n = a - ar^n$$
$$S_n(1-r) = a(1-r^n)$$
$$\therefore S_n = \frac{a(1-r^n)}{1-r} = \frac{a(r^n-1)}{r-1}$$

The second form is obtained by changing the signs in the numerator and denominator and is the form to be used if the common ratio r is greater than 1.

Geometric means

When three quantities are in geometric progression the middle term is called the *geometric mean* of the other two.

Let G be the geometric mean between a and b.

Then the common ratio $= \dfrac{G}{a} = \dfrac{b}{G}$

$$\therefore G^2 = ab$$
$$\therefore G = \sqrt{(ab)}$$

If we place a number of terms between two quantities a and b such that they form a g.p. with a and b, then all these terms are called *geometric means* of a and b.

Example 1 Insert four geometric means between 96 and 3.

We regard 96 as the first term and 3 as the sixth term of a g.p.

sixth term $= ar^5 = 3$
first term $= a = 96$

Dividing $r^5 = \dfrac{3}{96} = \dfrac{1}{32}$

$$\therefore r = \tfrac{1}{2}$$

The means are 48, 24, 12, 6

Example 2 Sum the series $\tfrac{2}{3} - 1 + \tfrac{3}{2} - \tfrac{9}{4} + \ldots$ to eight terms.

149 Geometrical progression

Common ratio $r = -\frac{3}{2}$

$$S_8 = \frac{a(1-r^n)}{1-r} = \frac{2}{3} \cdot \frac{1-(-\frac{3}{2})^8}{1-(-\frac{3}{2})}$$

$$= \frac{2}{3} \cdot \frac{1-\dfrac{3^8}{2^8}}{\dfrac{5}{2}} = \frac{4}{15}\left(1-\frac{6561}{256}\right)$$

$$= -\frac{4}{15} \times \frac{6305}{256} = -\frac{1261}{192}$$

Exercise 6c

For the series in questions 1–5 find:
(a) the common ratio   (b) the sixth term   (c) the nth term.

1   $1+3+9+\ldots$ 3 $8{\cdot}4-4{\cdot}2+2{\cdot}1-\ldots$

2   $5+\frac{5}{2}+\frac{5}{4}+\ldots$ 4 $1-\frac{1}{2}+\frac{1}{4}-\ldots$

5   $1{\cdot}2+0{\cdot}24+0{\cdot}048+\ldots$

6   If the second term of a series is $\frac{1}{4}$ and the eighth is 16, find the series.

7   Find the arithmetic mean and the geometric mean of $\frac{1}{3}$ and $\frac{1}{4}$.

8   Insert three geometric means between 5 and 80.

9   Insert four geometric means between 108 and $14\frac{2}{9}$.

10   Find the sum of the first eight terms of $4+8+16+\ldots$

11   Find the sum of the first eight terms of $\dfrac{1}{2}-\dfrac{1}{2^2}+\dfrac{1}{2^3}-\ldots$

12   The third term of a g.p. is 8 and the sixth term is -1. Find the sum of seven terms.

6d   The sum of an infinite number of terms of a g.p.

If we consider the series $1+2+4+8+\ldots$ etc. we can see that the sum gets larger and larger as we proceed. In fact each term is greater than the sum of all the preceding terms. The sum of an infinite number of these terms is infinitely great.

If we consider the series

$$1 + \tfrac{1}{2} + \tfrac{1}{4} + \tfrac{1}{8} + \ldots$$

then the sum of n terms is given by

$$S_n = \frac{a(1-r^n)}{1-r} = \frac{1\left(1 - \dfrac{1}{2^n}\right)}{1 - \dfrac{1}{2}}$$

$$= 2 - \frac{1}{2^{n-1}}$$

We may take as many terms as we like but the sum never gets beyond 2. By taking a large enough number of terms, that is by taking n large enough, we can make the fraction $\dfrac{1}{2^{n-1}}$ as small as we please. Thus by taking a sufficient number of terms we can make the sum differ from 2 by as little as we please. We say that 2 is the *sum to infinity* of the series $1 + \tfrac{1}{2} + \tfrac{1}{4} + \tfrac{1}{8} + \ldots$

In the general case of the series $a + ar + ar^2 + \ldots$ where the common ratio r is less than 1

$$S_n = \frac{a(1-r^n)}{1-r} = \frac{a}{1-r} - \frac{ar^n}{1-r}$$

Since r is less than 1, $\dfrac{ar^n}{1-r}$ continually decreases as n increases. By making n sufficiently large we can make S_n differ from $\dfrac{a}{1-r}$ by as little as we please.

This result is usually stated in the form that the sum of an infinite number of terms of a decreasing g.p. is $\dfrac{a}{1-r}$ or more briefly that the sum to infinity is $\dfrac{a}{1-r}$.

It may be written $\quad S_\infty = \dfrac{a}{1-r}$

where r is numerically less than 1.

We can illustrate the above geometrically by taking a length AB equal to 2 units.

Figure 79

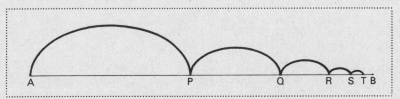

The sum of an infinite number of terms of a g.p.

We take a series of diminishing steps from A, the first, AP, being halfway to B, the second, PQ, being half the remaining distance to B, then QR, RS, etc. each halving the remaining distance to B.

The sum of these steps is the distance moved from A towards B and is represented by the series

$1+\frac{1}{2}+\frac{1}{4}+\frac{1}{8}+ \ldots$

This sum gets closer and closer to the length of AB which is 2 units but the sum can never exceed 2.

Clearly 2 is the sum to infinity of the series.

Example 1   Find the sum to infinity of the series

(a) $4+2+1+\frac{1}{2}+ \ldots$ (b) $2\frac{1}{4}-1\frac{1}{2}+1- \ldots$

(a) Here $a = 4$ and $r = \frac{1}{2}$

$$S_\infty = \frac{a}{1-r} = \frac{4}{1-\frac{1}{2}} = 8$$

(b) Here $a = 2\frac{1}{4}$ $r = \frac{-1\frac{1}{2}}{2\frac{1}{4}} = -\frac{3}{2}\times\frac{4}{9} = -\frac{2}{3}$

$$S_\infty = \frac{2\frac{1}{4}}{1-(-\frac{2}{3})} = \frac{9}{4} \times \frac{1}{1+\frac{2}{3}} = \frac{9}{4}\times\frac{3}{5} = \frac{27}{20}$$

Example 2   Express the recurring decimal $0\dot{6}3\dot{2}$ as a vulgar fraction.

$0\dot{6}3\dot{2} = 0\cdot632\,323\,2 \ldots$ etc.

$$= \frac{6}{10}+\frac{32}{1000}+\frac{32}{100\,000}+ \ldots \text{etc.}$$

$$= \frac{6}{10}+\frac{32}{10^3}+\frac{32}{10^5}+ \ldots$$

After the first term we have a g.p. with an infinite number of terms where

$a = \dfrac{32}{10^3}$ and $r = \dfrac{1}{10^2}$

$$\therefore 0\dot{6}3\dot{2} = \frac{6}{10}+\frac{a}{1-r}$$

$$= \frac{6}{10}+\frac{\dfrac{32}{10^3}}{1-\dfrac{1}{10^2}}$$

$$= \frac{6}{10}+\frac{32}{10^3}\times\frac{10^2}{99}$$

$$= \frac{6}{10} + \frac{32}{990} = \frac{594 + 32}{990}$$

$$= \frac{626}{990} = \frac{313}{495}$$

Exercise 6d

In questions 1–4 find the sum to infinity of

1 $6 + 3 + 1\frac{1}{2} + \ldots$ 2 $9 - 6 + 4 - \ldots$

3 $3 + \sqrt{3} + 1 + \ldots$ 4 $4 + 3 + 2\frac{1}{4} + \ldots$

5 If 9 is the second term and $\frac{81}{16}$ is the fourth term of a g.p., show that there are two possible series and give the first four terms of each.
   Calculate the sum to infinity in each case.

In questions 6–8 find the value as a vulgar fraction of

6 $0 \cdot \dot{8}$ 7 $0 \cdot 7\dot{2}\dot{3}$ 8 $0 \cdot 63\dot{1}\dot{2}$

9 The speeds of a machine tool are eleven in number varying from 20 r.p.m. to 640 r.p.m. If the speeds form a geometric progression find their values to the nearest whole numbers.

10 If the value of a machine originally valued at £2400 depreciates 15% each year calculate
   (a) its value after six years,
   (b) the number of years for its value to fall below £600.

11 A ball is dropped 12 m on to a horizontal surface and it rebounds to a height of 10 m. It continues to bounce, rebounding after each impact to a height of $\frac{5}{6}$ the distance fallen. Calculate the distance it travels before coming to rest.

12 The population of a town of 100 000 people increased by 4% after one year. If the population increased by this amount each year, what would the population be after eleven years? Give your answer correct to three significant figures.

6e The binomial series

A binomial is an expression containing two terms, just as a trinomial expression is one containing three terms.

153 The binomial series

Thus $a^2 + 5b^2$, $1+x$, $a+b$, $2t-16t^2$, are all binomials. The student will have expanded simple powers of binomials such as $(a+b)^2$ and $(a+b)^3$.

To find a general expression for the expansion of higher powers of binomials we work out by actual multiplication the expansions of $(1+x)^2$, $(1+x)^3$, etc. and set them out as below.

$$(1+x)^1 = 1+x$$
$$(1+x)^2 = 1+2x+x^2$$
$$(1+x)^3 = 1+3x+3x^2+x^3$$
$$(1+x)^4 = 1+4x+6x^2+4x^3+x^4$$
$$(1+x)^5 = 1+5x+10x^2+10x^3+5x^4+x^5$$
$$(1+x)^6 = 1+6x+15x^2+20x^3+15x^4+6x^5+x^6$$

We see that each gives a series of terms in ascending powers of x. It is fairly obvious that the expansion of $(1+x)^n$ where n is a positive whole number will give a similar series of terms in ascending powers of x and ending with the term x^n.

If we set out the coefficients only of the successive terms in x, x^2, x^3 etc. and include the first term which is 1 in each case, the way in which the coefficients are formed is indicated.

Powers of x	Coefficients
$(1+x)^0$	1
$(1+x)^1$	1 1
$(1+x)^2$	1 2 1
$(1+x)^3$	1 3 3 1
$(1+x)^4$	1 4 6 4 1
$(1+x)^5$	1 5 10 10 5 1
$(1+x)^6$	1 6 15 20 15 6 1

The first term in each case is 1 and the coefficient of the second term is the value of n in $(1+x)^n$.

To find the coefficient of the third term in each case we see that in

$$(1+x)^3 \quad \text{it is} \quad 3 = 2+1$$
$$(1+x)^4 \quad \text{it is} \quad 6 = 3+3 \quad = 1+2+3$$
$$(1+x)^5 \quad \text{it is} \quad 10 = 4+6 \quad = 1+2+3+4$$
$$(1+x)^6 \quad \text{it is} \quad 15 = 5+10 \quad = 1+2+3+4+5$$

and so on.

Thus in $(1+x)^n$ it would be $1+2+3+4+ \ldots +(n-1)$

This is an arithmetic progression whose sum $= \dfrac{n(n-1)}{2}$

We have finally, where n is a positive whole number

$$(1+x)^n = 1+nx+\frac{n(n-1)}{2}x^2+ \ldots +x^n$$

The series finishes after $n+1$ terms with the term x^n. Notice also from the triangle formed by the coefficients (known as Pascal's triangle) that the coefficients equidistant from each end of the series are equal.

The full expansion is given by the binomial theorem, but its proof is not attempted until volume 2.

The theorem states that

$$(1+x)^n = 1+nx+\frac{n(n-1)}{1.2}x^2+\frac{n(n-1)(n-2)}{1.2.3}x^3+$$

$$\frac{n(n-1)(n-2)(n-3)}{1.2.3.4}x^4+\ldots+x^n$$

We may write products such as $1.2.3.4$ as *factorial* 4 and write them for short as 4! or $\lfloor 4$

Thus $1.2.3.4.5$ is written 5!

and the product of all the integers from 1 to $r = 1 \times 2 \times 3 \times \ldots \times (r-1) \times r = r!$

The binomial theorem is then written

$$(1+x)^n = 1+nx+\frac{n(n-1)}{2!}x^2+\frac{n(n-1)(n-2)}{3!}x^3+\ldots+x^n$$

We have only dealt with cases where n has been a positive whole number. If n is fractional or negative the series does not end and we have an infinite series. In these cases the theorem is still true provided that x is numerically less than 1.

Example 1 Expand $(1+x)^6$

By the binomial theorem

$$(1+x)^6 = 1+6x+\frac{6.(6-1)}{2!}x^2+\frac{6.(6-1)(6-2)}{3!}x^3+\frac{6.(6-1)(6-2)(6-3)}{4!}x^4$$

$$+\frac{6.(6-1)(6-2)(6-3)(6-4)}{5!}x^5$$

$$+\frac{6.(6-1)(6-2)(6-3)(6-4)(6-5)}{6!}x^6$$

$$= 1+6x+\frac{6.5}{1.2}x^2+\frac{6.5.4}{1.2.3}x^3+\frac{6.5.4.3}{1.2.3.4}x^4+\frac{6.5.4.3.2}{1.2.3.4.5}x^5$$

$$+\frac{6.5.4.3.2.1}{1.2.3.4.5.6}x^6$$

$$= 1+6x+15x^2+20x^3+15x^4+6x^5+x^6$$

These coefficients agree with those in Pascal's triangle.

Example 2 Find a series for $\sqrt{(1+x)}$ in powers of x as far as the term in x^4, given that x is numerically less than 1.

$$\sqrt{(1+x)} = (1+x)^{\frac{1}{2}}$$

In the binomial expansion we put $n = \frac{1}{2}$ and the series does not terminate.

$$(1+x)^{\frac{1}{2}} = 1 + \tfrac{1}{2}x + \frac{\frac{1}{2}(\frac{1}{2}-1)}{1.2}x^2 + \frac{\frac{1}{2}(\frac{1}{2}-1)(\frac{1}{2}-2)}{1.2.3}x^3 + \frac{\frac{1}{2}(\frac{1}{2}-1)(\frac{1}{2}-2)(\frac{1}{2}-3)}{1.2.3.4}x^4 + \ldots$$

$$= 1 + \tfrac{1}{2}x + \frac{\frac{1}{2}(-\frac{1}{2})}{2}x^2 + \frac{\frac{1}{2}(-\frac{1}{2})(-\frac{3}{2})}{1.2.3}x^3 + \frac{\frac{1}{2}(-\frac{1}{2})(-\frac{3}{2})(-\frac{5}{2})}{1.2.3.4}x^4 + \ldots$$

$$= 1 + \tfrac{1}{2}x - \tfrac{1}{8}x^2 + \tfrac{1}{16}x^3 - \tfrac{5}{128}x^4 + \ldots$$

Determination of a particular term in the expansion

In the expansion of $(1+x)^n$ the

$$\text{third term} = \frac{n(n-1)}{2!}x^2$$

$$\text{fourth term} = \frac{n(n-1)(n-2)}{3!}x^3$$

$$\text{fifth term} = \frac{n(n-1)(n-2)(n-3)}{4!}x^4$$

Thus the rth term is $\dfrac{n(n-1)(n-2)\ldots(n-r+2)}{(r-1)!}x^{r-1}$

It is easier to remember a formula for the $(r+1)^{th}$ term.

The $(r+1)^{th}$ term is $\dfrac{n(n-1)(n-2)\ldots(n-r+1)}{r!}x^r$

Thus the eighth term of $(1+x)^{12}$ is

$$\frac{12.11.10\ldots(12-7+1)}{7!}x^7 = \frac{12.11.10.9.8.7.6}{7!}x^7$$

The expansion of $(a+x)^n$, n a positive integer.

From the series for $(1+x)^n$ we can easily obtain a series for $(a+x)^n$:

$$(a+x)^n = \left\{a\left(1+\frac{x}{a}\right)\right\}^n$$

$$= a^n\left(1+\frac{x}{a}\right)^n$$

$$= a^n\left\{1 + n\frac{x}{a} + \frac{n(n-1)}{2!}\left(\frac{x}{a}\right)^2 + \frac{n(n-1)(n-2)}{3!}\left(\frac{x}{a}\right)^3 + \ldots + \left(\frac{x}{a}\right)^n\right\}$$

$$= a^n + na^{n-1}x + \frac{n(n-1)}{2!}a^{n-2}x^2 + \frac{n(n-1)(n-2)}{3!}a^{n-3}x^3 + \ldots + x^n$$

This is a more general form for the binomial theorem.

Example 1   Expand by the binomial theorem

(a) $(3x+y)^5$

(b) $(a-2b)^4$

(a) $(3x+y)^5 = (3x)^5 + 5.(3x)^4.y + \frac{5.4}{1.2}(3x)^3y^2 + \frac{5.4.3}{1.2.3}(3x)^2y^3$

$$+ \frac{5.4.3.2}{1.2.3.4}3x.y^4 + \frac{5.4.3.2.1}{1.2.3.4.5}y^5$$

$$= 243x^5 + 405x^4y + 270x^3y^2 + 90x^2y^3 + 15xy^4 + y^5$$

(b) $(a-2b)^4 = a^4 + 4a^3(-2b) + \frac{4.3}{1.2}a^2(-2b)^2 + \frac{4.3.2}{1.2.3}a(-2b)^3$

$$+ \frac{4.3.2.1}{1.2.3.4}(-2b)^4$$

$$= a^4 - 8a^3b + 24a^2b^2 - 32ab^3 + 16b^4$$

Example 2   Write down the sixth term of

(a) $(1-x)^{11}$ (b) $(3x+2y)^9$

(a) sixth term $= \frac{11.10.9\ldots.(11-5+1)}{5!}(-x)^5$

$$= -\frac{11.10.9.8.7}{1.2.3.4.5}x^5 = -462x^5$$

(b) sixth term $= \frac{9.8.7.6.5}{1.2.3.4.5}(3x)^4(2y)^5$

$$= 126 \times 3^4 \times 2^5x^4y^5$$

$$= 326,592x^4y^5$$

Example 3   Find the value of $(1\cdot01)^8$ correct to five significant figures.

$(1\cdot01)^8 = 1 + 8 \times 0\cdot01 + \frac{8 \times 7}{1.2}(0\cdot01)^2 + \frac{8 \times 7 \times 6}{1.2.3}(0\cdot01)^3 + \ldots$

$$= 1 + 0\cdot08 + 0\cdot0028 + 0\cdot000056 + \ldots$$

$$= 1\cdot0829 \text{ to five significant figures}$$

If x is small then $(1+x)^n = 1 + nx + \frac{n(n-1)}{1.2}x^2 + \ldots$ and we can find the value of $(1+x)^n$ to any degree of approximation we require by taking say the first three terms in the expansion giving $(1+x)^n \simeq 1+nx+\dfrac{n(n-1)}{1.2}x^2$ or even taking only the the first two terms to give

$$(1+x)^n \simeq 1+nx$$

Exercise 6e

Expand questions 1–6 by the binomial theorem.

1 $(1-x)^5$ 　　　　　 2 $(1+3x)^4$ 　　　　　 3 $(2x-y)^4$

4 $\left(x-\dfrac{1}{x}\right)^6$ 　　　　 5 $(2+x)^4$ 　　　　　 6 $(1-t)^7$

Write out the series in questions 7–12 in ascending powers of x as far as the term containing x^3.

7 $(1+x)^{12}$ 　　　　 8 $(1-x)^{10}$ 　　　　 9 $(1+2x)^{20}$

10 $\sqrt{(1-x)}$ given x numerically less than 1.

11 $\dfrac{1}{1-x}$ given x numerically less than 1.

12 $\dfrac{1}{(1+2x)^2}$ given $2x$ numerically less than 1.

13 Find the fourth term of $(x+y)^{10}$

14 Find the fifth term of $(a+b)^{12}$

15 Find the fifth term of $(2x-3y)^8$

16 Find the seventh term of $\left(2x-\dfrac{1}{x}\right)^{11}$

17 Find the value of $(1{\cdot}01)^9$
(a) to two decimal places, 　　　 (b) to four decimal places.

18 Find the value of $(1{\cdot}002)^{10}$
(a) to three decimal places, 　　　 (b) to five decimal places.

Miscellaneous exercises 6

1 (a) The sum of n terms of an arithmetical series is $\frac{1}{2}(3n^2-n)$. Find the common difference.
(b) Find the sum of the first seven terms of the series $3\frac{3}{8}-2\frac{1}{4}+1\frac{1}{2}\ldots$

N.C.T.E.C.

2   (a) A man is employed at a commencing salary of £850 per annum and this is increased by £25 each year. What total sum of money will he have earned by the end of the tenth year?

(b) The speeds of a drilling machine are to be seven in number, varying from 20 to 200 r.p.m. If the speeds are to be in geometric progression find the common ratio and the middle term.

E.M.E.U.

3   (a) A man is appointed to a position at a starting salary of £800 per year, rising by £50 per year, reaching his maximum in ten years. What is his maximum salary and how much has he been paid in all by the end of the tenth year?

(b) The second term of a geometric progression is 6 and the fifth term is 162. Find the first term and the common ratio.

(c) Find the sum to infinity of the geometric series whose first term is 4 and whose third term is 3, all terms being positive.

E.M.E.U.

4   (a) The first three terms of a geometric progression are 1·1, 1·32, 1·584. Find the eleventh term and the sum of the first twenty terms.

(b) A contractor agrees to sink a shaft 40 m deep at a cost of £4 for the first metre, £4·30 for the second, and an extra 30p for each additional metre. Find the total cost and the cost of the last metre.

5   (a) In the series $-3, -2, -1, \ldots$ find the difference between the sum of the even terms and the sum of the odd terms when the total number of terms taken is 16.

(b) A ball, dropped on a floor from a height of 10 metres rebounds to a height of 6 metres and continues to fall and rebound. If after each rebound it rises to a height which is $\frac{3}{5}$ of the height it has just fallen, find (i) the total distance it moves before coming to rest on the floor and (ii) the distance moved from the point of release to the fourth impact.

D.T.C.

6   (a) If the first term of an arithmetical progression is 11 and the seventeenth is 31, find the sum of twenty-four terms.

(b) A machine cost £1000 when new. If it depreciated in value by 10% each year, after how many years would it be down to its scrap value of £20?

7   (a) Derive the general expression for the terms in an arithmetical progression, given that the first term is a and the common difference is d. Using this expression, find the fifteenth and twenty-first terms of the series

2, 7, 12 . . .

(b) At the end of a certain year a boy's height was 1·5 m. During the next year he grew 6 cm, and in each succeeding year his rate of growth was four-fifths of what it was in the previous year. Find his final height.

8   (a) Use the binomial theorem to obtain the first four terms of the expansion $(1-x)^9$ in ascending powers of x. Hence find the value of $(0.995)^9$ correct to four places of decimal.

     (b) Find the coefficient of x^7 in the expansion of $\left(2x-\dfrac{1}{6}\right)^{13}$

U.E.I.

9   Using the binomial theorem
     (a) Evaluate $(1.0007)^6$ correct to five decimal places.

     (b) Expand $\left(x-\dfrac{4}{x}\right)^5$, each term to be reduced to its simplest form.

     (c) Find, in its simplest form, the sixth term of $\left(3x+\dfrac{1}{x}\right)^9$.

U.E.I.

10   (a) Using the binomial expansion, evaluate $(1.04)^5$, correct to three places of decimals.

     (b) The sum of the first five terms of an arithmetical progression is 100 and the ninth term is 5. Find the first three terms.

     (c) The speeds of a drilling machine are 12 in number varying from 30 r.p.m. to 240 r.p.m. inclusive. If the speeds are in geometric progression, calculate the common ratio.

D.T.C.

11   (a) Neglecting powers of x above the first, find by means of the binomial theorem, an approximation to

$$\frac{(1+x)^{\frac{2}{3}}(1-2x)^{\frac{1}{2}}}{\left(1-\dfrac{5x}{6}\right)}$$

     (b) Using the binomial theorem find, to four places of decimals, an approximate value of $\sqrt[4]{(623)}$.

N.C.T.E.C.

12   (a) Using the binomial theorem

     i   expand $\left(x-\dfrac{1}{2y}\right)^5$

     ii find the sixth term of $\left(3a-\dfrac{1}{3b}\right)^{11}$

     iii find the value of $(1.0002)^5$ correct to five decimal places.

     (b) Simplify and express with positive indices

$$\sqrt[7]{\left(\frac{a^4b^{-6}b^3}{a^{-3}b^4}\right)} \div \left(\frac{d^5c^{-8}}{d^{-3}c^{-5}c}\right)^{0.25}$$

     (c) Using common logarithms, evaluate W in the following formula: $W = ae^{xy}$

U.E.I.

160   **Progressions and series**

13 (a) Solve $6^{1-4x}.4^{x+5} = 8$

(b) Using the binomial theorem

    i write down the expansion of $\left(3x - \dfrac{1}{x}\right)^8$ as far as the term independent of x.

    ii find the value of $(0.996)^4$ correct to five decimal places.

    iii write down the sixth term in the expansion of $\left(x + \dfrac{1}{2x}\right)^{10}$

U.E.I.

14 (a) Using the binomial theorem, expand $(2x - y)^4$

(b) The expression $a + bx + cx^2$ has the value 4·3 when $x = 1$, 7·8 when $x = 2$ and 12·3 when $x = 3$. Find the numerical values of a, b and c.

D.T.C.

15 (a) By using the binomial expansion to four terms find the cube root of 1·04 correct to four decimal places.

(b) The outer and inner radii of a hollow hemispherical casting are $2R$ and R respectively. A small thickness, t, is removed from both the inner and outer surfaces. Show that, if t^2 can be neglected compared with R^2, the weight removed is a fraction $\dfrac{15t}{7R}$ of the original weight.

E.M.E.U.

16 (a) Expand $(1 - x)^{-3}$ as far as the term in x^4. Using this expansion, find the value of $\dfrac{1}{(0.98)^3}$ to four places of decimals.

(b) Find the sum to infinity of the series $2 + \dfrac{2}{3} + \dfrac{2}{9} + \ldots$ proving the formula you use.

N.C.T.E.C.

17 (a) Use the binomial theorem to expand $(a + x)^5$, simplifying each term. Use this expression to evaluate to four decimal places $1.02^5 - 1.01^5$.

(b) The first three terms of a geometric series are 3, 1 and $\dfrac{1}{3}$. Find the sum of the first six terms and the sum of the infinite series.

U.L.C.I.

18 (a) If $f(x) = x^3 - 4x + 2$, find the value of (i) $f(3)$ (ii) $f(-2)$ (iii) $f(x+1)$

(b) The first term of a geometric progression is 3 and the fifth is 1,875. Show that there are two such series, and find them.

(c) Expand $(1 - x)^4$ by the binomial theorem and hence find the exact value of $(0.98)^4$

19 Write down and simplify the binomial expansion of $(1 + 3x)^{\frac{1}{2}}$ up to and including the term in x^3.

161   Miscellaneous exercises 6

By substituting $x = 0\cdot01$ in the series, calculate the value of $\sqrt{(1\cdot03)}$ correct to five decimal places.

U.L.C.I.

20   (a) Expand $\left(1+\dfrac{x}{4}\right)^{\frac{1}{2}}$ as far as the term in x^3 and hence evaluate $\sqrt{5}$ correct to three decimal places.

     (b) A radioactive element decays to half its mass every 6 hours. Use a geometric series to determine (i) what fraction of the original amount will be left after 2 days (ii) the approximate time to reduce its mass to only 1% of the original amount.

N.C.T.E.C.

7 Gradients and differentiation

7a The gradient of a curve

If a tangent is drawn at a point P on a curve then the gradient of this tangent is said to be the *gradient* of the curve at P.

Thus in fig. 80 the gradient of the curve at P is equal to the gradient of the tangent PT.

Figure 80

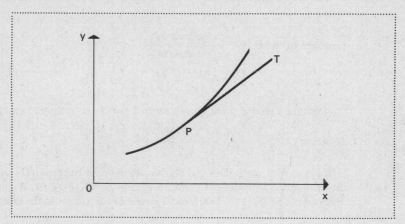

7b Calculation of the gradient

If we know the equation of a curve we can calculate the gradient at any point.

Method 1

Suppose we require the gradient of the curve $y = 4x^2$ at the point $(1, 4)$ on the graph.

Let P be the point $(1, 4)$ and Q_1 the point $(1\frac{1}{2}, 9)$ also on the curve.

In fig. 81 where PL and Q_1M are ordinates and PR is perpendicular to Q_1M then

Figure
81

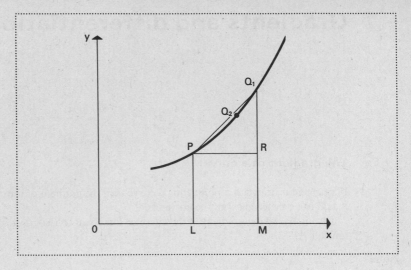

Gradient of chord $PQ_1 = \dfrac{\text{increase in } y}{\text{increase in } x}$

$$= \frac{RQ_1}{PR} = \frac{9-4}{1\frac{1}{2}-1} = 10$$

Now take a second point Q_2 (nearer to P) whose co-ordinates are $(1\cdot2, 5\cdot76)$

Gradient of $PQ_2 = \dfrac{5\cdot76-4}{1\cdot2-1} = \dfrac{1\cdot76}{0\cdot2} = 8\cdot8$

We next consider points Q_3, Q_4, etc. which move progressively closer and closer to P and consider the gradients of chords PQ_3, PQ_4, etc. We take their abscissae to be $1\cdot1$, $1\cdot01$, $1\cdot001$, etc. The results are shown in the table.

Abscissa of	$Q = OM$	1·5	1·2	1·1	1·01	1·001	1·0001
Ordinate of	$Q = MQ$	9	5·76	4·48	4·0804	4·008 004	4·000 800 04
Increase in	$y = RQ$	5	1·76	0·84	0·0804	0·008 004	0·000 800 04
Increase in	$x = PR$	0·5	·0·2	0·1	0·01	0·001	0·0001
Gradient of chord $= \dfrac{RQ}{PR}$		10	8·8	8·4	8·04	8·004	8·0004

Fig. 82 shows that as Q_1, Q_2, Q_3, etc. are taken nearer and nearer to P then the slope of the chord PQ approaches nearer and nearer to the slope of the tangent PT.

From the table we see that the slope of the tangent approaches nearer and nearer to the value 8.

Figure
82

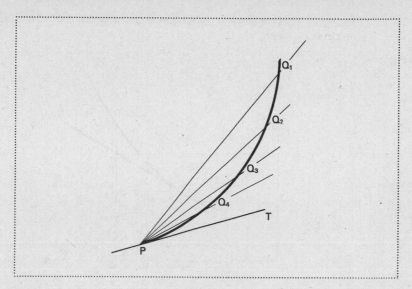

Method 2

In the above we took the value of the increase in x (= PR) to be successively 0·5, 0·2, 0·1, 0·01, etc. We can achieve the same result by letting the increase in x be h.

To find the gradient of the curve $y = 4x^2$ at the point P (1, 4) we choose a neighbouring point Q to be $[1+h, 4(1+h)^2]$.

Thus $QM = 4(1+h)^2$

$$\text{Gradient of chord } PQ = \frac{\text{increase in } y}{\text{increase in } x} = \frac{QM - PL}{PR}$$

$$= \frac{4(1+h)^2 - 4.1^2}{h}$$

$$= \frac{8h + 4h^2}{h}$$

$$= 8 + 4h$$

To find the gradient of the tangent at P from this gradient of chord PQ we let Q move nearer and nearer to P.

This is done by taking h smaller and smaller.

As h approaches zero the slope of the chord approaches 8 which may be taken as the slope of the tangent.

The symbol for approaches is $\rightarrow$ so that we write
As $h \rightarrow 0$, slope of $PQ \rightarrow 8$.

165   Calculation of the gradient

Example Find the slope of the tangent to the curve $y = 2x^2 - 3x$ at the point on the curve where $x = 2$.

Figure
83

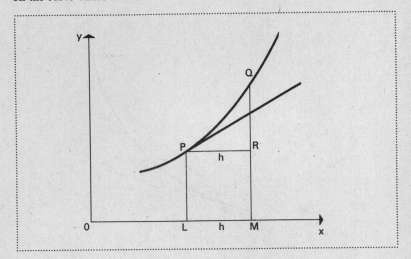

Referring to fig. 83 above, let P be the point whose abscissa is 2.
Then $OL = 2$ and $PL = 2.2^2 - 3.2 = 2$

Let point Q have abscissa $2 + h$
Then $QM = 2(2+h)^2 - 3(2+h)$

$$\text{Gradient of chord } PQ = \frac{\text{increase in } y}{\text{increase in } x} = \frac{QM - PL}{PR}$$

$$= \frac{2(2+h)^2 - 3(2+h) - 2}{h}$$

$$= \frac{8 + 8h + 2h^2 - 6 - 3h - 2}{h}$$

$$= \frac{5h + 2h^2}{h}$$

$$= 5 + 2h$$

As $h \to 0$ slope of $PQ \to 5$
Thus slope of tangent at P is 5.

Exercise 7b

1 P is the point $(2, 4)$ on the curve $y = x^2$.

Find the ordinates corresponding to points Q_1, Q_2, Q_3 on the curve with abscissae $2 \cdot 1$, $2 \cdot 01$, $2 \cdot 001$, respectively. As in worked example 1 on page 163 draw up a table to show the gradients of the chords PQ_1, PQ_2, PQ_3, and hence deduce the gradient of the tangent at P.

2   Find the gradient of the tangent to the curve $y = x^2$ at the point (2, 4) by first finding the gradient of the chord PQ where Q is the point on the curve whose abscissa is $2 + h$. Then let h approach zero to obtain the gradient of the tangent.

Apply the method of question 2 above (which is the method used in worked example of the text) to find the gradients of the curve at the point given in questions 3–6.

3   $y = 2x^2$ at point (2, 8)   4 $y = x^2 - 1$ at point (3, 8)

5   $y = 2x + x^2$ at point (1, 3)   6 $y = 5x^2$ at point (1, 5)

Figure
84

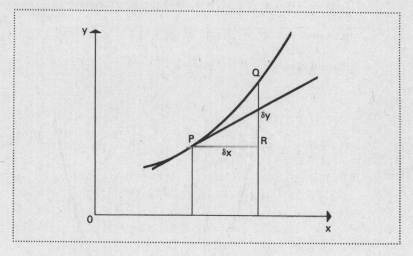

In finding the gradient of a chord as $\dfrac{\text{increase in } y}{\text{increase in } x}$ we used h for the increase in x.

It is customary to use δx as the symbol for a small increase in x. This is read as 'delta x' and is called the *increment* in x.

The corresponding increase in y is then δy.

Using this notation, we now proceed to find the gradient of a curve at any point $P(x, y)$, the working being set out as follows:

To find the gradient of the curve $y = x^2 - 2x$ at any point $P(x, y)$, when P is any point on the curve with co-ordinates (x, y).

Let Q be a neighbouring point co-ordinates $(x + \delta x, y + \delta y)$. Since Q lies on the curve

$$y + \delta y = (x + \delta x)^2 - 2(x + \delta x)$$

Also at P $y = x^2 - 2x$

Subtracting we get $\delta y = (x + \delta x)^2 - 2(x + \delta x) - (x^2 - 2x)$
$$= 2x\delta x + \delta x^2 - 2\delta x$$

$$\therefore \qquad \frac{\delta y}{\delta x} = 2x + \delta x - 2 = \frac{QR}{PR} \qquad \text{(See fig. 84.)}$$

Notice that this gives the gradient of chord PQ. The smaller δx becomes, the closer the gradient of PQ approaches the gradient of the tangent at P.

As $\delta x \to 0$, gradient of $PQ \to 2x - 2$

Thus we say that the gradient of the tangent at P is given by the value of $\frac{\delta y}{\delta x}$ as $\delta x \to 0$ and is $2x - 2$. It is called the 'limiting value' of $\frac{\delta y}{\delta x}$ as $\delta x \to 0$ and this value we write as $\frac{dy}{dx}$, read as 'dee y by dee x'. We write

gradient of curve at $P = \lim_{\delta x \to 0} \frac{\delta y}{\delta x} = \frac{dy}{dx}$

Figure 85

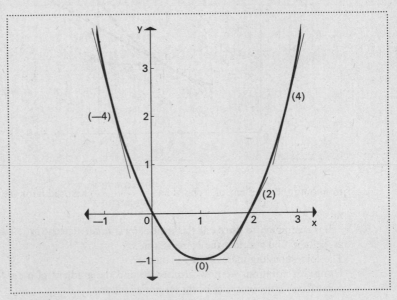

Hence for the curve $y = x^2 - 2x, \dfrac{dy}{dx} = 2x - 2$

and this gives the gradient of the curve at any point P in terms of the abscissa of that point.

Given the abscissa of any point on the curve we can now quickly find the gradient at that point.

Thus where (a) $x = 2$, the gradient is $2x - 2$ (where $x = 2$) $= 2(2) - 2 = 2$

(b) $x = 3$, the gradient is $2(3) - 2 = 4$

(c) $x = 1$, the gradient is $2(1) - 2 = 0$

and (d) $x = -1$, the gradient is $2(-1) - 2 = -4$

See fig. 85.

7d Differential coefficients and differentiation

$\dfrac{dy}{dx} = \lim\limits_{\delta x \to 0} \dfrac{\delta y}{\delta x}$ is derived from the equation of the curve and is called the *derivative of y with respect to x* or the *differential coefficient of y with respect to x.*

The process of obtaining $\dfrac{dy}{dx}$ where y is given as a function of x is called *differentiation* or more fully, *differentiating y with respect to x.*

We have seen that the gradient of a curve at any point is given by the value of $\dfrac{dy}{dx}$ at that point, but in finding $\dfrac{dy}{dx}$ we need not refer to any point on the graph, although we have based our method on it. To find $\dfrac{dy}{dx}$ for a given function we may proceed as follows:

Example 1 If $y = 3x^2 - 2x$, find $\dfrac{dy}{dx}$.

$$y = 3x^2 - 2x \dots (7.1)$$

Let x increase by δx and let δy be the corresponding increase in y.

Then $y + \delta y = 3(x + \delta x)^2 - 2(x + \delta x) \dots (7.2)$

Notice that we replace x wherever it occurs by $x + \delta x$. Subtracting equation (7.1) from equation (7.2) we get

$$\delta y = 6x\delta x + 3\delta x^2 - 2\delta x$$

$$\therefore \frac{\delta y}{\delta x} = 6x - 2 + 3\delta x$$

$$\frac{dy}{dx} = \lim\limits_{\delta x \to 0} \frac{\delta y}{\delta x} = 6x - 2$$

This method of finding $\frac{dy}{dx}$ is known as differentiating from first principles.

Example 2   Differentiate $\frac{1}{x}$ from first principles.

We write $\qquad y = \frac{1}{x}$

$$y + \delta y = \frac{1}{x + \delta x}$$

Subtracting $\delta y = \dfrac{1}{x + \delta x} - \dfrac{1}{x}$

$$= \frac{x - (x + \delta x)}{(x + \delta x)x}$$

$$= \frac{-\delta x}{x^2 + x\delta x}$$

$$\frac{\delta y}{\delta x} = \frac{-1}{x^2 + x\delta x}$$

$$\frac{dy}{dx} = \lim_{\delta x \to 0} \frac{\delta y}{\delta x} = -\frac{1}{x^2}$$

Example 3   Find the gradient of the curve $y = \frac{1}{x}$ at the point $(2, \frac{1}{2})$.

From example 2 above we know that for the function

$$y = \frac{1}{x}, \frac{dy}{dx} = -\frac{1}{x^2}$$

At $x = 2$, $\dfrac{dy}{dx} = -\dfrac{1}{2^2} = -\dfrac{1}{4}$

Thus the gradient of the curve at point $(2, \frac{1}{2})$ is $-\frac{1}{4}$.

Exercise 7d

In questions 1–8 differentiate from first principles

1	x^2	2	$3x^2 + x$	3	$2x + x^2$
4	$1 - 3x^2$	5	x^3	6	$\dfrac{1}{x^2}$
7	x	8	$\dfrac{1}{2x - 1}$		

9   Find the gradients of the curve $y = x^2$ at the points (2, 4) and $(-2, 4)$

10 Find the gradients of the curve $y = x^2$ at the points where it intersects the line $y = 2x+3$

11 Find the points on the curve $y = \dfrac{1}{x}$ where the gradient is $-\dfrac{1}{9}$

12 Find the point on the curve $y = 3x^2 - 2x$ at which the tangent is parallel to the x axis.

7e Differentiation of $y = x^n$ where n is a positive integer

The student, if he has worked through the examples, will have found that if

(a) $y = x$, $\dfrac{dy}{dx} = 1$

(b) $y = x^2$, $\dfrac{dy}{dx} = 2x$

(c) $y = x^3$, $\dfrac{dy}{dx} = 3x^2$

(d) $y = \dfrac{1}{x} = x^{-1}$, $\dfrac{dy}{dx} = -1.x^{-2} = -\dfrac{1}{x^2}$

These results are all included in the general case that if

$$y = x^n, \quad \frac{dy}{dx} = nx^{n-1}$$

This result is true for all values of n whether a whole number or fractional, whether positive or negative, but to start with we will prove it only for the case where n is any positive whole number.

Let $y = x^n \ldots (7.3)$

If δx is a small increase in x and δy the corresponding increment in y then

$y + \delta y = (x + \delta x)^n \ldots (7.4)$

Subtracting equation (7.3) from (7.4) we get

$\delta y = (x + \delta x)^n - x^n$

Expanding $(x + \delta x)^n$ by the binomial theorem we get

$$\delta y = x^n + nx^{n-1}.\delta x + \frac{n(n-1)}{1.2}x^{n-2}.(\delta x)^2 + \ldots + (\delta x)^n - x^n$$

$$= nx^{n-1}.\delta x + \frac{n(n-1)}{1.2}x^{n-2}(\delta x)^2 + \ldots + (\delta x)^n$$

$$\therefore \frac{\delta y}{\delta x} = nx^{n-1} + \frac{n(n-1)}{1.2}x^{n-2}.\delta x + \ldots + (\delta x)^{n-1}$$

$$= nx^{n-1} + \text{terms containing } \delta x \text{ and higher powers of } \delta x$$

Thus $\dfrac{dy}{dx} = \lim\limits_{\delta x \to 0} \dfrac{\delta y}{\delta x} = nx^{n-1}$ since every term after this will become zero

We may write $\dfrac{d}{dx}(x^n) = nx^{n-1}$

To differentiate x^n we multiply by the index n and reduce the index by 1 for the new index.

Notice if $y = Cx^n$ where C is any constant

$\dfrac{\delta y}{\delta x}$ will be $\dfrac{C(x+\delta x)^n - Cx^n}{\delta x}$

$$= C.\frac{(x+\delta x)^n - x^n}{\delta x}$$

which in the limit when $\delta x \to 0$ will give

$$\frac{dy}{dx} = Cnx^{n-1}$$

Thus if $y = 6x^2$ $\dfrac{dy}{dx} = 12x$

if $y = 4x^3$ $\dfrac{dy}{dx} = 12x^2$

if $y = 5x^7$ $\dfrac{dy}{dx} = 35x^6$

We have proved this rule only for n a positive integer, but the rule is still true when n is fractional or negative.

For example when $y = \dfrac{1}{x} = x^{-1}$ we showed from first principles earlier in the chapter that $\dfrac{dy}{dx} = -1.x^{-2}$ which is an example of the rule when x is negative.

Also if $y = \sqrt{x} = x^{\frac{1}{2}}$ then $\dfrac{dy}{dx} = \frac{1}{2}x^{\frac{1}{2}-1}$

$$= \tfrac{1}{2}x^{-\frac{1}{2}} = \frac{1}{2\sqrt{x}}, \text{ an example where } n \text{ is fractional.}$$

Some special cases

1. If $y = C$ where C is constant then $\dfrac{dy}{dx} = 0$

As y is a constant its value never alters whatever changes are made in the value of x

$\therefore \delta y = 0$ for all values of δx

$\therefore \dfrac{\delta y}{\delta x}$ is always zero and $\dfrac{dy}{dx} = 0$

Notice that the graph of $y = C$ is a straight line parallel to Ox and its gradient is zero.

2. *Differentiation of a sum*   Suppose $y = a + bx + cx^2 + dx^3$ where a, b, c and d are all constants

then $y + \delta y = a + b(x + \delta x) + c(x + \delta x)^2 + d(x + \delta x)^3$

and $\dfrac{\delta y}{\delta x} = b \cdot \dfrac{(x + \delta x) - x}{\delta x} + c \cdot \dfrac{(x + \delta x)^2 - x^2}{\delta x} + d \cdot \dfrac{(x + \delta x)^3 - x^3}{\delta x}$

and $\dfrac{dy}{dx}$ becomes $b + c \cdot 2x + d \cdot 3x^2$

Thus $\dfrac{dy}{dx}$ is the sum of the differential coefficients of the separate terms.

This is true generally.

For example if (a) $y = 5x^3 - 2x^2 + 6x - 3$

$$\frac{dy}{dx} = 5 \times 3x^2 - 2 \times 2x + 6 + 0$$

$$= 15x^2 - 4x + 6$$

(b) $y = 4x - 3x^5$

$$\frac{dy}{dx} = 4 - 3 \times 5x^4$$

$$= 4 - 15x^4$$

(c) $y = 2x + 5 + \dfrac{1}{x}$

$$\frac{dy}{dx} = 2 + 0 + (-1)x^{-2}$$

$$= 2 - \frac{1}{x^2}$$

Exercise 7e

In questions 1–12 differentiate with respect to x using the general rule.

1   x^5 2 $3x^6$ 3 $x - \dfrac{1}{x}$

4    $5x^3 + 3x$ 5 $2x^8 + 8x - 5$ 6 $x^3 - 3x^2 + 3x - 1$

7    $(x+2)^2$ 8 $3x^2 - \dfrac{1}{x}$ 9 $x + \dfrac{1}{x}$

10    $\dfrac{4}{3}\pi x^3$ 11 $4\pi x^2$ 12 $ax^2 + bx + c$

13   If $y = x^2 + 2x - 3$ find the value of x for which $\dfrac{dy}{dx}$ is zero.

14   Find the gradients of the curve $y = x^3 - 4x^2 + 6x - 3$ at the points $(0, -3)$, $(1, 0)$ and $(2, 1)$

15   Find the points on the graph of $y = x^3 - 3x$ at which the gradients are zero.

16   Find the gradients of the curve $y = x^2 - 2x - 1$ at the points where it intersects the line $y = x + 3$

17   Find the gradient of the curve $y = 2x^2 - 5x$ at the point $(1, -3)$ and obtain the equation of the tangent at this point.

7f   Further differentiation

If $y = x^5$ then $\dfrac{dy}{dx} = \dfrac{d}{dx}(x^5) = 5x^4$

We may continue and differentiate this result

$$\frac{d}{dx}\left(\frac{dy}{dx}\right) = \frac{d}{dx}(5x^4) = 5 \times 4x^3 = 20x^3$$

The expression $\dfrac{d}{dx}\left(\dfrac{dy}{dx}\right)$ is written $\dfrac{d^2y}{dx^2}$ and is called the second differential coefficient of y with respect to x.

Similarly $\dfrac{d}{dx}\left(\dfrac{d^2y}{dx^2}\right)$ is written $\dfrac{d^3y}{dx^3}$ and is called the third differential coefficient of y with respect to x, and so on.

174   Gradients and differentiation

Note that $\left(\dfrac{dy}{dx}\right)^2$ is not the same as $\dfrac{d^2y}{dx^2}$.

If $y = 5x^4$, $\dfrac{dy}{dx} = 5x^4$, $\left(\dfrac{dy}{dx}\right)^2 = 25x^8$ while $\dfrac{d^2y}{dx^2} = 20x^3$

Example 1   If $y = x^4$ find $\dfrac{dy}{dx}$ and $\dfrac{d^2y}{dx^2}$ and show that $4y\dfrac{d^2y}{dx^2} = 3\left(\dfrac{dy}{dx}\right)^2$

$$y = x^4, \quad \frac{dy}{dx} = 4x^3, \quad \frac{d^2y}{dx^2} = 12x^2$$

$$4y\frac{d^2y}{dx^2} = 4 \times x^4 \times 12x^2 = 48x^6$$

$$3\left(\frac{dy}{dx}\right)^2 = 3 \times 4x^3 \times 4x^3 = 48x^6$$

Therefore if $y = x^4$, $4y\dfrac{d^2y}{dx^2} = 3\left(\dfrac{dy}{dx}\right)^2$

Example 2   Find $\dfrac{d^2s}{dt^2}$ if $s = 12t - 16t^2$

$$s = 12t - 16t^2$$

$$\frac{ds}{dt} = 12 - 32t$$

$$\frac{d^2s}{dt^2} = -32$$

Example 3   If $\theta = 12 + 20t - 2t^3$ find $\dfrac{d\theta}{dt}$ and $\dfrac{d^2\theta}{dt^2}$ when $t = 2$

$$\theta = 12 + 20t - 2t^3$$

$$\frac{d\theta}{dt} = 20 - 6t^2$$

$$\frac{d^2\theta}{dt^2} = -12t$$

when $t = 2$, $\dfrac{d\theta}{dt} = 20 - 6(2)^2 = -4$

and $\dfrac{d^2\theta}{dt^2} = -12 \times 2 = -24$

Exercise 7f

Find $\dfrac{dy}{dx}$ and $\dfrac{d^2y}{dx^2}$ in questions 1–4.

1   $4x^5 - x^3$ 2 $6x^4 + 3x^2$

3   $(x^2 + 1)^2$ 4 $\dfrac{x^3 + 1}{x}$

In questions 5–8 differentiate with respect to the variable.

5   $r^4 - 3r^2 + 6$ 6 $\dfrac{1 + r^2}{r}$

7   $4t(t + 1)$ 8 $\theta + \dfrac{\theta^2}{2} + \dfrac{\theta^3}{3}$

9   If $y = x^3$ prove that $2x^2 \dfrac{dy}{dx} = y \cdot \dfrac{d^2y}{dx^2}$

10   If $y = x^2 - x$ prove that $\left(\dfrac{dy}{dx}\right)^2 = 2y \cdot \dfrac{d^2y}{dx^2} + 1$

11   Find $\dfrac{d^2s}{dt^2}$ if (a) $s = 40t - 16t^2$

                (b) $s = ut + \frac{1}{2}ft^2$
                  where u and f are constants.

12   Show that $\dfrac{d}{dx}\left(x^2 \dfrac{dy}{dx}\right) = 2x \dfrac{dy}{dx} + x^2 \dfrac{d^2y}{dx^2}$

    when $y = x^3 + 2x$

Miscellaneous exercises 7

1   (a) Differentiate from first principles
        $y = 2x^2 - 3x + 4$

    (b) Differentiate by inspection
        $y = \dfrac{5x^2}{3} - \dfrac{3x}{4} - 2 + \dfrac{3}{x} - \dfrac{2}{3x^2}$

    (c) For what values of x is the gradient of the graph of $2x^2 - 3x + 5$ equal to
        i -7,   ii 0,   iii 5
                                          U.E.I.

2   (a) Differentiate $3x^2 - x$ from first principles.

    (b) Find $\dfrac{dy}{dx}$ in the following cases

        i $y = x^3 - 2x^2 + x - 3$ ii $y = \dfrac{1}{x^2} - \dfrac{3}{x}$ iii $y = x^{\frac{2}{3}}$

    (c) Find the values of x which make $\dfrac{dy}{dx} = 0$

      if $y = x^3 - 6x^2 + 9x - 2$

3   (a) Differentiate the following with respect to x

      i $2x^5$,   ii $3\sqrt{x}$,   iii $\dfrac{5}{\sqrt{x}}$

    (b) If $y = 2x^3 - 3x + 6$, find the values of $\dfrac{dy}{dx}$ and $\dfrac{d^2y}{dx^2}$ when $x = 3$.

      For what values of x is $\dfrac{dy}{dx}$ equal to zero, and what are the corresponding values of y?

                                               N.C.T.E.C.

4   (a) Determine, from first principles, the expression for $\dfrac{d\theta}{dt}$ if $\theta = at^2$

    (b) A wheel rotates through θ radians in t seconds and $\theta = 15 + 16t - t^2$

      i Find $\dfrac{d\theta}{dt}$ when $t = 4$

      ii Find the number of radians through which it rotates in the first 7 seconds.

                                               U.L.C.I.

5   (a) Differentiate with respect to x

      $4x^3 - \dfrac{1}{x^4}$

    (b) Find the second derivative of $x^5 - 5x^4 + 2x$

    (c) Find the x co-ordinates of the points on the curve $y = x^3 + 3x^2 - 9x + 2$ at which the tangent is parallel to the x axis.

6   (a) Differentiate the following with respect to x

      i $3x^4 + \sqrt{x^3}$,   ii $\dfrac{7}{\sqrt{x}} + 6x + \dfrac{5}{x}$

    (b) Given that $y = ax^2 + 4x + 3$ and that $\dfrac{d^2y}{dx^2} = 6$, find the value of y when $x = 2$

                                                 N.C.T.E.C.

7　The equation of a curve is $y = 1 + 4x - 2x^2$
   (a) Find the co-ordinates of the point on the curve where the gradient is -2.
      Hence obtain the equation of the tangent to the curve at this point.
   (b) At what point on the curve does the tangent make an angle of $45°$ with the
      x axis?
   (c) What angle will the tangent to the curve at the point $x = \frac{5}{4}$ make with the
      x axis?

D.T.C.

8　(a) If $y = \dfrac{x}{2} + \dfrac{2}{x}$, find $\dfrac{d^2y}{dx^2}$

   (b) If $\dfrac{ds}{dt} = 40 - 32t$, find the value of $\dfrac{d^2s}{dt^2}$ when $t = 3$.
      Find the value of s in terms of t if $s = 0$ when $t = 0$.

9　(a) If $f(x) = x^2 - 3x$ find the value of

$$\lim_{x \to 0} \frac{f(x + \delta x) - f(x)}{\delta x}$$

   (b) Find the values of a and b if $y = ax^2 + bx + 2$ give n that when $x = 1, y = 4$
      and $\dfrac{dy}{dx} = 5$

10　(a) If $f(x) = 2x^2 + 1$, find the value of

$$\lim_{h \to 0} \frac{f(x + h) - f(x)}{h}$$

   (b) Derive the equation of the tangent to the curve $y = 2x^2 + 1$ at the point
      where $x = -1$

11　(a) If $y = x^4$ prove that $3x^3 \dfrac{dy}{dx} = y \dfrac{d^2y}{dx^2}$

   (b) Show that $\dfrac{d}{dx}\left(x^3 \dfrac{dy}{dx}\right) = 3x^2 \dfrac{dy}{dx} + x^3 \dfrac{d^2y}{dx^2}$ when $y = x^3 - 3x$

12　(a) i　Write down the first four terms of the expansion of $(1 + x)^n$
      ii　Hence expand completely $(1 + 2x)^3$
      iii　By differentiating the expansion of $(1 + 2x)^3$ show that

$$\frac{d}{dx}(1 + 2x)^3 = 6(1 + 2x)^2$$

   (b) If $y = 3x^2 + 6x$ find expressions for $\dfrac{dy}{dx}$ and $\dfrac{d^2y}{dx^2}$

      Hence show, by substitution, that $x^2 \dfrac{d^2y}{dx^2} = 2\left(x \dfrac{dy}{dx} - y\right)$

D.T.C.

8 Applications of differentiation

8a Rates of change

Suppose we are considering the motion of a stone falling freely. We define its velocity as the distance travelled divided by the time it takes, and this gives its average velocity for that time interval.

If the stone falls 78·4 m in 4 seconds we say that its average velocity for the 4 seconds is 19·6 m/s. This does not mean that each second the stone travelled 19·6 m. Its velocity is changing and would be found to increase each second of its fall.

If we want to find the actual velocity of the stone at any particular instant in time during its fall, we have to measure the distance moved in as short a time as our instruments allow. In the previous chapter we used the notation $\dfrac{\delta y}{\delta x}$ for the $\dfrac{\text{increase in } y}{\text{increase in } x}$. Using this same notation, let δs represent the distance moved by the stone in a small time interval δt.

Then the average velocity $= \dfrac{\delta s}{\delta t}$

The shorter the time interval the more accurately would this average velocity give the actual velocity of the stone at the instant we require the velocity.

Thus the velocity at the particular instant we are considering is the limit of the average velocity as the time interval approaches zero. This is given by

$$\lim_{\delta t \to 0} \frac{\delta s}{\delta t} = \frac{ds}{dt}$$

and this is known as the *instantaneous velocity*.

If the distance s the stone falls in a time t is given by the formula

$s = 4\cdot9t^2$ where s is in metres
and t is in seconds

then the velocity in m/s at any time t is given by

$$v = \frac{ds}{dt} = 9\cdot8t$$

The velocity at the end of 1 s $= 9 \cdot 8 \times 1 = 9 \cdot 8$ m/s.
The velocity at the end of 2 s $= 9 \cdot 8 \times 2 = 19 \cdot 6$ m/s.
The velocity at the end of 4 s $= 9 \cdot 8 \times 4 = 39 \cdot 2$ m/s.

If we draw the graph of distance and time, then the velocity at any instant is given by the gradient of the graph at the corresponding point.

Figure
86

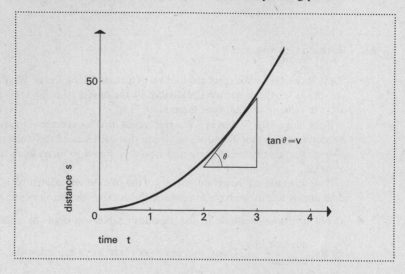

Acceleration

The acceleration of a body is the rate of change of velocity with respect to time. We find the average acceleration over a time interval by dividing the change in velocity by the time taken.

If v represents the velocity acquired in a time t the average acceleration $= \dfrac{\delta v}{\delta t}$ in the time interval δt and the acceleration at any instant is given by $\dfrac{dv}{dt}$.

If a velocity-time graph is drawn the acceleration at any instant is given by the value of the gradient of the tangent at that point.

velocity $\qquad v = \dfrac{ds}{dt}$

acceleration $f = \dfrac{dv}{dt} = \dfrac{d^2 s}{dt^2}$

Example 1 The distance s metres moved by a body in a time t seconds is given by the formula

$$s = t^3 - 3t^2 + 4t$$

180   Application of differentiation

Find the formulae for the velocity and acceleration at any instant in time and give their values after $t = 3$.

velocity $\quad v = \dfrac{ds}{dt} = 3t^2 - 6t + 4$

acceleration $f = \dfrac{dv}{dt} = 6t - 6$

When $t = 3$, velocity $= 3(3)^2 - 6(3) + 4 = 13$ m s^{-1}
 acceleration $= 6(3) - 6 = 12$ m s^{-2}

Other rates of change

If we have a quantity y which depends on and varies with a quantity x then, as y increases from y to $y + \delta y$ when x increases from x to $x + \delta x$, the rate of increase of y with respect to x is $\dfrac{\delta y}{\delta x}$.

This is an average rate over the interval δx.

$\dfrac{dy}{dx}$ gives the rate of increase of y with respect to x at the value x.

 x and y can be used to represent physical quantities other than time and distance, as will be seen from the examples and exercises that follow.

 Note that a rate of increase with respect to time is generally called 'the rate of increase', the phrase 'with respect to time' being dropped.

Example 2 The electrical resistance R of a wire at a temperature θ °C is given by $R = R_0(1 + a.\theta + b.\theta^2)$ where a and b are constants and R_0 is the resistance at 0 °C.

 Find the rate at which the resistance changes with temperature at 100 °C for a wire of resistance 200 ohm at 0 °C if $a = 0.0037$ and $b = 0.000\,006$ for the material of the wire.

$R = R_0(1 + a.\theta + b.\theta^2)$

Rate of change of resistance with respect to temperature

$= \dfrac{dR}{d\theta} = R_0(a + 2b\theta)$

At $\theta = 100$ °C $\quad \dfrac{dR}{d\theta} = 200(0.0037 + 2 \times 0.000\,006 \times 100)$

$= 0.98$ ohms per °C rise

Example 3 The area of a pool under a leaking water pipe is given by $A = 2t + \frac{t^2}{8}$ cm² where t is the time in minutes. Find the area and the rate it is growing after 10 minutes.

Area $A = 2t + \frac{t^2}{8}$

When $t = 10$, $A = 2 \times 10 + \frac{10^2}{8} = 32\frac{1}{2}$ cm²

Rate of increase of area $= \frac{dA}{dt} = 2 + \frac{t}{4}$ cm²/min

When $t = 10$, $\frac{dA}{dt} = 2 + \frac{10}{4} = 4\frac{1}{2}$ cm²/min

Example 4 The angle θ radians that a rotating wheel has turned after a time t seconds is given by

$$\theta = 50t - \frac{t^2}{4}$$

Find formulae for the angular velocity in rad/s and the angular acceleration in rad/s² in terms of the time t.

Show that the wheel has a constant retardation and find the angular velocity after 10 s and the total revolutions made by the wheel in that time.

Average angular velocity $= \dfrac{\text{increase in angle}}{\text{time taken}} = \dfrac{\delta\theta}{\delta t}$

Angular velocity at any instant $= \dfrac{d\theta}{dt}$

$$\theta = 50t - \frac{t^2}{4}$$

Angular velocity $w = \dfrac{d\theta}{dt} = 50 - \dfrac{t}{2}$ rad/s

Angular acceleration is the rate of change of angular velocity

$$= \frac{dw}{dt} = -\tfrac{1}{2} \text{ rad/s}^2$$

This is constant and is negative showing that the wheel is slowing down with a constant retardation of $\frac{1}{2}$ rad/s².

After 10 s angular velocity $w = 50 - \dfrac{10}{2} = 45$ rad/s

Angle wheel has turned through in 10 s

$$= \theta = 50 \times 10 - \frac{10^2}{4} = 475 \text{ radians}$$

1 revolution $= 2\pi$ radians
∴ total number of revolutions made by wheel in 10 s

$$= \frac{475}{2\pi} \text{ rev} = 75{\cdot}6 \text{ rev}$$

Exercise 8a

1   A body is moving along a straight line and its distance s metres from a fixed point on the line after a time t seconds is given by $s = 40t - 3t^2 + \frac{1}{3}t^3$. Find
    (a) its velocity after t seconds
    (b) its velocity at the start and after 3 seconds
    (c) its acceleration after t seconds and after 2 seconds
    (d) the distance travelled in the third second
    (e) the average velocity over the third second.

2   If the distance s metres a body moves after t seconds is given by $s = 120t - 16t^2$ find
    (a) its velocity after 2 seconds
    (b) its acceleration after 2 seconds
    (c) the time when the velocity is zero
    (d) the distance the body has travelled before coming to rest
    (e) the velocity after 5 seconds, and explain the significance of the sign of the velocity.

3   (a) The area of a circle is given by $A = \pi r^2$. Find the rate of change of area with respect to the radius.
    (b) The volume of a sphere is given by $V = \frac{4}{3}\pi r^3$. Find the rate of change of volume with respect to the radius.
    (c) If $y = x^5$ find the rate of change of y with respect to x.
    (d) If the pressure p and volume v of a given mass of gas are linked by a relationship of the form $pv = k$ where k is a constant, show that

    i the rate of change of pressure with respect to the volume $= -\dfrac{k}{v^2}$

    and ii the rate of change of volume with regard to the pressure $= -\dfrac{k}{p^2}$

4   The depth of water h cm in a tank at a time t minutes is given by

$$h = 4 + 5t - \frac{t^2}{8}$$

Find the rates at which the level is rising after 2 min and 10 min.

183   Rates of change

5   If the length of a rod of metal is given by the formula

$$L = 100 + 0 \cdot 002\theta - 0 \cdot 000\,003\theta^2$$

where θ °C is the temperature of the rod, find the rate at which the length changes with respect to temperature when the temperature is 80 °C.

6   The angle θ in radians which a wheel turns through in t seconds is given by the formula

$$\theta = 60t - \frac{t^2}{3}$$

Find the angular velocity at the start and after 2 seconds.
Show that the wheel has a constant retardation and find the time for it to come to rest.
How many revolutions will it have made in this time?

7   A pit is being dug by a party of men such that the volume V in cubic metres removed after t hours is given by $V = 10t - \dfrac{t^2}{3}$

Find the rate the soil is being removed in cubic metres per minute after 3 hours.

8   If the formula relating distance s travelled by a body in a time t is $s = 3t - \dfrac{3t^2}{2}$

show that the body is travelling twice as fast when $t = 3$ as when $t = 0$ but in the opposite direction.

9   If $y = \dfrac{x^3}{3} - 4x$ show that the rate of increase of y with respect to x when $x = 4$ is three times the rate of decrease when $x = 0$.
For what value of x is the rate of decrease equal to 3?

10 If the air resistance R N to a body moving with velocity v m s^{-1} is given by $R = \dfrac{v^3}{100}$, find the velocity when the rate of increase of resistance with respect to velocity is 12 N m^{-1}s

11 The distance s metres travelled by a body falling freely from rest under a gravitational acceleration of $9 \cdot 8$ m s^{-2} is given by $s = 4 \cdot 9t^2$ where t is the time in seconds.
(a) Find a formula for the velocity after t seconds.
(b) Find the velocity after 2 seconds.
(c) How long does the body take to fall 490 m?
(d) What is its velocity after falling 490 m?

12 A stone is thrown vertically upwards and its height h metres above the ground
    after t seconds is given by $h = 5(10t - t^2)$, approximately.
    (a) Find a formula for its velocity after t seconds.
    (b) What is its velocity after 2 seconds and 6 seconds and explain the signifi-
        cance of the signs of the velocities?
    (c) With what velocity was it thrown up?
    (d) What is its velocity at the top of its flight and when does this occur?
    (e) Find the greatest height reached by the stone and show that it reaches the
        ground again after 10 seconds.

8b Tangents and normals

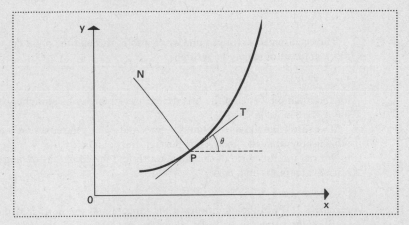

Figure
87

The normal at any point on a curve is the line which passes through the point
and is at right angles to the tangent.

In fig. 87 PT is the tangent at point P on the curve and PN is the normal.

If θ is the angle the tangent makes with the positive direction of the x axis
then the gradient of the tangent

$$\tan \theta = \frac{dy}{dx} \text{ for the point } P$$

We show earlier in the section on parallel lines and perpendicular lines
(page 139) that if two lines are at right angles then the product of their gradients
is -1.

Thus the gradient of the normal $= \dfrac{-1}{\dfrac{dy}{dx}}$

where the value of $\dfrac{dy}{dx}$ is its value at point P.

Example 1 Find the values of the gradients of the tangent and normal to the curve $y = x^3 - 5x + 3$ at the point $(2, 1)$.

$$y = x^3 - 5x + 3$$

$$\frac{dy}{dx} = 3x^2 - 5$$

At the point $(2, 1)$ $\frac{dy}{dx} = 3(2)^2 - 5 = 7$

$\therefore$ gradient of tangent $= 7$

and gradient of normal $= -\frac{1}{7}$

The equation of a straight line which passes through the point (x_1, y_1) and has a gradient of m may be written

$$y - y_1 = m(x - x_1)$$

for the equation, being of the first degree, must represent a straight line and it has a gradient of m.

If we substitute the co-ordinates x_1 for x and y_1 for y the equation is satisfied which shows that the line passes through the point (x_1, y_1).

We can use this form of the equation to find the equations of tangent and normal at a point on a curve.

Example 2 Find the equations of the tangent and the normal at the point $(2, 0)$ on the curve $y = x^2 - 2x$.

$$y = x^2 - 2x$$

$$\frac{dy}{dx} = 2x - 2$$

At the point $(2, 0)$ $\frac{dy}{dx} = 2 \times 2 - 2 = 2 =$ gradient m of tangent

Using the formula $y - y_1 = m(x - x_1)$ we have
equation of tangent is $y - 0 = 2(x - 2)$
i.e. $y = 2x - 4$

For the normal the value of m the gradient $= -\frac{1}{2}$
$\therefore$ equation of normal is $y - 0 = -\frac{1}{2}(x - 2)$
i.e. $y = -\frac{1}{2}x + 1$
or $x + 2y = 2$

Exercise 8b

For the following curves at the points given find
(a) the gradients of the tangents and the normals
(b) the equations of the tangents and the normals.

1   $y = x^2$ at the point $(1, 1)$

2   $y = 2x^2 - 3x$ at the point $(1, -1)$

3   $y = \dfrac{x^3}{3}$ at the point $(-1, -\frac{1}{3})$

4   $y = 1 + x - x^2$ at the point $(2, -1)$

5   $y = \dfrac{1}{x}$ at the point $(2, \frac{1}{2})$

8c   Maxima and minima

Consider the value of $\dfrac{dy}{dx}$ at various points on the curve shown in fig. 88.

Figure 88

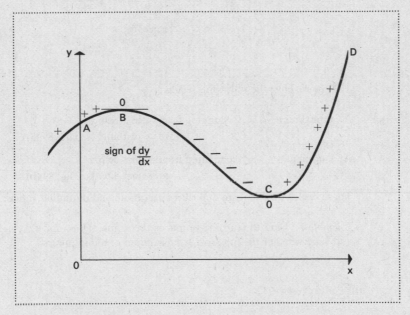

In the section from A to B the gradient of the curve is $+$ and y increases as x increases.

As we move along the curve to B the value of the gradient gradually becomes smaller and at B it is zero.

i.e. $\dfrac{dy}{dx} = 0$ at B

After B the gradient is $-$ and y decreases as x increases until point C is reached where again $\dfrac{dy}{dx}$ is zero.

From C onwards the gradient is $+$ and y increases again.

Points B and C on the graph are called *turning points*.

The value of y at B is greater than its value at neighbouring points at either side and y is said to be a *maximum* at this point.

Similarly at C the value of y is less than that at neighbouring points on either side and y is said to have a *minimum* value at C.

Figure 89

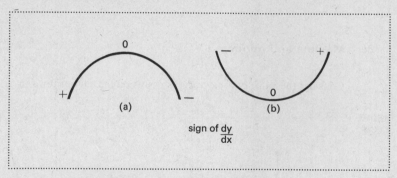

(a)

(b)

sign of $\dfrac{dy}{dx}$

Thus we have the following results:

At a maximum $\dfrac{dy}{dx} = 0$ changing from $+$ just before
to $-$ just after (see fig. 89 (a)).

At a minimum $\dfrac{dy}{dx} = 0$ changing from $-$ just before
to $+$ just after (see fig. 89 (b)).

These results enable us to determine maximum and minimum values.

Example 1 Find the turning points on the graph of $y = 2x^3 + 3x^2 - 12x - 4$ and state whether the function is a maximum or a minimum.

$y = 2x^3 + 3x^2 - 12x - 4$

$\dfrac{dy}{dx} = 6x^2 + 6x - 12$

At a turning point $\dfrac{dy}{dx} = 0$ i.e. $6x^2 + 6x - 12 = 0$

$$6(x^2 + x - 2) = 0$$
$$6(x-1)(x+2) = 0$$
$$\therefore \qquad\qquad x = 1 \text{ or } -2$$

At $\qquad\qquad x = 1, y = 2.1^3 + 3.1^2 - 12.1 - 4 = -11$

At $\qquad\qquad x = -2, y = 2(-2)^3 + 3(-2)^2 - 12(-2) - 4 = 16$

These are turning points; we now have to see how the sign of $\dfrac{dy}{dx}$ varies on each side of the turning points.

Consider the point $(1, -11)$

If x is slightly less than 1, $(x-1)$ is negative and $(x+2)$ is positive.

$\therefore \dfrac{dy}{dx} = 6(x-1)(x+2)$ is negative

If x is slightly greater than 1, $(x-1)$ is positive and $(x+2)$ is positive.

$\therefore \dfrac{dy}{dx}$ is positive

Hence as x increases through the value 1, $\dfrac{dy}{dx}$ changes sign from $-$ to $+$. Its shape is $-\ \cup\ +$.

Figure
90

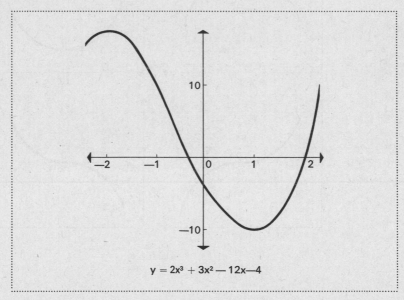

$y = 2x^3 + 3x^2 - 12x - 4$

Therefore the point $(1, -11)$ is a minimum point and $y = -11$ is a minimum value.

Consider the point $(-2, 16)$

When x is slightly less than -2, $(x+2)$ is negative and $(x-1)$ is negative.

$$\therefore \frac{dy}{dx} = (-) \times (-) = \text{positive}$$

When x is slightly greater than -2, $(x+2)$ is positive and $(x-1)$ is negative.

$$\therefore \frac{dy}{dx} = \text{negative}$$

Hence as x increases through the value -2, $\frac{dy}{dx}$ changes sign from $+$ to $-$, i.e. its shape is $+ \cap -$.

Therefore the point $(-2, 16)$ is a maximum point and $y = 16$ is a maximum value.

The graph of the function illustrates these results (fig. 90).

Figure
91

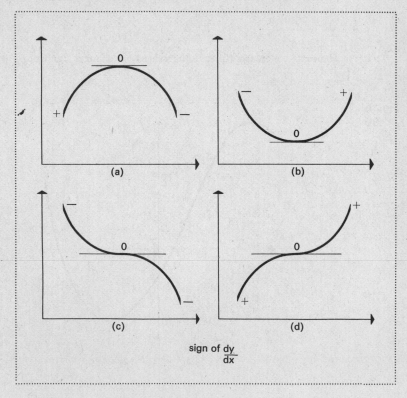

sign of $\frac{dy}{dx}$

Stationary points and turning points

A *stationary point* on a graph is any point where the gradient is zero. Since $\frac{dy}{dx}$ can be positive or negative on either side of a stationary point, there are four possibilities to consider. They are illustrated in fig. 91 (a) to (d). In cases (a) and (b) $\frac{dy}{dx}$ changes sign through the stationary point and these are the turning points we have considered, (a) being a maximum and (b) a minimum.

In cases (c) and (d) the values of y are stationary but they are not turning points. They are points where the curve changes its curvature, from concave on one side to convex and they are known as *points of contraflexure or inflexion.* $\frac{dy}{dx}$ is not necessarily zero at a point of contraflexure.

The use of $\frac{d^2y}{dx^2}$ to distinguish between maxima and minima

Figure
92

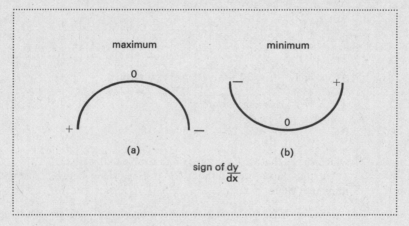

In passing through a maximum $\frac{dy}{dx}$ changes from $+$ to $-$ through zero and is therefore decreasing.

Thus the rate of change of $\frac{dy}{dx}$ as x increases is negative.

i.e. $\frac{d}{dx}\left(\frac{dy}{dx}\right) = \frac{d^2y}{dx^2}$ is $-$ at a maximum

In passing through a minimum $\frac{dy}{dx}$ changes from $-$ through zero to $+$ and is therefore increasing.

Its rate of change with respect to x is thus positive.

i.e. $\dfrac{d^2y}{dx^2}$ is $+$ at a minimum

This gives us a second test for deciding whether a stationary point is a maximum or a minimum.

If $\dfrac{dy}{dx} = 0$ and $\dfrac{d^2y}{dx^2}$ is $\begin{Bmatrix} \text{positive} \\ \text{negative} \end{Bmatrix}$ at $x = a$, then y is a $\begin{Bmatrix} \text{minimum} \\ \text{maximum} \end{Bmatrix}$ for this value of x

where the upper words or the lower words are taken together.

In example 1 worked out above, the turning points of $y = 2x^3 + 3x^2 - 12x - 4$ were at $x = 1$ and $x = -2$.

To investigate their nature we have only to find the sign of $\dfrac{d^2y}{dx^2}$ at these points.

As $\dfrac{dy}{dx} = 6x^2 + 6x - 12$

then $\dfrac{d^2y}{dx^2} = 12x + 6$

At $x = 1, \dfrac{d^2y}{dx^2} = 12 + 6 = 18$ which is positive

$\therefore$ $x = 1$ gives a minimum value.

At $x = -2, \dfrac{d^2y}{dx^2} = 12(-2) + 6 = -18$

which shows that we have a maximum value at this point.

We thus have two methods for distinguishing between maximum and minimum values.

For simple functions the second test involving $\dfrac{d^2y}{dx^2}$ is easier to apply than the first method which is that of examining the sign of $\dfrac{dy}{dx}$ as x goes through the stationary point. In some cases, however, the calculation of $\dfrac{d^2y}{dx^2}$ may involve much work and the first method is to be preferred.

Again it may happen that $\dfrac{d^2y}{dx^2} = 0$. In this case the nature of the stationary value must be decided by the first method.

Example 2   Find the turning points on the curve $y = 2x^3 + x^2 - 4x + 2$ and distinguish between them.

$$y = 2x^3 + x^2 - 4x + 2$$

$$\frac{dy}{dx} = 6x^2 + 2x - 4$$

$$= 2(3x - 2)(x + 1)$$

At a turning point $\dfrac{dy}{dx} = 0$

$\therefore \qquad 2(3x - 2)(x + 1) = 0$

$\therefore \qquad\qquad x = \frac{2}{3}$ or -1

At $\ x = \frac{2}{3}, y = 2(\frac{2}{3})^3 + (\frac{2}{3})^2 - 4(\frac{2}{3}) + 2 = \frac{10}{27}$
At $\ x = -1, y = 2(-1)^3 + (-1)^2 - 4(-1) + 2 = 5$

$$\frac{d^2y}{dx^2} = 12x + 2$$

At $\ x = \frac{2}{3}, \dfrac{d^2y}{dx^2} = 10 \quad \therefore$ a minimum point.

At $\ x = -1, \dfrac{d^2y}{dx^2} = -10 \quad \therefore$ a maximum point.

Thus when $\ x = \frac{2}{3}, y = \frac{10}{27}$ and is a minimum
and when $\ x = -1, y = 5$ and is a maximum.

Exercise 8c

Find the turning points of the curves in questions 1–4 and, for each point, decide whether the function is a maximum or a minimum by examining the sign change of $\dfrac{dy}{dx}$

1 $\ y = x^2 - 3x$ 　　　　　　2 $\ y = x^2 - 4x + 3$

3 $\ y = x^3 - x$ 　　　　　　4 $\ y = 3 + 3x^2 - x^3$

In questions 5–14, determine the maximum and minimum values.

5 $\ y = x + \dfrac{1}{x}$ 　　　　　　6 $\ y = x^3 + x^2$

7 $\ y = \dfrac{(x-1)(x-4)}{x}$ 　　　　8 $\ y = x^4$

9 $\ y = x + 2 + \dfrac{1}{x}$ 　　　　10 $\ y = 2x^3 - 15x^2 + 24x + 4$

11 $\ y = 3 + 12x + 3x^2 - 2x^3$ 　　12 $\ xy = 4x^2 + 1$

13    $A = t^2 + 8 - t$ 14 $A = 2l^2 + \dfrac{32}{l}$

15   The bending moment M of a beam of length l at a distance x from one énd is given by

$$M = \frac{wlx}{2} - \frac{wx^2}{2}$$

where w is the load per unit length.

Find the maximum bending moment and show that it occurs at the centre of the beam.

16   Find the stationary values of the curve $y = 2x^3 - x^6$ and investigate their nature.

8d   Problems involving maxima and minima

If we have to find the maximum or minimum value of a quantity which depends on one variable we can do this straight away by the methods of the previous section.

Example 1   An open box is to be made from a rectangular sheet of metal 16 by 6 units. Equal squares are cut from each of the corners and the sides are bent up to form the box. Find the dimensions of the box for it to have maximum volume.

Figure
93

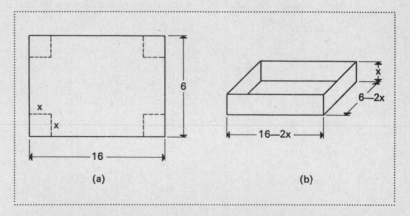

(a)   (b)

Let x be the sides of the squares removed from each corner of the sheet of metal.

The dimensions of the box will then be as shown in fig. 93.

Volume $V = (16-2x)(6-2x)x$

i.e. $\qquad V = 96x - 44x^2 + 4x^3$

$$\frac{dV}{dx} = 96 - 88x + 12x^2$$

If V is a maximum $\quad \dfrac{dV}{dx} = 0$

$\therefore \qquad 12x^2 - 88x + 96 = 0$

$\qquad\qquad 4(3x^2 - 22x + 24) = 0$

$\qquad\qquad 4(3x-4)(x-6) = 0$

$\qquad\qquad\qquad\qquad x = \frac{4}{3} \text{ or } 6$

$$\frac{d^2V}{dx^2} = -88 + 24x$$

When $x = \frac{4}{3}, \dfrac{d^2V}{dx^2} = -56 \quad \therefore V$ is a maximum at $x = \frac{4}{3}$

$x = 6$ is clearly inapplicable to the problem and gives no solution.

Taking $x = \frac{4}{3}$ then the dimensions of the box are $13\frac{1}{3}$ by $3\frac{1}{3}$ by $1\frac{1}{3}$ units deep.

In some problems we have to find the maximum or minimum value of a quantity which depends on two variables. In such cases a relationship between the two variables must exist, so enabling one to express the quantity involved in terms of one variable only.

Example 2 A wire 60 cm long is to be bent to form a rectangle. Find the lengths of the sides so that the area is as large as possible.

Let the sides of the rectangle by x cm and y cm.
Then area $A = xy$.

Here the quantity A depends on two variables x and y.
The fact that the perimeter is 60 cm gives us a relation between x and y and enables us to put y in terms of x.

$$\text{Perimeter} = 60 = 2x + 2y$$
$$x + y = 30$$
$$y = 30 - x$$

Substituting this in $\qquad A = xy$

we have $\qquad\qquad A = x(30-x) = 30x - x^2$

$\therefore \qquad\qquad\qquad \dfrac{dA}{dx} = 30 - 2x$

When A is a maximum $\quad \dfrac{dA}{dx} = 0$

$$30 - 2x = 0$$
$$x = 15$$

Also $\dfrac{d^2A}{dx^2} = -2$ so that the value is a maximum.

Hence for maximum area $x = 15$ cm and $y = 15$ cm and the wire is formed into a square.

Exercise 8d

1   If $x + y = 4$, find the least value of $x^2 + y^2$.

2   If the sum of two numbers is 8, find the least value of the sum of their squares.

3   If $2x + 3y = 8$, find the greatest value of xy.

4   If the sum of the height and base radius of a cylinder is to be 15 cm, find a a formula for the volume of the cylinder in terms of the radius. Find the dimensions if the volume is to be a maximum.

5   If the drag D on an aeroplane is given by

$$D = \frac{a}{q} + bq$$

where q is the variable depending on the velocity, and a and b are constants, find the minimum value of the drag.

6   The blade efficiency E of a particular turbine in terms of the blade speed u is given by the formula

$$E = \frac{2u(V - u)(1 + \cos \theta)}{V^2}$$

where V is the fixed velocity of the jet and θ is a constant for the blade.
Obtain the value of u for maximum efficiency and find this efficiency.

7   A closed box is to have a volume of 72 cm^3 and the length of the base is to be twice the depth.
Find the dimensions of the box so that the surface area shall be a minimum.

8   A post office regulation stated that the combined length and girth (distance round the middle) of a parcel for posting must not exceed 6 units.
If the cross-section of a parcel is a square of side x, find x and the volume of the parcel for the volume to be a maximum.

9   A closed tank with a square base of side x metres is to be made from sheet metal of total area 30 m^2.
Find the volume in terms of x. Hence find the largest possible volume of the tank.

10 A gardener has 100 metres of fencing which he uses to form three sides of a rectangular plot, whose fourth side is a long wall.

   If the fencing encloses the maximum possible area, what are the dimensions of the enclosed plot?

11 A rectangular crate with a square base and no lid is to be built so that its surface area is 100 m^2.

   Find its dimensions so that it will have the largest possible volume.

8e Small changes

If y is a function of x and we wish to find the approximate change in y corresponding to a small change δx in x we can use the result that

$$\frac{\delta y}{\delta x} \simeq \frac{dy}{dx}$$

or $\delta y \simeq \dfrac{dy}{dx} \times \delta x$

Example 1 If $y = 3x^2 - x$ find the approximate change in y if x changes from 2 to 2·03

$$y = 3x^2 - x$$

$$\frac{dy}{dx} = 6x - 1$$

Approximate change in $y = \delta y \simeq \dfrac{dy}{dx} \times \delta x$

$$\simeq (6x - 1)\delta x$$

When $x = 2$ and $\delta x = 0.03$

$$\delta y \simeq (6.2 - 1)\,0.03$$
$$\simeq 11 \times 0.03 \simeq 0.33$$

Note that the exact value of δy may be obtained by working out the value of y when $x = 2.03$

Thus $\delta y = \{3(2.03)^2 - 2.03\} - \{3(2)^2 - 2\}$
       $= 10.3327 - 10 = 0.3327$

Example 2 Find the possible error in calculating the area of a circle whose radius is found to be 8 cm, with a possible error in measurement of $\pm \frac{1}{50}$ cm.

In this problem we have a change δr of $\frac{1}{50}$ cm in radius r and we require δA the change in area.

197 Small changes

$$A = \pi r^2 \qquad \frac{dA}{dr} = 2\pi r$$

$$\delta A \simeq \frac{dA}{dr}.\delta r$$

$$\simeq 2\pi r.\delta r$$

When $r = 8$ and $\delta r = \frac{1}{50}$
then $\delta A \simeq 2\pi \times 8 \times \frac{1}{50}$

$$\simeq \frac{16\pi}{50} \simeq 1{\cdot}0054$$

The possible error in the area $= 1{\cdot}005 \text{ cm}^2$ approx.

The percentage error $\simeq \dfrac{16\pi}{50 \times \pi.8^2} \times 100 = \frac{1}{2}$

The error is approximately $\frac{1}{2}\%$

Exercise 8e

1   If $y = 2x^2$ find the approximate change in y if x changes from 6 to 6·03.

2   Find the change in y if x changes from 4 to 4·02
    (a) when $y = x - x^2$
    (b) when $y = \dfrac{4}{x}$

3   The sides of a cube are x metres. Find the approximate increase in
    (a) the volume
    (b) the surface area
    if the side x increases from 2 metres to 2·03 metres.

4   The radius of a sphere decreases from 3 cm to 2·98 cm. Find
    (a) the approximate change in surface area
    (b) the approximate change in volume.

5   The time of swing of a pendulum is given by $T = k\sqrt{l}$ where T is a constant. Find the percentage change in the time of swing if the length of the pendulum changes from 39·1 to 39·0.

6   The pressure p and volume v of a mass of gas are related by the formula $pv = 40$. If the pressure increases from 30 to 30·5, find the approximate change in the volume of the gas.

Miscellaneous exercises 8

1   (a) Derive from first principles the differential coefficient of $\dfrac{4}{x^2}$ with respect to x.

   (b) Find the co-ordinates of the turning points on the curve $y = x^3 - 2x^2 + x + 3$. Distinguish between the maximum and the minimum points.

   D.T.C.

2   (a) From first principles differentiate with respect to x the function $y = 2x^2 + 1$.

   (b) Use the standard rules to differentiate the following with respect to x

   (i) $5x^2 + 2x - 3$ (ii) $\sqrt{x} - \dfrac{1}{\sqrt{x}}$ (iii) $x(1 - 4x^{-2})$

   (c) Find the length of the sides of an equilateral triangle whose area increases at the rate of 15 cm^2 per cm increase in its side.

3   A body moves along a straight line in such a way that its distance S metres from its starting point at the end of t seconds is given by

   $$S = 6t^2 - 2t + 3$$

   Find
   (a) the distance it travels from 5 seconds to 5·6 seconds
   (b) the average speed during the same interval
   (c) the velocity when t is 7 seconds
   (d) the acceleration.

4   The relationship between the displacement x metres and the time t seconds of a moving body is $x = 2t^3 - 9t^2 + 12t + 4$. Find
   (a) when it comes to rest
   (b) when its acceleration is zero
   (c) the velocity when the acceleration is zero
   (d) the acceleration when the velocity is zero.

5   A body moves through a distance s metres in t seconds where

   $$s = 15 + 8t + 9t^2 - t^3$$

   Find by means of the calculus
   (a) its velocity at the end of 3 s
   (b) its acceleration at the end of 2·5 s
   (c) the value of t when the velocity is 23 m s^{-1}
   (d) the value of t when the velocity is zero
   (e) the value of t when the acceleration is zero.

6   (a) Differentiate $3x^2$ from first principles.

(b) Find $\dfrac{dy}{dx}$ in the following cases

i $y = x^3 - 3x + 2$ ii $y = \dfrac{1}{x^3} - \dfrac{3}{x}$ iii $y = x^{\frac{4}{3}}$

(c) Find the maximum and minimum values of the expression $x^3 - 6x^2 + 9x + 4$.

D.T.C.

7   (a) Find the co-ordinates of the point on the curve $y = 3x - x^2$, where the gradient is 1. Find also the gradient of the curve at the origin. Sketch the curve.

- (b) Find the maximum and minimum values of the function $y = 5 - 3x + x^3$ and sketch the curve.

N.C.T.E.C.

8   A particle P moves along a straight line. At time t seconds its velocity is v m/s and its distance from a fixed point in the line is x metres.

Given that $v = 2t + \dfrac{1}{t^2}$, find

(a) the distance travelled by P in the fourth second
(b) the acceleration when $t = 2$
(c) the minimum velocity of P.

9   (a) Differentiate with respect to x

$$3x^{\frac{4}{3}} + x^{-\frac{1}{2}} + 5x^{1\cdot2} + 4$$

(b) A flywheel rotates according to the law $\theta = 28t - 3t^2$, θ giving the angular rotation in radians taking place in t seconds. Find expressions for the angular velocity $\left(\dfrac{d\theta}{dt}\right)$ and the angular acceleration $\left(\dfrac{d^2\theta}{dt^2}\right)$. What is the value of t when $\dfrac{d\theta}{dt} = 0$? Find the value of θ for this value of t.

U.L.C.I.

10   Find the maximum and minimum values of the expression

$$x^3 - x^2 - 8x + 12$$

Distinguish between these values.
    Draw very carefully the graph of

$$y = x^3 - x^2 - 8x + 12$$

from $x = -4$ to $x = +4$, taking 2 cm as the unit for x and 0·2 cm as the unit for y.

11   (a) The depth h cm of water in a tank at a time t min is given by

$$h = 10 + 6t - \frac{t^2}{4}$$

Find the rates at which the level is rising after 1 min and after 8 min.

(b) A prism has a square base of side x cm and has a height of 8 cm. Find its volume in terms of x and find $\dfrac{dV}{dx}$.

If x changes from 4 to 3·98 cm, what is the approximate change in V?

12   (a) A body is thrown vertically upwards and its equation of motion is

$$S = 120t - 16t^2$$

where S is the distance travelled and t the time.

Find (i) the velocity of the body when $t = 3$, (ii) the time taken to reach its greatest height.

(b) Find the dimensions of the largest rectangular piece of ground that can be enclosed by 240 hurdles each 5 m long, if an existing fence is utilized to form one side.

13   (a) A point moves along a straight line so that its distance s metres from a fixed point at time t seconds is given by $s = 3·5 - 4t + 16t^2 - t^3$. Find its velocity and acceleration at the end of $3s$.

(b) The power W given to an external circuit by a generator of internal resistance r and e.m.f. E, when the current is I is $W = IE - I^2 r$. Find for what current the power is a maximum when $E = 24$ V and $r = 1·8\Omega$. Calculate the value of the power when the current has this value.

14   An open metal tank with a square base is to contain 108 m³ of liquid. Taking the side of the base as x metres show that the total surface area A of metal is given by $A = x^2 + \dfrac{432}{x}$. Find the dimensions of the tank for a minimum surface area.

15   If $y = x^3 + 6x^2 - 15x + 20$, find the slope of the curve when $x = 2$ and also the co-ordinates of the turning points of the curve.

U.L.C.I.

16   (a) Find the values of a and b if $y = ax^3 + bx$, given that when $x = 0·5$, $y = 2$ and $\dfrac{dy}{dx} = 6$

(b) Find the co-ordinates of the turning points on the curve $y = 27x - x^3$. Distinguish between the maximum and minimum points.

D.T.C.

17   The cost per hour of running a ship at a speed of v is £ $\left(9 + \dfrac{v^3}{2058}\right)$

Find an expression for the total cost of a voyage of distance 3000 units covered at a speed v. By differentiation, find the speed which makes this total cost a minimum, testing that the value you have obtained is a minimum and not a maximum.

18   (a) Find the differential coefficient of $2x^3$ from first principles.
(b) The displacement s of a body moving in a straight line is given at time t by

$$s = 160t - 16t^2$$

Show by differentiation that it moves with constant retardation and describe briefly the way in which the body moves from $t = 0$ to $t = 10$.

9 Mensuration

9a The circle

Many of the following relationships will be familiar to the student. Some have already been proved in the section on degrees and radians (page 68).

r = radius, d = diameter, and in working out examples we take the value of π to be 3·1416.

Figure 94

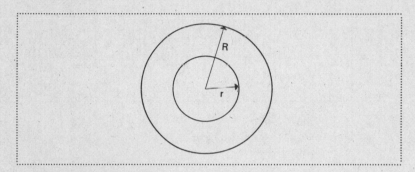

(a) *Circumference of circle* $= 2\pi r = \pi d$

(b) *Area of circle* $\doteq \pi r^2 = \dfrac{\pi d^2}{4}$

(c) *Area of circular annulus* (see fig. 94)

= area between two concentric circles
$= \pi R^2 - \pi r^2$
$= \pi(R^2 - r^2)$
$= \pi(R+r)(R-r)$

(d) *Length of arc ABC* (see fig. 95)

$s = r\theta$ where θ radians is the angle subtended at the centre of the circle.

If the angle subtended at the centre is $\alpha°$ we convert it to radians by multiplying by $\dfrac{\pi}{180°}$ to give

$$\text{arc } s = \frac{r\pi\alpha°}{180°}$$

(e) *Area of a sector of a circle* A sector of a circle is the figure bounded by two radii and the arc between them. (See fig. 95.)

Figure 95

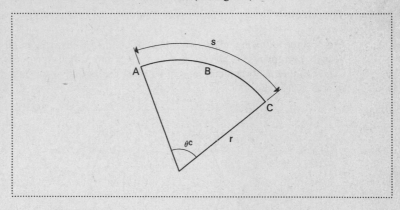

$$\text{area} = \tfrac{1}{2}r^2\theta$$

Since arc $s = r\theta$ we also have

$$\text{area} = \tfrac{1}{2}rs$$

(f) *Area of a segment of a circle* Consider the segment ABC in fig. 96 bounded by the arc ABC and the chord AC.

Figure 96

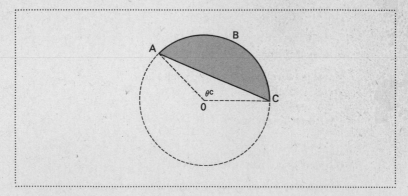

area = area of sector OAC − area of triangle OAC

$= \frac{1}{2}r^2\theta - \frac{1}{2}AO.CO \sin AOC$

$= \frac{1}{2}r^2\theta - \frac{1}{2}r^2 \sin \theta$

$= \frac{1}{2}r^2(\theta - \sin \theta)$

If the angle at the centre θ is given in degrees then again we convert to radians by multiplying by $\frac{\pi}{180°}$.

In looking up the sine of the angle, the conversion is not needed as the tables give trigonometric ratios for angles expressed in degrees.

(g) *A plane lune* is the area between two segments of circles having a common chord and on the same side of it.

Figure 97

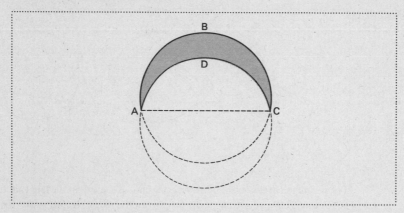

The area of the lune $ABCD$ can be found by calculating the areas of the two segments ABC and ADC and taking their difference (fig. 97).

Approximate formulae

There are many useful approximations for lengths of arcs and areas of segments in terms of chord distances.

Figure 98

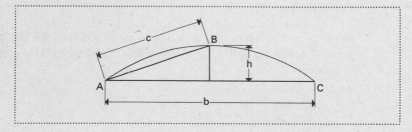

(a) Length of arc AC
$\qquad = \frac{1}{3}(8c - b)$ approx. (Huygens' rule)
$\qquad$ where $\quad c =$ chord of half the arc $= AB$
$\qquad$ and $\qquad b =$ chord of whole arc $= AC$

(b) Area of segment ABC

$\qquad$ i Area $= \dfrac{h(6b + 8c)}{15}$ approx. where $h =$ height of segment.

$\qquad$ ii Area $= \dfrac{h}{6b}(3h^2 + 4b^2)$ approx. (Newton's rules.)

Intersecting chords

Figure 99

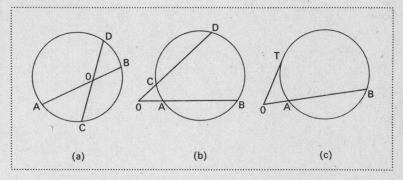

$\qquad$ (a) $\qquad\qquad\qquad\qquad$ (b) $\qquad\qquad\qquad\qquad$ (c)

The geometrical theorem of intersecting chords (based on the fact that triangles OAD and OCB are similar with proportionate sides, fig. 99) states that if two chords intersect either inside or outside a circle the product of the segments of one is equal to the product of the segments of the other.

$\qquad$ Thus referring to fig. 99 (a) and (b) we have

$$AO.OB = CO.OD$$

$\qquad$ Also if the chord CD rotates about O until C and D coincide at T and the chord becomes a tangent (see fig. 99 (c)), then

$$OA.OB = OT^2$$

Example 1 The height of a segment of a circle is 10 and the chord of the segment is 40. Find (a) the radius, (b) the length of the arc, (c) the area of the segment.

(a) By the intersecting chords property
$\qquad\qquad AD \times DC = BD.DE \quad$ (fig. 100)
$\qquad\qquad\quad 20 \times 20 = 10(2R - 10)$

$$\therefore \quad 2R-10 = \frac{400}{10} = 40$$

$$\therefore \text{ Radius } R = 25$$

Figure 100

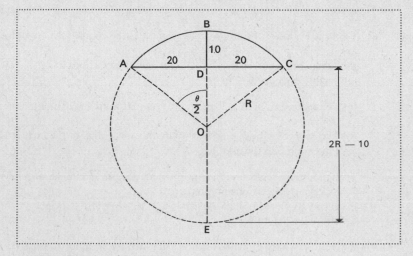

(b) If θ is the angle subtended by arc ABC at centre O then

$$\sin AOB = \sin \frac{\theta}{2} = \frac{AD}{AO} = \frac{20}{25} = \frac{4}{5}$$

From the tables $\quad \frac{\theta}{2} = 53°8' = 0.9274^c$

and $\qquad\qquad\quad \theta = 1.8548^c$

Length of $\quad$ arc $ABC = r\theta = 25 \times 1.8548 = 46.37$

(c) Area of segment = area of sector $OABC -$ area $\triangle OAC$

$$\begin{aligned} &= \tfrac{1}{2}R^2\theta - \tfrac{1}{2}AC \times DO \\ &= \tfrac{1}{2}\,25^2 \times 1.8548 - \tfrac{1}{2} \times 40 \times 15 \\ &= 579.7 - 300 \\ &= 279.7 \end{aligned}$$

Exercise 9a

1 The diameter of the piston of a steam engine is 28 cm and the mean steam pressure on it is 150 kN m^{-2}. Find the thrust on the piston.

2 A reservoir is supplied from a pipe 36 cm in diameter. How many pipes of 12 cm diameter would supply the same quantity assuming the velocity of flow to be the same?

3   The circumference of a circle is 50 m. Calculate its area.

4   A circle circumscribes a square. Compare their areas.

5   A square is inscribed in a circle of area 400 cm^2. Find the side of the square.

6   Find the radius of the circle if the height and the chord of an arc of the circle are
(a) height 1 m, chord 6 m   (b) height 3 m, chord 24 m
(c) height 5 m, chord 12 m

7   (a) The span of an arch is 30 m and the rise of the arch is 10 m. Find the radius of the arch.
(b) The span of a bridge arch is 70 m and the radius of the arch is $125\frac{1}{2}$ m. Find the rise in the middle.

8   Using Huygens' rule, find the approximate lengths of circular arcs having the following dimensions in metres
(a) chord 30, chord of half the arc 15·3   (b) chord 8, height 3
(c) chord 24, height 9.

9   Two circles whose radii are 1 m and 3 m touch one another externally. Find the length of a band that will just pass round them.

10   Calculate the areas of the circular segments having the following dimensions in metres
(a) radius 4, angle at centre 60°   (b) radius 5, angle at centre 30°
(c) radius 10, angle at centre 120°   (d) radius 10, angle at centre 240°
(e) radius 15, angle at centre 210°

11   The height of a segment of a circle is 3 cm and the chord is 8 cm. Find the area of the segment using one of the approximate rules.

12   A segmental arch has a span of 30m and a rise of 8 m. If the arch is to be filled with brickwork, calculate the approximate area.

13   Two segments of circles have a common chord 20 cm long and the heights of the segments are 2 cm and 5 cm. Find the area of the lune.

14   A sector of an annulus is 9 cm broad and its bounding arcs are 31 cm and 49 cm. Find its area.

15   Two circles each of radius 5 cm have a common chord of 8 cm. Find the area common to both.

16   Find the areas of the two segments into which a circle of 15 cm diameter is divided by a chord 12 cm long.

17   A church doorway with a pointed arch is 5 m wide and is rectangular for a height of 8 m. The total height is 13 m and the centres of the circular arcs forming the arch are 8 m from the ground. Calculate the radius of each arc and find the area of the doorway.

9b   Prisms, cylinders and their frusta

A prism is a solid bounded by plane figures, the two ends being parallel and equal figures and the side faces, called lateral faces, being parallelograms.

Figure 101

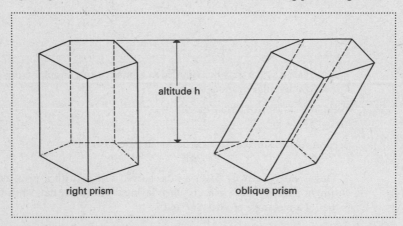

altitude h

right prism   oblique prism

    The prism is said to be *right* if the lateral faces are perpendicular to the ends so making the lateral faces rectangles.

    Other prisms are said to be *oblique*.

    A *regular* prism has ends which are regular polygons with all the sides and all the angles equal.

    The altitude or height *h* of a prism is the perpendicular distance between the two parallel ends.

    The volume of any prism is equal to the area of its base multiplied by its altitude. This is true for both right and oblique prisms:

volume = base × altitude

    The volume of an oblique prism is also given by multiplying the area of a transverse section by the length of the prism.

    A *transverse section* is one made perpendicular to the lateral or side edges. It may be regarded as dividing the prism into two parts and on fitting the base to the top face the two parts form a right prism standing on the transverse section as base and of height equal to the length of an edge.

Hence volume of any prism = area of transverse section × length

Figure
102

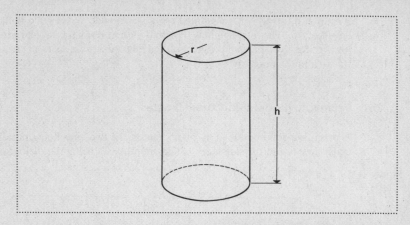

A *circular cylinder* may be regarded as a prism with a circular cross-section. For a right circular cylinder we have:

volume V = area of base × height
$\quad\quad = \pi r^2 h$

Area of curved surface A = perimeter of base × height
$\quad\quad\quad\quad\quad\quad\quad\quad = 2\pi rh$

This is easily seen by covering the curved surface with a piece of paper, cutting it parallel to the axis and then laying it out on the flat, when the area is that of a rectangle of sides $2\pi r$ and h.

Frustum of a prism

If a prism is cut by two planes inclined to one another, the solid contained between them is called a frustum of the prism.

The volume of the frustum of any triangular prism is equal to the average length of the lateral edges multiplied by the area A of the transverse section.

$$\text{Volume} = \frac{l_1 + l_2 + l_3}{3} . A$$

Figure
103

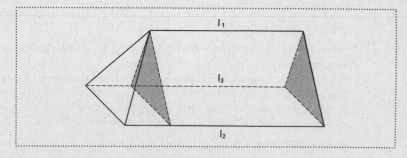

This may be shown by dividing the frustum into a triangular prism and a pyramid with a quadrilateral base (see fig. 103) and adding the two volumes. (See the next section for the volume of a pyramid.)

The volume of the frustum of a regular prism is found by multiplying the area of the transverse section by the average length of the edges.

For the regular prism in fig. 104

Figure 104

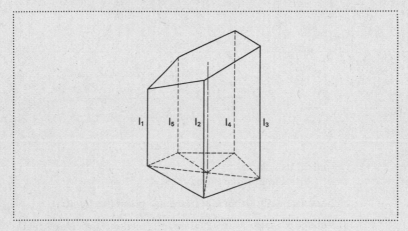

$$\text{volume} = \frac{l_1 + l_2 + l_3 + l_4 + l_5}{5} . A$$

$$= L.A$$

where A = area of transverse section
and L = length of the axis within the frustum

Both these formulae may be obtained by dividing the section into triangles and using the formula for the volume of the frustum of a triangular prism.

The area of the lateral surface of the frustum of a regular pyramid is given by multiplying the perimeter of the transverse section by the mean length of the edges. For fig. 104

$$\text{area} = \frac{l_1 + l_2 + l_3 + l_4 + l_5}{5} . p$$

$$= L.p$$

where p = perimeter of transverse section

The volume of the frustum of a circular cylinder follows from that of a regular prism (see fig. 106).

Volume = area of cross-section × length of axis
$$= \pi r^2 h$$

Area of curved surface = $2\pi r h$

Example 1 The base of a wedge is 3 m by $\frac{2}{3}$ m; its height is 3 m and top edge $1\frac{1}{2}$ m.

Figure 105

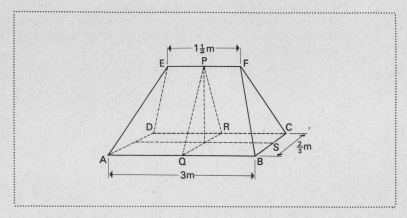

Find (a) its volume,
   (b) its total surface area.

The wedge is a frustum of a triangular prism (see fig. 105).

(a) Volume of wedge = area of transverse section × average of lengths of edges.
The transverse section PQR is a triangle base $\frac{2}{3}$ m height 3 m

$$\therefore \text{ area of transverse section} = \tfrac{1}{2} \times \tfrac{2}{3} \times 3 = 1 \text{ m}^2$$

$$\text{Average of lengths of edges} = \frac{AB + DC + EF}{3} = \frac{3 + 3 + 1\frac{1}{2}}{3}$$
$$= 2\tfrac{1}{2} \text{ m}$$
$$\text{Volume} = 1 \times 2\tfrac{1}{2} = 2\tfrac{1}{2} \text{ m}^3$$

(b) Area of trapezium $ABFE = \tfrac{1}{2}(AB + EF)PQ$
$$PQ = \sqrt{\{3^2 + (\tfrac{1}{3})^2\}} = \sqrt{9\tfrac{1}{9}} = 3{\cdot}018 \text{ m}$$
$\therefore$ area of trapezium $ABFE = \tfrac{1}{2}(3 + 1\tfrac{1}{2})3{\cdot}018 = 6{\cdot}791 \text{ m}^2$
Area of triangle $FBC = \tfrac{1}{2} \text{ base } BC \times \text{ height } FS$
$$= \tfrac{1}{2}\left(\tfrac{2}{3}\right)\sqrt{\{3^2 + (\tfrac{3}{4})^2\}} = \tfrac{1}{2} \times \tfrac{2}{3} \times 3{\cdot}092 \text{ m}^2$$
$$= 1{\cdot}031 \text{ m}^2$$

Total surface area = area of base $ABCD + 2 \times$ trapezium $ABFE$
$$+ 2 \times \text{triangle } FBC$$
$$= 3 \times \tfrac{2}{3} + 2 \times 6{\cdot}791 + 2 \times 1{\cdot}031$$
$$= 17{\cdot}64 \text{ m}^2$$

Example 2 A frustum 4 m long is cut from a circular cylinder whose radius is 1 m 75 cm. Find its curved surface and volume.

Figure
106

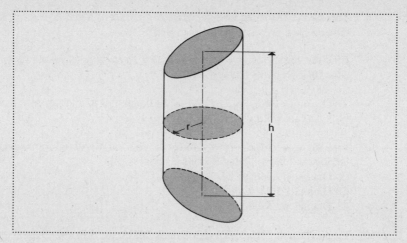

Referring to fig. 106 we have

radius $r = 1\frac{3}{4}$ m and length of axis $h = 4$ m

Therefore

Curved surface $= 2\pi rh$

$$= 2 \times 3{\cdot}1416 \times \frac{7}{4} \times 4 \text{ m}^2$$

$$= 43{\cdot}98 \text{ m}^2$$

Volume of frustum $= \pi r^2 h$

$$= 3{\cdot}1416 \times \left(\frac{7}{4}\right)^2 \times 4 \text{ m}^3$$

$$= 38{\cdot}48 \text{ m}^3$$

Exercise 9b

1   A ditch is 100 m long and 4 m deep. Its breadth at the top is 5 m and at the bottom 4 m; find the number of cu. m of water that it will hold.

2   Find the volume of a right prism of length 9 cm with an equilateral triangle of side 3 cm as base.

3   What is the volume of a right hexagonal prism 6 m long and side of base 2 m?

4   A ditch is to be dug 300 m long, 10 m wide at the top and 3 m deep. The sides slope at 45°. Find the number of cu. metres to be excavated.

5   Find the area of the whole surface and the volume of a right triangular prism of length 4 m, each side of the base being 75 cm.

213   Prisms, cylinders and their frusta

6 The sum of the three parallel edges of a wedge is 50 cm and the area of the cross-section is 35 cm^2. Find the volume.

7 Find the volume of a wedge whose base is 16 cm long and $4\frac{1}{2}$ cm broad, its top edge $10\frac{1}{2}$ cm and its height 7 cm.

8 The base of a wedge is 3 m by 1 m; its height is 4 m and top edge 3 m 50 cm. Calculate its volume.

9 Find the areas of the curved surfaces and the volumes of right circular cylinders having the following dimensions in metres
(a) Diameter 2, length 20
(b) Diameter 10, length 25
(c) Diameter 3·5, length 6·75

10 Find the whole surface of a right cylinder of length 20 m and circumference 6 m.

11 A hollow cast iron column is 5 m high. It is of octagonal section measuring 20 cm between opposite corners, the central hollow being cylindrical of diameter 16 cm. If the density of cast iron is 7·2 g cm^{-3}, find the weight of the column.

12 The transverse section of a prism is a regular hexagon of side 4 cm. If the mean length of the frustum is 36 cm find
(a) the area of the sides
(b) the volume.

13 Find the volume of the frustum of the circular cylinder shown in fig. 107.

Figure 107

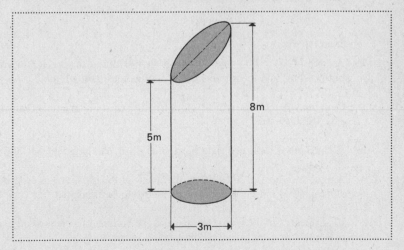

5m 8m 3m

14 For the frustum of the cylinder of fig. 107 find
   (a) the area of the curved surface   (b) the total surface area.

15 The right-angled elbow-joint shown in fig. 108 is a bend in a cylindrical air
   duct. The dimensions are in cm.
   Find the area of the sheet metal required to make the joint.
   If the ends are sealed what would be the total volume of the solid?

Figure
108

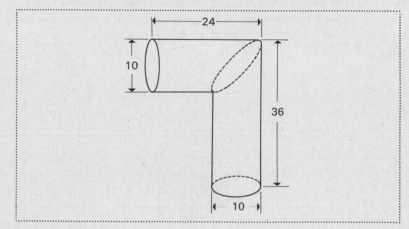

16 A cubic metre of copper is drawn into a wire 2 mm diameter. Find its length.

17 A cylindrical boiler is 3 m in diameter and 10 m long, its axis being horizontal.
   Find the number of cubic metres of water it contains when
   (a) half full
   (b) filled to three-quarters of its depth.

9c Pyramids, cones and their frusta

A *pyramid* is a solid with a plane polygon as base and the sides triangles with
a common vertex.

Figure
109

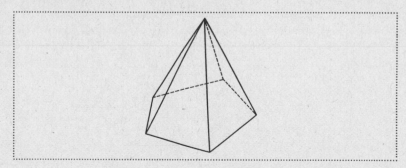

The polygon is called the base and the triangles are called the lateral faces. The *altitude* is the perpendicular distance from the vertex to the base. A *regular* pyramid has a regular polygon for base and the sides isosceles triangles.

The volume of a pyramid

The volume of any pyramid $= \frac{1}{3}$ area of base × altitude.

We may demonstrate this by considering first a triangular pyramid. Let $PABC$ be a triangular pyramid as in fig. 110.

Figure 110

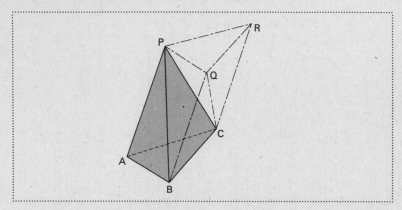

Through B and C draw parallels to AP and cut them at Q and R respectively by a plane drawn parallel to the base ABC. Join QC.

We now have a triangular prism $ABCPQR$ and it consists of three pyramids $PABC$, $CPQR$, and $PBCQ$. When taken in pairs these stand on equal bases and have equal altitudes.

Figure 111

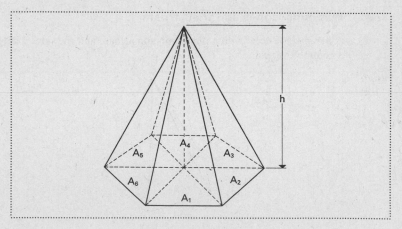

The three pyramids are equal in volume and therefore each has a volume equal to one third the volume of the prism.

$\therefore$ volume of pyramid $= \frac{1}{3}$ area of base $\times$ altitude

Since any pyramid with a plane polygon as base can be divided into a set of pyramids on triangular bases A_1, A_2, A_3, etc. all with the same altitude h (see fig. 111) then

$$\text{volume of pyramid} = \frac{1}{3}hA_1 + \frac{1}{3}hA_2 + \ldots \text{etc.}$$
$$= \frac{1}{3}h(A_1 + A_2 + \ldots)$$
$$= \frac{1}{3}h \cdot A$$

where $A = A_1 + A_2 + A_3 + \ldots$
$\qquad\quad = \text{area of base}$

$\therefore$ volume of pyramid on any base $= \frac{1}{3}$ area of base $\times$ height

A *cone* may be regarded as the limiting case of a pyramid with a regular polygon as base, when the number of sides of the polygon increases indefinitely.

Volume of cone $= \frac{1}{3}$ area of base $\times$ height
$$= \frac{1}{3}\pi r^2 h$$

Figure 112

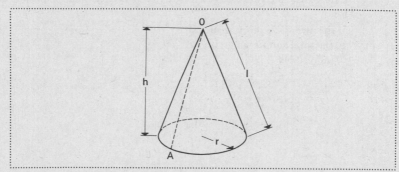

The area of the curved surface may be obtained by supposing the cone to be cut along a line *AO* (fig. 112) and then unrolled on a plane. The surface will take the form of a sector OA_1A_2 where the radius $OA_1 = $ slant height l (fig. 113) and the

Figure 113

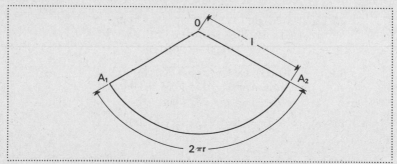

arc $A_1 A_2$ = circumference of base of cone

$\qquad = 2\pi r$

$\therefore$ area of curved surface $= \frac{1}{2}$ arc $\times$ radius

$\qquad\qquad\qquad\qquad = \pi r l$

Example 1   Find the volume of a pyramid whose altitude is 9 m and base a triangle whose sides are 11, 7 and 8 m.

Area of base $= \sqrt{\{s(s-a)(s-b)(s-c)\}}$ where $\begin{aligned} a &= 11 & s-a &= 2 \\ b &= 7 & s-b &= 6 \\ c &= 8 & s-c &= 5 \\ \hline 2s &= 26 \end{aligned}$

$\qquad\qquad\quad = \sqrt{(13 \times 2 \times 6 \times 5)}$
$\qquad\qquad\quad = \sqrt{780}$
Volume $= \frac{1}{3}Ah = \frac{1}{3}\sqrt{780} \times 9 = 3\sqrt{780}$
$\qquad\qquad = 83{\cdot}8 \text{ m}^3$

Example 2   A right cone has a base radius of 5 cm and an altitude of 12 cm. Find

(a) the area of the curved surface
(b) the total surface area
(c) the volume.

Figure 114

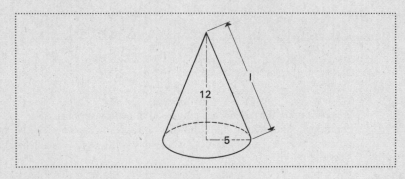

(a) The slant height $l = \sqrt{(12^2 + 5^2)} = 13$ cm
$\qquad$ curved surface $= \pi r l = \pi \times 5 \times 13 \text{ cm}^2$
$\qquad\qquad\qquad\qquad = 65\pi = 204{\cdot}2 \text{ cm}^2$

(b) $\qquad$ Area of base $= \pi r^2 = 25\pi \text{ cm}^2$
$\qquad \therefore$ total surface area $= 25\pi + 65\pi = 90\pi$
$\qquad\qquad\qquad\qquad\quad = 282{\cdot}7 \text{ cm}^2$

(c) Volume $= \frac{1}{3}\pi r^2 h = \frac{1}{3} \times 25\pi \times 12 = 100\pi$
$\qquad\qquad\quad = 314{\cdot}2 \text{ cm}^3$

$\qquad$ The *frustum of a pyramid* is the portion cut off between the base and a plane parallel to it. It is sometimes called a truncated pyramid.

The volume of a frustum of a pyramid

Suppose the frustum to be formed by cutting away the upper pyramid of height h and base area A_2 from the original pyramid of height H and base area A_1.

Let the perpendicular drawn from vertex V to the base meet the base of the frustum at X and the top at Y. (See fig. 115.)

Figure
115

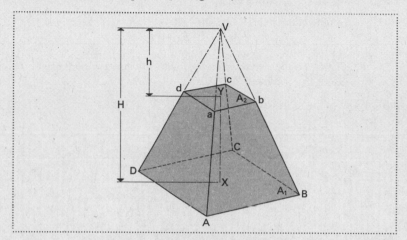

The base and top of the frustum are similar figures since their sides are formed by the intersection of parallel planes with the triangular sides of the original pyramid.

The areas A_1 and A_2 are proportional to the squares of the lengths of corresponding sides.

$$\frac{\text{Area of top}}{\text{Area of bottom}} = \frac{A_2}{A_1} = \frac{(ab)^2}{(AB)^2} = \frac{(Vb)^2}{(VB)^2} \text{ by similar triangles}$$

$$= \frac{(VY)^2}{(VX)^2} = \frac{h^2}{H^2}$$

Thus
$$\frac{A_2}{h^2} = \frac{A_1}{H^2}$$

Let each ratio $= k \ (= \text{a constant})$

Then $A_2 = kh^2$ and $A_1 = kH^2$

$$
\begin{aligned}
\text{Volume of frustum} &= \text{volume of whole pyramid} \\
&\quad - \text{volume of part removed} \\
&= \tfrac{1}{3}A_1 H - \tfrac{1}{3}A_2 h \\
&= \tfrac{1}{3}kH^3 - \tfrac{1}{3}kh^3 \\
&= \tfrac{1}{3}k(H^3 - h^3) \\
&= \tfrac{1}{3}k(H-h)(H^2 + Hh + h^2) \\
&= \tfrac{1}{3}(H-h)(kH^2 + kHh + kh^2) \\
&= \tfrac{1}{3}(H-h)\{A_1 + \sqrt{(A_1 A_2)} + A_2\}
\end{aligned}
$$

where $\quad H - h =$ altitude of frustum
and $\quad A_1$ and $A_2 =$ areas of ends

Frustum of a cone

Applying the formula for the volume of a frustum of a pyramid to the case of a conical frustum we get

$$\text{volume of frustum} = \tfrac{1}{3} \text{ height } \{\pi R^2 + \sqrt{(\pi R^2 \pi r^2)} + \pi r^2\}$$
$$= \tfrac{1}{3}\pi h (R^2 + Rr + r^2)$$

The area of the curved surface $= \pi s (R + r)$ where $s =$ slant height. This is easily shown by referring to fig. 116.

Figure 116

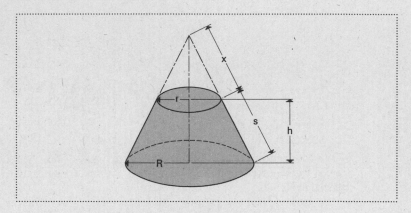

Required area $=$ curved surface of larger cone
$\qquad\qquad\qquad\; -$ curved surface of smaller cone
$$= \pi R(s + x) - \pi r x$$
$$= \pi R s + \pi (R - r)x$$

By similar triangles $\quad \dfrac{r}{R} = \dfrac{x}{x + s}$

from which $\qquad\qquad x = \dfrac{rs}{R - r}$

$\therefore$ area of curved surface of frustum $= \pi R s + \pi (R - r) . \dfrac{rs}{R - r}$

$$= \pi R s + \pi r s$$
$$= \pi s (R + r)$$

Example 1 Find the volume of the frustum of a square pyramid of height 8 m, each side of the base being 4 m and each side of the top 3 m.

$$\text{Volume} = \frac{h}{3}\{A_1 + \sqrt{(A_1 A_2)} + A_2\}$$

$$= \frac{8}{3}\{4^2 + \sqrt{(4^2 \times 3^2)} + 3^2\}$$

$$= \frac{8}{3}(16 + 12 + 9) = 98\tfrac{2}{3} \text{ m}^3$$

Example 2 A bucket in the form of a frustum of a right circular cone is 18 cm deep and the top and bottom diameters are 16 cm and 10 cm respectively. Find the total surface area of the bucket and the number of litres of water it will hold.

Figure 117

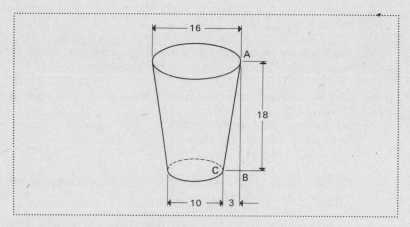

Slant height $s = AC = \sqrt{(AB^2 + BC^2)}$ (fig. 117)
$$= \sqrt{(18^2 + 3^2)}$$
$$= \sqrt{333}$$
$$= 18{\cdot}25 \text{ cm}$$

Area of curved surface $= \pi s(R+r)$
$$= 3{\cdot}1416 \times 18{\cdot}25 \times 13$$
$$= 745{\cdot}2 \text{ cm}^2$$

Area of base $= \pi r^2 = 25\pi = 78{\cdot}5 \text{ cm}^2$

Total surface area $= 745{\cdot}2 + 78{\cdot}5 = 823{\cdot}7 \text{ cm}^2$

Volume $= \tfrac{1}{3}\pi h(R^2 + Rr + r^2)$
$$= \tfrac{1}{3} \times 3{\cdot}1416 \times 18(8^2 + 8 \times 5 + 5^2)$$
$$= 3{\cdot}1416 \times 6 \times 129 \text{ cm}^3$$

$$= \frac{3{\cdot}1416 \times 6 \times 129}{1000} \text{ litres}$$

$$= 2{\cdot}43 \text{ litres}$$

$\therefore$ capacity of bucket $= 2{\cdot}43$ litres

Exercise 9c

1 Find the volume of a pyramid of altitude 10 cm and base a triangle whose sides are 5, 12 and 13 cm.

2 A regular pyramid stands on a square base and all its edges are 5 m. Find its volume and total surface area.

3 The altitude of a pyramid is 6 m and its base is an equilateral triangle of side 2 m. Find its volume.

4 Find the volume of a regular hexagonal pyramid of height 20 cm and side of base 9 cm.

5 The side of the base of a regular hexagonal pyramid is 10 cm and the vertical height is 30 cm. Find the total area of the lateral faces.

6 Find the total surface areas and the volumes of the right cones having the following dimensions in metres
(a) diameter of base 10, altitude 12
(b) diameter of base 5, altitude 9
(c) diameter of base $8\frac{1}{2}$, altitude $7\frac{1}{2}$.

7 Find the volume of the frustum of a pyramid, the ends being squares of sides 8 cm and 6 cm and the thickness 3 cm.

8 Find the volume of a frustum of a triangular pyramid the sides of the top and base being 3, 4, 5 m and 9, 12, 15 m respectively, the height being 12 m.

9 Find the volumes of the frusta of cones with dimensions
(a) altitude 10 m, diameter of ends 10 m and 6 m
(b) altitude 5 m diameter of ends 5 m and 10 m

10 Find the areas of the curved surfaces of the frusta of the cones in question 9.

11 A cylindrical steel vessel, open at the top, is 9 cm high and 16 cm in diameter (outside measurements). The metal is $\frac{1}{2}$ cm thick and has a density of $7 \cdot 8 \, g \, cm^{-3}$. Find its mass.
  The vessel is filled with sand which is then poured on to a bench to form a conical heap 8 cm high. Find the diameter of the circular base of the sand.

12 A concrete bed for a machine is in the form of a frustum of a pyramid whose base is a square of side 4 m and is of height 3 m, the upper surface being a square of side 2 m. Find the volume of the concrete bed and the area of wood required to board up the sides.

13 A tumbler is in the form of a truncated cone. Its height is 10 cm and the bottom is 5 cm diameter. Find the diameter of the top if it holds half a litre.

14 A timber spar 12 m long is 42 cm diameter at one end and tapers uniformly to 30 cm diameter at the other end. Its mass is 526 kg. If a 3 m length is cut off the smaller end, find the mass of the remainder.

9d   The sphere

This is the solid generated by the revolution of a semicircle about its diameter as axis. It may also be defined as a solid such that every point on its surface is a constant distance, called the *radius*, from a fixed point, called the *centre*.

Figure
118

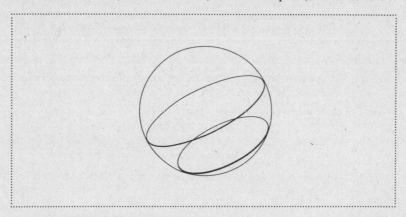

Any line passing through the centre and terminated by the surface is a *diameter*.

The section of a sphere by a plane is a circle. When the plane passes through the centre the section is a *great circle*; all other plane sections are small circles.

Useful formulae are given below.

They are difficult to prove at this stage and will be proved in volume II, when the student has done more calculus.

Area of curved surface $= 4\pi r^2 = \pi D^2$ (r = radius, D = diameter)

$$\text{Volume} = \tfrac{4}{3}\pi r^3 = \frac{\pi D^3}{6}$$

The *circumscribing cylinder* of a sphere is a right circular cylinder of the same diameter as the sphere, whose ends touch the sphere, and whose axis passes through the centre. See fig. 119.

Figure
119

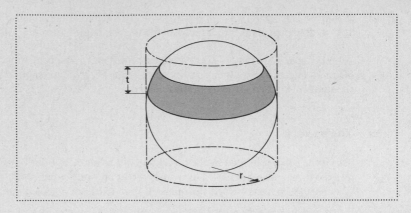

The area of its curved surface = circumference of base × height
$$= 2\pi r \times 2r = 4\pi r^2$$
$$= \text{area of enclosed sphere}$$

A frustum of a sphere is the portion intercepted between two parallel planes.
A *zone* is the curved surface of a frustum.

The area of a zone = $2\pi rt$ where t
= distance between planes
= area of corresponding cylindrical belt on the circumscribing cylinder.   (See fig. 119.)

A segment or cap is the portion of a sphere cut off by a single plane (fig. 120).

Figure
120

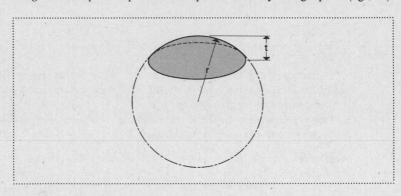

The area of the curved surface = $2\pi rt$
where r = radius of the sphere
t = height of segment

A sector of a sphere is the solid subtended at the centre of a sphere by a segmental cap (fig. 121).

Figure
121

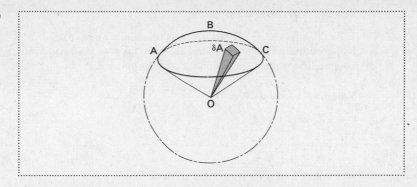

Consider the sector $OABC$. If we divide the surface of the cap into small elements of area, say δA_1, δA_2, etc., each may be considered the base of a pyramid whose vertex is at the centre and whose height is the radius of the sphere.

Volume of any such pyramid $= \frac{1}{3}$ area of base $\times$ height
$$= \frac{1}{3}r.\delta A$$
$\therefore$ volume of sector $=$ sum of volumes of small pyramids
$$= \frac{1}{3}r.\delta A_1 + \frac{1}{3}r.\delta A_2 + \frac{1}{3}r.\delta A_3 + \ldots$$
$$= \frac{1}{3}r(\delta A_1 + \delta A_2 + \delta A_3 + \ldots)$$
$$= \frac{1}{3}r.A \quad \text{where} \quad A = \text{area of cap} = 2\pi rt$$
$$= \frac{2}{3}\pi r^2 t \quad \text{(See fig. 120.)}$$

Notice that if we are given the area of the whole surface of the sphere as $4\pi r^2$ then the volume of the sphere may be deduced as

Volume $= \frac{1}{3}r[4\pi r^2] = \frac{4}{3}\pi r^3$

The volume of a segment may be found by taking the difference between the volume of the solid sector and the solid cone on the base of the cap. See fig. 122.

Figure
122

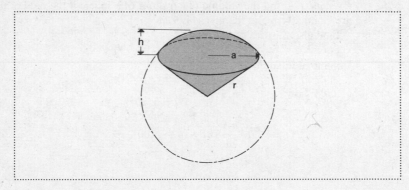

$$\text{Volume} = \tfrac{1}{3}r(2\pi rh) - \tfrac{1}{3}\pi a^2 (r-h)$$

By the intersecting chords property of a circle we have $a^2 = h(2r-h)$. By substituting firstly for a^2 and secondly for r we get two formulae for the volume. The student should check these for himself.

$$\text{Volume of segment} = \pi h^2 \left(r - \frac{h}{3}\right)$$

$$= \frac{\pi h}{6}(3a^2 + h^2)$$

The volume of a frustum of a sphere

Figure 123

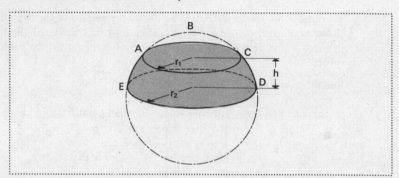

The volume of the frustum $ACDE$ in fig. 123 may be found by taking the difference between segment EBD and segment ABC. This gives the formula for the frustum.

$$\text{Volume} = \frac{\pi h}{6}(h^2 + 3r_1^2 + 3r_2^2)$$

Example 1 Find the volume of a frustum of a sphere if the radii of the ends are 7 and 20 cm and the height is 9 cm.

Find also the area of the zone.

$$\text{Volume of frustum} = \frac{\pi h}{6}(h^2 + 3r_1^2 + 3r_2^2) \tag{a}$$

$$= \frac{\pi . 9}{6}(9^2 + 3 . 7^2 + 3 . 20^2)$$

$$= \frac{\pi . 9}{6}(81 + 147 + 1200)$$

$$= 2142\pi$$

$$= 6729 \text{ cm}^3 \tag{b}$$

226   Mensuration

Figure
124

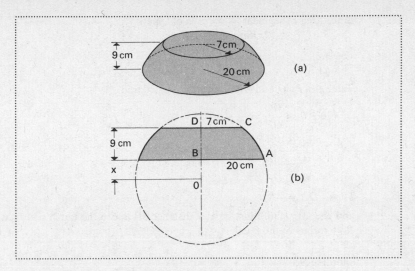

(a)

(b)

To find the area of the zone we require the radius of the sphere.

Referring to fig. 124 (b) let $OB = x$ cm

$$OA^2 = OC^2 \quad \therefore \quad OB^2 + BA^2 = OD^2 + DC^2$$
$$x^2 + 20^2 = (x+9)^2 + 7^2$$
$$x^2 + 400 = x^2 + 18x + 81 + 49$$
$$\therefore 18x = 270$$
$$x = 15$$
$$\therefore \text{ radius of sphere } R = \sqrt{(x^2 + 20^2)} = \sqrt{(15^2 + 20^2)}$$
$$= 25 \text{ cm}$$

$$\text{Area of zone} = 2\pi Rh = 2\pi \times 25 \times 9 = 450\pi$$
$$= 1414 \text{ cm}^2$$

Example 2   How high above the Earth must an astronaut be to see three-eighths of the surface?

Let A be the position of the observer. He will see the surface of segment PBQ where AP and AQ are tangential to the sphere (fig. 125).

Let R be the radius of the sphere and h the height of the segment.

Figure
125

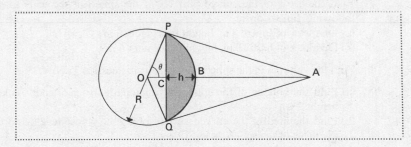

Since area of segment $= \frac{3}{8} \times$ area of sphere

$$2\pi Rh = \frac{3}{8} \times 4\pi R^2$$

$\therefore \qquad\qquad h = \dfrac{3 \times 4\pi R^2}{8 \times 2\pi R} = \frac{3}{4}R = CB$

Triangles PCO and APO are right-angled and

$$\cos \theta = \frac{OC}{OP} = \frac{OP}{OA}$$

$\therefore \qquad\qquad \dfrac{\dfrac{R}{4}}{R} = \dfrac{R}{OA}$

Thus $\quad OA = 4R$

and the astronaut must be at a distance $3R$ above the Earth's surface, where $R =$ radius of the Earth.

Exercise 9d

1 Calculate the surface area and volume of a sphere of diameter 9 m.

2 Assuming the earth to be a sphere of diameter 12·8 Mm, find its approximate surface area.

3 Find the diameter of a hemisphere if the area of its curved surface is 71·5 m^2.

4 The area of a sphere is 1224 m^2. Find its radius.

5 Show that the volume of a spherical shell of inner and outer radii r and R is $\frac{4}{3}\pi t\,(R^2 + Rr + r^2)$ where t is the thickness.
    If R and r are nearly equal, show that this volume is approximately given by $4\pi R^2 t$.

6 A hemispherical vessel, made of metal with a density of 7·5 g cm^{-3} is 40 cm in internal diameter and mass 55 kg. Find its external diameter.
    If the vessel is filled with sand and the sand is emptied on to a table forming a cone 20 cm high find the diameter of the base of the cone.

7 Find the areas of the curved surfaces of the spherical segments having the following dimensions
    (a) Diameter of sphere 7 m, height of segment 3 m
    (b) Diameter of base 16 m, height of segment 6 m

8 Find the volumes of the spherical segments in question 7 above.

9 (a) Find the volume of the spherical frustum, diameter of ends 3 and 4 cm, height 2 cm.
    (b) Find the area of the curved surface of a zone whose height is 3 cm, the diameter of the sphere being 12 cm.

10 Find the area of the curved surface and the volume of the spherical frustum, diameter of ends 12 and 20 cm, and height 8 cm.

11 Calculate the proportion of the Earth's surface that lies between the tropics, $23\frac{1}{2}°$ north latitude to $23\frac{1}{2}°$ south latitude.

12 What proportion of the Earth's surface lies within the Arctic Circle i.e. north of latitude $66\frac{1}{2}°$ north?

13 What portion of a sphere 12 cm in diameter is contained between two parallel planes distant 2 and 4 cm from the centre and on the same side of it?

14 To what height above the Earth's surface must an astronaut ascend to see one-third of its surface?

15 If a point light source were placed 4 m from the centre of a sphere of radius 2 m, what proportion of the surface would be illuminated?

16 A hemispherical cistern, internal diameter 1·25 m is filled with water. Standing in it is a solid cone whose vertex just reaches the surface and whose diameter of base is 0·5 m. Find the volume of water in the cistern.

9e Areas of irregular figures

The area of a plane surface bounded wholly or partly by a free curve is often required; a surveyor may require the area of a plot of land with curved boundaries, or a naval architect the areas of the water planes and transverse sections of a ship. Below are three rules all giving reasonable approximations to the area.

1 The mid-ordinate rule

Figure 126

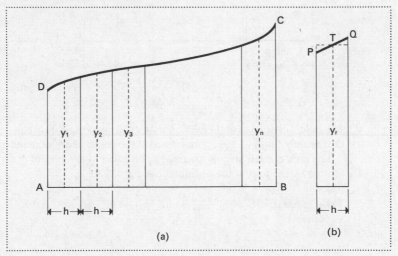

(a)   (b)

Suppose the area required is that of *ABDC* in fig. 126. The base *AB* is divided into a number of equal parts of width h and at the centre of each, the mid-ordinates $y_1, y_2, y_3 \ldots, y_n$, are erected and each carefully measured.

The area of each strip is assumed to be approximately equal to the area of a rectangular strip of equal width and length equal to that of the mid-ordinate. See fig. 126 (b).

The sum of all such areas is approximately equal to the area required.

$$\text{Area } ABDC = hy_1 + hy_2 + hy_3 + \ldots + hy_n$$
$$= h(y_1 + y_2 + y_3 + \ldots + y_n)$$

h is the width of each strip and is known as the common interval.

$$h = \frac{\text{length of base}}{\text{number of mid-ordinates}}$$

2   The trapezoidal rule

Figure 127

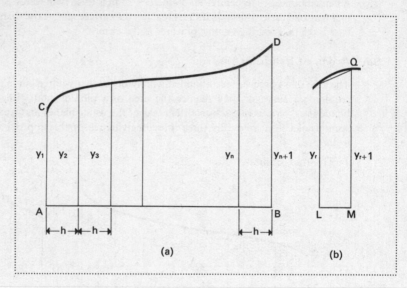

(a)   (b)

The base is divided as in the mid-ordinate rule, into a number of equal intervals. Ordinates $y_1, y_2, y_3 \ldots y_{n+1}$ are erected at the points of division and measured.

The area of each strip is assumed to be equal to the area of the trapezium formed by the join of the ordinates (see fig. 127 (b)).

$$\text{Thus } \text{area } ABDC = h.\frac{y_1 + y_2}{2} + h.\frac{y_2 + y_3}{2} + h.\frac{y_3 + y_4}{2} + \ldots + h.\frac{y_n + y_{n+1}}{2}$$

$$= h\left(\frac{y_1}{2} + y_2 + y_3 + \ldots + y_n + \frac{y_{n+1}}{2}\right)$$

$$= h \left(\frac{y_1 + y_{n+1}}{2} + y_2 + y_3 + \ldots + y_n \right)$$

= common interval (half the sum of the first and last
+ sum of remaining ordinates)

When the bounding curve is partly concave and partly convex the errors in finding areas by both the mid-ordinate and trapezoidal rule will tend to cancel out. When the bounding curve is wholly concave or convex to the base line the errors for each strip will all be of the same sign and will be additive, and could accumulate to give a serious error. The third rule, known as Simpson's rule, is devised to overcome this drawback.

3 Simpson's rule

The rule is obtained by assuming that the small arcs of the curve between ordinates are portions of parabolas.

The area is divided into an *even* number of strips of equal width and therefore has an odd number of ordinates at the division points.

The formula is

$$\text{area} = \frac{h}{3}(A + 2B + 4C)$$

where h = common interval
A = sum of first and last ordinates
B = sum of the remaining odd ordinates (third, fifth, seventh, ... etc.)
C = sum of the even ordinates (second, fourth, sixth, ... etc.)

Figure
128

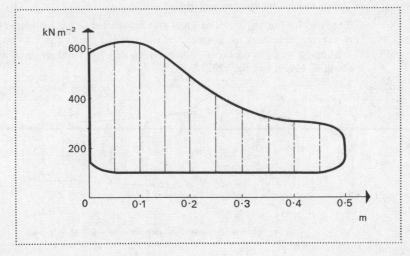

231   **Areas of irregular figures**

Example Fig. 128 shows the indicator card of a steam engine. Using Simpson's rule find
(a) the area enclosed by the curve   (b) the mean steam pressure.

The lengths of the ordinates are tabulated below.

Number of ordinate	Length of ordinate	Simpson's multipliers	Totals
1	410	1	410
2	530	4	2120
3	520	2	1040
4	500	4	2000
5	390	2	780
6	300	4	1200
7	280	2	560
8	230	4	920
9	220	2	440
10	200	4	800
11	80	1	80

$$\text{Sum} = 10\,350$$

$$\text{area} = 10\,350 \times \frac{h}{3} = 10\,350 \times \frac{1}{20} \times \frac{1}{3} = 172\tfrac{1}{2}\frac{\text{kN}}{\text{m}^2} \times \text{m}$$

$$\text{mean pressure} = \frac{\text{area}}{\text{base}} = \frac{172\tfrac{1}{2}\dfrac{\text{kN}}{\text{m}^2} \times \text{m}}{0\cdot5\ \text{m}} = 345\ \text{kN m}^{-2}$$

9f   Volumes of irregular solids

The rules for finding irregular areas may be applied to find volumes of solids of varying sections when bounded by two parallel planes.

Suppose we have the cross-sectional areas of a tree trunk at equal intervals along its length (see fig. 129).

Figure 129

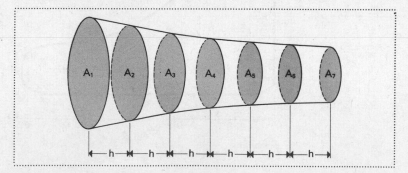

Then the approximate volume of the first portion may be taken as length × average of end sections

$$= h.\frac{A_1+A_2}{2}$$

Adding the volumes of each of the portions we get a formula for the volume which corresponds to the *trapezoidal rule.*

$$\text{Volume} = h.\frac{A_1+A_2}{2}+h.\frac{A_2+A_3}{2}+ \ldots +h.\frac{A_6+A_7}{2}$$

$$= h\left(\frac{A_1+A_7}{2}+A_2+A_3+ \ldots +A_6\right)$$

In a similar manner Simpson's rule would give

$$\text{Volume of trunk} = \frac{h}{3}\{A_1+A_7+2(A_3+A_5)+4(A_2+A_4+A_6)\}$$

Example　The underwater portion of a vessel is divided by vertical sections 10 m apart, the area of the sections being 1·2, 24·5, 51·3, 75·0, 92·4, 86·5, 63·2, 30·2, 5·1 m². Find the underwater volume.

As there are an odd number of ordinates evenly spaced then the vessel is divided into an even number of sections and we can use Simpson's rule to find the volume.

Number of section	Area of section	Simpson's multipliers	Totals
1	1·2	1	1·2
2	24·5	4	98·0
3	51·3	2	102·6
4	75·0	4	300·0
5	92·4	2	184·8
6	86·5	4	346·0
7	63·2	2	126·4
8	30·2	4	120·8
9	5·1	1	5·1

Sum 1284·9

$$\text{Volume} = \frac{h}{3}\times 1284\cdot9 = \frac{10}{3}\times 1284\cdot9 = 4283 \text{ m}^3$$

If the cross-sectional areas are given but are not at equal intervals along the solid, we may plot a graph of areas against the distance from one end. Then the total area under this curve found by any of the three rules will give an

Figure
130

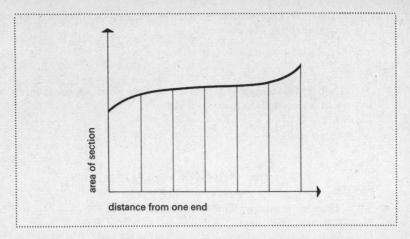

approximate value for the volume of the solid. In fig. 130 the area under the graph will give the volume of the solid whose sections are plotted against distance from one end.

The prismoidal formula

If we apply Simpson's rule to a solid divided by three equidistant parallel planes we obtain an important formula for the volume.

Figure
131

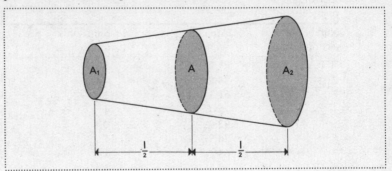

Let A_1 and A_2 be the areas of the ends and A the area of the mid-section. See fig. 131.

Applying Simpson's rule we get

$$\text{volume} = \frac{1}{3}.\frac{l}{2}.(A_1 + A_2 + 4A)$$

$$= \frac{l}{6}(A_1 + 4A + A_2) \quad \text{where } l = \text{length of solid}$$

234   Mensuration

This is known as the *prismoidal formula* and in many cases gives an exact value for the volume. The pyramid, cone, sphere, wedge and prismoid are some for which the formula is exact.

A *prismoid* is a solid having two parallel plane figures for its ends and all its other faces trapeziums. The ends are therefore equiangular polygons, but not necessarily similar (see fig. 132).

Figure 132

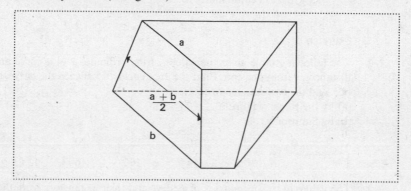

Example A railway embankment is built across a flat-bottomed valley 200 m across. The ends slope out of the valley at 10° to the horizontal. The embankment is 15 m high, 10 m wide at the top and its side slope at 1 vertical to 2 horizontal. Find the volume of the embankment in cubic metres.

Figure 133

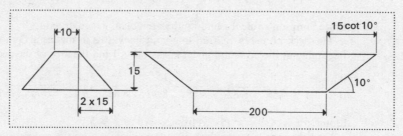

The embankment is a prismoid and the formula for the volume is exact.

$$\text{Volume} = \frac{h}{6}(A_1 + 4A + A_2)$$

A_1 = area of base = $200 \times (10 + 2 \times 30) = 200 \times 70 = 14\,000$ m²
A_2 = area of top = $10 \times (200 + 2 \times 15 \cot 10°) = 10 \times 370 \cdot 1$
$\qquad = 3701$ m²

The mid-section is a rectangle with sides

$$\frac{10 + 70}{2} \quad \text{and} \quad \frac{200 + 370 \cdot 1}{2}$$

i.e. 40 m and 285·1 m

$$A = \text{area of mid-section} = 40 \times 285 \cdot 1 = 11404 \text{ m}^2$$

$$\text{volume} = \frac{15}{6}(14000 + 4 \times 11404 + 3701)$$

$$= 158293 \text{ cubic metres}$$

Exercise 9f

1 The following table gives the values of the ordinates y of a curve and their distances x from one end. Find the area enclosed between the curve, the axis of x and the two extreme ordinates
(a) by the trapezoidal rule
(b) by Simpson's rule.

x	0	5	10	15	20	25	30
y	0	10·5	14·5	16·2	16	13·6	8·6

2 The values of the ordinates y of a curve and their distances x from the origin are given in the table below. Plot the graph and by taking 8 mid-ordinates find the area under the curve.

x	0	13	23	30	45	58	69	80
y	15	20	30	40	46	41	22	17

3 State Simpson's rule for finding the area of an irregular figure.

The deck of a ship is 30 m long and its widths in metres at 3 m intervals beginning at the bows are given in the table. Find the area of the deck.

0	3	6	9	12	15	18	21	24	27	30
0	2·4	4·56	6·62	8·15	8·90	8·68	8·02	6·71	5·10	3·0

4 Plot a graph of $y = x^2(5-x)$ from $x = 0$ to $x = 5$.

Find the area between the curve, the axis of x, and the ordinates at $x = 0$ and $x = 5$.

5 Estimate in cubic metres the volume of earth removed in excavating a portion of a canal, the areas of seven equidistant sections each 3 m apart being 27, 28·5, 29·3, 30·7, 31·5, 30 and 29·2 m².

6 A wooden spar is 10 m long and of variable circular cross-section. The following table gives its diameter at distances on either side of the middle point of its length about which it is symmetrical. Find its volume.

Distance m	0	1	2·5	3·5	4	5
Diameter cm	20	18·8	17·4	16·4	15·6	12

7   A small reservoir is in the form of a prismoid, the bottom being a rectangle 14 m long by 12 m broad and the top a rectangle 26 m long by 20 m broad. If the depth is 8 m, find the number of cubic metres of water that the reservoir will hold.

8   Using the prismoidal formula find
    (a) the volume of a sphere
    (b) the volume of a cone

9   Find the capacity of a coal bunker, the top being 20 m by 8 m, the bottom 16 m by 7 m, and the depth 6·5 m.

10   Find the capacity of a trough the top of which is 6 m long by 4 m broad and the bottom 4 m long by 3·5 m broad, the depth being 3 m.

11   A straight embankment is constructed across a valley which has a level bottom 100 m wide with sides sloping up at 1 vertical to 2 horizontal. The embankment is 5 m high, 8 m wide at the top, and has side slopes 1 to 1. Calculate its volume in cubic metres.

Miscellaneous exercises 9

1   A tunnel is to be constructed with straight vertical sides of height 5·5 m, a horizontal floor 7 m wide and a roof which is the arc of a circle. The tangents to the roof at the points where it meets the sides are inclined at 42° to the horizontal.
    Calculate (a) the distance of the highest point of the roof above the floor, (b) the area of cross section of the tunnel.

2   It is estimated that the debris from a shaft sinking will be 237 160 cubic metres. This debris is to be stacked in the form of a frustum of a cone, such that the vertical height must not exceed 21 m and the area of the base must not exceed four times the area of the top. What area will the stack occupy?

3   (a) ABC is a triangle having $BC = 5·6$ cm, $CA = 4·4$ cm and angle $BCA = 72°$. With centre C and radius CA a circular arc is described outside the triangle to meet BC produced in D. Calculate the area of $BCDA$.
    (b) A tank 4 m deep has plane sloping sides. The top and bottom sections are horizontal rectangles 7 m by 6 m and 5 m by 3·5 m respectively. Calculate the area of the section midway between the top and the bottom; hence, using the prismoidal rule, find the capacity of the tank.

4 A cooling tower is in the form of a frustum of a square pyramid. The base has side 32 m, the top has side 20 m, and the height is 16 m. Calculate (a) the total external area of the walls, (b) the length of the join of two adjacent walls, (c) the volume of the tower.

5 Y is the midpoint of the chord AB, of length 6 cm, of the circle of centre O and of radius 4 cm. C is a point on AB produced 2 cm from B. The tangent from C is drawn to touch the circle at Z. ZY is produced to cut the circle at X (fig. 134).

Figure 134

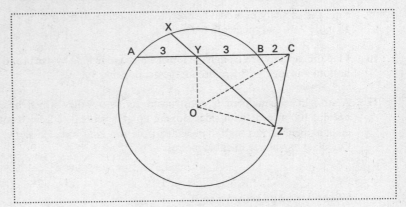

(a) Calculate the lengths of CZ, OC and OY
(b) Calculate the angle YCZ and hence find the lengths of ZY and YX

6 The site for a washery plant is bounded on two sides by roads OP and OQ at right angles and by a river in the form of a curve. The following are the ordinates in metres measured at 50 m intervals along OQ and starting at OP: 300, 290, 280, 265, 240, 216, 188, 152, 110, 60, 0.
    Calculate the area of the site.

7 (a) A 20 cm diameter steel shaft, 2·4 m long, has a keyway 3 cm wide by 2 cm deep cut along its length. Calculate the mass of metal removed, assuming the density of steel is 7·8 g cm^{-3}.
   (b) An oblique section of an 8 cm diameter cylinder has an area of 63 cm^2 Calculate the angle between the plane of the section and the axis of the cylinder. Show this angle in a neat sketch.

8 In order to find the area of a field a surveyor takes the measurements as shown in fig. 135. The distances between the ordinates are equal and the lengths of the ordinates are given in the following table:

Figure 135

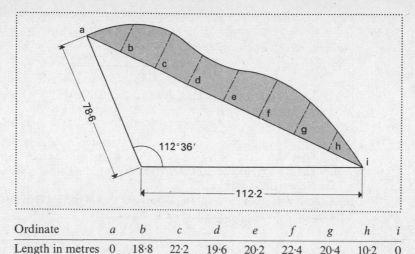

Ordinate	a	b	c	d	e	f	g	h	i
Length in metres	0	18·8	22·2	19·6	20·2	22·4	20·4	10·2	0

Calculate the area of the field to the nearest square metre.

9   A frustrum of a cone is 4 cm long and its end radii are 2 cm and 3 cm respectively. Find the height of the cone of which the frustum is a part. Hence or otherwise find the volume of the frustum and the area of its curved surface giving both answers to three significant figures.

10   The area of the cross-section of a pithead coal bunker is A m² at a distance x m from one end. Values of x and A are

x	0	10	20	30	40	50	60
A	16	25	24	22	26	23	23

Plot A vertically and x horizontally. Estimate in cubic metres the volume of the bunker, the total length of which is 60 m.

11   (a) A hemisphere, radius R, is cut by a plane parallel to the plane surface through the centre of the hemisphere so that the height of the segment (or cap) is equal to the height of the zone of the sphere.

i Show that the radius r of the section $= \dfrac{\sqrt{3}}{2}R$. Hence show that the volume of the segment is $\frac{5}{16}$ of that of the hemisphere.

Note Volume of segment (or cap) $= \dfrac{\pi h}{6}(3r^2 + h^2)$ where r = radius and h = height of the segment.

Figure
136

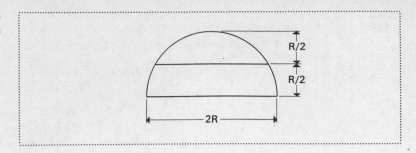

ii What is the relationship between the curved surface areas of the segment and the zone in this case?

(b) A sheet-metal cone, to be of the dimensions shown in fig. 137, is made from a sector of sheet tin. Calculate the sector angle θ.

D.T.C.

Figure
137

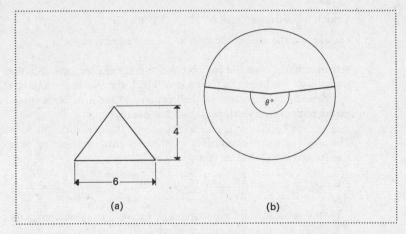

(a) (b)

12 A 12 cm deep tumbler is 8 cm diameter at the bottom and 12 cm at the top and is filled with water to a depth of 7 cm. Calculate the surface area of the water. A sphere submerged in the water increases the depth to 8 cm. Calculate the diameter of the sphere.

13 A pulverized fuel hopper has an open top 8 m square, a base 4 m square and a depth of 6 m. Find an expression for the volume it contains when filled to a depth of y m. Calculate the total capacity of the hopper and the area of one of the sloping sides.

14 (a) *OP*, *OQ* are radii of a circle radius r and the angle *POQ* is θ radians. State and prove the formula for the area of the sector *POQ*.

(b) Two circles of radii 8 and 10 cm, having centres A and B, intersect in C and D. AB is 12 cm. Find the angles of the triangle ABC in radians and calculate the area bounded by the two shorter circular arcs from C to D.

15   An embankment with a level top 5 m wide is to be built across a depression of varying depth. Fig. 138 shows a transverse vertical section across the em-

Figure 138

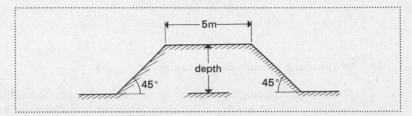

bankment. The table below gives the depth of the existing ground level below the top of the embankment at intervals of 2 m along the centre line. Calculate the cross-sectional areas at the 2 m intervals, and hence, using Simpson's rule, calculate the volume of earth in the embankment in cubic metres.

Distance (m)	0	20	40	60	80	100	120	140	160	180	200
Depth (m)	0	1·5	1·7	2·0	2·2	1·9	1·8	1·6	1·3	0·6	0

16   A horizontal cylindrical tank has hemispherical ends. The internal diameter is 3 m and the length of the cylindrical portion is 8 m. Calculate the volume of liquid in the tank if it is filled to a depth of 2 m.

17   The table shows the diameter of a piece of timber 8 m long of varying circular section, at stated distances from one end.
      Find its volume in cubic metres.

Distance (m)	0	1	2	3	4	5	6	7	8
Diameter (m)	24·2	24·7	25·5	26·2	27·1	28·0	29·2	30·4	31·8

18   A mound of earth has a rectangular base 60 m by 40 m, a rectangular top, side slopes of 45° and end slopes of 60°. It is 15 m high.
      Calculate its volume in cubic metres and the area of its surface in square metres.

10 Graphs and laws of graphs

10a Graphical solution of equations

In an earlier section (page 50) we plotted graphs of quadratic functions and used them to solve quadratic equations. When we cannot solve an equation using factors then a graphical method is often the only method we can use. This is especially true in the case of trigonometric equations.

Example 1 Solve the equation

$$2x^3 - 5x^2 - 10x + 3 = 0$$

This is known as a cubic equation since the highest power of x is the third. Just as a quadratic equation can have two roots, a cubic can have up to three real roots.

If we plot the graph of $y = 2x^3 - 5x^2 - 10x + 3$, then the values of x which make y zero, i.e. where the graph cuts the x axis, are the required values. These are the roots or solutions of $2x^3 - 5x^2 - 10x + 3 = 0$.

We prepare a table of values of x and y as follows

x	-3	-2	-1	0	1	2	3	4
$2x^3$	-54	-16	-2	0	2	16	54	128
$-5x^2$	-45	-20	-5	0	-5	-20	-45	-80
$-10x$	30	20	10	0	-10	-20	-30	-40
$+3$	3	3	3	3	3	3	3	3
y	-66	-13	6	3	-10	-21	-18	11

The graph is plotted as shown in fig. 139.
The graph cuts $x_1 Ox$ in points where $x = -1.5, 0.27$, and 3.73.

And hence $2x^3 - 5x^2 - 10x + 3 = 0$ when x is approximately
-1.5 or 0.3 or 3.7.

If we wish to find any particular root more accurately, say the root between 0 and 1, we can plot this section of the curve more accurately and to a larger scale by finding the values of y for additional values of x between 0 and 1.

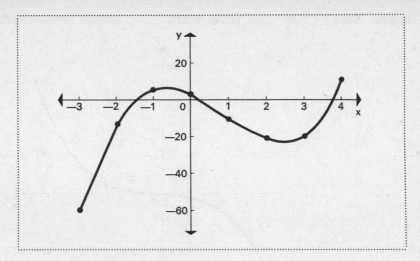

Figure 139

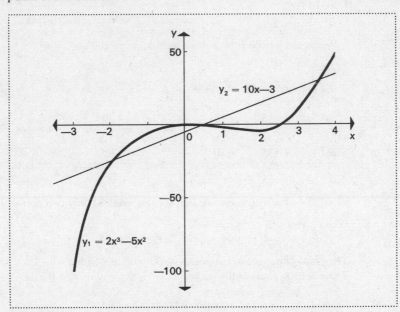

Figure 140

An alternative graphical method of solving the equation is as follows:

Write the equation $2x^3 - 5x^2 - 10x + 3 = 0$
as $2x^3 - 5x^2 = 10x - 3$

We then plot the graphs of $y_1 = 2x^3 - 5x^2$ and $y_2 = 10x - 3$ and find their points of intersection.

Figure
141

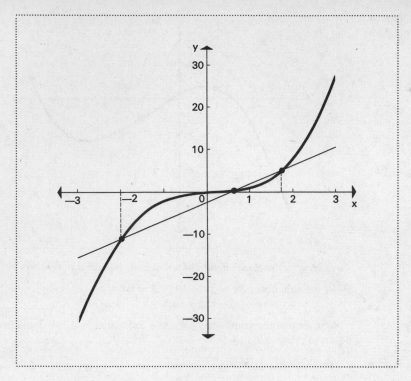

Where the graphs intersect we have $y_1 = y_2$ and so

$2x^3 - 5x^2 = 10x - 3$

We prepare a table of values for $y_1 = 2x^3 - 5x^2$ as before

x	-3	-2	-1	0	1	2	3	4
$2x^3$	-54	-16	-2	0	2	16	54	128
$-5x^2$	-45	-20	-5	0	-5	-20	-45	-80
y_1	-99	-36	-7	0	-3	-4	9	48

$y_2 = 10x - 3$ is a straight line and for this we need only two points

When $x = -3 \qquad y_2 = -33$
$\qquad\quad x = 4 \qquad y_2 = 37$

The graphs intersect in the points A, B and C at which $x = -1 \cdot 5$, $0 \cdot 3$, and $3 \cdot 7$.
These are the roots of the equation $2x^3 - 5x^2 - 10x + 3 = 0$

Example 2 · Solve the equation $x^3 - 4x + 2 = 0$

Writing the equation as $x^3 = 4x - 2$ we have to plot graphs of $y_1 = x^3$ and $y_2 = 4x - 2$.

x	-3	-2	-1	0	1	2	3
y_1	-27	-8	-1	0	1	8	27

The graph of $y_2 = 4x - 2$ is a straight line

When $x = -3$ $y_2 = -14$
      $x = 3$ $y_2 = 10$

The roots are approximately $-2.3, 0.6, 1.64$ (fig. 141)

Example 3   Draw the graph of $y = \sin 2x$ where the angle is in radians, for values of x from 0 to $\dfrac{\pi}{2}$. Use the graph to find a solution of the equation $0.5 + \sin 2x = x$ in this range.

The given equation $0.5 + \sin 2x = x$ can be written $\sin 2x = x - 0.5$ which is satisfied by the values of x where the graphs of $y = \sin 2x$ and $y = x - 0.5$ intersect.

We plot these graphs from $x = 0$ to $\dfrac{\pi^c}{2} = 1.571^c$ noting that x is in radians.

The student will find a page giving the sine of an angle when the angle is in radians in most school mathematical tables.

Remember that for an angle x greater than 1.57^c or $90°$, $\sin x$ is equal to $\sin(\pi - x) = \sin(3.142 - x)$

Thus when $x = 1.0^c$, $\sin 2x = \sin 2.0 = \sin(3.142 - 2.0)$
                               $= \sin 1.14 = 0.909$

Alternatively, if the student finds it easier, the x axis may be divided into degrees for plotting $y = \sin 2x$.

x^c	0	0.2	0.4	0.6	0.8	1.0	1.2	1.4	$\dfrac{\pi}{2}$
$y = \sin 2x$	0	0.389	0.717	0.932	0.999	0.909	0.674	0.334	0

The graph of $y = x - 0.5$ is a straight line and we need only find two points on it.

When $x = 0, y = -0.5$
When $x = 1.4 (= 80° \ 13'), y = 0.9$

The two graphs intersect at point A where $x = 1.19^c$

This is the required solution of $0.5 + \sin 2x = x$ (fig. 142.)

Figure
142

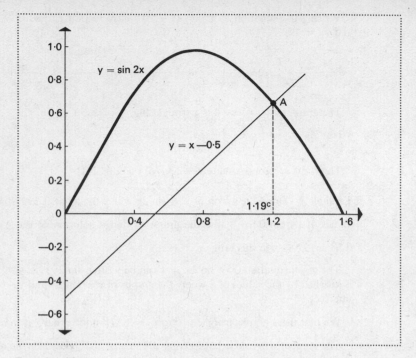

Exercise 10a

1 Solve the equation $x^3 - 5x - 2 = 0$ by drawing the graphs of $y = x^3$ and $y = 5x + 2$ for values of x between -3 and $+3$

2 By drawing the graphs of $y = x^3$ and $y = 15x + 2$ for values of x between -4 and 4, solve the equation $x^3 - 15x - 2 = 0$

3 By plotting suitable graphs for values of x between -3 and $+3$, find the roots of the equation $x^3 - x^2 - 5x + 2 = 0$

4 Find by a graphical method the roots of the equation $x^3 - 6x + 5 = 0$. Check your answer using the remainder theorem.

5 Solve the equation $x^2 + 4(1 - x)^2 = 9$ by drawing the graphs of $x^2 + y^2 = 9$ and $2x + y = 2$

6 Find a solution of the equation $2 \sin \theta - \theta = 0$ by drawing graphs of $\sin \theta$ and $\dfrac{\theta}{2}$ for values of x from $\dfrac{\pi}{3}$ to $\dfrac{2\pi}{3}$

7 Solve the equation $2x - \sin 2x = \pi + 1$ by drawing graphs of $y = 1 + \sin 2x$ and $y = 2x - \pi$ where the angle is in radians, for values of x from 0 to π

8   On the same axes and to the same scales draw graphs of $y = \tan x$ and $y = \pi - 2x$, the angle being measured in radians for values of x from 0 to $\dfrac{5\pi}{12}$

Hence find a value of x satisfying the equation $2x + \tan x = \pi$

9   Solve the equation $2 \cos x = x$ where x lies in the range 0 to $\dfrac{\pi}{2}$

Use your graph to solve the equation $4 \cos x - 2x + 1 = 0$

10   (a) If $y = x^3 - 3x + 1$, find the values of y when $x = 0, \frac{1}{2}, 1, 1\frac{1}{2}$, and 2. Draw the graph of $y = x^3 - 3x + 1$ for these values of x and from your graph find two roots of the equation $x^3 - 3x + 1 = 0$.

(b) On the same axes draw the graph of $y = x$, and find the values of x where it cuts the cubic curve. Of what cubic equation are these values of x the solutions?

D.T.C.

10b   Determination of laws of graphs

When we have obtained experimentally in the laboratory a number of pairs of corresponding values of two variables, it is often of great value if we can find the mathematical relationship between the two variables. This relationship is known as the *law of the graph*.

Example 1   The following table gives the force P which, applied to a lifting machine, overcomes a corresponding load W.

Figure 143

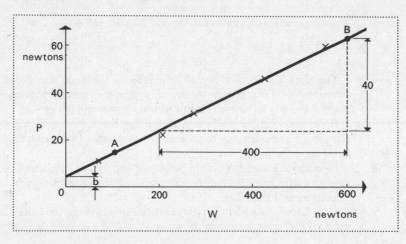

P N	10	20	30	45	60	67
W N	60	160	270	420	550	640

Plot the values and find the relationship between P and W.

On plotting P vertically against W horizontally we find that the points lie approximately on a straight line. See fig. 143.

The equation of this line is of the form

$P = aW + b$

where a is the gradient of the line and b is the intercept on the vertical or P axis, i.e. the value of P when $W = 0$.

From the graph we see that $b = 4$ and $a = \frac{40}{400} = \frac{1}{10}$

An alternative method of finding a and b, and perhaps a better method, is to take two points, one at each end of the line, and substitute their co-ordinates in the equation $P = aW + b$, to obtain two simultaneous equations for a and b.

Convenient points are A at $W = 100$ N and B at $W = 600$ N and the distance between these points is a convenient divisor.

Consider point B, $W = 600$, $P = 64$. Then $64 = 600a + b \dots (10.1)$
Consider point A, $W = 100$, $P = 14$. Then $14 = 100a + b \dots (10.2)$

$$\text{Subtracting these equations} \quad \overline{50 = 500a}$$

$\therefore a = \frac{50}{500} = \frac{1}{10}$

Substituting this value of a in equation (10.2) we get

$$14 = 100 \times \frac{1}{10} + b$$

$\therefore b = 4$

Thus the relationship between P and W for the machine is

$$P = \frac{1}{10}W + 4$$

The plotted points will not all lie exactly on a straight line due to experimental errors. To determine the law of the graph all that is necessary is that a straight line can be drawn so as to run evenly through the points.

If the observed value of one variable, say the x, is correct, the probable error in y may be determined by seeing what change in y is required to put the point on to the line.

In example 1 the relationship between P and W was linear, and the values gave a straight line. This only happens occasionally when we plot one variable directly against the other.

If we know or suspect the type of relationship between the variables then if necessary we must rearrange the equation so that a straight line will result.

Example 2 The following values of x and y are believed to follow a law of the form $y = ax^2 + b$. Test this and if true find the approximate values of a and b.

x	0	2	4	6	8	10
y	3·9	5·9	12·2	21·8	35·6	53·5

It is no use plotting y against x as a curved graph may represent any one of a number of laws and it is impossible by inspection to identify the relationship.

If, however, we plot y against a new variable $X = x^2$ and a straight line results, we know the law is linear between y and X; i.e. $y = aX + b$ and we can then find a and b. Replacing X by x^2 gives $y = ax^2 + b$

We prepare a new table as below and plot y against X (fig. 144).

$X = x^2$	0	4	16	36	64	100
y	3·9	5·9	12·2	21·8	35·6	53·5

Since the values lie on a straight line then the relation between y and X must be of the form $y = aX + b$.

i.e. $y = ax^2 + b$

Figure 144

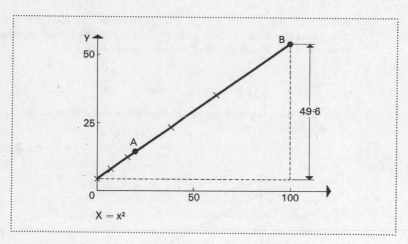

To find the law we select two points A and B on the line.

Consider point B, $X = 100$, $y = 54$ $\therefore$ $54 = 100a + b$ . . . (10.3)
Consider point A, $X = 20$, $y = 13·8$ $\therefore$ $13·8 = 20a + b$ . . . (10.4)
$\qquad\qquad\qquad$ Subtracting $\overline{40·2} = \overline{80a}$

$\therefore a = \dfrac{40·2}{80} = 0·5025$

Substituting in equation (10.4) $13 \cdot 8 = 20 \times 0 \cdot 5025 + b \ldots$ (10.4)

$$\therefore b = 3 \cdot 75$$

Thus the required law between x and y is

$$y = 0 \cdot 50x^2 + 3 \cdot 75$$

In general if we wish to test a suspected relationship between corresponding values of x and y this can be done provided the equation can be rearranged in the form $Y = aX + b$ where X and Y are modified forms of the variables containing x and y, and a and b are constants to be determined.

For example if we believe x and y follow a law of the form $xy = a + bx$, we divide the equation by x to give $y = \dfrac{a}{x} + b$

If we write $X = \dfrac{1}{x}$ this becomes $y = aX + b$

If the graph of y against X gives a straight line then the suspected relationship is correct and we proceed to find a and b as in the examples above. If we do not obtain a straight line then the relationship is not true.

In some cases the equation can be put in a suitable form only by taking logarithms, as in the following example.

Example 3   The following table gives corresponding experimental values of two quantities x and y. Test whether they are connected by an equation of the form $y = ax^n$ and if so find probable values for a and n.

x	2	3	4	5	6·5	8	9·5	11·0
y	24·7	12·9	8·2	5·8	3·8	2·7	2·1	1·7

If x and y are related by a law of the form $y = ax^n$ then taking logarithms of both sides

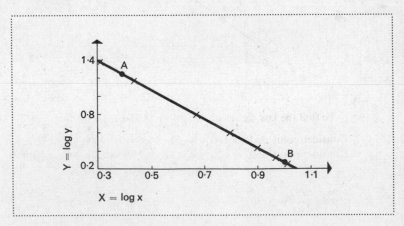

$$\log y = \log a + \log (x^n)$$
$$= \log a + n \log x$$

If we write $\log x = X$ and $\log y = Y$ we get

$$Y = nX + \log a$$

This has a straight line graph if X is plotted against Y. We therefore prepare a table of values of $\log x$ against $\log y$ and plot the graph in the usual way.

Since the graph is a straight line (fig. 145) then X and Y are connected by a linear relationship of the form

$$Y = nX + \log a$$

Taking two points A and B on the line

A is point $X = 0.4$, $Y = 1.24$ $\therefore$ $1.24 = n\,0.4 + \log a$
B is point $X = 1.0$, $Y = 0.28$ $\therefore$ $\underline{0.28 = n\,1 \ + \log a}$
$\qquad$ Subtracting $\quad 0.96 = -0.6\,n$

$$n = -\frac{0.96}{0.6} = -1.60$$

Substituting for n $\quad \log a = 0.28 + 1.60 = 1.88$
$$\therefore a = 75.9$$

Thus $\quad \log y = -1.60 \log x + \log 75.9$
and $\qquad y = 75.9\,x^{-1.60}$ is the required relationship.

10c Use of log–log and log–linear graph sheets

If a set of values of x and y are believed to follow a law of the form $y = Ax^n$ we may check this by plotting corresponding values directly on to special graph paper drawn with logarithmic scales on both axes. This paper is known as log–log graph paper and distances along the x and y axes are proportional to the logarithms of the numbers. Values of x and y which obey the law $y = Ax^n$ i.e. $\log y = n \log x + \log A$ will lie on a straight line when plotted directly on to this paper.

With common logarithms where the base is 10, we have $\log 1 = 0$, $\log 10 = 1$, $\log 100 = 2$, $\log 1000 = 3$, etc. This means that on logarithmic ruled paper the distance from 1 to 10 equals the distance from 10 to 100, and from 100 to 1000, etc. Each of these distances is called one cycle. In using log–log graph paper to plot laws of the type $y = Ax^n$ a suitable paper must be chosen, depending upon the number of cycles needed on each axis.

Example 4 The following values of x and y are believed to be related by a law of the form $y = Ax^n$:

x	2	8	25	62	98	326	566	840
y	5·85	9·3	13·6	18·4	21·4	32·0	38·4	43·8

Check this and find values of A and n.

Since x ranges from 2 to 840 we have values in the three ranges 1 to 10, 10 to 100, 100 to 1000.

Thus we need three cycles along the x axis to cover all the values. We need two cycles to cover the values of y which lie in the two ranges 1 to 10 and 10 to 100.

The most suitable log–log paper to select would be "log 2 cycles × 3 cycles". The graph is indicated in fig. 146.

Figure
146

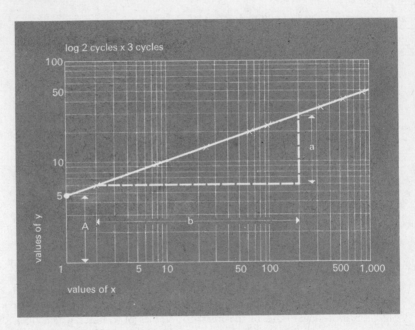

To determine the law directly from the graph

If the value of y when $x = 1$ can be read directly on the graph then this gives the value of A since $y = A$ when $x = 1$ if $y = Ax^n$

From fig. 146 $A = 4·64$

To find n we measure the slope of the line.

Provided the lengths of a cycle of logs on each axis are equal we divide the vertical rise (a) by the corresponding horizontal distance (b).

Here $n = 0·33$ and x and y are related by the law $y = 4·64\,x^{0·33}$

If the values of A and n cannot be determined by this method, we proceed as in example 3 worked out previously. We substitute two sets of values in the equation $\log y = n \log x + \log A$ and solve the two simultaneous equations which result.

If the suspected relationship between x and y is of the form $y = An^x$, where $\log y = x \log n + \log A$, then plotting $\log y$ against x would result in a straight line if the relationship is true.

In this case we may plot x and y directly onto graph paper which has ordinary linear divisions on the x axis and logarithmic divisions on the y axis. This paper is known as log-linear, semi-logarithmic, or logarithmic one-way graph paper.

If a straight line results then the values are related by a law of the form $y = An^x$. The value of y at $x = 0$ gives A and n is generally best found by substituting one value of x and y in the equation $\log y = x \log n + \log A$ and solving.

Exercise 10c

1   Rearrange the following into a linear form of the type $Y = aX + b$, where X and Y are functions of x and y. For example, if $xy = ax + b$ then $y = a + \dfrac{b}{x}$, and writing $Y = y$, $X = \dfrac{1}{x}$ we get the linear relationship $Y = bX + a$

   (a) $y = a + bx^2$ (b) $xy = ax + by$ (c) $y = ax + bx^2$
   (d) $y = ax^n$ (e) $y + a\sqrt{(x^2 + y^2)} = b$ (f) $y = ma^x$
   (g) $y = a^{x+b}$

2   Variables x and y are known to be connected by a law of the form $y = ax + b$ where a and b are constants.
   When $x = 1$, $y = -0.8$ and when $x = 6$, $y = -16.8$

   Find the law connecting x and y.

3   The following table gives the effort P to lift a load W with a small lifting machine.

W newtons	10	20	30	40	50	60
P newtons	5·1	6·4	8·1	9·6	10·9	12·4

   Plot W horizontally against P vertically and show that the values lie approximately on a straight line. Determine the probable relationship connecting P and W in the form $P = aW + b$.

4   In an experiment the speed N r.p.m. of a flywheel slowly coming to rest were recorded against the time t in minutes. Plot the results and show that N and t

are connected by an equation of the form $N = at+b$. Find probable values of a and b.

t min	2	4	6	8	10	12	14
N r.p.m.	372	333	292	255	210	177	132

5 The following corresponding values of x and y were measured. There may be errors of observation. Test if there is a probable law of the form $y = a+bx^2$ and if this is the case find values of a and b.

x	1·0	1·5	2·0	2·3	2·5	2·7
y	1·54	2·10	3·00	3·54	4·06	4·50

6 Show that the following values of x and y are connected by an equation of the form $y = ax^n$ and find probable values of a and n.

x	1·2	2·5	4·0	6·3	10·7	14·5
y	2·8	10	17·8	38	91	138

7 The following observations were made in experiments on towing a barge; P being the pull and V the speed.

V	2·1	2·5	3·2	3·7	4·3	4·9
P	152	207	326	424	550	701

Plot V against P on log–log paper or plot log V against log P on squared paper and give an approximate formula connecting P and V.

8 The table gives corresponding experimental values of two quantities x and y which are known to be connected by an equation of the form $y = ax+bx^2$
Find the values of a and b.

x	2	4	6	8	10	12
y	5·6	6·4	2·4	$-6·5$	$-20·0$	$-46·4$

9 Values of x and y are believed to follow a law of the form $y = ax^n$. Find the number of log-cycles required on each axis of log–log graph paper when plotting the following values
(a) x ranges from 4 to 354 and corresponding values of y are from 6 to 43
(b) x ranges from 0·3 to 6·5 and y from 4·2 to 57.

10 State the most suitable type of logarithmic ruled paper to be used when plotting the following relationships
(a) $R = fv^n$ where v has values from 1·5 m s^{-1} to 18 m s^{-1} and R has values from 6·9 N to 1200 N.
(b) $\theta = Ae^{bt}$ where t ranges from 0 to 30 min and θ from 180 °C to 73 °C
(c) $pv^{1·4} = 1000$ where v ranges from 3 to 40.

Miscellaneous exercises 10

1   (a) Draw the graph of $y = \frac{1}{3}(3+3x-x^2)$, between values of $x = -1$ and $x = +5$, and find the roots of $3y = 0$.

    (b) On the same axes draw the graph of $y = 3-x$ and find the points where this graph cuts the other curve.

    (c) For what equation are these points the possible solutions?

U.E.I.

2   Plot a graph of $y = 3x^2-5x+7$ between the values of $x = -2$ and $x = +4$.

    (a) Using the trapezoidal rule determine the area enclosed by the graph line, the x axis and the end ordinates.

    (b) From the graph determine the gradient of the curve when $x = 2\cdot5$, and also find the value of x when the curve has zero slope.

    (c) Use the graph to solve the equation

$$3x^2-5x-12 = 0$$

U.E.I.

3   Plot to a large scale the graph of $y = x^3$ for values of x between $+1\cdot5$ and $-1\cdot5$.

    By plotting other graphs on the same figure, solve the equations

    (a) $x^3 = 2x+1$

    (b) $x^3 = -4x+6$

E.M.E.U.

4   On the same axes and to the same scales, plot graphs of the functions x^3+5x^2+3 and $17-x$ for values of x between -5 and $+2$.

    Hence, solve the equation $x^3+5x^2+x-14 = 0$

U.E.I.

5   Solve graphically the equation

$$x^3-2x^2-11x+12 = 0$$

given that the roots lie within the range ±5.

U.L.C.I.

6   (a) Plot a graph of $y = x^3-7x^2+9x+15$ between the values of $x = 0$ and $x = 6$.

    (b) Using the trapezoidal rule determine the area enclosed by the graph line, the x axis, and the end ordinates.

    (c) From the graph determine the gradient of the curve when $x = 1\cdot5$, and also find the values of x when the curve has zero slope.

U.E.I.

7   Solve graphically the equation $\sin 2x = \dfrac{x}{3\pi}$, for all values of x between 0 and $\dfrac{3\pi}{2}$ radians. Give your answers (a) in radians (b) in degrees.

N.C.T.E.C.

8   Draw carefully in one diagram the graphs of the curve $y = \sin x$ (where x is in radians), and the line $y = \frac{1}{2}x - 1$, for values of x in the range $0 \leq x \leq 2\pi$.
     Deduce from the graph the root of the equation

$$1 + \sin x = \tfrac{1}{2}x$$

correct to one decimal place.   *U.L.C.I.*

9   Find graphically the solutions of the equation

$$\tan x = 2 - x^2$$

(where x is measured in radians), which lie between 0 and π.   *E.M.E.U.*

10   With the same axes and to the same scales, draw graphs of $y = \dfrac{1}{x}$ and $y = \tan x$

(the angle being measured in radians) for values of x from $\dfrac{\pi}{12}$ to $\dfrac{5\pi}{12}$. Find a

value of x, correct to two significant figures, satisfying the 'theory of sound' equation $x \tan x = 1$.

11   By plotting a suitable graph, show that the values of p and V in the following table are related by the law $p = a\sqrt{V} + b$, where a and b are constants. Determine the probable values of a and b.

p	8·69	9·715	11·005	11·76	12·782	13·1
V	5	7	10	12	15	16

N.C.T.E.C.

12   It is believed that power (p) and velocity (v) are connected by a law of the form: $p = cv^3 + k$. The following observations were made during a test

Power	p	89	211	325	695	966	1719
Velocity	v	3	5	6	8	9	11

     Check by drawing a suitable graph if the law is true, and find the probable values of the constants c and k.
     Using the law determine the velocity v when the power is 500.

13   The table gives corresponding values of p, the pressure of saturated steam and v, the volume of unit mass.

p	5	10	15	20	25	30	35	40	45
v	62·5	38·4	28·5	21·7	17·6	15·2	13·2	11·5	10·4

An approximate formula connecting the values of p and v is $\dfrac{1}{v} = a + bp$ where a and b are constants. By plotting suitable variables, test the validity of the law, and by means of the graph or otherwise, determine the values of a and b.

14 Two quantities W and H are believed to be connected by a law of the form

$$W = \frac{m}{\sqrt{H}} + c$$

The following values of W and H were obtained by experiment

W	5·1	4·64	4·37	4·18	4·04	3·94
H	4	6	8	10	12	14

Draw a suitable graph to test if W and H are connected by the law, and determine the probable values of m and c.

15 In an experiment the resistance, R, of copper wire of various diameters, d, was measured and the following readings were obtained

d mm	0·19	0·21	0·27	0·32	0·37	0·46
R ohm	1·25	0·95	0·57	0·40	0·26	0·14

It is believed that R and d are connected by an approximate equation of the type

$$R = a + \frac{b}{d^2}$$

where a and b are constants. By suitably modifying the above table obtain a graph which approximates to a straight line and thus verify that the equation is approximately satisfied. Find the best values of a and b.

E.M.E.U.

16 The power P required to drive a certain vessel at speed V, and the speed V are connected by an equation of the form $P = a + bV^3$ where a and b are constants. Corresponding values of P and V are given in the table below.

V	8	10	12	14	15
P	830	1390	2220	3390	4120

By plotting suitable variables, test the validity of the law, and by means of the graph or otherwise, determine the values of a and b.

17 When air is compressed adiabatically, the law connecting the absolute temperature, T, and the pressure, p, is of the form $T = ap^n$, where a and n

are constants. Verify that the following experimental values fit this law approximately and find the best values of a and n.

Pressure p	20	40	50	60	80	90
Temperature T	513	631	673	717	785	810

18 The following table gives values of x and y

x	1	2	3	4	5	6
y	2·65	2·44	2·23	2	1·73	1·41

It is believed that x and y have a relationship in the form of $y^2 = a - bx$. Draw a suitable graph and hence determine the probable value of a and b. Use this relationship to determine the probable value of y when $x = 7$.

U.E.I.

19 Two quantities x and y are connected by a law $y = \dfrac{a}{1 - bx^2}$ where a and b are constants.

Related values of x and y are given in the table. Confirm the truth of the law and determine the values of a and b.

(Use tables correct to two significant figures.)

x	6	8	10	11	12
y	5·50	6·76	9·10	11·60	16·67

D.T.C.

20 The values of pressure, p, and volume, v, are given below

p	68	25·5	13·3	8·3	6·5
v	1·5	3·0	4·8	6·7	8·0

They are believed to be connected by a law of the form $pv^n = c$, where n and c are constants. By plotting $\log p$ against $\log v$, test the law and obtain the values of n and c.

U.L.C.I.

11 Compound angles and trigonometric equations

In this chapter we obtain a number of identities which may at first sight seem to be of theoretical interest only. In actual fact they are of great importance and a knowledge of them is essential.

11a The addition and subtraction theorems

Consider triangle PQR as in fig. 147. PL is drawn perpendicular to QR forming the right-angled triangles PLQ and PLR. Let $\angle LPQ = A$, $\angle LPR = B$, $PQ = a$, $PR = b$.

Figure 147

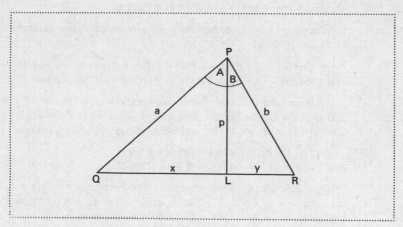

Then $QL = x = a \sin A$, $RL = y = b \sin B$
and $PL = p = a \cos A = b \cos B$

Area of triangle PQR = sum of areas of triangles PLQ and PLR
$$\therefore \tfrac{1}{2}ab \sin (A+B) = \tfrac{1}{2}xp + \tfrac{1}{2}yp$$
$$= \tfrac{1}{2}a \sin A . b \cos B + \tfrac{1}{2}b \sin B . a \cos A$$

Dividing both sides by $\tfrac{1}{2}ab$ we have the first formula

$$\sin (A+B) = \sin A \cos B + \cos A \sin B$$

By applying the cosine rule to triangle PQR we get

$$\cos (A+B) = \frac{a^2+b^2-(x+y)^2}{2ab}$$

$$= \frac{a^2+b^2-x^2-y^2-2xy}{2ab}$$

$$= \frac{(a^2-x^2)+(b^2-y^2)-2xy}{2ab}$$

$$= \frac{2p^2-2xy}{2ab} \quad \text{by Pythagoras' theorem}$$

Substituting $p = a \cos A = b \cos B$, and $x = a \sin A$, $y = b \sin B$

we get $\quad \cos (A+B) = \dfrac{a \cos A.b \cos B - a \sin A.b \sin B}{ab}$

$\therefore \ \cos (A+B) = \cos A \cos B - \sin A \sin B$

The two formulae

$\sin (A+B) = \sin A \cos B + \cos A \sin B$
$\cos (A+B) = \cos A \cos B - \sin A \sin B$

are clearly true when A and B are acute angles.

If we replace A by its complement $90° - A$ which is also an acute angle the formulae still hold.

$$\sin (90°-A+B) = \sin (90°-A) \cos B + \cos (90°-A) \sin B$$
$$\text{and} \quad \cos (90°-A+B) = \cos (90°-A) \cos B - \sin (90°-A) \sin B$$

We have seen that the sine of the complement is the cosine of the angle and that the cosine of the complement is the sine of the angle; also that $90° - A + B = 90° - (A - B)$; so we can obtain two more formulae:

$$\cos (A-B) = \cos A \cos B + \sin A \sin B$$
$$\text{and} \quad \sin (A-B) = \sin A \cos B - \cos A \sin B$$

These four identities are important. The proofs given above hold only for the cases where A and B are acute angles. A more general method of proof applicable to angles of any magnitude is the following:

Consider the lines OP and OQ each of length r, making angles A and B respectively with the initial line Ox (fig. 148).

P has co-ordinates $(r \cos A, r \sin A)$ and Q $(r \cos B, r \sin B)$ and distance $PQ^2 = (r \cos A - r \cos B)^2 + (r \sin A - r \sin B)^2$ by Pythagoras' theorem or see the section on co-ordinates, page 126.

By the cosine rule

$$PQ^2 = OP^2 + OQ^2 - 2OP.OQ \cos POQ$$
$$\therefore \ (r \cos A - r \cos B)^2 + (r \sin A - r \sin B)^2 = r^2 + r^2 - 2r^2 \cos (A-B)$$

Figure 148

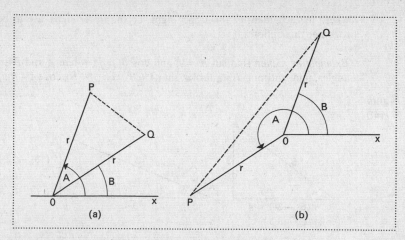

(a)   (b)

Dividing through by r^2

$\cos^2 A - 2\cos A \cos B + \cos^2 B + \sin^2 A - 2\sin A \sin B + \sin^2 B$
$$= 2 - 2\cos(A - B)$$
since $\cos^2 A + \sin^2 A = 1 = \cos^2 B + \sin^2 B$ we get
$$\cos(A - B) = \cos A \cos B + \sin A \sin B \dots (1)$$

The formula is true for all values of A and B both positive and negative.

If we replace B by $-B$ and remember that

$$\sin(-B) = -\sin B, \text{ and } \cos(-B) = \cos B$$

we get

$$\cos(A + B) = \cos A \cos B - \sin A \sin B \dots (2)$$

The formula for $\sin(A + B)$ can be obtained by replacing B by $(90° - B)$ in (1) since

$$\sin(90° - B) = \cos B, \cos(90° - B) = \sin B$$
and $\cos\{A - (90° - B)\} = \cos(A + B - 90°) = \cos\{90° - (A + B)\}$
$$= \sin(A + B)$$
so giving

$$\sin(A + B) = \sin A \cos B + \cos A \sin B \dots (3)$$

Replacing B by $-B$ in this result gives

$$\sin(A - B) = \sin A \cos(-B) + \cos A \sin(-B)$$
i.e. $\sin(A - B) = \sin A \cos B - \cos A \sin B \dots (4)$

If we summarize these four results known as the addition and subtraction formulae we have

$$\sin(A \pm B) = \sin A \cos B \pm \cos A \sin B$$
and $\cos(A \pm B) = \cos A \cos B \mp \sin A \sin B$

where in each identity the upper signs, or the lower signs, are to be taken together throughout.

Example 1   Given that $\sin A = \frac{3}{5}$ and $\cos B = \frac{12}{13}$ where A and B are acute angles, find, without using tables, $\sin (A+B)$, $\cos (A+B)$, $\cos (A-B)$.

Figure 149

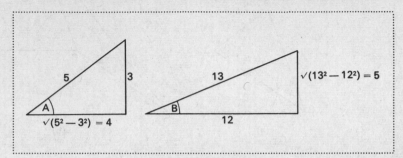

$$\sin (A+B) = \sin A \cos B + \cos A \sin B$$
$$= \frac{3}{5} \times \frac{12}{13} + \frac{4}{5} \times \frac{5}{13} = \frac{36+20}{65}$$
$$= \frac{56}{65}$$

$$\cos (A+B) = \cos A \cos B - \sin A \sin B$$
$$= \frac{4}{5} \times \frac{12}{13} - \frac{3}{5} \times \frac{5}{13} = \frac{48-15}{65}$$
$$= \frac{33}{65}.$$

$$\cos (A-B) = \cos A \cos B + \sin A \sin B$$
$$= \frac{48+15}{65}$$
$$= \frac{63}{65}$$

Example 2   Find the values of $\sin 75°$ and $\cos 75°$ without using tables.

$$\sin 75° = \sin (45°+30°) = \sin 45° \cos 30° + \cos 45° \sin 30°$$
$$= \frac{1}{\sqrt{2}} \times \frac{\sqrt{3}}{2} + \frac{1}{\sqrt{2}} \times \frac{1}{2} = \frac{\sqrt{3}+1}{2\sqrt{2}}$$

$$\cos 75° = \cos (45°+30°) = \cos 45° \cos 30° - \sin 45° \sin 30°$$
$$= \frac{1}{\sqrt{2}} \times \frac{\sqrt{3}}{2} - \frac{1}{\sqrt{2}} \times \frac{1}{2} = \frac{\sqrt{3}-1}{2\sqrt{2}}$$

Example 3 Use the addition theorems to simplify

$\sin (270° + \theta)$, $\cos (90° + \theta)$, $\cos (270° + \theta)$

$$\begin{aligned}
\sin (270° + \theta) &= \sin 270° \cos \theta + \cos 270° \sin \theta \\
&= -1 \times \cos \theta + 0 \times \sin \theta \\
&= -\cos \theta \\
\cos (90° + \theta) &= \cos 90° \cos \theta - \sin 90° \sin \theta \\
&= 0 \times \cos \theta - 1 \times \sin \theta \\
&= -\sin \theta \\
\cos (270° + \theta) &= \cos 270° \cos \theta - \sin 270° \sin \theta \\
&= 0 \times \cos \theta - (-1) \sin \theta \\
&= \sin \theta
\end{aligned}$$

To prove $\tan (A+B) = \dfrac{\tan A + \tan B}{1 - \tan A \tan B}$

$$\tan (A+B) = \frac{\sin (A+B)}{\cos (A+B)} = \frac{\sin A \cos B + \cos A \sin B}{\cos A \cos B - \sin A \sin B}$$

Dividing numerator and denominator by $\cos A \cos B$ gives

$$\tan (A+B) = \frac{\dfrac{\sin A \cos B}{\cos A \cos B} + \dfrac{\cos A \sin B}{\cos A \cos B}}{\dfrac{\cos A \cos B}{\cos A \cos B} - \dfrac{\sin A \sin B}{\cos A \cos B}}$$

$$= \frac{\tan A + \tan B}{1 - \tan A \tan B}$$

Also by substituting $(-B)$ for B and remembering that
$\tan (-B) = -\tan B$ we get

$$\tan (A-B) = \frac{\tan A - \tan B}{1 + \tan A \tan B}$$

Example (a) If $\tan A = \frac{1}{3}$ and $\tan B = \frac{3}{4}$ find $\tan (A + B)$
(b) If $\tan \theta = m_1$ and $\tan \phi = m_2$ find a formula for $\tan (\theta - \phi)$

(a) $\tan (A+B) = \dfrac{\tan A + \tan B}{1 - \tan A \tan B} = \dfrac{\frac{1}{3} + \frac{3}{4}}{1 - \frac{1}{3} \times \frac{3}{4}} = \dfrac{\frac{4+9}{12}}{1 - \frac{1}{4}}$

$\qquad = \dfrac{13}{12} \times \dfrac{4}{3} \qquad\qquad = \dfrac{13}{9}$

(b) $\tan (\theta - \phi) = \dfrac{\tan \theta - \tan \phi}{1 + \tan \theta \tan \phi} = \dfrac{m_1 - m_2}{1 + m_1 m_2}$

Exercise 11a

1   Verify the formulae

$$\sin (A+B) = \sin A \cos B + \cos A \sin B$$
$$\text{and} \quad \cos (A+B) = \cos A \cos B - \sin A \sin B$$

(a) when $A = 30°$ and $B = 60°$ (b) when $A = 30°$ and $B = 40°$

2   Given that $\cos A = \frac{3}{5}$ and $\cos B = \frac{5}{13}$, find without using tables the values of $\sin (A+B)$, $\sin (A-B)$, $\cos (A+B)$, $\cos (A-B)$.

3   Show that (a) $\sin (A+60°) + \sin (A-60°) = \sin A$
     (b) $\sin (60°+A) + \sin (60°-A) = \sqrt{3} \cos A$

4   Use the addition theorems to simplify

(a) $\cos (270°-\theta)$ (b) $\sin (180°+\theta)$ (c) $\cos (360°-\theta)$

5   Find the value of (a) $\sin (A+B) + \sin (A-B)$
     (b) $\cos (A-B) + \cos (A+B)$

6   Without using tables find the value of

(a) $\sin 45° \cos 15° - \cos 45° \sin 15°$
(b) $\sin 63° \cos 27° + \cos 63° \sin 27°$
(c) $\cos 125° \cos 35° + \sin 125° \sin 35°$

7   Prove that

$$\sin (45°+A) \cos (45°-B) + \cos (45°+A) \sin (45°-B) = \cos (A-B)$$

8   Given $\tan A = \frac{3}{4}$ and $\cos B = \frac{12}{13}$, find without using tables, $\cos (A-B)$, and $\tan (A-B)$.

9   Show that (a) $\tan \left(\dfrac{\pi}{4} + \theta \right) = \dfrac{1 + \tan \theta}{1 - \tan \theta}$

(b) $\tan (45° - A) = \dfrac{\cos A - \sin A}{\cos A + \sin A}$

10   If $\tan A = \frac{1}{3}$ and $\tan B = \frac{3}{4}$ find $\tan (A+B)$ and $\tan (A-B)$.

11   If $\sin A = 0.6$ and $\sin B = 0.4$ find $\tan (A+B)$ and $\cos (A-B)$.

12   If $\sin A = 0.5$ and $\cos B = 0.6$ find $\sin (A+B)$ and $\cos (A+B)$.

13   If $\tan A = 2$ and $\tan (A-B) = 0.75$, find $\tan B$.

264   Compound angles and trigonometric equations

14 Prove that $\sqrt{2} \sin\left(x - \dfrac{\pi}{4}\right) = \sin x - \cos x$.

15 By expanding $\cos\left(x + \dfrac{\pi}{3}\right)$ express

$4\cos\left(x + \dfrac{\pi}{3}\right)$ in the form $a\cos x + b\sin x$, finding the values of a and b.

16 Find the values of $\sin 15°$, $\cos 15°$, $\tan 15°$, $\sin 75°$, $\cos 75°$, $\tan 75°$ without using tables given that

$$\sin 30° = \frac{1}{2}, \quad \cos 30° = \frac{\sqrt{3}}{2} = 0 \cdot 8660,$$

and $\sin 45° = \cos 45° = \dfrac{1}{\sqrt{2}} = 0 \cdot 7071$.

11b Multiple and submultiple angles

If in the addition formula for $\sin(A + B)$ we write $A = B$

we get $\sin(A + A) = \sin A \cos A + \cos A \sin A$
Thus $\sin 2A = 2\sin A \cos A$

Similarly in $\cos(A + B) = \cos A \cos B - \sin A \sin B$, substituting A for B
gives $\cos 2A = \cos^2 A - \sin^2 A$

Since $\sin^2 A = 1 - \cos^2 A$ $\cos 2A$ may also be written

$$\cos 2A = 2\cos^2 A - 1$$

or writing $\cos^2 A = 1 - \sin^2 A$ we get a third form for $\cos 2A$

$$\cos 2A = 1 - 2\sin^2 A$$

Also $\tan(A + B) = \dfrac{\tan A + \tan B}{1 - \tan A \tan B}$ when $A = B$ becomes

$$\tan 2A = \frac{2\tan A}{1 - \tan^2 A}$$

All the above double-angle formulae are important and are true for all values of A. They will be true if instead of A we write $\dfrac{A}{2}$.

Thus $\sin A = 2\sin\dfrac{A}{2}\cos\dfrac{A}{2}$

$\cos A = 2\cos^2\dfrac{A}{2} - 1$

265   Multiple and submultiple angles

$$= 1 - 2 \sin^2 \frac{A}{2}$$

$$= \cos^2 \frac{A}{2} - \sin^2 \frac{A}{2}$$

$$\tan A = \frac{2 \tan \frac{A}{2}}{1 - \tan^2 A}$$

In the same way writing $2A$ for A then

$$\sin 4A = 2 \sin 2A \cos 2A$$

and we could go on in this manner

$$\sin 8A = 2 \sin 4A \cos 4A \quad \text{and so on.}$$

Example 1 If θ is an acute angle and $\sin \theta = 0{\cdot}6$, find $\sin 2\theta$, $\cos 2\theta$ and $\tan 2\theta$ without using trigonometric tables.

$$\sin \theta = 0{\cdot}6 = \frac{3}{5}$$

Figure 150

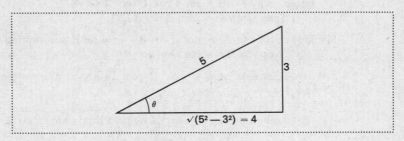

$\sqrt{(5^2 - 3^2)} = 4$

$$\sin 2\theta = 2 \sin \theta \cos \theta = 2 \times \frac{3}{5} \times \frac{4}{5}$$

$$= \frac{24}{25}$$

$$\cos 2\theta = 1 - 2 \sin^2 \theta = 1 - 2 \times \left(\frac{3}{5}\right)^2 = 1 - \frac{18}{25} = \frac{7}{25}$$

$$\tan 2\theta = \frac{2 \tan \theta}{1 - \tan^2 \theta} = \frac{2 \times \frac{3}{4}}{1 - (\frac{3}{4})^2} = \frac{\frac{3}{2}}{1 - \frac{9}{16}}$$

$$= \frac{3}{2} \times \frac{16}{7} = \frac{24}{7}$$

Example 2 Find $\sin 3A$ and $\cos 3A$ in terms of $\sin A$ and $\cos A$.

266 Compound angles and trigonometric equations

(a) $\sin 3A = \sin (2A+A)$
$$= \sin 2A \cos A + \cos 2A \sin A$$
$$= (2 \sin A \cos A) \cos A + (1-2 \sin^2 A) \sin A$$
$$= 2 \sin A \cos^2 A + \sin A - 2 \sin^3 A$$

Writing $\cos^2 A = 1 - \sin^2 A$

$$\sin 3A = 2 \sin A (1 - \sin^2 A) + \sin A - 2 \sin^3 A$$
$$= 3 \sin A - 4 \sin^3 A$$

(b) $\cos 3A = \cos (2A+A)$
$$= \cos 2A \cos A - \sin 2A \sin A$$
$$= (2 \cos^2 A - 1) \cos A - (2 \sin A \cos A) \sin A$$
$$= 2 \cos^3 A - \cos A - 2 \sin^2 A \cos A$$
$$= 2 \cos^3 A - \cos A - 2 (1 - \cos^2 A) \cos A$$
$$= 4 \cos^3 A - 3 \cos A$$

By continuing in this way we could find the sines and cosines of $4A$, $5A$, etc. in terms of $\sin A$ and $\cos A$.

11c   To convert $a \sin \theta + b \cos \theta$ to $r \sin (\theta + \alpha)$

It is very useful to be able to trace the changes in the sign and the magnitude of the sum of two wave forms such as $a \sin \theta + b \cos \theta$. We show that this sum can be written as a sine wave of the form $r \sin (\theta + \alpha)$ where r and α are constants depending on the values of a and b.

Let $a \sin \theta + b \cos \theta = r \sin (\theta + \alpha)$
$$= r \sin \theta \cos \alpha + r \cos \theta \sin \alpha$$

These are identical if $r \cos \alpha = a$
and $r \sin \alpha = b$

Squaring and adding

$$r^2 \cos^2 \alpha + r^2 \sin^2 \alpha = a^2 + b^2$$
i.e. $r = \sqrt{(a^2 + b^2)}$ since $\cos^2 \alpha + \sin^2 \alpha = 1$

Dividing $$\frac{r \sin \alpha}{r \cos \alpha} = \frac{b}{a}$$

i.e. $\tan \alpha = \dfrac{b}{a}$

Figure 151

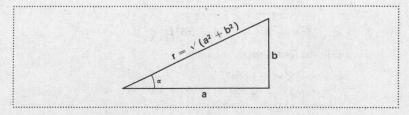

The relationship between the constants a, b, r and α are indicated in fig. 151. Thus we have

$$a \sin \theta + b \cos \theta = \sqrt{(a^2 + b^2)} \sin (\theta + \alpha)$$

where α is the angle whose tangent is $\dfrac{b}{a}$

This may be written $\alpha = \tan^{-1} \dfrac{b}{a}$

Example 1   Convert $3 \sin \theta + 4 \cos \theta$ into the form $r \sin (\theta + \alpha)$

Here $r = \sqrt{(3^2 + 4^2)} = 5$

and $\tan \alpha = \frac{4}{3} = 1.333$ $\therefore \alpha = 53° 8'$

$\therefore 3 \sin \theta + 4 \cos \theta = 5 \sin (\theta + 53° 8')$

Example 2   Express $3 \sin \theta - 5 \cos \theta$ in the form $r \sin (\theta + \alpha)$

Let $3 \sin \theta - 5 \cos \theta = r \sin (\theta + \alpha)$
$$= r \sin \theta \cos \alpha + r \cos \theta \sin \alpha$$

$\therefore r \cos \alpha = 3$

and $r \sin \alpha = -5$ (see fig. 152)

Figure 152

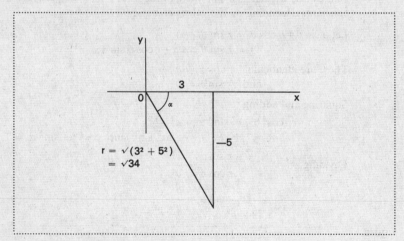

$r = \sqrt{\{3^2 + (-5)^2\}} = \sqrt{34} = 5.831$

α is in the fourth quadrant since

$\tan \alpha = -\frac{5}{3} = -1.6667$
$\qquad \alpha = -59° 2'$ or $360° - 59° 2' = 300° 58'$
$\therefore 3 \sin \theta - 5 \cos \theta = 5.831 \sin (\theta - 59° 2')$

Example 3 Find the greatest value of 3 sin $\theta - 5 \cos \theta$ and the value of θ at which this occurs.

Since 3 sin $\theta - 5 \cos \theta = 5{\cdot}831 \sin (\theta - 59° \ 2')$ then we require the greatest value of $5{\cdot}831 \sin (\theta - 59° \ 2')$.

The greatest value of $\sin (\theta - 59° \ 2')$ is 1 when $\theta - 59° \ 2' = 90°$. Thus the greatest value of the expression is $5{\cdot}831$ when $\theta = 90° + 59° \ 2' = 149° \ 2'$.

We could, if we wish, convert $a \sin \theta + b \cos \theta$ into the form $r \cos (\theta - \beta)$ as follows:

Let $\quad a \sin \theta + b \cos \theta = r \cos (\theta - \beta)$
$$= r \cos \theta \cos \beta + r \sin \theta \sin \beta$$
These are identical if $\quad r \cos \beta = b$
$$\text{and} \quad r \sin \beta = a$$

Thus $\quad r = \sqrt{(a^2 + b^2)} \quad$ and $\quad \tan \beta = \dfrac{a}{b} \quad$ (see fig. 153)

Figure 153

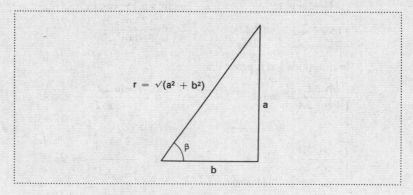

Notice that β is the complement of α in

$a \sin \theta + b \cos \theta = \sqrt{(a^2 + b^2)} \sin (\theta + \alpha)$

Hence $\quad a \sin \theta + b \cos \theta = \sqrt{(a^2 + b^2)} \cos (\theta - \beta)$

where $\quad \tan \beta = \dfrac{a}{b} \quad$ i.e. $\quad \beta = \tan^{-1} \dfrac{a}{b}$

Example 4 Convert 3 sin $\theta + 4 \cos \theta$ into the form $r \cos (\theta - \beta)$

Here $\quad r = \sqrt{(3^2 + 4^2)} = 5$
and $\quad \tan \beta = \tfrac{3}{4} = 0{\cdot}75 \therefore \beta = 36° \ 52'$

$\therefore$ 3 sin $\theta + 4 \cos \theta = 5 \cos (\theta - 36° \ 52')$

Compare this with the result in example 1 above.

269 To convert a sin $\theta + b$ cos θ to r sin $(\theta + \alpha)$

Exercise 11c

1   Write down the three forms for cos 2A.
    Find the value of sin 22½° and cos 22½° without using trigonometric tables, given that $\cos 45° = \dfrac{1}{\sqrt{2}} = 0.7071$.

2   Given $\tan A = \frac{4}{3}$, find sin 2A, cos 2A and tan 2A.

3   If sin 2A = 0.8, find sin A and $\sin \dfrac{A}{2}$ without evaluating the angles.

4   Given that $\sin 30° = \dfrac{1}{2}$, $\cos 30° = \dfrac{\sqrt{3}}{2} = 0.8660$, and $\sin 45° = \cos 45° = \dfrac{1}{\sqrt{2}} = 0.7071$, find the values of

    (a) $1 - 2 \sin^2 15°$ (b) sin 15° cos 15°

    (c) $\cos^2 22\frac{1}{2}° - \sin^2 22\frac{1}{2}°$ (d) $\dfrac{2 \tan 22\frac{1}{2}°}{1 - \tan^2 22\frac{1}{2}°}$

In questions 5–11, prove that

5   $\dfrac{\sin 2A}{1 + \cos 2A} = \tan A$

6   $\dfrac{\sin 2A}{1 - \cos 2A} = \cot A$

7   $\dfrac{1 - \cos 2A}{1 + \cos 2A} = \tan^2 A$

8   $\dfrac{2 \tan \dfrac{A}{2}}{1 + \tan^2 \dfrac{A}{2}} = \sin A$

9   $\dfrac{1 - \cos \theta}{1 + \cos \theta} = \tan^2 \dfrac{\theta}{2}$

10   $\dfrac{\cos 2\theta}{\cos \theta + \sin \theta} = \cos \theta - \sin \theta$

11   $(\cos A - \sin A)^2 = 1 - \sin 2A$

12   By expanding the right-hand side of the identity show that

$$\sin x + \cos x = \sqrt{2} \sin\left(x + \frac{\pi}{4}\right)$$

Convert the expressions in questions 13–16 into the form $r \sin (\theta + \alpha)$

13   $8 \sin \theta + 6 \cos \theta$

14   $2 \sin \theta + 3 \cos \theta$

15   $4 \sin \theta - 3 \cos \theta$

16   $12 \sin \theta - 5 \cos \theta$

17 Express $4 \cos \theta + 7 \sin \theta$ in the form $r \cos (\theta - \beta)$

18 Express $15 \sin 100t - 20 \cos 100t$ in the form $r \sin (100t - \alpha)$, finding the values of r and α.

19 Write down the greatest and the least values of $a \sin \theta + b \cos \theta$.

20 Find the greatest value of $5 \sin \theta + 12 \cos \theta$ and find the smallest positive value of θ at which it occurs.

Sketch the graph of $y = 5 \sin \theta + 12 \cos \theta$.

11d Solution of trigonometric equations

Trigonometric equations differ from algebraic in that they often have an unlimited number of solutions. For example consider the equation $\sin x = \frac{1}{2}$.

Figure 154

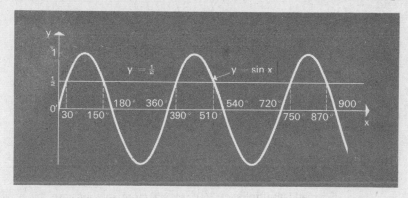

If we draw the graph of $y = \sin x$ and find the values of x which make $y = \frac{1}{2}$ we find that the solutions are given by the intersections of the line $y = \frac{1}{2}$ with the graph of $y = \sin x$ (see fig. 154).

We see that $\sin x = \frac{1}{2}$ at $x = 30°, 150°, 360 + 30°, 360 + 150°, \ldots$ etc.

Since the curve repeats itself we need only find the roots of the equation between $0°$ and $360°$. We then have only to add multiples of $360°$ to find all the other solutions.

Some equations can only be solved by a graphical method, but if we can simplify the equation sufficiently we can solve it without drawing a graph.

Example 1   Solve $3 \sin x = 2$

Here $\sin x = \frac{2}{3} = 0.6667$

There are two possible solutions between $0°$ and $360°$. Since the sine is positive the angle must lie in the first quadrant or the second quadrant.

From the tables the acute angle whose sine is 0·6667 is 41° 49′.

The angle in the second quadrant is $180° - 41° 49′ = 138° 11′$. Other solutions are obtained by adding multiples of 360° to these values.

Thus the solutions are 41° 49′, 138° 11′, 401° 49′, 498° 11′, ... etc.

Example 2 Solve $2 \tan x + 3 = 0$

We write this $\tan x = -1·5$

Since the tangent is negative the angle must lie in the second or fourth quadrants (fig. 155).

The acute angle whose tangent is 1·5 is 56° 19′ from the tables.

Figure 155

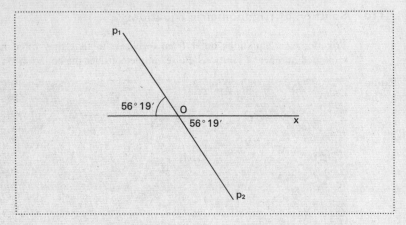

The solutions between 0° and 360° are $180° - 56° 19′$ and $360° - 56° 19′$ i.e. 123° 41′ and 303° 41′.

If we add multiples of 360° we get more solutions which are 483° 41′, 663° 41′, 843° 41′ ... etc.

In solving trigonometric equations we try to reduce the given equation to one of the standard equations given below, where $α°$ is the numerical value of the smallest positive angle satisfying the equation. There are always two angles between 0° and 360° corresponding to a possible value for a trigonometric ratio.

(1) $\sin x = \sin α°$

Solutions are $x = α°, 180° - α°, 360° + α°, 540° - α°$, etc.

(2) $\cos x = \cos α°$

Solutions are $x = α°, 360° - α°, 360° + α°, 720° - α°$, etc.

(3) $\tan x = \tan α°$

Solutions are $x = α°, 180° + α°, 360° + α°, 540° + α°$, ... etc.

272 **Compound angles and trigonometric equations**

Example 3 Find all the angles between $0°$ and $360°$ which satisfy the equation $2 \sin^2 \theta - \cos \theta - 1 = 0$.

By substituting $1 - \cos^2 \theta$ for $\sin^2 \theta$ we can change the equation into a quadratic equation in $\cos \theta$.

$$2(1 - \cos^2 \theta) - \cos \theta - 1 = 0$$
$$\text{i.e.} \quad 2 - 2\cos^2 \theta - \cos \theta - 1 = 0$$
$$\text{And re-arranging} \quad 2\cos^2 \theta + \cos \theta - 1 = 0$$
$$\therefore (2 \cos \theta - 1)(\cos \theta + 1) = 0$$
$$\text{Thus} \quad \cos \theta = \tfrac{1}{2} \quad \text{or} \quad \cos \theta = -1$$

(a) If $\cos \theta = \tfrac{1}{2}$ then θ may be in the first or fourth quadrants. (Fig. 156)

Figure
156

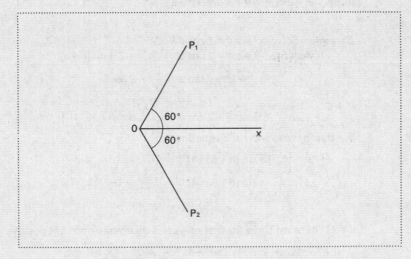

$$\cos \theta = \tfrac{1}{2} = \cos 60°$$
$$\therefore \theta = 60° \text{ or } 360° - 60° = 300°$$

(b) If $\cos \theta = -1 = \cos 180°$
$$\text{then} \quad \theta = 180°$$

The next solution $360° - 180° = 180°$ and there is only one solution between $0°$ and $360°$.

The required solutions are $60°, 180°, 300°$.

Example 4 Find the angles between $0°$ and $360°$ which satisfy the equation $2 \sin 2x = \cos 2x$
Dividing both sides by $2 \cos 2x$ gives

$$\tan 2x = \tfrac{1}{2}$$
$$= \tan 26° 34' \text{ from the tables.}$$

Here $2x$ is either in the first or third quadrants.

$$\therefore 2x = 26° 34', 180° + 26° 34', 360° + 26° 34', 540° + 26° 34', \ldots \text{etc.}$$
$$= 26° 34', 206° 34', 386° 34', 566° 34', \text{etc.}$$

On dividing by 2 we find that the solutions between $0°$ and $360°$ are

$$x = 13° 17', 103° 17', 193° 17', 283° 17'$$

The equation $a \sin \theta + b \cos \theta = c$

Equations of this type can be solved by first converting $a \sin \theta + b \cos \theta$ into

form $\sqrt{(a^2 + b^2)} \sin (\theta + \alpha)$ where $\tan \alpha = \dfrac{b}{a}$.

Example Solve $3 \sin \theta + 2 \cos \theta = 2.5$

If we write $3 \sin \theta + 2 \cos \theta = \sqrt{(3^2 + 2^2)} \sin (\theta + \alpha)$

where $\tan \alpha = \dfrac{2}{3} = 0.6667$

i.e. $\alpha = 33° 41'$

$$\therefore 3 \sin \theta + 2 \cos \theta = \sqrt{13} \sin (\theta + 33° 41')$$

We thus have to solve the equation

$$\sqrt{13} \sin (\theta + 33° 41') = 2.5$$
$$\sin (\theta + 33° 41') = \frac{2.5}{\sqrt{13}} = 0.6933$$
$$= \sin 43° 54'$$

$\theta + 33° 41'$ must lie in the first or second quadrants since it is positive.

$$\therefore \theta + 33° 41' = 43° 54', 180° - 43° 54', 360° + 43° 54', \text{etc.}$$
$$= 43° 54', 136° 6', 403° 54', \text{etc.}$$
$$\therefore \theta = 43° 54' - 33° 41', 136° 6' - 33° 41', 403° 54' - 33° 41',$$
$$= 10° 13', 102° 25', 370° 13', \text{etc.}$$

The solutions between $0°$ and $360°$ are $10° 13'$ and $102° 25'$

Exercise 11d

Solve the equations in questions 1–19 for all values of the angle between $0°$ and $360°$

1 $\cos x = 0.8660$	2 $\sin^2 x = \frac{1}{4}$	3 $4 \tan x + 3 = 0$
4 $\cot \theta = 1$	5 $\sec \theta = 2$	6 $\sin x - \cos x = 0$
7 $4 \cos x = \sec x$	8 $\sin 2x = \sin x$	9 $3 \sin (x + 30°) = 2$

10    $2 \cos (\theta - 25°) - 1 = 0$ 11 $2 \sin 2\theta + 1 = 0$

12    $\cos 3\theta = \frac{1}{2}$ 13 $3 \tan^2 \theta - 4 \tan \theta + 1 = 0$

14    $2 \tan \theta + 1 - \cot \theta = 0$ 15 $2 \sin^2 \theta + 3 \cos \theta - 3 = 0$

16    $\cos^2 \theta - \sin \theta - \frac{1}{4} = 0$ 17 $\operatorname{cosec} \theta - 2 = 3 \sin \theta$

18    $4 \sin \theta + 3 \cos \theta = 2$ 19 $15 \sin \theta + 8 \cos \theta = 10$

20   Find the values of θ between $0°$ and $360°$ that satisfy both the equations in each of the following

(a) $\cos \theta = \dfrac{1}{\sqrt{2}}$ and $\tan \theta = -1$ (b) $\sin \theta = \dfrac{-1}{2}$ and $\tan \theta = \dfrac{1}{\sqrt{3}}$

(c) $\sin \theta = \dfrac{\sqrt{3}}{2}$ and $\cos \theta = \dfrac{-1}{2}$

Miscellaneous exercises 11

1   Write down the expansion of $\sin (A + B)$ in terms of the sines and cosines of the angles A and B.

If $\tan A = \frac{12}{5}$, $\sin B = \frac{4}{5}$ and A and B are both acute angles, obtain the value of $\sin (A + B)$ without using tables.

U.L.C.I.

2   (a) Prove the formula for $\cos (A + B)$ in terms of sines and cosines of A and B, when A, B, and $A + B$ are positive acute angles. Deduce the formula for $\cos 2A$ in terms of $\cos A$.

(b) Using the ratios of $45°$ and $30°$, find the values of $\cos 75°$, $\cos 22\frac{1}{2}°$ and $\sin 22\frac{1}{2}°$ without using tables and leaving the answers in surd form.

D.T.C.

3   Prove the following

(a) $\dfrac{2 \tan B}{1 + \tan^2 B} = 2 \sin B \cos B$

(b) Solve the equation $2 \cos^2 x + \cos x = 1$, giving all possible values of x between $0°$ and $360°$.

U.L.C.I.

4   (a) Prove that $\sin (A + B) = \sin A \cos B + \cos A \sin B$ where A and B are each less than $90°$.

(b) Find the values of $\sin 15°$, $\cos 15°$ and $\tan 15°$, using the standard relationships for $60°$ and $45°$.

E.M.E.U.

5 (a) Express tan $2A$ as a function of tan A and hence show without tables that $\tan 22\tfrac{1}{2}° = \sqrt{2}-1$.

(b) Prove the identity $\dfrac{\sin 2A}{1+\cos 2A} = \tan A$

(c) Determine the values of θ between $0°$ and $360°$ which satisfy the equation $6\sin^2\theta - \cos\theta = 4$.

N.C.T.E.C.

6 (a) Show that $\cos(A+B) = \cos A\cos B - \sin A\sin B$.

(b) If $\sin A = 0.6$ and $\cos B = 0.4$, determine the values of $\sin(A+B)$ and $\cos(A-B)$, without evaluating the angles A and B

(c) Express $6.8\sin 3t + 5.4\cos 3t$ in the form: $A\sin(3t+C)$.

U.E.I.

7 (a) If $\cos B = 0.6$, calculate the values of $\sin 2B$, $\cos 2B$, and $\tan 2B$ without evaluating the angle B.

(b) Solve the following equation for all values of x between $0°$ and $360°$: $2\sin^2 x + 5\cos x + 1 = 0$.

(c) Prove the following identity:

$$2\sin^2 x(\cot x - 1) + 1 = \sin 2x + \cos 2x$$

U.E.I.

8 (a) If $\sin A = \tfrac{1}{5}$, find the values of $\sin 2A$, $\cos 2A$ and $\sin 4A$.

(b) Prove the identity $\operatorname{cosec}^2 A + \sec^2 A = 4\operatorname{cosec}^2 2A$.

(c) Solve the equation $\cos 2\theta - 3\cos\theta + 2 = 0$ for values of θ from $0°$ to $360°$.

D.T.C.

9 Give the expansions of $\sin(A+B)$ and $\cos(A-B)$. Show that the expression $R\sin(\theta+\alpha)$ can be put in the form $a\sin\theta + b\cos\theta$.

If R is 7 and α is $\dfrac{\pi}{6}$ obtain the values of a and b.

U.L.C.I.

10 (a) Assuming the formulae for $\sin(A+B)$ and $\cos(A+B)$, find the formulae for (i) $\tan(A+B)$ and (ii) $\sin 2A$.

(b) If $a\sin\theta + b\cos\theta = R\cos(\theta - a)$ find the values of R and $\tan a$ in terms of a and b.

(c) Find all the values of θ from $0°$ to $180°$ which satisfy the equations (i) $2\cos 3\theta = 1$, (ii) $\sin 3\theta = \cos 3\theta$.

D.T.C.

11 (a) Assuming the expansion of $\cos(A+B)$, prove that $\cos 2A = 1 - 2\sin^2 A$. Hence find the value of $\sin 15°$ and $\tan 15°$.

(b) Solve the equation $\sin 2x = 0.56$ for all values of x between $0°$ and $360°$.

N.C.T.E.C.

12 (a) i Write down the expansions of $\sin(A-B)$ and $\cos(A-B)$.

ii Show that $\sin(x-150°) + \sin(x-330°) = 0$.

(b) Solve the following equation for all values of x from $0°$ to $360°$:

$\cos 2x + \sin 2x = 1$

(c) Prove that $\dfrac{1 + \cos 2A}{\sin 2A} = \cot A$

U.E.I.

13   (a) Find all the values of x between $0°$ and $360°$ which satisfy the equation

$6 \sin^2 x - 7 \sin x = -2$

(b) Prove that

$\sin (45° + A) \sin (45° - A) = \tfrac{1}{2} \cos 2A$

E.M.E.U.

14   (a) If $\cos \theta = \tfrac{4}{5}$, find without tables the values of $\sin 2\theta$ and $\cos 2\theta$.

(b) Find the smallest positive value of θ which satisfies the expression

$$\sin \theta + \sin \left(\theta + \frac{\pi}{4}\right) - \cos \left(\theta + \frac{\pi}{4}\right) = 1{\cdot}25$$

(c) Express $5 \sin \theta + 12 \cos \theta$ in the form $R \sin (\theta + \alpha)$ and solve the equation
$5 \sin \theta + 12 \cos \theta = 6{\cdot}5$ for values of θ between $0°$ and $360°$.

U.L.C.I.

15   (a) Prove that

$$\frac{\cot A + \tan B}{\tan A + \cot B} = \cot A \tan B$$

(b) Solve the equation

$$\sec^2 x - \frac{2}{\sqrt{3}} \tan x - 2 = 0$$

giving all possible solutions between $0°$ and $360°$.

(c) If $\sin A = \tfrac{3}{5}$ and $\tan B = \tfrac{8}{15}$ calculate without tables
i $\sin (A + B)$
ii $\cos (A + B)$

E.M.E.U.

16   Show that $A \sin \theta + B \cos \theta$ may be expressed in the form $R \sin (\theta + \alpha)$. Find
the values of R and α if $A = 4$ and $B = 3$. Hence solve $4 \sin \theta + 3 \cos \theta = 3{\cdot}5$
for values of θ between $0°$ and $360°$.

U.L.C.I.

17   (a) Prove that

$\sin A + \sin (A + 120°) + \sin (A + 240°) = 0$

(b) Express $v = 24 \sin x + 7 \cos x$ in the form $v = R \sin (x + \alpha)$ giving the
values of R and α. Hence, find the positive value of $x < 90°$ when $v = 20$.

D.T.C.

277   Miscellaneous exercises 11

18 (a) Simplify $5 \sin (x+60°)-3 \cos (x+30°)$
    (b) Find $\tan (\alpha-\beta)$ in terms of m_1 and m_2 given that $\tan \alpha = m_1$ and $\tan \beta = m_2$.
        If, in addition, $m_1 m_2 = -1$, find the value of $(\alpha-\beta)$.

                                                                    N.C.T.E.C.

19 Express $12 \sin \theta+5 \cos \theta$ in the form $K \sin (\theta+a)$.
       Hence find the values of θ between $0°$ and $360°$ which will satisfy the
    equation $12 \sin \theta+5 \cos \theta = 9{\cdot}75$
       Sketch the graph of $12 \sin \theta+5 \cos \theta$ for one complete cycle.

                                                                    D.T.C.

20 (a) Solve the equation

        $$5(1-\sin x) = 2(\cos 2x + \cos^2 x)$$

        giving all values of x between $0°$ and $360°$

    (b) After a pendulum 48 cm long has swung through a certain angle from the
        vertical, the bob is 8 cm higher than its lowest position. Without using
        tables, find how much higher the bob will be when the pendulum has
        swung through an angle from the vertical twice as large as the first.

12 Integration

12a   Integration as the reverse of differentiation

The two earlier sections on calculus, pp. 163–202, were mainly concerned with differentiation where, given y as a function of the variable x, one finds $\dfrac{dy}{dx}$.

The reverse process, that of finding y when given $\dfrac{dy}{dx}$, is called *integration*.

For example, if $\dfrac{dy}{dx} = 6x$, then $y = 3x^2$ is a solution. This is not the only answer, however, for if $y = 3x^2 + 1$ or $y = 3x^2 - 5$ then in each case $\dfrac{dy}{dx} = 6x$.

The complete answer to the problem $\dfrac{dy}{dx} = 6x$ is $y = 3x^2 + c$ where c is a constant which may have any value whatever. For this reason c is called an arbitrary constant.

As a second illustration suppose $\dfrac{dy}{dx} = 8x^3$ then $y = 2x^4 + c$ is the solution. We can easily check this by differentiating this value of y.

If $\quad \dfrac{dy}{dx} = x^n \quad$ then $\quad y = \dfrac{x^{n+1}}{n+1} + c$

This is obviously true, for differentiating

$$y = \frac{x^{n+1}}{n+1} + c \quad \text{we get} \quad \frac{dy}{dx} = \frac{(n+1)x^{n+1-1}}{n+1} = x^n$$

The rule holds for all values of n except -1, for applying the rule to $\dfrac{dy}{dx} = \dfrac{1}{x} = x^{-1}$ we get $y = \dfrac{x^{-1+1}}{-1+1} + c = \dfrac{x^0}{0} + c$ which is not a solution.

Example 1   Given the following values of $\dfrac{dy}{dx}$ find y.

(a) $\dfrac{dy}{dx} = x^5$ 　　　　　　(b) $\dfrac{dy}{dx} = Ax^5$ 　where A is any constant

(c) $\dfrac{dy}{dx} = 4$ (d) $\dfrac{dy}{dx} = \dfrac{1}{x^2}$

(a) $\dfrac{dy}{dx} = x^5$ then $y = \dfrac{x^6}{6} + c$

(b) $\dfrac{dy}{dx} = Ax^5$ then $y = \dfrac{Ax^6}{6} + c$

The presence of the constant A merely multiplies the answer.

(c) $\dfrac{dy}{dx} = 4$ $y = 4x + c$

This is best shown by differentiating the answer. It can be obtained from the general rule by writing

$$\dfrac{dy}{dx} = 4 = 4 \times x^0 \quad \text{since} \quad x^0 = 1$$

and the rule gives $y = 4 \times \dfrac{x^{0+1}}{0+1} + c = 4x + c$

(d) $\dfrac{dy}{dx} = \dfrac{1}{x^2} = x^{-2}$

Then $y = \dfrac{x^{-2+1}}{-2+1} + c = \dfrac{x^{-1}}{-1} + c$

$$= -\dfrac{1}{x} + c$$

In differentiating a sum of several terms we differentiate each term separately. Hence, reversing the process, to integrate a sum we integrate each term separately as in the following example.

Example 2   If $\dfrac{dy}{dx} = 3x^3 - 5x^2 + x + 4$

then $y = \dfrac{3}{4}x^4 - \dfrac{5}{3}x^3 + \dfrac{x^2}{2} + 4x + c$

This result can easily be checked by differentiating y to obtain $\dfrac{dy}{dx}$ and then comparing with the original value.

The constant of integration, the arbitrary constant c which appears on integration, can be found in a particular problem if a corresponding pair of values of x and y are known.

Example 3 Find y given $\dfrac{dy}{dx} = 3x^2 + 4x$ and that $y = 2$ when $x = 1$.

$$\frac{dy}{dx} = 3x^2 + 4x \ \therefore \ y = x^3 + 2x^2 + c$$

When $x = 1 \ y = 2 \ \therefore \ 2 = 1^3 + 2.1^2 + c$
$$\therefore \ c = 2 - 3 = -1$$
$$\therefore \ y = x^3 + 2x^2 - 1$$

Example 4 Find the equation of a curve which passes through the origin, given that its gradient is $4x^2$.

Since the gradient of a curve at any point on it is given by $\dfrac{dy}{dx}$ at the point in question, then for this curve

$$\frac{dy}{dx} = 4x^2$$

$$\therefore \ y = \frac{4x^3}{3} + c$$

As the curve passes through the origin then $y = 0$ when $x = 0$

$$\therefore \ 0 = 0 + c \quad \text{and} \quad c = 0$$

Required equation is $y = \dfrac{4x^3}{3}$

Exercise 12a

In questions 1 to 10 find the general value for y from the expression for $\dfrac{dy}{dx}$.

1 $\dfrac{dy}{dx} = x^4$ 2 $\dfrac{dy}{dx} = 4x$ 3 $\dfrac{dy}{dx} = 3x^2 + 2$

4 $\dfrac{dy}{dx} = x^2 - 8x + 5$ 5 $\dfrac{dy}{dx} = \dfrac{1}{x^4}$ 6 $\dfrac{dy}{dx} = \sqrt[3]{x}$

7 $\dfrac{dy}{dx} = x^2(1 - x)$ 8 $\dfrac{dy}{dx} = (2x - 1)^2$ 9 $\dfrac{dy}{dx} = \dfrac{x^3 - 2x}{x}$

10 $\dfrac{dy}{dx} = \left(x + \dfrac{1}{x}\right)^2$

In questions 11 to 15 find the value of y.

11 $\dfrac{dy}{dx} = 3x^2 - 2$ and $y = 0$ when $x = 0$

12    $\dfrac{dy}{dx} = 4(1+x)$ and $y = 3$ when $x = 1$

13    $\dfrac{dy}{dx} = 5x^4 - 2x$ and $y = 2$ when $x = 1$

14    $\dfrac{dy}{dx} = 1 - \dfrac{4}{x^3}$ and $y = 4$ when $x = 3$

15    $\dfrac{dy}{dx} = (x+2)(x-1)$ and $y = 5$ when $x = 2$

16   Find the equation of a curve which passes through the origin, given that the gradient is $6x(x-1)$.

17   A curve has a gradient of $2x-1$. If the curve passes through the point $x = 1$, $y = 3$ find its equation.

18   If $\dfrac{ds}{dt} = 10 - 2t$ and $s = 40$ when $t = 3$, find an expression for s.

19   If $\dfrac{dp}{dv} = 5v - 2$ and $p = 10$ when $v = 1$, find the value of p when $v = 3$.

20   If $\dfrac{dA}{dt} = 2 + \dfrac{2}{5}t$ and $A = 6$ when $t = 2$, find the value of A when $t = 4$.

12b   The integral sign

The problem of finding y when given $\dfrac{dy}{dx}$ we called integration. There is a symbol for this reverse process, known as the integral sign, and it is written as follows:

If $\dfrac{dy}{dx} = f(x)$ then $y = \displaystyle\int f(x)\,dx$

Thus if $\dfrac{dy}{dx} = 4x^2 - 3x + 1$ then $y = \displaystyle\int (4x^2 - 3x + 1)\,dx$

The statement

if $\dfrac{dy}{dx} = x^n$ then $y = \dfrac{x^{n+1}}{n+1} + c$

may now be written

$$\int x^n dx = \frac{x^{n+1}}{n+1} + c$$

This is true for all values of n except $n = -1$.

Example Find (a) $\int (3x^2 - 6x + 2)\,dx$ (b) $\int (4x - \sqrt{x})\,dx$ (c) $\int \left(\frac{4 - x^2}{x^2}\right) dx$

(a) $\int (3x^2 - 6x + 2)\,dx = \dfrac{3x^3}{3} - \dfrac{6x^2}{2} + 2x + c$

$$= x^3 - 3x^2 + 2x + c$$

(b) $\int (4x - \sqrt{x})\,dx = \int (4x - x^{\frac{1}{2}})\,dx = \dfrac{4x^2}{2} - \dfrac{x^{\frac{3}{2}}}{\frac{3}{2}} + c$

$$= 2x^2 - \frac{2}{3}x^{\frac{3}{2}} + c$$

(c) $\int \left(\dfrac{4 - x^2}{x^2}\right) dx = \int \left(\dfrac{4}{x^2} - \dfrac{x^2}{x^2}\right) dx = \int (4x^{-2} - 1)\,dx$

$$= \frac{4x^{-1}}{-1} - x + c$$

$$= -\frac{4}{x} - x + c$$

12c   Acceleration, velocity and distance

If s is the distance travelled in a time t and v the velocity at the time t we saw in chapter 8 that

$$v = \frac{ds}{dt}$$

Thus if v is given in terms of t then by integration it is possible to obtain the distance in terms of t.

Also the acceleration at any instant is given by $\dfrac{dv}{dt}$ and if the acceleration is given in terms of the time t then integrating will give velocity.

Example 1   A body starts from rest and its velocity in m s^{-1} after a time t seconds is given by $v = 20 + 12t$. Find the distance from the starting point (a) after a time t and (b) after 3 seconds.

$$\text{velocity } v = \frac{ds}{dt} = 20 + 12t$$

$$\therefore \text{ distance } s = \int (20 + 12t)dt$$

$$= 20t + 6t^2 + c$$

But when $\quad t = 0, s = 0 \therefore c = 0$

$\therefore$ (a) distance $= 20t + 6t^2$

When $\quad t = 3, s = 20 \times 3 + 6 \times 3^2 = 114$

$\therefore$ (b) distance after 3 seconds $= 114$ metres

Example 2 A body starts with an initial velocity of 5 m s^{-1} and its acceleration is given by $6 + 4t \text{ m s}^{-2}$ where t is the time from the start. Find formulae for the velocity and for the distance travelled after t seconds.

Calculate the velocity after 2 s and the distance travelled in 6 s.

$$\text{Acceleration } a = 6 + 4t = \frac{dv}{dt}$$

$$\therefore \text{ velocity } v = \int (6 + 4t)dt = 6t + 2t^2 + c$$

When $\quad t = 0$, velocity $v = 5 \text{ m s}^{-1}$

$$\therefore 5 = c$$

$$\therefore \text{ velocity } v = 6t + 2t^2 + 5$$

$$v = \frac{ds}{dt} = 6t + 2t^2 + 5$$

$$\therefore \text{ distance } s = \int (6t + 2t^2 + 5)dt$$

$$= 3t^2 + \frac{2}{3}t^3 + 5t + c$$

When $\quad t = 0$, the body is at the starting point and $s = 0$

$$\therefore 0 = c$$

$$\therefore \text{ distance } s = 3t^2 + \frac{2}{3}t^3 + 5t$$

When $\quad t = 2$ s velocity $= 6.2 + 2.2^2 + 5$

$$= 25 \text{ m s}^{-1}$$

When $\quad t = 6$ s distance $= 3.6^2 + \frac{2}{3}.6^3 + 5.6$

$$= 282 \text{ m}$$

Exercise 12c

In questions 1–12 find the integrals.

1 $\displaystyle\int 5x^4\,dx$

2 $\displaystyle\int 6x^2\,dx$

3 $\displaystyle\int \frac{dx}{x^3}$

4 $\displaystyle\int \frac{dx}{x^2}$

5 $\displaystyle\int (4-x)^2\,dx$

6 $\displaystyle\int (ax+b)^2\,dx$

7 $\displaystyle\int (t^2-6t)\,dt$

8 $\displaystyle\int (r^3-2r)\,dr$

9 $\displaystyle\int \sqrt{m}\,dm$

10 $\displaystyle\int (u^2-7)\,du$

11 $\displaystyle\int \frac{dp}{\sqrt{p}}$

12 $\displaystyle\int (2-u^2)\,du$

13 A body starts from rest and its velocity v in m s^{-1} after a time t seconds is given by $v = 3+2t$. Find a formula for the distance s.

14 If the velocity v of a body is given by $v = 5+t$ and distance $s = 0$ when $t = 0$, find a formula for the distance in terms of t.

15 If velocity $v = 3t^2-6t$, and distance $s = 4$ when $t = 1$ find s when $t = 4$.

16 If a body has an acceleration $a = 2t$ m s^{-2} after t seconds, find its velocity after time t if its initial velocity when $t = 0$ is 3 m s^{-1}.

17 If the acceleration a of a body is given by $a = t+2$ m s^{-2}, find a formula for the velocity v at any time t if the initial velocity is 16 m s^{-1}.

18 If $v = 100-32t$ find s if when $t = 0$, $s = 0$. Find the acceleration.

19 If the acceleration $a = 32$, find expressions for velocity v and distance travelled s if when $t = 0$, $v = 10$ and $s = 0$.

20 Find expressions for v and s if $a = 3t+1$ and $v = 5$ and $s = 2$ when $t = 0$.

Figure
157

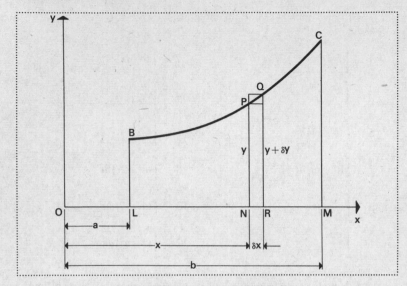

Fig. 157 shows the graph of $y = f(x)$. We wish to find the area $BCML$ which is the area bounded by the curve, the x axis and the ordinates at $x = a$ and $x = b$.

Point P, coordinates x and y, is any point on the arc BC.

Let the area $BPNL$ be represented by A.

If the ordinate PN moves a small distance δx to the position QR then the area A increases by a small amount $PQRN$ which we denote by δA.

Ordinate $QR = y + \delta y$

Then δA lies between the values of the areas of two rectangular strips, each of width δx, one of height y and the other of height $y + \delta y$.

δA lies between $y \cdot \delta x$ and $(y + \delta y) \cdot \delta x$

i.e. $\dfrac{\delta A}{\delta x}$ lies between y and $y + \delta y$

If we make δx smaller and smaller to approach zero then $y + \delta y$ approaches y and $\dfrac{\delta A}{\delta x}$ approaches $\dfrac{dA}{dx}$.

$\therefore \lim\limits_{\delta x \to 0} \dfrac{\delta A}{\delta x} = \dfrac{dA}{dx} = y$

Hence $\quad A = \displaystyle\int y\,dx = \int f(x)\,dx$

Let the value of this integral be denoted by $F(x)+c$. Since we measure the area A starting at $x = a$ then $A = 0$ when $x = a$.

Putting $x = a$ in $F(x)+c$ must give zero.

$F(a)+c = 0$ and $c = -F(a)$

Thus area $BPNL = F(x)-F(a)$

The area $BCML$ is given by putting b for x in this

$$= F(b)-F(a)$$
$$= \text{value of} \int f(x)\,dx \text{ when } x = b$$

minus the value of $\int f(x)\,dx$ when $x = a$.

This is written $\int_a^b f(x)\,dx$

Thus required area $= \int_a^b f(x)\,dx$

Example 1 Find the area bounded by the graph of $y = 3x^2+2x$, the x axis and the ordinates at $x = 1$ and $x = 3$.

Required area $= \int_1^3 (3x^2+2x)\,dx$

We integrate this and write it down as follows

$$\int_1^3 (3x^2+2x)\,dx = \left[x^3+x^2+'c \right]_1^3$$

Substituting in the values of the limits

$$= [3^3+3^2+c]-[1^3+1^2+c]$$
$$= 34$$

There is no need to bring in the arbitrary constant c in problems of this kind as it always disappears in the subtraction.

Example 2 Calculate the area bounded by the curve $y = x^2+4$, the x axis and the ordinates $x = 2$ and $x = 4$.

Required area $= \int_2^4 (x^2+4)\,dx = \left[\dfrac{x^3}{3}+4x \right]_2^4$

$$= \left[\frac{64}{3}+16 \right]-\left[\frac{8}{3}+8 \right] = 26\tfrac{2}{3}$$

12e The definite integral

The expression $\int_a^b f(x)\,dx$ which represents the value of $\int f(x)\,dx$ when $x = b$ minus the value of $\int f(x)\,dx$ when $x = a$ is called a *definite* integral. The arbitrary constant is not introduced as it automatically disappears in the subtraction.

Example Evaluate the definite integrals

(a) $\displaystyle\int_0^3 (x^2-2)\,dx$ (b) $\displaystyle\int_4^9 \sqrt{x}\,dx$ (c) $\displaystyle\int_1^2 \frac{dx}{x^3}$

(a) $\displaystyle\int_0^3 (x^2-2)\,dx = \left[\frac{x^3}{3} - 2x\right]_0^3 = \left(\frac{27}{3} - 6\right) - (0) = 3$

(b) $\displaystyle\int_4^9 \sqrt{x}\,dx = \int_4^9 x^{\frac{1}{2}}\,dx = \left[\frac{2}{3}x^{\frac{3}{2}}\right]_4^9 = \frac{2}{3}(27-8) = 12\frac{2}{3}$

(c) $\displaystyle\int_1^2 \frac{dx}{x^3} = \int_1^2 x^{-3}\,dx = \left[\frac{x^{-2}}{-2}\right]_1^2 = \left[\frac{-1}{2x^2}\right]_1^2$

$= \left(\frac{-1}{8}\right) - \left(\frac{-1}{2}\right) = \frac{1}{2} - \frac{1}{8} = \frac{3}{8}$

Exercise 12e

Evaluate the integrals in questions 1–10.

1 $\displaystyle\int_1^2 x\,dx$

2 $\displaystyle\int_0^3 x^2\,dx$

3 $\displaystyle\int_0^3 (x-1)\,dx$

4 $\displaystyle\int_1^2 (x^2-3x+3)\,dx$

5 $\displaystyle\int_0^4 2\sqrt{x}\,dx$

6 $\displaystyle\int_2^3 \frac{dx}{x^2}$

7 $\displaystyle\int_1^3 (t^2-2t)\,dt$

8 $\displaystyle\int_{-1}^2 (2x+1)\,dx$

9 $\displaystyle\int_1^9 3\sqrt{u}\,du$

10 $\displaystyle\int_0^a (ax-x^2)\,dx$

In questions 11 to 17 find the area bounded by the given curve, the x axis and the given ordinates.

11 $y = x^2$; $x = 0$, $x = 2$

12 $y = x^2 + 2x$; $x = 0$, $x = 2$

13    $y = 3x - x^2$; $x = 0$, $x = 3$ 14 $y = x^2 + x$; $x = 1$, $x = 4$

15    $y = x + \dfrac{1}{x^2}$; $x = 1$, $x = 4$ 16 $y = (x - 2)^2$; $x = -1$, $x = 2$

17    $y^2 = x$; $x = 1$, $x = 4$

18   Fig. 158 represents the graph of $y = 6x - x^2$. Find the area cut off from the curve by the x axis.

Figure 158

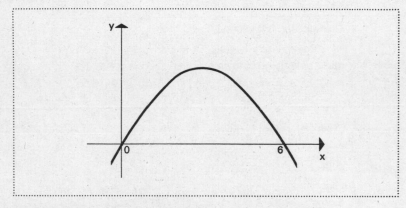

19   Fig. 159 shows a sketch of the graph $y = x^2$ and $y = x + 6$.
Find the co-ordinates of the points of intersection P and Q.
Find the area enclosed between the curves $y = x^2$ and $y = x + 6$.

Figure 159

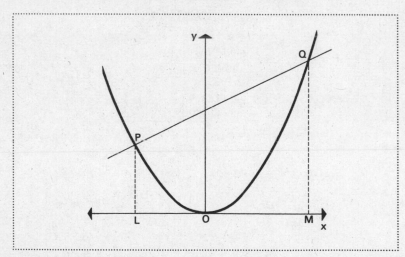

20   Find the area between the curve $y = 10x - x^2$ and the line $y = 4x$.

12f The trigonometric functions sin x and cos x

When sin x and cos x appear in calculus, the angle is always taken to be in radians unless it is stated otherwise.

The differential coefficient of sin x

Let $\qquad y = \sin x$

Then $\quad y + \delta y = \sin(x + \delta x)$

Consider fig. 160 where

$$\angle POx = x \text{ radians}$$

and $\quad \angle POQ = \delta x \text{ radians}$

$$\sin x = \frac{PM}{OP}$$

$$\sin(x + \delta x) = \frac{QL}{OQ}$$

And $\qquad \delta x = \dfrac{\text{arc } PQ}{OP}$

$$\therefore \quad \frac{\delta y}{\delta x} = \frac{\sin(x + \delta x) - \sin x}{\delta x} = \frac{QL - PM}{\text{arc } PQ}$$

$$= \frac{QR}{\text{arc } PQ} = \frac{QR}{\text{chord } PQ} \times \frac{\text{chord } PQ}{\text{arc } PQ}$$

$$= \cos PQR \times \frac{\text{chord } PQ}{\text{arc } PQ}$$

If $\quad \delta x \to 0 \quad$ then $\quad \dfrac{\text{chord } PQ}{\text{arc } PQ} \to 1$

$$\angle PQR = \angle PQO - \angle LQO = \left(\frac{\pi}{2} - \frac{\delta x}{2}\right) - \left(\frac{\pi}{2} - x - \delta x\right)$$

$$= x + \frac{\delta x}{2}$$

$$\therefore \text{ as } \delta x \to 0, \quad \frac{\delta y}{\delta x} \to \cos\left(x + \frac{\delta x}{2}\right) \times 1$$

$$\therefore \lim_{\delta x \to 0} \frac{\delta y}{\delta x} = \frac{dy}{dx} = \cos x$$

The differential coefficient of cos x

Figure 160

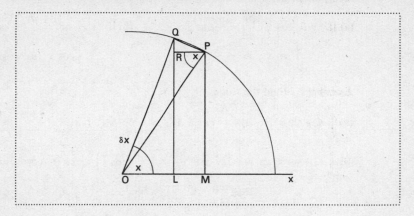

Referring to fig. 160 we have

$$y = \cos x = \frac{OM}{OP}$$

$$y + \delta y = \cos(x + \delta x) = \frac{OL}{OQ}$$

and as before $\quad \delta x = \dfrac{\text{arc } PQ}{OP}$

$$\therefore \frac{\delta y}{\delta x} = \frac{OL - OM}{\text{arc } PQ} = \frac{-RP}{\text{arc } PQ}$$

$$= \frac{-RP}{\text{chord } PQ} \times \frac{\text{chord } PQ}{\text{arc } PQ}$$

$$= -\sin PQR \times \frac{\text{chord } PQ}{\text{arc } PQ}$$

As $\quad \delta x \to 0 \quad \dfrac{\text{chord } PQ}{\text{arc } PQ} \to 1 \quad$ and $\quad \angle PQR \to x$

$$\therefore \lim_{\delta x \to 0} \frac{\delta y}{\delta x} = \frac{dy}{dx} = -\sin x$$

Example 1   If $y = 2 \sin x - 3 \cos x$ find $\dfrac{dy}{dx}$

$$\frac{dy}{dx} = 2 \cos x - 3(-\sin x)$$

$$= 2 \cos x + 3 \sin x$$

291   The trigonometric functions sin x and cos x

Integrals of sin x and cos x

(a) If $y = \cos x$ $\quad \dfrac{dy}{dx} = -\sin x$

$\therefore \displaystyle\int \sin x \; dx = -\cos x + c$

(b) If $y = \sin x$ $\quad \dfrac{dy}{dx} = \cos x$

$\therefore \displaystyle\int \cos x \; dx = \sin x + c$

Example 2 Find the values of

(a) $\displaystyle\int_0^{\frac{\pi}{2}} (2 + \sin x)\, dx$ (b) $\displaystyle\int_{\frac{\pi}{3}}^{\frac{\pi}{2}} \cos x \, dx$

(a) $\displaystyle\int_0^{\frac{\pi}{2}} (2 + \sin x)\, dx = \left[\, 2x - \cos x \,\right]_0^{\frac{\pi}{2}} = \left(\pi - \cos \frac{\pi}{2}\right) - \left(2 \times 0 - \cos 0\right)$

$\qquad\qquad = (\pi - 0) - (0 - 1) = \pi + 1$
$\qquad\qquad = 4 \cdot 142$

(b) $\displaystyle\int_{\frac{\pi}{3}}^{\frac{\pi}{2}} \cos x \, dx = \left[\, \sin x \,\right]_{\frac{\pi}{3}}^{\frac{\pi}{2}} = \sin \frac{\pi}{2} - \sin \frac{\pi}{3}$

$\qquad\qquad = 1 - 0 \cdot 8660 = 0 \cdot 134$

Exercise 12f

In questions 1–6, differentiate with respect to x

1   $5 \sin x$

2   $2 \cos x$

3   $\sin x + \cos x$

4   $2 \sin x - \cos x$

5   $3 \cos x - 4 \sin x$

6   $2x - \sin x$

In questions 7–12, integrate

7   $2 \cos x$

8   $3 \sin x$

9   $\sin x - \cos x$

10   $2 \cos x - \sin x$

11   $a \sin x + b \cos x$

12   $3x^2 + \cos x$

13   If $y = \sin x$ find $\dfrac{d^2 y}{dx^2}$

14   If $y = 2 \sin \theta + \cos \theta$ find $\dfrac{d^2 y}{d\theta^2}$

15   Evaluate (a) $\displaystyle\int_0^{\frac{\pi}{3}} 3 \cos x \, dx$ (b) $\displaystyle\int_0^{\frac{\pi}{2}} 2 \sin x \, dx$

16   Evaluate $\displaystyle\int_0^{\frac{\pi}{3}} (\sin x + \cos x)\, dx$

17   Find the area between the curve $y = \sin x$, the x axis, and the ordinates at $x = 0$ and $x = \dfrac{\pi}{4}$

18　Find the area bounded by the graph of $y = 3 \cos x$, the x axis and the ordinates at $x = \dfrac{\pi}{6}$ and $x = \dfrac{\pi}{3}$

Miscellaneous exercises 12

1　(a) Differentiate from first principles $y = \sin x$.

(b) Differentiate by inspection

$$y = \frac{5x^3}{6} - \frac{2x}{3} + 3 - \frac{4}{3x^2} + \frac{4}{9x^3}$$

(c) Find expressions for y given

ⅰ $\dfrac{dy}{dx} = 6x^2 - 3$ and $y = 3$ when $x = 0$

ⅱ $\dfrac{dy}{dx} = \dfrac{3}{x^2} + 1$ and $y = 8\frac{1}{2}$ when $x = 6$

U.E.I.

2　Integrate the following

(a) $\displaystyle\int (x^2 - 2\sqrt{x})\, dx$ 　(b) $\displaystyle\pi \int_0^r (r^2 - x^2)\, dx$ 　(c) $\displaystyle\int_1^2 \left(x^3 + \frac{1}{x^3}\right) dx$

U.L.C.I.

3　(a) Integrate the following with respect to x

(i) $4x^3$ 　(ii) $5\sqrt{x}$ 　(iii) $\dfrac{7}{x^2}$ 　(iv) $(2x+1)^2$

(b) If $\dfrac{dy}{dx} = 4x^3 + 2x + 7$, find y in terms of x given that when $x = 0$, $y = 8$

N.C.T.E.C.

4　(a) Differentiate by inspection

$$y = \frac{5x^3}{2} - \frac{3x}{4} - \frac{2}{3} + \frac{3}{5x} - \frac{4}{3x^3}$$

(b) Differentiate from the first principles $y = \cos x$

(c) ⅰ $\displaystyle\int (7x^2 + 4x - 6)\, dx$

ⅱ $\displaystyle\int \left(\frac{8x^3}{5}\right) dx$

ⅲ Find y if $\dfrac{dy}{dx} = \dfrac{3}{x^2} - x + 2$ and $y = 3$ when $x = 3$

U.E.I.

5   Integrate the following

(a) $\int \left(2+3\sqrt{x}-\dfrac{1}{x^2}\right) dx$ (b) $\int_1^8 x^{\frac{1}{3}} dx$ (c) $\int_0^a (a^3-x^3) dx$

U.L.C.I.

6   A curve passes through the origin and the gradient at a point (x, y) on the
curve is $3-2x$.
Find (a) the equation of the curve
        (b) the points where the curve cuts the x axis
        (c) the area enclosed between the curve and the x axis.

7   (a) Integrate   i $\int (a+2x^{\frac{1}{3}}) dx$ ii $\int_{\frac{\pi}{6}}^{\frac{\pi}{3}} \sin x \, dx$

(b) Solve the equation $5x-4-x^2 = 0$. Hence find the area enclosed between
the curve $y = 5x-4-x^2$ and the x axis.

U.L.C.I.

8   (a) Integrate with respect to x

i $3x^2+3\sqrt{x}$ ii $\dfrac{5}{x^3}+5$

(b) The slope of a curve which passes through the origin is $2x^2+5x$. Determine the equation to the curve and the value of x at the points where the
tangent to the curve is parallel to the x axis. Sketch the curve.

N.C.T.E.C.

9.   (a) Differentiate from first principles $y = \sin x$
(b) Find the values of the following

i $\int 3x^4 dx$ ii $\int \dfrac{5dx}{x^3}$ iii $\int (3x^2-2x+5) dx$

U.E.I.

10   (a) Integrate with respect to x

i $4x^3+\sqrt{x}$ ii $\dfrac{1}{x^2}+(x+1)^2$

(b) Given that $\dfrac{dr}{dt} = -\dfrac{50}{t^2}$ and that $r = 2$ when $t = 10$, find the value of r
when $t = \frac{1}{2}$.

(c) Given that $pv^{1.1} = 60$, find $\int p \, dv$.

N.C.T.E.C.

Appendix A

Ordinary National Certificate Mathematics examination papers

Examination paper 1

Time allowed: 3 hours. Answer SIX questions.

1   (a) Solve the equation $7^{x+2} = 8^{2x-1}$

     (b) Given that $\dfrac{2p+1}{p+2} = \dfrac{3p+1}{p+3}$, find two possible values of $\dfrac{p^2-p+1}{p^2+p+1}$

     (c) Solve the simultaneous equations
$$x+y+z = 13$$
$$x+2y+2z = 18$$
$$3x-y-2z = 8$$

2   (a) i Write down the expansions of $\sin(A-B)$ and $\cos(A-B)$
       ii Show that: $\sin(x-150°) + \sin(x-330°) = 0$
     (b) Solve the following equation for all values of x from $0°$ to $360°$
$$2\sin 2x + 1 = 0$$
     (c) Prove that: $\dfrac{\sin 2A}{1+\cos 2A} = \tan A$

3   Plot a graph of $y = 3\sin x$ and a graph of $y = 2\cos x$ for values of x between $45°$ and $150°$ at intervals of $15°$.

     Hence or otherwise draw the graph of $y = 3\sin x + 2\cos x$ and determine from the graph approximate values for P and Q in the expression

$$3\sin x + 2\cos x = P\sin(x+Q)$$

4   On the same axes and to the same scales, plot graphs of the functions $17-4x-2x^2$ and $2x+16$ between the values of $x = -4$ and $x = 2$
     (a) Using the graphs, solve the equation

$$0 = 1-6x-2x^2$$

     (b) Using the trapezoidal rule, determine the area enclosed by the graph of the function $17-4x-2x^2$, the x axis and the end ordinates.

5   (a) Differentiate from the first principles

$$y = x^2 - 2x$$

(b) Differentiate by inspection

$$y = \frac{x^3}{3} - bx - 7 + \frac{2}{3x} - \frac{1}{3x^3}$$

(c) Obtain the integrals

  (i) $\displaystyle\int x\left(1 + \frac{1}{x^4}\right) dx$ (ii) $\displaystyle\int (x-1)(x+2)\, dx$

6   (a) Resolve into factors the following:
    i $21x^2 + 2y(5x - 8y)$ ii $12ac - 8bc + 9ad - 6bd$ iii $a^2 - 9b^2 + 6bc - c^2$
  (b) A 900 litre tank can be filled with water flowing through two pipes in 18 minutes. The pipes have different bores and the larger one can fill the tank in 15 minutes less than the smaller one. Find the time taken by each.

7   Two quantities W and H are believed to be connected by a law of the form:

$$W = \frac{m}{\sqrt{H}} + c$$

  The following values of W and H were obtained by experiment:

W	5·02	4·59	4·33	4·15	4·02	3·92
H	4	6	8	10	12	14

  Draw a suitable graph to test if W and H are connected by the law, and determine the probable values of m and c.
  Using the law, find the value of H when $W = 4\cdot25$.

8   The following table gives the values of $f(x)$ for $x = -2(1)6$.

x	-2	-1	0	1	2	3	4	5	6
$f(x)$	-32	-11	-2	1	4	13	34	73	136

Tabulate the finite differences as far as the fourth order. Show that $f(x)$ is of the form $ax^3 + bx^2 + cx + d$ and find the function.

9   (a) Using the binomial theorem:
    i expand $\left(x + \dfrac{1}{2y}\right)^4$ ii find the sixth term of $\left(a - \dfrac{1}{2b}\right)^{10}$
    iii find the value of $(1\cdot0002)^5$ correct to five decimal places.
  (b) Simplify and express with positive indices:

$$\sqrt[3]{\left(\frac{27a^4b^{-5}}{a^{-2}b^4}\right)} \div (4a^2b^4)^{-0\cdot5}.$$

10 (a) A wheel of a locomotive engine is 1·5 m diameter and the engine is travelling at 35 km/h. What is the angular velocity of the wheel?

   (b) A point moves so that its displacement s metres at a given time t seconds is given by $s = 16+48t-t^3$.

   Find when and where it will stop and reverse its motion and its acceleration at this point.

Examination paper 2

Time allowed: 3 hours. Answer SIX questions.

1 (a) By means of the substitution $u = e^x$ solve
   $$e^{2x}-7e^x+12 = 0$$

   (b) Solve
   $$\left(\log_e x\right)^2 - 5\log_e x+6 = 0$$

   (c) Solve the simultaneous equations
   $$4x+5y = 0$$
   $$2x^2+xy-y^2 = 14$$

2 (a) Find the value of T from the formula
   $$T = 2\pi\sqrt{\left(\frac{h^2+k^2}{hg}\right)}$$
   if $h = 1\cdot581, k = 1\cdot162, g = 32\cdot18, \pi = 3\cdot142$.

   (b) Rearrange the formula to make k the subject.

   (c) The perimeter of a rectangular template is 40 cm and its length is 3 cm longer than its breadth. Find its dimensions.

3 (a) The fifth term of an arithmetic progression is 17 and the eleventh term is 35. Find the fifteenth term.

   (b) A lathe is to have 7 spindle speeds varying from 50 r.p.m. to 650 r.p.m. Find the intermediate speeds, assuming they are in geometric progression.

4 (a) A certain law of motion is
   $$s = \tfrac{2}{3}t^3 - \tfrac{5}{2}t^2+3t+1.$$

   Find expressions for $\dfrac{ds}{dt}, \dfrac{d^2s}{dt^2}$.

   From these expressions, find the times at which
   i the velocity is zero   ii the acceleration is zero.

   (b) A metal tank with an open top and square base is to have a volume of 32 m^3. Representing the side of the base by x, express the height of the tank in terms of x. Deduce a formula for the total surface area A of the tank. Determine the value of x for which A is a minimum.

5 (a) Obtain i $\int \left(3x^2 - \frac{1}{x^2} + 5\right) dx$

ii $\int (x^2 - \sqrt{x})^2 \, dx.$

(b) A body passes a datum point at a velocity of 5 m s^{-1} and immediately starts accelerating at the rate of 3 m s^{-2}. The time at which the body passes the datum point is taken to be $t = 0$.

i Find an expression for the velocity of the body at any time t.

ii How far is the body from the datum point after 12 seconds?

6 The following table contains values derived from an experiment on pulleys

T (N)	56·8	196·2	358	848	1,392
θ (radians)	2	3·3	4·2	5·95	7·1

By drawing a suitable graph, verify that these quantities satisfy a law of the form

$T = a\theta^n$

where a and n are constants, and obtain values for a and n.

7 (a) Solve the equation

$5 \cos \theta + 3 \sin^2 \theta = 5$

giving all the solutions in the range $0° - 360°$.

(b) The centres of each of three holes A, B and C lie on a circle radius 2 m, where $AB = 3·8$ m, $BC = 3·65$ m.

If O is the centre of the circle, calculate the acute angle AOC.

8 Draw, on the same axes, the graphs of $y = \cos 2x$, $y = \sin 3x$, and $y = \cos 2x + \sin 3x$ for x between 0 and 360°.

Hence solve the equation

$\cos 2x = \sin 3x$

in this range.

From your graph find the value of x for which $\cos 2x + \sin 3x$ is greatest and find the greatest value.

9 (a) Soundings taken across a river at intervals of 10 m are shown

Distance from bank (m)	0	10	20	30	40	50	60	70	80
Depth (m)	0	2	3	7	10	13	10	8	4

Use Simpson's rule to estimate the area of this cross-section of the river.

(b) A 2 m length of metal pipe of outside diameter 12 cm weighs 18 kg. If the density of the metal is 7·5 g cm^{-3}, find the thickness of the metal.

10 Find values of a, b and c if the following relationships are simultaneously true:

$$16a + 5b - c = 86$$
$$4a - b + 3c = 38\cdot8$$
$$2\cdot4a + 4\cdot5b + 2c = 67\cdot3$$

Examination paper 3

Time allowed: 3 hours. Answer SIX *questions.*

1 (a) Solve (correct to two decimal places) the following equation:

$$x(x-2)^2 = (x-1)^3$$

(b) A solid cylinder is 6 cm high and has a total surface area of 288 cm². Calculate its diameter and volume.

2 (a) Given $\sqrt{63} = 7\cdot9373$, express as a decimal, correct to three decimal places:

$$\frac{\sqrt{9} - \sqrt{7}}{\sqrt{9} + \sqrt{7}}$$

(b) When water flows through a pipe the loss of head due to friction is directly proportional to the length, to the square of the velocity and inversely proportional to the diameter.

The loss of head is 68 cm in a length of 20 m, when the velocity is $1\cdot5$ m s⁻¹ and pipe diameter is 10 cm.

Determine the loss of head when water flows at a velocity of $1\cdot2$ m s⁻¹ through a pipe of 15 cm diameter and length 36 m.

3 (a) Use Napierian logarithms to find:
   i $\log_e 0\cdot0347$

   ii the number whose Napierian logarithm is $\overline{4}\cdot476$
   (b) Evaluate H in the following formula

$$V^2 = \frac{64\cdot4\,DH}{D + 4fl}$$

   when $V = 12\cdot3, f = 0\cdot0085, l = 350$ and $D = 1\cdot75$

4 (a) Use the binomial theorem to obtain the first four terms of the expansion $(1+x)^{10}$ in ascending powers of x. Hence find the value of $(1\cdot005)^{10}$ correct to four places of decimal.

(b) Find the coefficient of x^7 in the expansion of $\left(2x - \dfrac{1}{5}\right)^{11}$

5　The following table gives values of x and y.

x	1	2	3	4	5	6
y	19·6	18·4	16·4	13·6	10	5·6

It is believed that x and y have a relationship in the form of $y^2 = a - bx^2$. Draw a suitable graph and hence determine the probable values of a and b. Use this relationship to determine the probable value of y when $x = 7$.

6　(a) Prove $\cot 2x = \dfrac{1 - \tan^2 x}{2 \tan x}$ using the formulae for $\sin 2x$ and $\cos 2x$. If $\cot 2x = 0·5$, find without using tables the values of $\tan x$.

(b) Given $\tan A = 0·8$ and $\tan (A - B) = 0·3$, find $\tan B$.

7　(a) Draw the graph of $y = \frac{1}{2}(2 + 5x - x^2)$, between values of $x = -1$ and $x = +5$, and find the roots of $y = 0$.

(b) On the same axes draw the graph of $2(x - y) = 1$ and find the points where this graph cuts the other curve.

(c) For what equation are these points the possible solutions?

8　A bucket in the shape of a frustum of a cone of end radii 18 cm and 12 cm and depth 28 cm is filled to the top with water. The water is then poured into a vessel in the shape of a sphere of radius 10 cm. Find the volume of water remaining in the bucket after the sphere is filled.

Find also the external surface area of the bucket.

9　(a) If $a = \dfrac{4b + 5}{5b + 4}$, and $b = c - 3$, express c in terms of a.

(b) Solve the equation: $3·8^{x-2} = 5·3^x$

(c) The function $x^3 - 2x^2 - 9x + 18$ has a zero value when $x = -3$. Find the other two values of x when the function is zero.

10　(a) For what value of x is the gradient of the graph of $6x^2 - 3x - 4$ equal to $7·5$?

(b) The distance s moved by a body in time t is given by the equation
$$s = t^3 - 2·5t^2 - 12t + 72$$
Determine the time, displacement and acceleration when the velocity is zero.

(c) Find an expression for y, given $\dfrac{dy}{dx} = 3x^2 - \dfrac{2}{3} + \dfrac{3}{x^2}$ and $y = 20$ when $x = 3$.

Appendix B
Answers

1a

1. 2
2. 8
3. 2
4. 4
5. 9
6. $\frac{1}{9}$
7. 1
8. x^5
9. x^6
10. 9

11. 32
12. $\frac{1}{5}$
13. $\frac{1}{25}$
14. 3
15. 4
16. 32
17. $\frac{1}{2}$
18. 16
19. $3\dfrac{x}{y^2}$

20. 27
21. 12
22. $\dfrac{1}{a}$
23. (a) $3 \cdot 6 \times 10^4$
    (b) $6 \cdot 723 \times 10^{-5}$
    (c) 5×10^5
24. (a) 4×10^5
    (b) 10^3

1b

1. 3
2. 4
3. 3
4. 3
5. -1
6. -2
7. -3
8. -3
9. $1 \cdot 5$
10. $\frac{1}{3}$
11. $\frac{1}{2}$
12. -3
13. $3 \log 2$
14. $\log 3 + \log 5$
15. $3 \log 3 + \log 5 + \log 2$
16. $3 \log 3 + \frac{1}{3} \log 5 - 4 \log 2$

17. $3 \log 3 + \frac{4}{3} \log 2$
18. $4 \log 3 + 3 \log 2 + \frac{3}{2} \log 5$
19. (a) 100
    (b) 32
    (c) $\frac{1}{9}$
    (d) 6
    (e) 3
    (f) $-\frac{1}{3}$
20. (a) $1 \cdot 3010$
    (b) $2 \cdot 3010$
    (c) $0 \cdot 9030$
    (d) $-1 \cdot 6990$
    (e) $6 \cdot 3010$
21. 5
22. $0 \cdot 9030 ; 1 \cdot 2552$

1c

1. $665 \cdot 9$
2. 192
3. $135 \cdot 5$
4. $0 \cdot 014 \, 55$

5. 5742
6. $0 \cdot 5$
7. $0 \cdot 026 \, 77$
8. 1066

9. $26 \cdot 93$
10. $19 \cdot 72$

1e 2. 1·234
3. (a) 2·008
   (b) 1·76
   (c) 3·029

4. (a) 1066
   (b) 1212
   (c) 0·4343
5. (a) 2241
   (b) 2·222
   (c) 1553

6. 1·485
7. 2·079
8. −1·987
9. 0·89
10. $x = 1.52, y = 3.23$

1g 2. 37·2
3. 15·05 cm

4. 4·40 cm
6. 144·0 cm

7. 22·37

1h 1. 5.95×10^{27}
2. 54·46 ; 53·56 ; 54
3. $t = \left(\dfrac{1+2s^2}{1-s^2}\right)q$; 2.53×10^4

4. (a) $h = \dfrac{sR}{R+\pi sT}$

   (b) $h = \dfrac{x(x-2l)}{2l}$

   (c) $h = 2\sqrt{\left(\dfrac{P+fT}{\pi f}\right)}$

5. 80
6. 0·004 44 m
7. $r = tE\left\{\left(\dfrac{v}{p}\right)^2 - \dfrac{1}{2k}\right\}$; 4·30

Miscellaneous exercises 1

1. (a) (i) 1·94 (ii) 5·57
   (b) 4.01×10^{-3}
2. (a) 1·099
   (b) 1·29
3. (a) (i) $13a^2b^3$ (ii) $5a^3b^2$
   (b) $9m^2n$
   (c) 10 920
4. (a) (i) 1, −3 (ii) 1·709
   (b) 13·55, 2·297
5. (a) 7·3776
   (b) $\bar{1}$·2576, 0·013 38
   (c) 20 180
6. (a) 0·002 553
   (b) 2·539
   (c) 2·486
7. (a) (i) $\bar{1}$·5814 (ii) 0·039 24
   (b) 10·34
8. (a) 1480 (b) $\log b = \log a + 0.4343\left(\dfrac{L}{2c}-1\right)$

9. $r = de\left(\dfrac{1}{4} - \dfrac{L}{0.000\,644}\right)$; 0·692
10. (a) 0·0764
   (b) $\dfrac{1}{\sqrt{(v^2k^2lg-1)}-1}$
11. 471 ; 4%
12. (a) $A = \dfrac{qs\sqrt{d}}{\sqrt{(2ghD+q^2d)}}$
   (b) 4·69
13. $n = 1.11$; $c = 519$
14. (b) (i) 1·2 (ii) 1·2
   (c) −1·5
   (d) 0·8343
15. (a) $\frac{1}{5}$
   (b) 0·1076
   (c) 1·099
   (d) 2·988

16. (a) 4·96

(b) $T = \sqrt{\left\{\left(\dfrac{\pi f d^2}{16} - M\right)^2 - M^2\right\}}$

17. 8·40
18. 3·46
19. $\bar{x} = 209$ cm

2a

1. $4\sqrt{2}$
2. $5\sqrt{3}$
3. $9\sqrt{3}$
4. $3\sqrt[3]{3}$
5. $2\sqrt[3]{2}$
6. $-2\sqrt[3]{2}$
7. $13\sqrt{3}$
8. $10\sqrt{5}$
9. $6\sqrt{2}$
10. $7\sqrt{3}$
11. $4\sqrt{5}$
12. $2\sqrt{3}$
13. $39\sqrt{3}$
14. $-6\sqrt{5}$
15. $6\sqrt[3]{4}$
16. 7
17. $-4\sqrt{6}$
18. 4·243
19. 1·155
20. 4·899
21. 5·476
22. 4·181

2b

1. 2
2. 2
3. 3
4. 10
5. $14\sqrt{2} + 10\sqrt{3}$
6. 53
7. $5 + 2\sqrt{2} + 3\sqrt{3} + \sqrt{6}$
8. $28 + \sqrt{105} - 4\sqrt{21} - 3\sqrt{5}$
9. y^2
10. 1
11. $2 - \sqrt{3}$
12. $3 - 2\sqrt{2}$
13. $3 - 2\sqrt{2}$
14. $1 + \sqrt{5}$
15. $\dfrac{2\sqrt{7} - \sqrt{13}}{5}$
16. $8(\sqrt{3} - 1) + 6(\sqrt{6} - \sqrt{2})$
17. -2
18. $\dfrac{5 - \sqrt{3}}{2}$
19. 0
20. 0·252
21. 0·343
22. 2·094
23. 3·415
24. 4·098
25. 1
26. 8
27. 14

2c

1. 350 kg
2. 0·5, 1·5, 3
3. 18
4. $\frac{4}{7}$
5. $\frac{4}{7}$
6. 4
7. $\frac{3}{2}, \frac{2}{3}$
9. 15, 20
10. 42, 49
11. 28, 44
12. $\frac{7}{2}$
13. 82, 65, 58
14. 1100, 540, 360

2d

1. $y = \frac{2}{3}x,\ y = 6$
2. $y = 6$
3. $z = 4$
4. $y = 3x + \dfrac{3}{2x}$
6. 3·3
7. $40\frac{1}{2}$ kg
8. 27 cm
9. 18 N
10. 30 km
11. 40 cm
12. $E = \pounds75N + \pounds450$

2e(i)

1. $x^2+6x+9 = (x+3)^2$
2. $x^2+4x+4 = (x+2)^2$
3. $x^2-6x+9 = (x-3)^2$
4. $2x^2-x+\frac{1}{8} = 2(x-\frac{1}{4})^2$
5. $3x^2+x+\frac{1}{12} = 3(x+\frac{1}{6})^2$
6. $3, 2$
7. $-3, -7$
8. $5, -1$
9. $-4, 6$
10. $4, \frac{1}{2}$
11. $0\cdot2, 0\cdot3$
12. $3, 4$
13. $0\cdot9, -2$
14. $7\cdot9, -1\cdot9$
15. $2\cdot65, -0\cdot45$
16. $3\cdot73, 0\cdot27$
17. $1, \frac{4}{5}$
18. $3\cdot46, -1\cdot73$
19. $-\frac{3}{5}, \frac{4}{5}$
20. $4\frac{1}{2}, -\frac{3}{5}$
21. $2, -\frac{9}{5}$
22. $-4, 3\frac{1}{2}, 9$
23. 2 or -3
24. 4
25. $k \geqslant 6$ or $k \leqslant -2$
26. $0, 1$
27. $1, 2\cdot32$
28. $\pm1, \pm\sqrt{2}$
29. $12\cdot58$ or $7\cdot42$
30. 155 cm
31. $79\cdot7$
32. $9\cdot52$

2e(ii)

1. $\frac{1}{2}$ or $4\frac{1}{2}$
2. $-4, -1\frac{1}{2}$ or $2\frac{1}{2}$
3. (a) $1\frac{1}{4}$
   (b) $-\frac{1}{2}$ or 1
   (c) -1 or $1\frac{1}{2}$
4. $3\cdot121, -1\cdot121$
5. $1\frac{3}{4}$
6. $-3\cdot158, 0\cdot158$

2g

1. $x = 6, y = 4$
2. $M_1 = 4\cdot2, M_2 = 0\cdot6$
3. $x = 5, y = 4\frac{1}{2}$
4. $a = \frac{3}{25}, b = 12$
5. $x = 1, y = -1, z = 2$
6. $l = 3, m = -2, n = 4$
7. $a = \frac{1}{3}, b = -1, c = \frac{1}{2}$
8. $i_1 = 0\cdot5, i_2 = 0\cdot25, i_3 = -0\cdot2$
9. $y = 2x^2-3x+1$
10. $a = 3, b = -6, c = -10$
11. $x = 3, y = 1$ or $x = 1, y = 5$
12. $x = 2, y = 1; x = \frac{1}{2}, y = 4$

13. $x = 3, y = 1; x = -3, y = -1$
14. $x = 2, y = 1; x = \frac{1}{2}, y = 4; x = -2, y = -1; x = -\frac{1}{2}, y = -4$
15. $x = 1\cdot32, y = -0\cdot46, z = 1\cdot69$

2h

1. $9, -3, 2, -6$
2. $-24, 0, -36, 0, -10$
3. $4, 9\frac{1}{2}, 28$
4. $24, 24$
5. (a) $(x+h)(2x+2h+1)$
   (b) $2(x+h)-1$
6. $-\dfrac{1}{2x(x+h)}$
7. $f(12) = 1,452$
8. $f(1) = -4$
9. $f(2) = 4$
10. $a = 2, b = -3, c = -1$
11. $s = 2t-t^2$

2i

1. (a) 92
   (b) 32
   (c) 16
2. -9
3. $(x+1)(x+2)(x+3)$
4. $(x-2)(x+2)(x-3)$
5. $(x-2)(x+3)(x-4)$
6. $(x-1)(x-3)(x-5)$
7. $(x+1)(x-2)(x-4)$
8. $(x-1)(x-2)(2x-1)$
9. $(x+2)(x-3)(x-6)$
10. $a = 20, b = -39$

Miscellaneous exercises 2

1. (a) $x^{\frac{5}{4}}$
   (b) $x = 5, y = -1, z = 3$
2. (a) (i) $xy(y+13)(y-7)$
   (ii) $(a-3b+4)(a-3b-4)$
   (iii) $(5a-b)(a+5b)$
   (iv) $27(a-2b)(a^2+2ab+4b^2)$
   (b) 5
   (c) $V = \dfrac{hA}{3}$; 24 cm^3
3. (a) (i) $-4(2a-b)(a-b)$
   (ii) $3(7x-5)(5x+4)$
   (iii) $(3a-5b)(9a^2+15ab+25b^2)$
   (b) 2
4. (a) $x = -32$ or -8
   $y = -8$ or -32
   (b) $x = 12, y = 9, z = -3$
   (c) $x = 4.11$ or -0.61
5. (a) $x = 2, 1\frac{2}{3}, -2$
   (b) $i_1 = -1.576, i_2 = 2.272$
   $i_3 = 0.168$
6. (a) $1, -2, 1\frac{1}{2}$
   (b) $c = -6; 1\frac{1}{2}, -\frac{1}{2}$
7. (a) $x = 9, y = -2, z = 4$
   (b) 1.82 or 0.34

8. (a) $\dfrac{2ab}{a^2+b^2}$
   (b) $(2b-1)(b+3)$
9. (a) -3
   (b) (i) $(x-1)(x-3)(x+2)$
   (ii) $\pi\left(d-\dfrac{1}{3}\right)\left(d^2+\dfrac{d}{3}+\dfrac{1}{9}\right)$
10. (a) $a = -1, b = 1, c = 1$
    (b) $x = 5\frac{1}{2}, y = -\frac{5}{6}$
11. (a) 2.57 or -0.91
    (b) 35 km/h, 40 km/h
12. (a) (i) $2y(5x+14)(2x-3)$
    (ii) $4(a-b)(a-4b)$
    (iii) $(4a+5b)$
    $\quad(16a^2-20ab+25b^2)$
    (b) 16.6 cm, 10.6 cm
13. (a) 1 or -3
    (c) 1.55 or -0.80
14. (a) $0.868, -0.218$
    (b) $x = 7\frac{1}{2}, y = \frac{9}{10}$
    (c) $\frac{3}{2}$
15. (a) 6.54 or 0.46
    (b) 21.37 or -3.37
    (c) $x = 7\frac{1}{2}, y = -\frac{9}{10}$

3a

1. (a) 1.0472^c
   (b) 3.0674^c
   (c) 1.0159^c
   (d) 9.4248^c
2. (a) $60°$
   (b) $147° 50'$
   (c) $36° 40'$
   (d) $150°$

3. (a) $1.885^c, 108°$
   (b) $2.094^c, 120°$
   (c) $2.244^c, 128.6°$
   (d) $2.356^c, 135°$
4. (a) 2.356^c
   (b) 1.833^c
5. 3.25^c
6. 6.3 Mm
7. $1° 49' 8''$

8. (a) 26.18 cm^2
   (b) 150.8 cm^2
   (c) 240 m^2
9. (a) 7.5 m^2
   (b) 9.05 m
10. $0.3^c, 17° 11'$
11. 1087 cm^2
12. $75.4, 543$

3c

1. $\cos\theta = \frac{4}{5}$; $\operatorname{cosec}\theta = \frac{5}{3}$; $\tan\theta = \frac{3}{4}$; $\sec\theta = \frac{5}{4}$; $\cot\theta = \frac{4}{3}$
2. $\sin\theta = \frac{15}{17}$; $\tan\theta = \frac{15}{8}$
3. $\sin\theta = \dfrac{p}{\sqrt{(p^2+q^2)}}$; $\cos\theta = \dfrac{q}{\sqrt{(p^2+q^2)}}$
4. $\sin\theta = \sqrt{(1-x^2)}$; $\tan\theta = \dfrac{\sqrt{(1-x^2)}}{x}$

17. $\sin\theta = \dfrac{2t}{1+t^2}$; $\cos\theta = \dfrac{1-t^2}{1+t^2}$
18. $\frac{2}{3}$
19. $4\frac{2}{9}$

3e 2. $45°, 135°$; $30°, 120°$; $40° 45', 130° 45'$;

  $\dfrac{3\pi}{10}, \dfrac{4\pi}{5}$; $-65°, 25°$; $120°$; $210°$

8. $23° 50'$
9. $0·7193$
10. $227·3$

3. (a) 1
   (b) 2

3f 1. $8·01$ m
2. $5° 2'$
3. $66\frac{2}{3}$ m
4. $23·7$ m
5. 48 m
6. 561 m

7. 284 m; $40° 52'$ west of north
8. 1 km 652 m
9. (a) $25·9$ cm
   (b) $65·0$ cm
10. (a) 202 cm
    (b) 213 cm

3g 1. (a) $-0·7660$
   (b) $1·1918$
   (c) $-1·5557$
   (d) $-1·7321$
   (e) $-0·3640$
   (f) $-0·9397$
   (g) $-0·6428$
   (h) $0·9848$
   (i) $-5·6713$
   (j) $-0·9848$

2. (a) $\cos \theta$
   (b) $-\sin \theta$
   (c) $\tan \theta$
   (d) $-\cos \theta$
   (e) $-\tan \theta$
   (f) $\tan \theta$
   (g) $-\cos \theta$
   (h) $\cos \theta$

4. (a) $120°, 240°$
   (b) $240°, 300°$
   (c) $45°, 225°$

3i 1. (a) 4; $120°, \dfrac{2\pi}{3}$

   (b) 2; $72°, \dfrac{2\pi}{5}$

   (c) 3; $720°, 4\pi$

   (d) 100; $240°, \dfrac{4\pi}{3}$

   (e) 5; $180°, \pi$

   (f) a; $\dfrac{360°}{w}, \dfrac{2\pi}{w}$

2. (a) $45°, \dfrac{\pi}{4}$

   (b) $60°, \dfrac{\pi}{3}$

   (c) $\dfrac{180°}{p}, \dfrac{\pi}{p}$

3. (a) $15, \dfrac{\pi}{10}$

   (b) $240, \dfrac{\pi}{50}$

   (c) $34, \dfrac{\pi}{5}$

   (d) $y_0, \dfrac{2\pi b}{a}$

5. (a) $90°, 330°$
   (b) $150°, 270°$
9. (a) $0°, 60°, 180°$
   (b) $32° 33'$
   (c) $126° 22'$
10. $39° 27'$

Miscellaneous exercises 3

1. (a) (i) 0·866 (ii) −0·8569
   (b) (i) $\frac{56}{65}$ (ii) $\frac{53}{72}$

2. (a) $\frac{7}{9}$
   (b) (i) sin A (ii) 1

3. (a) Complements 27° 48′, $\frac{\pi}{3}$, −46°, 140°

   Supplements 117° 48′, $\frac{5\pi}{6}$, 44°, 230°

4. (a) $\frac{5\pi}{12}$ (b) $\frac{a}{\sqrt{(b^2-a^2)}}$, $\frac{b}{\sqrt{(b^2-a^2)}}$, $\frac{\sqrt{(b^2-a^2)}}{a}$

5. (a) 2° 10′ 58″
7. 93 m; 97·4 m
8. 56·3 m
9. 7·3 m
10. 2·73 km
11. 23·1 m
12. 36·6 m; 59° 27′, 37° 6′
13. 51·6 m

14. (a) 27° 52′ (b) 8·7 m
15. 1·16 km
16. 1020 m
17. 5, 2π; 2, $\frac{2\pi}{3}$; 2π
18. (b) 15° 34′, 121° 18′
19. 34° 36′
20. $50\frac{1}{2}$°; 33°, $68\frac{1}{2}$°

4a

1. (a) $a = 9.70, b = 11.0$
   (b) $b = 6.56$
2. (a) 24·8 cm²
   (b) 26·6 cm²
   (c) 99·3 cm²
   (d) 76·8 cm²
3. 12·1 cm
4. 34·97 cm²; 0·9991
5. (a) 24
   (b) 30
   (c) 1·732 cm²

6. $b = c \cos A + a \cos C$
   $c = a \cos B + b \cos A$
7. $\tan C = \dfrac{c \sin A}{b - \cos A}$;

   $\tan A = \dfrac{a \sin B}{c - a \cos B}$
8. 95·1 cm²; 16·18, 11·76 cm
9. 119·9 cm²
10. 22·6 cm²

4b

1. $C = 63°, a = 15.0, c = 13.7$
2. $b = 15.5, A = 55° 56′, B = 84° 4′$
3. $A = 110° 26′, B = 42° 44′, C = 26° 50′$
4. $C_1 = 26.9°, A_1 = 138.1°, a_1 = 10.3$
   $C_2 = 153.1°, A_2 = 11.9°, a_2 = 3.18$
5. 59° 4′, 71° 26′, 22·9
6. 71°, 10·0, 18·3
7. 51° 18′, 59° 10′, 69° 32′
8. 11·3, 59° 51′, 85° 9′; 19·0, 120° 9′, 24° 51′
9. (a) 6·92 m (b) 45° 21′

4c
  1.   35° 16′
  2.   5·076 m²
  3.   122 cm²
  4.   93·5 m²
  5.   (a) 158·8 m
       (b) 22·3°

  6. $2·37 \times 10^5$ m³
  7.   20′ 42′
  8.   (a) 25° 55′
       (b) 25° 40′

  9.   (a) 70° 32′
       (b) 75° 58′
 10.   (a) 79° 6′
       (b) 84° 30′

4d
  1.   0·002 62
  2.   0·007 56
  3.   0·003 49

  4.   0·011 93
  5.   0·004 36
  6.   0·002 91

  7.   5·4 km
  8.   11·6 m

Miscellaneous exercises 4

  1. $A = 29° 6′, B = 23° 52′, C = 127° 2′$, Area $= 39\,780$
  2.   72·2; 128° 24′; 37° 10′; 4952
  3. $B = 107° 55′, C = 29° 47′, c = 25·7$ m, Area $= 425$ m²
  4. $B_1 = 74° 30′, C_1 = 62° 30′, c_1 = 8·19$
       $B_2 = 105° 30′, C_2 = 31° 30′, c_2 = 4·83$
  5. $A = 37° 54′, B = 79° 22′, C = 62° 44′, c = 21·7$ cm
  6.   64 900 tonnes
  7. $A = 82° 49′, B = 55° 46′, C = 41° 25′, p = 3·31$
  8.   (a) 241° 51′ or $4·221^c$, 298° 9′ or $5·204^c$
       (b) 0·902 km, 4° 25′
  9.   (b) 37·7 km
 10.   (a) 38° 40′
       (b) 3·25 m, 29° 36′
       (c) 3 m
       (d) 52°
       (e) 35·9 m²
 11.   241 m; 18 m
 12.   560 m
 13.   309 m
 14.   40·7 m, 21° 39′

 15.   (a) 1·581
       (b) (i) 3·6   (ii) 2π (iii) $-0·59^c$
 16.   (a) 70° 32′
       (b) 34° 27′
       (c) 23° 4′
 17.   1·43 m
 18.   (a) 2·4 cm
       (b) 64° 23′
       (c) 5·55 cm

5a
  3.   (a) (4·33, 2·5)
       (b) (5, 53° 8′)
  4. A (5, 126° 52′)
       B (5, 233° 8′)
       C (5, 306° 52′)
  5.   (2, −3·464) (−1, −1·732) ($2\frac{1}{2}$, −4·33)
  6.   (a) 5
       (b) 13
       (c) 5
       (d) 10

  7.   5; 6; 5·656
  8.   5; 5; 4·472
  9.   34
 10.   (a) 5·39   (b) 4·36   (c) 4·33
 11.   (a) (10, 53° 8′) (5, 233° 8′)
       (b) (−2·828, 2·828); (5·196, −3)

5b   *1.*   (a) 4, 0, 0, -12
          (b) ± 2, ± 3, ± 1
          (c) $(2, 0)$, $(-2, 0)$
          (d) $(0, 4)$
          (e) $(1, 3)$, $(-2, 0)$

5.   (a) y small and positive
       (b) y small and negative
       (c) y very large and positive
       (d) y very large and negative

6. $-30, -8, 0, 0, -2, 0, 12, 40$

5c   *1.* $(-1, -2)$; $(3, 6)$
          2. $(2 \cdot 414, 6 \cdot 828)$; $(-0 \cdot 414, 1 \cdot 172)$
          3. $(1\frac{4}{5}, 43\frac{1}{5})$; $(-1\frac{1}{3}, 30\frac{2}{3})$

4. $(1, 0)$
5. $(0, 0)$ $(1, 0)$ $(3, -18)$

5d   *1.*   (a) 4
          (b) 2
          (c) $\frac{2}{3}$
          (d) $-\frac{1}{3}$
          (e) $-\dfrac{a}{b}$
          (f) $-\dfrac{p}{q}$

2.   (a) $45°$
       (b) $26° \, 34'$
       (c) $135°$
       (d) $123° \, 41'$
       (e) $116° \, 34'$

3.   (a) $\frac{3}{2}$
       (b) $-\frac{3}{4}$
       (c) 1
       (d) $-\frac{4}{3}$

5e   *1.* $y = 2x + 3$
          2. $y = 3x - 2$
          3. $y = -x + 2\frac{1}{2}$
          4. $y = \dfrac{x}{3} - \dfrac{1}{3}$

5. $y = 2x - 4$
6. $y = 2x + 4$
7. $m = \frac{3}{2}$, $(0, -4)$
8. $x + y = 3$

10.   (a) $y = 2x - 3$
        (b) $2x + 3y = 4$

5f   *1.*   Parallel (a), (d), (f)
          Perpendicular (b), (c), (e)

2.   (a) $y = 3x + 2$
       (b) $3y + x = 6$

3. $x + y + 2 = 0$
4. $4x + 3y = 10$

Miscellaneous exercises 5

1. $0 \cdot 999$
2.   (a) 9
       (b) $(1 \cdot 57, 68°)$
3.   (a) (i) $(4, 6)$ (ii) 8
4. $y = 3$ at $x = 1$
5. $(5, 25)$, $(-3, 9)$

6.   (a) $\frac{1}{4}$
       (b) $a = \frac{1}{4}$, $b = 1$
7. $\frac{1}{2}$; $(0, 1\frac{1}{2})$
       $2y = x + 4$
8.   (a) $5 \cdot 24$, $0 \cdot 36$
       (b) -5 at $x = 3$; 4

10. $2 \cdot 1$, $1 \cdot 6$, $-1 \cdot 8$
11. $0 \cdot 52$, $-3 \cdot 19$
12. $y = 2x^2 - 3x - 2$
13. $(1, 2)$ $(0 \cdot 36, -1 \cdot 2)$

6a   *1.*   14, 17
          2.   11, 7
          3.   48, 96
          4. $1\frac{1}{2}$, $-\frac{3}{4}$
          5. $\frac{1}{8}$, $\frac{1}{16}$

6.   81, -243
7.   21, 34
8.   (a) $2n$
       (b) $2n - 1$
       (c) n^2

9.   5, 7, 9, 11
10.   3, 6, 12, 24

6b

1. $47, 820$
2. $13\frac{1}{2}, 135$
3. $4 \cdot 05$
4. $15\frac{3}{4}, 106\frac{1}{2}$
5. $\dfrac{-2}{3}, \dfrac{-2}{3}$
6. $2, 20$
7. $3 \cdot 38, 48\frac{1}{2}$
8. $-5 \cdot 5, -52\frac{1}{2}$
9. $3 + 6 + 9 + 12 + \ldots$
10. $69 + 65 + 61 + 57 + \ldots$
11. 2500
12. 1275
13. 21
14. $17, 23, 29, 35, 41, 47$
15. $15, 18, 21, 24$
16. $\frac{5}{12}$
17. £366, £3210
18. £73·20
19. $\dfrac{n(n+1)}{2}$; 1702
20. (a) 93·1 m
    (b) 490 m

6c

1. (a) 3
   (b) 243
   (c) 3^{n-1}
2. (a) $\frac{1}{2}$
   (b) $\frac{5}{32}$
   (c) $\dfrac{5}{2^{n-1}}$
3. (a) $-\frac{1}{2}$
   (b) $-0 \cdot 2625$
   (c) $8 \cdot 4 \times (-\frac{1}{2})^{n-1}$
4. (a) $-\frac{1}{2}$
   (b) $-\frac{1}{32}$
   (c) $(-\frac{1}{2})^{n-1}$
5. (a) $0 \cdot 2$
   (b) $0 \cdot 000\,384$
   (c) $1 \cdot 2 \times (0 \cdot 2)^{n-1}$
6. $\frac{1}{8}, \frac{1}{4}, \frac{1}{2}, 1, \ldots$
7. $\dfrac{7}{24}$; $\dfrac{1}{2\sqrt{3}}$
8. $\pm 10, 20, \pm 40$
9. $72, 48, 32, 21\frac{1}{3}$
10. 1020
11. $\frac{85}{256}$
12. $21\frac{1}{2}$

6d

1. 12
2. $5\frac{2}{5}$
3. $4\frac{1}{2} + \frac{3}{2}\sqrt{3}$
4. 16
5. $\pm 12, 9, \pm \frac{27}{4}, \frac{81}{16}$; $48, -\frac{48}{7}$
6. $\frac{8}{9}$
7. $\frac{358}{495}$
8. $\frac{2083}{3300}$
9. $20, 28, 40, 57, 80, 113, 160,$ $226, 320, 452, 640$
10. (a) £1064
    (b) 9 years
11. 132 m
12. $154\,000$

6e

1. $1 - 5x + 10x^2 - 10x^3 + 5x^4 - x^5$
2. $1 + 12x + 54x^2 + 108x^3 + 81x^4$
3. $16x^4 - 32x^3 y + 24x^2 y^2 - 8xy^3 + y^4$
4. $x^6 - 6x^4 + 15x^2 - 20 + \dfrac{15}{x^2} - \dfrac{6}{x^4} + \dfrac{1}{x^6}$
5. $16 + 32x + 24x^2 + 8x^3 + x^4$
6. $1 - 7t + 21t^2 - 35t^3 + 35t^4 - 21t^5 + 7t^6 - t^7$
7. $1 + 12x + 66x^2 + 220x^3 + \ldots$
8. $1 - 10x + 45x^2 - 120x^3 + \ldots$
9. $1 + 40x + 760x^2 + 9120x^3 + \ldots$
10. $1 - \frac{1}{2}x - \frac{1}{8}x^2 - \frac{1}{16}x^3 \ldots$
11. $1 + x + x^2 + x^3 + \ldots$
12. $1 - 4x + 12x^2 - 32x^3 + \ldots$
13. $120\, x^7 y^3$
14. $495\, a^8 b^4$
15. $90\,720\, x^4 y^4$
16. $\dfrac{14\,784}{x}$
17. (a) $1 \cdot 09$
    (b) $1 \cdot 0937$
18. (a) $1 \cdot 020$
    (b) $1 \cdot 020\,18$

Answers

Miscellaneous exercises 6

1. (a) 3
    (b) $\frac{463}{216}$
2. (a) £9625
    (b) $\sqrt[6]{10} = 1\cdot47$; $63\cdot2$
3. (a) £10250
    (b) $a = 2, r = 3$
    (c) $8(2+\sqrt{3}) = 29\cdot86$
4. $6\cdot81$; $205\cdot5$
    (b) £394; £15·7
5. (a) 8
    (b) (i) 40 m (ii) $33\frac{13}{25}$ m
6. (a) 609
    (b) 37 years
7. (a) 72, 102   (b) 1.8 m
8. (a) $1-9x+36x^2-84x^3+\ldots$; $0\cdot9559$
    (b) $\frac{1144}{243}$
9. (a) $1\cdot004\,21$

    (b) $x^5 - 20x^3 + 160x - \dfrac{640}{x} + \dfrac{1280}{x^3} - \dfrac{1024}{x^5}$

10. (a) $1\cdot217$
    (b) 25, $22\frac{1}{2}$, 20
    (c) $r = 1\cdot208$
11. (a) $1 + \dfrac{x}{2}$

    (b) $4\cdot9960$

12. (a) (i) $x^5 - \dfrac{5}{2}\dfrac{x^4}{y} + \dfrac{5}{2}\dfrac{x^3}{y^2} - \dfrac{5}{4}\dfrac{x^2}{y^3} + \dfrac{5}{16}\dfrac{x}{y^4} - \dfrac{1}{32y^5}$

    (ii) $-1386\dfrac{a^6}{b^5}$ (iii) $1\cdot001\,00$

    (b) $\dfrac{ac}{bd^2}$

    (c) $\log W = \log a + 0\cdot4343xy$
13. (a) $x = 1\cdot15$
    (b) (i) $6561x^8 - 17\,496x^6 + 20\,412x^4 - 13\cdot608x^2 + 5670$
    (ii) $0\cdot984\,01$ (iii) $\frac{63}{8}$
14. (a) $16x^4 - 32x^3y + 24x^2y^2 - 8xy^3 + y^4$
    (b) $a = 1\cdot8, b = 2, c = 0\cdot5$
15. (a) $1\cdot0132$
16. (a) $1 + 3x + 6x^2 + 10x^3 + 15x^4$; $1\cdot0625$
    (b) 3
17. (a) $a^5 + 5a^4x + 10a^3x^2 + 10a^2x^3 + 5ax^4 + x^5$; $0\cdot0531$
    (b) $4\frac{40}{81}$; $4\frac{1}{2}$

18. (a) (i) 17 (ii) 2 (iii) $x^3 + 3x^2 - x - 1$
    (b) 3, ± 15, 75, ± 375, ...
    (c) $1 - 4x + 6x^2 - 4x^3 + x^4$; 0·922 368 16

19. $1 + \dfrac{3}{2}x - \dfrac{9}{8}x^2 + \dfrac{27}{8}x^3$; 1·014 89

20. (a) $1 + \dfrac{x}{8} - \dfrac{x^2}{128} + \dfrac{x^3}{1024}$; 2·236

    (b) (i) $\frac{1}{256}$
        (ii) 40 hours approx.

7b
1. 4·41, 4·0401, 4·004 001 ; 4·1, 4·01, 4·001 ; 4
2. 4th ; 4   4. 6   6. 10
3. 8   5. 4

7d
1. $2x$
2. $6x + 1$
3. $2 + 2x$
4. $-6x$
5. $3x^2$
6. $-\dfrac{2}{x^3}$
7. 1
8. $\dfrac{-2}{(2x-1)^2}$
9. 4, -4
10. 6, -2
11. $(3, \frac{1}{3})$, $(-3, -\frac{1}{3})$
12. $(\frac{1}{3}, -\frac{1}{3})$

7e
1. $5x^4$
2. $18x^5$
3. $1 + \dfrac{1}{x^2}$
4. $15x^2 + 3$
5. $16x^7 + 8$
6. $3x^2 - 6x + 3$
7. $2x + 4$
8. $6x + \dfrac{1}{x^2}$
9. $1 - \dfrac{1}{x^2}$
10. $4\pi x^2$
11. $8\pi x$
12. $2ax + b$
13. $x = -1$
14. 6, 1, 2
15. $(1, -2)(-1, 2)$

16. 6 at $(4, 7)$; -4 at $(-1, 2)$ 17. -1, $x + y + 2 = 0$

7f
1. $20x^4 - 3x^2$; $80x^3 - 6x$
2. $24x^3 + 6x$; $72x^2 + 6$
3. $4x^3 + 4x$; $12x^2 + 4$
4. $2x - \dfrac{1}{x^2}$; $2 + \dfrac{2}{x^3}$
5. $4r^3 - 6r$
6. $1 - \dfrac{1}{r^2}$
7. $8t + 4$
8. $1 + \theta + \theta^2$
11. (a) -32
    (b) f

Miscellaneous exercises 7

1. (a) $4x - 3$

   (b) $\dfrac{10x}{3} - \dfrac{3}{4} - \dfrac{3}{x^2} + \dfrac{4}{3x^3}$

   (c) (i) -1 (ii) $\frac{3}{4}$ (iii) 2

2. (a) $6x - 1$

   (b) (i) $3x^2 - 4x + 1$

   (ii) $-\dfrac{2}{x^3} + \dfrac{3}{x^2}$ (iii) $\dfrac{2}{3x^{\frac{3}{2}}}$

   (c) $1 ; 3$

3. (a) (i) $10x^4$ (ii) $\dfrac{3}{2\sqrt{x}}$

   (iii) $-\dfrac{5}{2x^{\frac{3}{2}}}$

   (b) $51, 36$

   $x = \dfrac{1}{\sqrt 2}, y = 6 - \sqrt 2$

   $x = -\dfrac{1}{\sqrt 2}, y = 6 + \sqrt 2$

4. (a) $2at$

   (b) (i) 8 (ii) 63

5. (a) $12x^2 + \dfrac{4}{x^5}$

   (b) $20x^3 - 60x^2$

   (c) $1, -3$

6. (a) (i) $12x^3 + \dfrac{3}{2}\sqrt x$

   (ii) $-\dfrac{7}{2x^{\frac{3}{2}}} + 6 - \dfrac{5}{x^2}$

   (b) 23

7. (a) $(1\frac{1}{2}, 2\frac{1}{2}), 4x + 2y = 11$

   (b) $(\frac{3}{4}, 2\frac{7}{8})$

   (c) $135°$

8. (a) $\dfrac{4}{x^3}$

   (b) $-32, s = 40t - 16t^2$

9. (a) $2x - 3$

   (b) $a = 3, b = -1$

10. (a) $4x$

    (b) $4x + y + 1 = 0$

12. (a) (i) $1 + nx + \dfrac{n(n-1)}{2!}x^2 + \dfrac{n(n-1)(n-2)}{3!}x^3$

    (ii) $1 + 6x + 12x^2 + 8x^3$

    (b) $6x + 6, 6$

8a

1. (a) $40 - 6t + t^2 \text{ ms}^{-1}$
   (b) $40 \text{ ms}^{-1}, 31 \text{ ms}^{-1}$
   (c) $2t - 6 \text{ ms}^{-2}, -2 \text{ ms}^{-2}$
   (d) $31\frac{1}{3} \text{ m}$
   (3) $31\frac{1}{3} \text{ ms}^{-1}$

2. (a) 56 ms^{-1}
   (b) -32 ms^{-2}
   (c) $3\frac{3}{4} \text{ s}$
   (d) 225 m
   (e) -40 ms^{-1}

3. (a) $2\pi r$
   (b) $4\pi r^2$
   (c) $5x^4$

4. $4\frac{1}{2} \text{ cm/min} ; 2\frac{1}{2} \text{ cm/min}$

5. $0{\cdot}001\,52$ per °C rise

6. $60 \text{ rad s}^{-1} ; 58\frac{2}{3} \text{ rad s}^{-1}$
   $90 \text{ s} ; 430 \text{ rev}$

7. $0{\cdot}13 \text{ m}^3 \text{ min}^{-1}$

9. $x = 1$

10. 20 ms^{-1}

11. (a) $9{\cdot}8t \text{ ms}^{-1}$
    (b) $19{\cdot}6 \text{ ms}^{-1}$
    (c) 10 s
    (d) 98 ms^{-1}

12. (a) $50 - 10t \text{ ms}^{-1}$
    (b) $30, -10 \text{ ms}^{-1}$
    (c) 50 ms^{-1}
    (d) 0, after 5 s
    (e) 125 m

8b
1. (a) $2; -\frac{1}{2}$
    (b) $y = 2x - 1; x + 2y = 3$
2. (a) $1; -1$
    (b) $y = x - 2; x + y = 0$
3. (a) $1; -1$
    (b) $y = x + \frac{2}{3}; x + y + \frac{4}{3} = 0$

4. (a) $-3; \frac{1}{3}$
    (b) $3x + y = 5; 3y = x - 5$
5. (a) $-\frac{1}{4}; 4$
    (b) $x + 4y = 4; y = 4x - 7\frac{1}{2}$

8c
1. $(1\frac{1}{2}, -2\frac{1}{4})$ min.
2. $(2, -1)$ min.
3. $\left(\dfrac{\sqrt{3}}{3}, -\dfrac{2\sqrt{3}}{9}\right)$ min.; $\left(-\dfrac{\sqrt{3}}{3}, \dfrac{2\sqrt{3}}{9}\right)$ max.
4. $(0, 3)$ min.; $(2, 7)$ max.
5. minimum $= 2$ at $x = 1$, maximum $= 2$ at $x = -1$
6. maximum $= 0$ at $x = 0$, minimum $= \frac{4}{27}$ at $x = -\frac{2}{3}$
7. minimum $= -1$ at $x = 2$, maximum $= -9$ at $x = -2$
8. minimum $= 0$ at $x = 0$
9. minimum $= 4$ at $x = 1$, maximum $= 0$ at $x = -1$
10. maximum $y = 15$ at $x = 1$, minimum $y = -12$ at $x = 4$
11. maximum $y = 23$ at $x = 2$, minimum $y = -4$ at $x = -1$
12. maximum $y = -4$ at $x = -\frac{1}{2}$, minimum $y = 4$ at $x = \frac{1}{2}$
13. minimum $A = 7\frac{3}{4}$ at $t = \frac{1}{2}$
14. minimum $A = 24$ at $l = 2$
15. $\dfrac{wl^2}{8}$ at $x = \dfrac{l}{2}$
16. maximum at $x = 1$, $y = 1$; point of inflexion at $(0, 0)$

8d
1. 8
2. 32
3. $2\frac{2}{3}$
4. $V = \pi r^2(15 - r)$, $r = 10$ cm, $h = 5$ cm
5. $2\sqrt{(ab)}$
6. $u = \dfrac{V}{2}; \dfrac{1 + \cos\theta}{2}$

7. 3 cm $\times$ 4 cm $\times$ 6 cm
8. $x = 1; v = 2$
9. $V = \dfrac{x(15 - x^2)}{2}; 5\sqrt{5}$ m³
10. 50 m $\times$ 25 m
11. $2 \cdot 89$ m $\times$ $2 \cdot 89$ m $\times$ $5 \cdot 77$ m

8e
1. $0 \cdot 72$
2. (a) $-0 \cdot 14$
    (b) $-0 \cdot 005$

3. (a) $0 \cdot 36$ m³
    (b) $0 \cdot 72$ m²
4. (a) $-1 \cdot 51$ cm²
    (b) $-2 \cdot 26$ cm³

5. $0 \cdot 128\%$ less
6. $0 \cdot 022$

Miscellaneous exercises 8

1. (a) $-\dfrac{8}{x^3}$

   (b) max. $\left(\dfrac{1}{3}, 3\dfrac{4}{27}\right)$; min. $(1, 3)$

2. (a) $4x$

   (b) (i) $10x + 2$

   (ii) $\dfrac{1}{2\sqrt{x}} + \dfrac{1}{2\sqrt{x^3}}$

   (iii) $1 + \dfrac{4}{x^2}$

   (c) 17.32 cm

3. (a) 36.96 m
   (b) $61.6\ \mathrm{m\,s}^{-1}$
   (c) $82\ \mathrm{m\,s}^{-1}$
   (d) $12\ \mathrm{m\,s}^{-2}$

4. (a) 1 s and 2 s
   (b) $1\frac{1}{2}$ s
   (c) $-1\frac{1}{2}\ \mathrm{m\,s}^{-1}$
   (d) $-6\ \mathrm{m\,s}^{-1}$ at $t = 1$ s,
       $6\ \mathrm{m\,s}^{-1}$ at $t = 2$ s

5. (a) $35\ \mathrm{m\,s}^{-1}$
   (b) $3\ \mathrm{m\,s}^{-2}$
   (c) 1 s and 5 s
   (d) 6.42 s
   (e) 3 s

6. (a) $6x$

   (b) (i) $3x^2 - 3$ (ii) $\dfrac{3}{x^2} - \dfrac{3}{x^4}$ (iii) $\dfrac{4}{5\sqrt[5]{x}}$

   (c) max. 8, min. 4

7. (a) $(1, 2)$; 3
   (b) max. 7; min. 3

8. (a) $7\frac{1}{12}$ m
   (b) $1\frac{3}{4}\ \mathrm{m\,s}^{-2}$
   (c) $3\ \mathrm{m\,s}^{-1}$

9. (a) $\dfrac{2}{\sqrt[3]{x}} - \dfrac{1}{2x^{\frac{3}{2}}} + 6x^{0.2}$

   (b) $28 - 6t$ rad/s; -6 rad/s^2; $4\frac{2}{3}$ s; $65\frac{1}{3}$ rad

10. max $17\frac{1}{3}$; min 0

11. (a) $5\frac{1}{2}$ cm/min; 2 cm/min

    (b) $V = 8x^2$; $\dfrac{dV}{dx} = 16x$; -1.28 cm^3

12. (a) (i) 24 (ii) $3\frac{3}{4}$
    (b) $300\ \mathrm{m} \times 600\ \mathrm{m}$

13. (a) $65\ \mathrm{m\,s}^{-1}$; $14\ \mathrm{m\,s}^{-2}$
    (b) $6\frac{2}{3}$; 80

14. $6\ \mathrm{m} \times 6\ \mathrm{m} \times 3\ \mathrm{m}$

15. 21; min $(1, 12)$; max $(-5, 120)$

16. (a) $a = 4$, $b = 3$
    (b) max $(3, 54)$; min $(-3, 54)$

17. £3000 $\left(\dfrac{9}{v} + \dfrac{v^2}{2058}\right)$

    $v = 21$

18. (a) $6x^2$

9a

1. 9·24 kN
2. 9 pipes
3. 198·9 m^2
4. $\pi : 2$
5. 15·9 cm
6. (a) 5 m
   (b) 25$\frac{1}{2}$ m
   (c) 6·1 m
7. (a) 16$\frac{1}{4}$ m
   (b) 5 m

8. (a) 30·8 m
   (b) 10·6 m
   (c) 32 m
9. 21·6 m
10. (a) 1·45 m^2
    (b) 0·295 m^2
    (c) 61·42 m^2
    (d) 252·8 m^2
    (e) 468·6 m^2

11. 17·71 cm^2
12. 168·5 m^2
13. 43·04 cm^2
14. 360 cm^2
15. 22·4 cm^2
16. 25·2, 151·8 cm^2
17. 6$\frac{1}{4}$ m, 57·5 m^2

9b

1. 1800 m^3
2. 35·1 cm^3
3. 41·6 m^3
4. 5520
5. 5·22 m^2 ; 0·974 m^3
6. 583$\frac{1}{3}$ cm^3
7. 223·1 cm^3
8. 6·33 m^3
9. (a) 125·7 m^2, 62·8 m^3
   (b) 785·4 m^2, 1964 m^3
   (c) 74·2 m^2, 64·9 m^3

10. 126 m^2
11. 294 kg
12. (a) 864 cm^2
    (b) 1497 cm^3
13. 45·95 m^3
14. (a) 61·3 m^2
    (b) 78·3 m^2
15. 1570 cm^2, 3920 cm^3
16. 318 km
17. (a) 35·4 m^3
    (b) 56·9 m^3

9c

1. 100 cm^3
2. 29·5 m^3, 34·2 m^2
3. 3·46 m^3
4. 1403 cm^3
5. 937 cm^3
6. (a) 282·7 m^2, 314·2 m^3
   (b) 93·0 m^2, 58·9 m^3
   (c) 171·8 m^2, 142 m^3
7. 148 cm^3

8. 312 m^3
9. (a) 513 m^3
   (b) 229 m^3
10. (a) 256 m^2
    (b) 132 m^2
11. 2·4 kg; 26·6 cm
12. 28 m^3 ; 37·94 m^2
13. 8·28 cm
14. 426 kg

9d

1. 254·5 m^2, 381·7 m^3
2. 5·1 × 10^8 sq. km
3. 6·75 m
4. 9·87 m
6. 45·1 cm, 56·6 cm
7. (a) 65·97 m^2
   (b) 314·2 m^2

8. (a) 70·7 m^3
   (b) 716 m^3
9. (a) 23·8 cm^3
   (b) 113 cm^2
10. 503 cm^2, 1980 cm^3
11. 0·3987
12. 0·0415

13. 168 cm^3
14. 2R
15. $\frac{1}{4}$ surface
16. 0·47 m^3

9f *1.* (a) 375·5
     (b) 385·6
2. 2470 sq. units
3. 183·4 m^2

4. 52·1 sq. units
5. 534·9 m^3
6. 0·23 m^3
7. 2624 m^3

9. $879\frac{2}{3}$ m^3
10. $56\frac{1}{2}$ m^3
11. 6742 m^3

Miscellaneous exercises 9

1. (a) 6·85 m
    (b) 89·9 m^2
2. 4840 m^2

3. (a) 30 cm^2
    (b) 116 m^3

4. (a) 1777 m^2
    (b) 18·1 m
    (c) 11 008 m^3

5. (a) $CZ = 4$ cm, $OC = 4\sqrt{2}$ cm, $OY = \sqrt{7}$ cm
    (b) $YCZ = 72° 53'$, $YZ = 5·41$ cm, $XY = 1·66$ cm
6. 97 800 m^2
7. (a) 11·44 kg
    (b) 52° 54'
8. 6801 m^2
9. 12 cm; 79·6 cm^3; 64·8 cm^2
10. 1395 m^3
11. (a) (ii) equal
    (b) 216°
12. 83·9 cm^2; 5·49 cm
13. $V = 16y + \frac{8}{3}y^2 + \frac{4}{27}y^3$; 224 m^3, 38 m^2
14. $A = 0·9733^c$, $B = 0·7726^c$, $C = 1·4456^c$; 55·2 cm^2
15. 1990 m^3
16. 50·5 m^3
17. 0·474 m^3
18. 19 900 m^3; 3470 m^2

10a *1.* 2·14, −2, −0·14
     2. −3·82, −0·13, 3·95
     3. 2·63, 0·38, −2
     4. −2·79, 1, 1·79
     5. −0·48, 2·1
     6. 1·9^c

7. 1·8^c
8. 0·91^c
9. 1·03^c, 1·22^c
10. (a) 0·30, 1·55
    (b) 0·25, 1·8; $x^3 - 4x + 1 = 0$

10c *1.* (a) $Y = y, X = x^2$; $Y = bX + a$

(b) $Y = y, X = \dfrac{y}{x}$; $Y = bX + a$

(c) $Y = \dfrac{y}{x}, X = x$; $Y = bX + a$

(d) $Y = \log y, X = \log x$; $Y = nX + \log a$
(e) $Y = y, X = \sqrt{(x^2 + y^2)}$; $Y = -aX + b$
(f) $Y = \log y, X = x$; $Y = X \log a + \log m$
(g) $Y = \log y, X = x$; $Y = X \log a + b \log a$

2. $y = -3 \cdot 2x + 2 \cdot 4$
3. $P = 0 \cdot 15W + 3 \cdot 5$
4. $N = -20t + 410$
5. $a = 1 \cdot 08, b = 0 \cdot 48$
6. $a = 2 \cdot 14, n = 1 \cdot 55$
7. $P = 39 \cdot 8 \, V^{1 \cdot 8}$
8. $a = 4, b = -0 \cdot 6$

9. (a) 2 cycles × 3 cycles
    y range first
(b) 2 cycles × 2 cycles
10. (a) 4 cycles × 2 cycles
(b) semi-log 2 cycles
(c) 3 cycles × 2 cycles

Miscellaneous exercises 10

1. (a) $3 \cdot 79, -0 \cdot 79$
  (b) $4 \cdot 73, 1 \cdot 27$
  (c) $x^2 - 6x + 6 = 0$
2. (a) 40
  (b) $10; x = \frac{5}{6}$
  (c) $3, -\frac{4}{3}$
3. (a) $-1, -0 \cdot 62$
  (b) $1 \cdot 14$
4. $-3 \cdot 0, 1 \cdot 4$
5. $-3, 1, 4$
6. (b) 72
  (c) $-5, 0 \cdot 8, 3 \cdot 9$
7. (a) $1 \cdot 49^c, 3 \cdot 32^c$
  (b) $85 \frac{1}{2}°, 190°$

8. $2 \cdot 8$
9. $0 \cdot 88, 2 \cdot 02$
10. $0 \cdot 86$
11. $a = 2 \cdot 48, b = 3 \cdot 2$
12. $c = 1 \cdot 32, k = 60; v = 6 \cdot 93$
13. $a = 0 \cdot 006, b = 0 \cdot 002$
14. $m = 5, c = 2 \cdot 6$
15. $a = -0 \cdot 08, b = 0 \cdot 047$
16. $a = 225, b = 1 \cdot 11$
17. $a = 207, n = 0 \cdot 30$
18. $a = 8 \cdot 0, b = 1 \cdot 0; y = 1$
19. $a = 4 \cdot 5, b = 0 \cdot 0050$
20. $n = 1 \cdot 39, c = 118$

11a
2. $\frac{56}{65}, -\frac{16}{65}, -\frac{33}{65}, \frac{63}{65}$
4. (a) $-\sin \theta$
  (b) $-\sin \theta$
  (c) $\cos \theta$
5. (a) $2 \sin A \cos B$
  (b) $2 \cos A \cos B$
6. (a) $\frac{1}{2}$
  (b) 1
  (c) 0

8. $\frac{63}{65}, \frac{16}{63}$
10. $\frac{13}{9}, -\frac{1}{3}$
11. $2 + \dfrac{\sqrt{7}}{3}, \dfrac{6 + 4\sqrt{21}}{25}$
12. $\dfrac{3 + 4\sqrt{3}}{10}, \dfrac{3\sqrt{3} - 4}{10}$
13. $\frac{1}{2}$
15. $a = 2, b = -2\sqrt{3}$

16. $\dfrac{\sqrt{3} - 1}{2\sqrt{2}}, \dfrac{\sqrt{3} + 1}{2\sqrt{2}}, 2 - \sqrt{3}, \dfrac{\sqrt{3} + 1}{2\sqrt{2}}, \dfrac{\sqrt{3} - 1}{2\sqrt{2}}, 2 + \sqrt{3}$

11c

1. 0·3827, 0·9239
2. $\frac{24}{25}, -\frac{7}{25}, -\frac{24}{7}$
3. 0·4472, 0·2298
4. (a) 0·8660
   (b) $\frac{1}{4}$
   (c) 0·7071
   (d) 1
13. $10 \sin (\theta + 36° 52')$

14. $\sqrt{13} \sin (\theta + 56° 19')$
15. $5 \sin (\theta - 36° 52')$
16. $13 \sin (\theta - 22° 37')$
17. $\sqrt{65} \cos (\theta - 60° 15')$
18. $25 \sin (100t - 53° 8')$
19. $\sqrt{(a^2 + b^2)}, -\sqrt{(a^2 + b^2)}$
20. $13 ; 22° 37'$

11d

1. 30°, 330°.
2. 30°, 150°, 210°, 330°
3. 143° 8′, 323° 8′
4. 45°, 225°
5. 60°, 300°
6. 45°, 225°
7. 60°, 120°, 240°, 300°
8. 0°, 60°, 180°, 300°
9. 11° 49′, 108° 11′
10. 85°, 325°
11. 105°, 165°, 285°, 345°

12. 20°, 100°, 140°, 220°, 260°, 240°
13. 18° 26′, 45°, 198° 26′, 225°
14. 26° 34′, 135°, 206° 34′, 315°
15. 0°, 60°, 300°, 360°
16. 30°, 150°
17. 19° 28′, 160° 32′, 270°
18. 119° 33′, 346° 43′
19. 7° 58′, 115° 54′
20. (a) 315°
    (b) 210°
    (c) 120°

Miscellaneous exercises 11

1. $\frac{56}{65}$
2. $\frac{\sqrt{3}-1}{2\sqrt{2}}, \frac{1}{2}\sqrt{(2+\sqrt{2})},$
   $\frac{1}{2}\sqrt{(2-\sqrt{2})}$
3. 60°, 180°, 300°
4. $\frac{\sqrt{3}-1}{2\sqrt{2}}, \frac{\sqrt{3}+1}{2\sqrt{2}}, 2-\sqrt{3}$
5. 60°, 131° 49′, 228° 11′, 300°
6. (b) 0·9733, 0·8700
   (c) $8.68 \sin (3t + 38° 27')$
7. (a) $\frac{24}{25}, -\frac{7}{25}, -\frac{24}{7}$
   (b) 120° and 240°
8. (a) 0·3919, 0·92, 0·7212
   (c) 0°, 60°, 300°, 360°
9. $a = 6.06, b = 3.5$

10. (b) $R = \sqrt{(a^2 + b^2)}, \tan \alpha = \frac{a}{b}$
    (c) (i) 20°, 100°, 140°
       (ii) 15°, 75°, 135°
11. (a) $\frac{\sqrt{3}-1}{2\sqrt{2}} = 0.2588, 2 - \sqrt{3} = 0.2679$
    (b) 17° 2′, 72° 58′, 197° 2′, 252° 58′
12. (b) 0°, 45°, 180°, 225°, 360°
13. (a) 30°, 41° 49′, 138° 11′, 150°
14. (a) $\frac{24}{25}, \frac{7}{25}$
    (b) 31° 11′
    (c) $13 \sin (\theta + 67° 23')$, 82° 37′, 322° 37′
15. (b) 60°, 150°, 240°, 330°
    (c) (i) $\frac{77}{85}$ (ii) $\frac{36}{85}$
16. $R = 5, \alpha = 36° 52'$; 7° 33′, 98° 43′

17. (b) $R = 25$, $\alpha = 16°\ 16'$; $36°\ 52'$, $110°\ 36'$

18. (a) $4 \sin x + \sqrt{3} \cos x$

    (b) $\dfrac{m_1 - m_2}{1 + m_1 m_2}$, $90°$

19. $13 \sin(\theta + 22°\ 37')$; $25°\ 58'$, $108°\ 48'$

20. (a) $19°\ 28'$, $30°$, $150°$, $160°\ 32'$

    (b) $21 \cdot 3$ cm

12a

1. $\dfrac{x^5}{5} + c$

2. $2x^2$

3. $x^3 + 2x + c$

4. $\dfrac{x^3}{3} - 4x^2 + 5x + c$

5. $-\dfrac{1}{3x^3} + c$

6. $\tfrac{3}{4}x^{\frac{4}{3}} + c$

7. $\dfrac{x^3}{3} - \dfrac{x^4}{4}$

8. $\tfrac{4}{3}x^3 - 2x^2 + x + c$

9. $\dfrac{x^3}{3} - 2x + c$

10. $\dfrac{x^3}{3} + 2x - \dfrac{1}{x} + c$

11. $x^3 - 2x$

12. $4x + 2x^2 - 3$

13. $x^5 - x^2 + 2$

14. $x + \dfrac{2}{x^2} + \dfrac{7}{9}$

15. $\dfrac{x^3}{3} + \dfrac{x^2}{2} - 2x + 4\tfrac{1}{3}$

16. $y = 2x^3 - 3x^2$

17. $y = x^2 - x + 3$

18. $10t - t^2 + 19$

19. 26

20. $12\tfrac{2}{3}$

12c

1. $x^5 + c$

2. $2x^3 + c$

3. $\dfrac{-1}{2x^3} + c$

4. $-\dfrac{1}{x} + c$

5. $16x - 4x^2 + \dfrac{x^3}{3} + c$

6. $\dfrac{a^2 x^3}{3} + abx^2 + b^2 x + c$

7. $\dfrac{t^3}{3} - 3t^2 + c$

8. $\dfrac{r^4}{4} - r^2 + c$

9. $\tfrac{2}{3}m^{\frac{3}{2}} + c$

10. $\dfrac{u^3}{3} - 7u + c$

11. $2\sqrt{p} + c$

12. $2u - \dfrac{u^3}{3} + c$

13. $s = 3t + t^2$

14. $s = 5t + \dfrac{t^2}{2}$

15. 22

16. $v = t^2 + 3 \text{ m s}^{-1}$

17. $v = \dfrac{t^2}{2} + 2t + 16 \text{ m s}^{-1}$

18. $s = 100t - 16t^2$; $a = -32$

19. $v = 32t + 10$; $s = 16t^2 + 10t$

20. $v = \dfrac{3t^2}{2} + t + 5$; $s = \dfrac{t^3}{2} + \dfrac{t^2}{2} + 5t + 2$

12e

1. $1\frac{1}{2}$
2. 9
3. $1\frac{1}{2}$
4. $\frac{5}{6}$
5. $10\frac{2}{3}$
6. $\frac{1}{6}$
7. 1
8. 6
9. 52
10. $\dfrac{a^3}{6}$
11. $2\frac{2}{3}$
12. $6\frac{2}{3}$
13. $4\frac{1}{2}$
14. $28\frac{1}{2}$
15. $8\frac{1}{4}$
16. 9
17. $4\frac{2}{3}$
18. 36
19. $(-2, 4)$ and $(3, 9)$; $20\frac{5}{6}$
20. 36

12f

1. $5\cos x$
2. $-2\sin x$
3. $\cos x - \sin x$
4. $2\cos x + \sin x$
5. $-3\sin x - 4\cos x$
6. $2 - \cos x$
7. $2\sin x + c$
8. $-3\cos x + c$
9. $-\cos x - \sin x + c$
10. $2\sin x + \cos x + c$
11. $-a\cos x + b\sin x + c$
12. $x^3 + \sin x + c$
13. $-\sin x$
14. $-2\sin\theta - \cos\theta$
15. (a) 3
    (b) 2
16. 1·366
17. 0·293
18. 1·098

Miscellaneous exercises 12

1. (a) $\cos x$

   (b) $\dfrac{5}{2}x - \dfrac{2}{3} + \dfrac{8}{3x^3} - \dfrac{4}{3x^4}$

   (c) (i) $2x^3 - 3x + 3$ (ii) $x + 3 - \dfrac{3}{x}$

2. (a) $\dfrac{x^3}{3} - \dfrac{4}{3}x^{\frac{3}{2}} + c$

   (b) $\frac{2}{3}\pi r^3$

   (c) $4\frac{1}{8}$

3. (a) (i) $x^4 + c$ (ii) $\dfrac{10}{3}x^{\frac{3}{2}} + c$

   (iii) $-\dfrac{7}{x} + c$

   (iv) $\dfrac{4}{3}x^3 + 2x^2 + x + c$

   (b) $y = x^4 + x^2 + 7x + 8$

4. (a) $\dfrac{15}{2}x^2 - \dfrac{3}{4} - \dfrac{3}{5x^2} + \dfrac{4}{x^4}$

   (b) $\dfrac{dy}{dx} = -\sin x$

   (c) (i) $\dfrac{7x^3}{3} + 2x^2 - 6x + c$

   (ii) $\dfrac{2}{5}x^4 + c$

   (iii) $-\dfrac{3}{x} - \dfrac{x^2}{2} + 2x + 2\frac{1}{2}$

5. (a) $2x + 2x^{\frac{3}{2}} + \dfrac{1}{x} + c$

   (b) $18\frac{3}{5}$
   (c) $\frac{3}{4}a^4$

6. (a) $y = 3x - x^2$
   (b) $(0, 0)$ and $(3, 0)$
   (c) $4\frac{1}{2}$

7. (a) (i) $ax + \frac{3}{2}x^{\frac{4}{3}} + c$ (ii) $0\cdot 366$
   (b) $x = 1$ and $4, 4\frac{1}{2}$

8. (a) (i) $x^3 + 2x^{\frac{3}{2}} + c$ (ii) $5x - \dfrac{5}{2x^2} + c$
   (b) $y = \frac{2}{3}x^3 + \frac{5}{2}x^2$; $x = -2\frac{1}{2}, x = 0$

9. (a) $\dfrac{dy}{dx} = \cos x$
   (b) (i) $\dfrac{3}{5}x^5 + c$ (ii) $-\dfrac{5}{2x^2} + c$
   (iii) $x^3 - x^2 + 5x + c$

10. (a) (i) $x^4 + \dfrac{2}{3}x^{\frac{3}{2}} + c$
    (ii) $-\dfrac{1}{x} + \dfrac{x^3}{3} + x^2 + x + c$
    (b) 97
    (c) $-\dfrac{600}{v^{0\cdot 1}} + c$

Examination paper 1

1. (a) $2\cdot 70$
   (b) $3, \frac{1}{3}$
   (c) $x = 8, y = -6, z = 11$
2. $105°, 165°, 285°, 345°$
3. $P = 3\cdot 61, Q = 33° \, 41'$
4. (a) $-3\cdot 16, 0\cdot 16$
   (b) 76
5. (a) $2x - 2$
   (b) $x^2 - 6 - \dfrac{2}{3x^2} + \dfrac{1}{x^4}$
   (c) (i) $\dfrac{x^2}{2} - \dfrac{1}{2x^2} + c$
   (ii) $\dfrac{x^3}{3} + \dfrac{x^2}{2} - 2x + c$

6. (a) (i) $(7x + 8y)(3x - 2y)$
   (ii) $(3a - 2b)(4c + 3d)$
   (iii) $(a + 3b - c)(a - 3b + c)$
   (b) 30 min, 45 min
7. $m = 4\cdot 72, c = 2\cdot 66$; $8\cdot 8$
8. $x^3 - 3x^2 + 5x - 2$
9. (a) (i) $x^4 + \dfrac{2x^3}{y} + \dfrac{3}{2}\dfrac{x^2}{y^2} + \dfrac{x}{2y^3} + \dfrac{1}{16y^4}$
   (ii) $-\dfrac{63}{8}\dfrac{a^5}{b^5}$
   (b) $\dfrac{6a^3}{b}$
10. (a) 124 rev/min
    (b) $t = 4s, s = 144$ m $f = -24$ ms^{-2}

Examination paper 2

1. (a) $1\cdot 386, 1\cdot 099$
   (b) $7\cdot 39, 20\cdot 1$
   (c) $x = \pm 5, y = \mp 4$
2. (a) $1\cdot 73$
   (b) $k = \dfrac{1}{2\pi}\sqrt{(ghT^2 - 4\pi^2 h^2)}$
   (c) $11\frac{1}{2}$ cm $\times \, 8\frac{1}{2}$ cm
3. (a) 47
   (b) $76\cdot 7, 117\cdot 6, 180\cdot 3, 276\cdot 5, 423\cdot 8$

4. (a) $2t^2 - 5t + 3, 4t - 5$
   (i) $1, 1\frac{1}{2}$ (ii) $\dfrac{5}{4}$
   (b) $\dfrac{32}{x^2}; \dfrac{128}{x} + x^2; 4$
5. (a) $x^3 + \dfrac{1}{x} + 5x + c$; $\dfrac{x^5}{5} - \dfrac{4}{7}x^{\frac{7}{2}} + \dfrac{x^2}{2} + c$
   (b) $v = 3t + 5$; 276 m

6. $a = 10, n = 2 \cdot 5$

7. (a) $0°, 48° 11', 311° 49', 360°$
   (b) $84° 42'$

8. $18°, 90°, 162°, 234°, 306°$;
   $21°, 159°$; $1 \cdot 63$

9. (a) $566 \cdot 7$
   (b) $0 \cdot 341$ cm

10. $a = 3 \cdot 5, b = 8 \cdot 2, c = 11 \cdot 0$

Examination paper 3

1. (a) $1 \cdot 62, 0 \cdot 62$
   (b) $8 \cdot 81$ cm, 366 cm^3

2. (a) $0 \cdot 063$
   (b) $52 \cdot 2$ cm

3. (a) (i) $\bar{4} \cdot 6350$ (ii) $0 \cdot 029\,48$
   (b) $18 \cdot 3$

4. (a) $1 + 10x + 45x^2 + 120x^3$; $1 \cdot 0511$
   (b) $\dfrac{8448}{125}$

5. $y^2 = 20 - 0 \cdot 4x^2$; $0 \cdot 4$

6. (a) $\dfrac{-1 \pm \sqrt{5}}{2}$
   (b) $0 \cdot 403$

7. (a) $5 \cdot 37, -0 \cdot 37$
   (b) $3 \cdot 79, -0 \cdot 79$
   (c) $x^2 - 3x - 3 = 0$

8. $15\,870$ cm^3, 3152 cm^2

9. (a) $c = \dfrac{11a - 7}{5a - 4}$
   (b) $-8 \cdot 03$
   (c) $3, 2$

10. (a) $\dfrac{7}{8}$
    (b) $3, 40 \cdot 5, 13$
    (c) $y = x^3 - \dfrac{2}{3}x - \dfrac{3}{x} - 4$

Index